MW00994128

CHRONICLE OF THE
7. PANZERKOMPANIE
1. SS-PANZER DIVISION
"LEIBSTANDARTE"

CHRONICLE OF THE 7. PANZER-KOMPANIE 1.SS-PANZER DIVISION "LEIBSTANDARTE"

Ralf Tiemann

Schiffer Military History
Atglen, PA

Book Design by Robert Biondi.
Translated from the German by Allen Brandt.
The publisher wishes to thank Mark Yerger for his assistance with this project.

Library of Congress Catalog Number: 97-80199.

Printed in the United States of America.
ISBN: 0-7643-0463-1

We are interested in hearing from authors with book ideas on related topics.

Published by Schiffer Publishing Ltd.
4880 Lower Valley Road
Atglen, PA 19310
Phone: (610) 593-1777
FAX: (610) 593-2002
E-mail: Schifferbk@aol.com.
Please write for a free catalog.
This book may be purchased from the publisher.
Please include $3.95 postage.
Try your bookstore first.

7. Panzerkompanie LAH

Exactly 50 years after the formation of our company the chronicle of our company history has become an actual reality.

I lay the documentation in the hands of my old comrades, it has become a decisive chapter in the history of their young lives.

They will find within these pages the confirmation, that despite all of the malicious defamation, that this chapter of their lives was engraved with a devotion to their homeland.

May foreigners who read this chronicle recognize from the continuously required preparedness for action described herein, that it was always an honor for our troops to be clean and brave soldiers.

Ralf Tiemann
June, 1992

PROLOGUE

In this year of 1992 our proud 7. Panzerkompanie celebrates the 50th anniversary of its formation:

– 4 years of combat on the battlefields of the Second World War and
– 46 years of post-war time during which the former members of our company have continued to gather, thus confirming our firmly bound camaraderie.

This 50 year anniversary of the formation should be the birthday of our,

COMPANY CHRONICLE.

With this chronicle we lay the history of our company in the hands of our company comrades and it should help to awaken the memories of happy and successful days, but also memories of the difficult days of complete disappointment.

To all the comrades who helped enable us to compile this chronicle with reports, photos and documents, we express our sincere thanks.

Hans Behrend
Manfred Thorn
Hans Siptrott
Neustadt on the Aisch, June, 1992
The Company Troop

FOREWORD

The 3. Panzerkompanie (3rd Tank Company) of the Panzerabteilung (Tank Battalion) "LAH," later 7. Panzerkompanie, was one of the first Panzer companies of the Waffen-SS.

During the course of actions of the Second World War, the history of the SS-Panzer Divisions began. During the three years of their actions on all fronts, during all the hazards of battle conducted by the army and the paratroopers, the term "SS-Panzer Division" has established a firm place at the top of the opponent's list in terms of respect – yesterday and today!

During the formation of the Panzer Battalion in January, 1942, the strengthened infantry regiment (motorized) "LAH" was promoted in status to a Panzer Grenadier Division. In later years of the war – during the formation of the Panzer Regiment – the Division was again promoted in status and re-equipped to form a Panzer Division.

Throughout the war, on all battlefields in the east, in the south and in Western Europe, in all battle conditions, whether in attack or later during the retreat battles, the 7. Panzerkompanie held its place in the focal point of the battles in which the "Leibstandarte" had to fight.

This chronicle should serve to report about the experiences of the company in words and pictures. And for those surviving former members of this company it should awake memories of not only the successful tank battles, but also the days of the later retreats of the lost war, which were marked with bitter and severe disappointment.

With this chronicle we remember our killed and missing comrades.

This chronicle should serve to quell any doubt that to this very day, despite all of the disappointment, demonization and defamation of our great experience, that there is one thing that actively remained in us: THE CAMARADERIE.

CONTENTS

PART I

THE COMPANY HISTORY

1942
Wildflecken – Haustenbeck – Stalino – Paris – Evreux – Orbec

WILDFLECKEN

By the order of the Supreme Command of the Army, General Halder (Commander of the General Staff of the Army), the motorized infantry divisions "Großdeutschland" and "LSSAH," among other plans for formations, are each ordered to form a Panzer Battalion. This is the official day of formation for the framework of the Panzer Battalion of the LAH and also for the 3. (later 7.) Panzerkompanie.

This historic day has a small and unofficial, pre-history.

Ralf Tiemann, the first adjutant of the Panzer Battalion, reports as follows:

> At the beginning of January, 1942 I arrived at the Lichterfeld concern after being released from the field hospital where I was supposed to report to the replacement battalion. In order to freshen myself after the long trip and to have a drink for the first time in a long time, I went in the casino and met my old battalion commander Sturmbannführer Mohnke in the "watering-hole." Mohnke had just been released from the field hospital in Hohenlychen.
>
> We were very excited to see each other again and Sturmbannführer Mohnke, in his usual extreme vitality, developed his plan to build a Panzer battalion for the LAH.
>
> As the future commander of this planned battalion, it was his first "official duty" to appoint me as his adjutant.
>
> He then informed me that the Führungshauptamt was against the plan and that Obergruppenführer Jüttner had rudely sent him on his way.
>
> I therefore received, as the first battalion order, the task of "illegally" recruiting NCOs and enlisted men throughout the concern for the new Panzerabteilung.
>
> I visited Hauptsturmführer Wellershaus' clothing depot and fit myself into a black Panzer uniform from the supplies of the reconnaissance battalion. I appeared wearing the uniform as often as possible in the different quarters of the concern in order to awake the curiosity of the "Alte Hasen."
>
> One after another I visited all of the company quarters of the replacement battalion, the VII. (guard) Battalion and the reserve company consisting of men recovering from their wounds which was situated in the chapel.

Everyone I spoke to displayed a keen interest in the new Panzer Battalion and without exception wanted to be transferred to the unit and put on the list of "volunteers."

By the time I attracted the wrath of Sturmbannführer Schiller and Sturmbannführer Schuldt and was "grounded to my quarters" due to my "illegal recruiting activities," it was already too late. My improvised formation of personnel was already so extensive that two companies could be formed from the "enlisted volunteers."

Just after his wedding on January 14, 1942, Obergruppenführer Sepp Dietrich (commander of the LAH), invited all his commanders who were present to a toast in the "Leroux-Building" in order to present his young new wife to the circle of commanders.

Sturmbannführer Mohnke used this opportunity to have the Obergruppenführer sign his personnel list, which in the meantime had been changed into a transfer order. At first Dietrich was a bit startled and could not consent to this "illegal" deed, but he soon gave into Mohnke's pressuring and signed the order.

Because of this "Sepp Dietrich Order," Obergruppenführer Jüttner finally sanctioned the "unauthorized action" and decreed the official formation of a Panzer Battalion for the LAH. He ordered that equivalent detachments be formed for "Reich" and "Wiking" as well. Jüttner then proclaimed that the work that had taken place thus far be continued at the training grounds in WILDFLECKEN/RHÖN.

After the Führungshauptamt's final consent for the formation of the Panzer Battalion, officers, NCOs and members of the forming Panzerabteilung were gathered in the quarters of the replacement battalion.

The issuing of available Panzer uniforms from the supplies of the reconnaissance battalion then began.

The equipping of the unit with vehicles and sidearms also continued.

On **January 18, 1942,** the Führungshauptamt instructed the unit to prepare for a transfer to WILDFLECKEN, which would take place in the beginning of February.

On **January 24, 1942**, after receiving the OKH-Order (Supreme Command of the Army Order), the order to prepare to load up for a rail transport was issued.

The departure of the Battalion began on **February 6, 1942**.

The train carrying the personnel of the future 3. Panzerkompanie departed on **February 7, 1942,** from Lichterfeld/East. It traveled through Halle, Erfurt, Weimar,

Eisenach, Bebra and Fulda, and after 36 hours reached its new quarters on **February, 9, 1942,** at the training grounds in WILDFLECKEN.

On **February 10, 1942,** a march company, consisting of new recruits and recovering soldiers from several Waffen-SS units, arrived from the camp in Beneschau.

They brought with them some Panzer vehicles of the type "Hotchkis" as exercise tanks.

The tactical formation of the detachment was final at this stage and consisted of a

Staff, Staff Company, Panzer Maintenance Platoon and
3 intermediate Panzer companies

each company consisted of : 1 company troop with 2 Panzer IVs
1 light platoon with 3 Panzer IIs
2 intermediate platoons with 4 (short-barrel) Panzer IVs each

The leadership of the 1. Panzerkompanie was overtaken by the commander of the march company, Hauptsturmführer Manfred Schmidt.

The command position of the 2. Panzerkompanie remained unoccupied for the time being.

The leadership of the 3. Panzerkompanie was provisionally taken over by Obersturmführer Astegher.

Light Platoon	(Panzer IIs)	Untersturmführer Fröhlich
1st Platoon	(Panzer IVs)	Untersturmführer von Ribbentrop
	Half-Platoon	Oberjunker Berg
2nd Platoon	(Panzer IVs)	Untersturmführer Janke
	Half-Platoon	Oberjunker Eckardt

The Stabsscharführer (staff sergeant) of the march company, Michael Meschnarz, stepped up to the position as "Spieß" within the 3. Kompanie.

The 3. Panzerkompanie received the field post number 31820.

On **February 11, 1942,** the initial issue of Panzers arrived by transport.

On the same day the tactical Panzer training was taken over by the commando of the Army Panzer Regiment 1 from Erfurt.

The supervision and inspection of the entire training (LAH, Wiking, Reich) was to be led by Hauptmann Philipp. Oberleutnant Eichberg was to be responsible for the Battalion of the LAH.

On **February 12, 1942,** training for the entire company began with tank driving classes on the icy and hilly streets, radio training with UKW radio telephones, and No. 1 gunner target practice.

Following that:

> Combat driving (solo and in platoon formation), platoon radio exercises, and the first shooting exercises with the tank-mounted machine-gun and the main gun on the snow-covered inclines of the Rhön firing ranges.

On **February 20, 1942,** Hauptsturmführer Lamprecht arrived from the front and reported as the newly declared leader of the 2. Panzerkompanie.

Hauptsturmführer Lamprecht reported that Sturmbannführer Mohnke had been relieved of the command of the Panzer Battalion and that Sturmbannführer Schönberger (Sturmgeschütz Battalion) was on his way from the front to take over the command of the Panzer Battalion.

Ralf Tiemann reports about this change in command and the personnel changes associated with it:

> Sturmbannführer Mohnke was, as so many times in the past, driven to Berlin, to "raise hell," as he put it. The sluggish delivery of supplies and weapons, particularly of the special vehicles and tanks, stirred his annoyance.
>
> This time he was away for a long time and didn't send any messages.
>
> As Hauptsturmführer Lamprecht appeared with the order that Sturmbannführer Mohnke had been relieved and that the somewhat indecisive Sturmbannführer Schönberger was to be promoted to the position of the new commander, I became very worried indeed. I called the Führungshauptamt (the SS Leadership Main Office) and found out that after having vehement arguments with Jüttner, Sturmbannführer Mohnke had been sent to the psychiatric ward of the military hospital in Würzburg, as a "result of his wounds, which had caused him to lose control of himself."
>
> While I was deeply regretting the fate of Sturmbannführer Mohnke, it seemed that it was going to be even more unbearable to serve at the side of Sturmbannführer Schönberger as his adjutant.
>
> In a snap decision I completed a Battalion order which appointed me as the leader of the 3. Panzerkompanie and Obersturmführer Astegher as the Battalion's adjutant. With the order prepared in just this way, I then set off immediately to Würzburg. At the military hospital I asked my way through to Sturmbannführer Mohnke, whom I found to be completely disheartened.
>
> He completely understood the measures that I had prepared and without

hesitating he signed the order. I didn't see Sturmbannführer Mohnke again until the Ardennes Offensive, during which he was my commander.

With the order in my pocket I set off on the trip home where I informed the displeased Obersturmführer Astegher about his new assignment. I then took over the 3. Panzerkompanie. With that began a period of battlefield engagements which will remain in my memory as the most unforgettable experiences of my life as a front-line combat soldier.

On **February 26, 1942,** Sturmbannführer Schönberger arrived in WILDFLECKEN and overtook the leadership of the Battalion.

The training with tank weaponry, radios, and driving tracked vehicles in action as well as tank shooting exercises continued with intensity until the end of March. At this time the training commando of Army Panzer Regiment 1 determined that the Panzer companies could be trusted with the fundamentals of tank action.

A special occurrence during training has remained in the memory of Hans Behrend:

The training was greatly hindered by the winter storm conditions. The accommodations were cramped and the number of soldiers who called in sick was very high due to the many colds.

These conditions were worsened by the insufficient supply of rations. Constant rations of Kinzinger artificial honey and tubes of cheese were unable to raise anyone's spirits.

Therefore everyone tried to come into possession of bread coupons to stock up on supplemental rations of fruit bread in the cantina.

The mass of fruit bread consumed during the two and a half months in Wildflecken insured the need to go on living.

Despite these and other inadequacies, the Panzer training objectives were indeed reached, which helped form the men's battle spirit forever.

A funny occurrence had especially impressed me. Comrade von Wildenegg was assigned the position of Unteroffizier von Dienst.[1] One of his tasks as Unteroffizier von Dienst was to remind the company commander, Obersturmführer Tiemann, that it was time to go to lunch when the time came.

The company would sit in the instruction area and von Wildenegg would knock on the table and then cross the room to give the company commander the appropriate message — an occurrence which repeated itself every day. This time, however, comrade von Wildenegg, in his haste to do his duty, put his helmet on backwards. The company commander, noticing this, became dumbfounded. The entire company almost fell off their chairs laughing and comrade von Wildenegg received quite an ovation.

For further training within in the framework of the Company and also within the framework of the Battalion, a transfer to the training grounds in SENNELAGER was foreseen.

On **April, 13, 1942,** the order was given to load a transport of trains bound for PADERBORN.

Heinz Freiberg wrote in his diary:

Better an ass full of tacks than another day in WILDFLECKEN.

HAUSTENBECK AND PARIS

On **April 15, 1942,** the train transport departed with the 3. Panzerkompanie from GERSFELD and traveled through FULDA and GIESSEN on the way to PADERBORN. There the company arrived on **April 16, 1942**, unloaded and continued the journey in a motorized march through BAD LIPPSPRINGE into the abandoned village of HAUSTENBECK and onto the training grounds.

The 3. Panzerkompanie set up camp with the entire Battalion in this village after which groups took shelter in the empty houses.

The first days in HAUSTENBECK were spent setting up company quarters, undergoing one-on-one infantry training under the auspices of an experienced soldier, undergoing weaponry training (building and maintaining weapons) and then there was physical training.

At the end of April the company commenced Panzer sharp shooting in platoon formation at the training ground's firing range.

At the beginning of May came the combat training within the framework of the company with:

> Execution of wide-area combat simulation exercises employing radio equipment and fire-escape exercises with live ammunition.
>
> The tank driving school continued as well and the tank drivers obtained their driver's license for tracked vehicles over 10 tons.

In May the company threw a garden party with Chinese lanterns, music and a dance in the railway attendant's home in HIDDESEN.

The public pool in BAD LIPPSPRINGE was a popular visiting place for a large part of the company after the conclusion of duties.

On **June 13, 1942,** the 1st Platoon picked up their new tanks (KWK F2, 7.5, L48) at the army ordnance depot BURG nearby Magdeburg.

The 2nd Platoon received short-barreled tanks for the time being.

The **20th of June 1942** remains the symbol of the visit of Divisional Commander Sepp Dietrich.

He inspected all of the companies and attended the firing exercises. During the conclusion of his visit he expressed his satisfaction with the training completed thus far.

HAUSTENBECK is a name associated with some of Hans Behrend's most notable memories:

> By having arrived in HAUSTENBECK, we had escaped the winter. In the cleared village we made Spartan quarters in the empty houses. Every platoon had its own house. In the neighboring gardens we attentively observed the slowly growing berry bushes and the slow growth of their fruits, which we had already spiritedly worked into our meal plan.
>
> When the transfer to Russia came, we had to chow them down as fast as possible, even though they were only half ripe.
>
> To increase our rations and overcome the constant, intense hunger common to youths of our age, we used tube mustard – already taken out of the tubes and put into small pots – to considerably improve the quality of the skinned potatoes. Supposedly there were even attempts by the even hungrier among us to hunt rabbits with .38 pistols. But more commonplace was the hunt for bread coupons, because in Bad Lippspringe one coupon received a double portion of plumb tarts for a single coupon. The path to the place where the tarts were issued was far away and one had to travel over the heath to get there. Therefore we would always rotate the task among ourselves and went in groups. However, we lived in constant fear that the group fetching the plum tarts would not be able to overcome their natural impulses during their march over the heath and that the plumb tarts would never reach their destination.
>
> But the "hunger camaraderie" was stronger, and our fears were for nothing.
>
> To support the discipline and the preparedness for action, inspections were carried out on a continual basis. Naturally a few comrades were always singled out after the end of duties and had to take part in the "march in the memory of Kaiser-Wilhelm," which would assemble before the unit weapon and equip-

ment stores. There they were equipped with the necessary "marching utensils" – normally two full cases of handgrenades per man – and were sent on their way to the main camp in Paderborn after hearing a few friendly words.

A plan not included in the march orders (taking a short-cut) was an impossibility, since the guards at the main camp had been informed of the arriving tourists.

Over time we all became experts in "running to the heath."

More pleasant was the drive to shower in the camp at Staumühle. One time during the ride there in an Opel-Blitz, the truck tipped over with its freshly showered passengers after a curve was executed too sharply.

The actually hum-drum training with live ammunition on the firing range became spicy now and then, especially when we filled our little mess tins with gun powder from the 2 cm armored cars and set the heath in the target area on fire. Putting out fires also became a part of the practical training.

I especially remember one occurrence:

One day our "Spieß" Michel Meschnarz must have killed that last nerve in our very correct company commander with some sort of stupidity.

After that the "Spieß" was read the "word of the day" while lined up with the rest of the company:

"Meschnarz, I am going to let you sit on top of the front of my Panzer so you can play the role of hood ornament during the first attack!"

With that the "Spieß" was dumfounded, which was a seldom occurrence for a pure-blooded Austrian such as himself.

After a final company war-game which consisted of an attack while making a bee-line under fire or with live ammunition and a Panzer radio exercise, of all leaders for the action in closed Battalion formation, the training was considered concluded. The order was then issued to remain ready to load up for transport to join the troops in the field in the east.

The entraining of the 3. Panzerkompanie followed on **June 17, 1942,** at the freight train station in PADERBORN.

As a bid farewell, Heinz Freiburg noted in his diary:

Der Hergott erschuf in seinem Zorn
das Sennelager bei Paderborn
The Lord created in his rage
the mountain pasture camp in Paderborn

The ride went through Brackel, Nordheim, Dresden, Ratibor, Krakau, Lemberg, Bobrinskaja, Dnepropetrovsk and Mariopol in the area of Stalino, where, on **July 8, 1942**, after an eight-day train-ride, the troops were able to unload .

The company moved into field positions (foxholes under the Panzers), fought against dysentery, suffered through temperatures of 86º F in the shade while waiting for events that were about to take place. With this the integration of the Panzer Battalion into the field troops of the LAH was completed.

Rumors were circling that the Division was going to be transported to the West shortly, since it was predicted that there would be an Allied landing on the French coast of the Channel.

A Battalion company commander conference took place at the command post On **July 11, 1942**, during which the Battalion commander was informed that "due to feared enemy landings, the LAH was at the disposal of the Supreme Commander of the Supreme Commander West (OB West) and that the Division was subordinated to his command. (see Appendix 1).

On **July 13, 1942,** the 3. Panzerkompanie of the Battalion was to load up at the train station in STALINO with the rest Battalion for a trip to the West. The ride went through Ivanovka, Losovaja, Kiev, Kovel, Warsaw, Glogau, Frankfurt, Saarbrücken, Montreux until reaching MELUN (50 km south of Paris), where the Battalion unloaded on **July 21, 1942**. The Battalion set up camp in a small Chateau on the edge of the city, high over the Seine River.

Hans Behrend remembers:

> In spite of the large cleaning operations there was still enough time to reconnoiter the near vicinity. Behind the chateau there were several terraces that extended out to the bank of the Seine River. The shortest way to the river was naturally a jump over the retaining wall from terrace to terrace.
>
> The water called. A comrade took a run, elegantly jumping over the walls, then suddenly there was a clattering of glass – then silence. He had jumped through the glass roof of a green house, but no important body parts were hurt.
>
> Realization: the shortest way is not always the best.

The rudder boat rides on the Seine during which we purposely tipped over the boats are still remembered.

Soon the message spread that the Division was to take part in an impressive parade right through Paris. The purpose of the parade was take away any desire the enemy had for a landing.

Everything was made "parade-ready" with car-care products and "rag-cleaning."

On **July 28, 1942,** the 3. Panzerkompanie marched with the rest of the Battalion on National Street #36 until LANG. SOUR MARINE (20 km east of Paris) and moved up to the eastern edge of Paris on **July 29, 1942.**

The long march across the country with Panzers over asphalt roads took its toll on the tank tracks, and cotter pins had to be continually beat back into place.

The march then went right through Paris, through the Place de la Bastille, along the Louvre river until reaching the Place de la Concorde. Here began the parade which ran through Champs Elysée, past the Oberbefehlshaber West, General Field Marshal von Runstedt, the commanding general of the SS-Panzer Korps, Obergruppenführer Hausser and the commander of the LAH – Obergruppenführer Sepp Dietrich.

The parade lasted a full 6 hours for the entire Division.

The 3. Panzerkompanie passed the review at 1400 hours, rounded the Arc de Triomphe and rolled from the Place de l'Etoile further in the direction of MANTES. In NANTERRE the company stopped for supplies and food and a short overnight nap on the vehicles.

The march continued at dawn on **July 30, 1942,** on the National Street #13. During the early afternoon the company reached it new quarters in EVREUX after a march of 80 km, during which cotter pins had to be continually beat back into place. In EVEREUX the company took quarters in the French combat engineer barracks there.

EVREUX and ORBEC

The 3. Panzerkompanie's training routine began on the first day after arriving at the concern in EVREUX.

After **August 2, 1942,** the Panzer training moved along at full speed.

In the meadowlands of BOUNEVILLE the company had the possibility to practice combat actions and to drive in simulated combat in company-wedge and company-wide-wedge formation.

The land was also well-suited for wide range radio-simulated Panzer exercises.

Due to the lack of a firing range for sharp-shooting with targets, the company built a model Panzer stage in the backyard of the concern. Terrain sections were built in a 4 X 3 M sandbox, which gradually rose in the rear. Simulated enemy positions, complete with all equipment and weapons, were constructed at a scale of 1:50.

Panzer commanders, no. 1 gunners and radio operators could exercise the procedure of locating targets, giving orders from their tanks and carrying out main gun aiming exercises.

These practical exercises proved to be extremely valuable in later actions.

On **August 10, 1942,** the Supreme Commander of the 15th Army, General Haase, visited the Battalion and inspected the companies. He also stayed to observed a battalion leader communications exercise.

On **August 19, 1942,** the 3. Panzerkompanie received the order that it was at "Alarm Grade II" and was to be ready to march off at any minute.

The order instructed that the enemy had landed on the DIEPPE in a strength of 2 battalions.

The coastal defense stood in successful defensive battle. Five-hundred Canadians had been just taken prisoner.

After an hour and a half the alarmed Panzer battalion left EVREUX but was stopped just west of the edge of the city.

Heinz Freiberg noted the following about the alarm in his notebook:

> After we had departed from Evreux, were stopped shortly before the edge of the city.
>
> In the vicinity of the Panzer of Oberjunker Vockelmann of the 2. Panzerkompanie, a smoke candle had ignited. Due to the developing heat a fire started and the Panzer IV blew up with a bang. None of the comrades were wounded, but the Battalion had its first tank loss. From this day on the entire Battalion knew comrade Vockelmann.

From **August 23, 1942,** on the company strengthened its skills by taking part in unit exercises simulating attacks at close distances and breaking into enemy positions.

Exercises simulating fighting were conducted in company-wide and company-wedge formation with flank protection by a light platoon. Radio exercises, during which orders were issued over the radio for the men fighting in battalion formation, were also conducted.

Heinz Freiberg remembers these days:

> Company orientation marches during the day and at night.
> The fruit gardens bring a change of vitamin content.
> Obersturmführer Tiemann is in one of his moods and "rules" very strictly.
> Every fourth day the company has guard duty at the concern's gates.

Theater visit in Evreux where "Maria Stuart" is playing.
While on guard duty I had to report Spieß Meschnarz for ignoring curfew. In the end he was mad at me, which I completely understand. From then on my Spieß gave me a hard time.
Here in Evreux our company earned the name "moonshine-company." Reason: when the other comrades got ready to go to bed, we stood in the back yard of the concern and performed drill exercises.

On **September 20, 1942,** the battalion participated in a large sport festival at the sport field in EVREUX.

The 3. Panzerkompanie was the victor in handball and the 4 x 100 meter relay events.

The fastest man of the entire company was our Rudi Hoffrichter.

During this time the bicycle racer Hans Stuck visited the battalion on **September 21, 1942,** and told us stories from his life as a bicycle racer in the soldier's mess hall.

Until **October 10, 1942,** the Battalion took part in uninterrupted training.

Battalion attack from the movement in battalion-wedge formation and battalion-wide-wedge formation in coordination with the Schützenpanzerbataillon (armored semi-tracked vehicle battalion).

On **October 10, 1942,** the Battalion cleared out of the concern in EVREUX, to make room for a new formation.

The Battalion transferred 60 km to the west in the village of ORBEC (20 km southeast of LISIEUX) and took quarter in the palace of MERVILLY.

On **October 14, 1942,** a complete Panzer regiment was formed for the Panzer Division LAH. Obersturmbannführer Schönberger was assigned to be the leader of the regiment.

The commander of the 3. Kompanie, Obersturmführer Tiemann, was assigned the position of regimental adjutant.

The regimental staff set up its command-post in the palace of BOULY MORIN (directly north of Evreux).

The I. Panzer Battalion was built from portions of the Sturmgeschütz Battalion and filled with recruits.

Sturmbannführer Wünsche, until now the commander of Sturmgeschütz Battalion, was given the command.

The Battalion set up quarters in the concern in Evreux.

The previous Panzer battalion became the II. Panzer Battalion under the leadership of Sturmbannführer Martin Groß.

The Battalion now consisted of the 5th, 6th, and 7th Panzer Companies, where the previous 3. Panzerkompanie became the 7. Panzerkompanie.

Obersturmführer Schütz overtook the leadership of the 7. Panzerkompanie for Obersturmführer Tiemann, since the latter transferred to a new position. However, Schütz was transferred shortly thereafter to the 13. (Tiger) Kompanie in Fallingbostel. Obersturmführer Alt then took over the leadership of the Company.

The leadership of the platoons remained unchanged with the exception of Untersturmführer Sternebeck, who stepped into the position of half-platoon leader within the 1st Platoon.

On **October 15, 1942,** the Division was informed that according to an intercepted English spy message, the Allies intended to undertake a landing west of the mouth of Seine, with the intent of advancing in the direction of Bayeux. Their ultimate goal was to cut off the half-island of Cotentin.

On **October 17, 1942** the order to prepare to march was issued under the key word "Herbstlaub" (Fall Leaf). On **October 18, 1942,** this forewarning was raised again.

On **October 20, 1942,** the training program was re-initiated. This time the troops concentrated on exercising night battles.

On **November 7, 1942,** the Divisional order to "make emergency preparations for the emergency case 'Anton'" was issued.

Sea and air reconnaissance units reported: "Enemy convoys in the western Mediterranean Sea."

Tank tracks were loaded up and transported to the line of demarcation of unoccupied France. The 7. Panzerkompanie reached LISIEUX in a motorized march to load up at the freight train station located there.

On **November 9, 1942,** at 2300 hours the company finished loading and waited at the train station until **November 13, 1942.**

Hans Behrend remembers:

> The transport stood at the train station in Lisieux. Going out was absolutely forbidden, since the departure time was not yet known.
>
> But two comrades were nabbed during their attempt to go out. They were promptly instructed to build a compartment and had guards posted before the door to oversee them.
>
> In spite of this, some crews from the 1st Platoon (under Rudolf von Ribbentrop) took the opportunity to take a prowl through the city. It went well – Rudolf von Ribbentrop's dad said, "don't get caught!"
>
> Comrade Reinhold Gienke (Panzer driver), who had guard duty at the

train transport, fetched us from a local bar (where we were hanging out with some comrades from the Luftwaffe) just in time before the train departed.

Heinz Freiberg can remember these days as well:

> During the evening the night guard Spieß Meschnarz asked us all if we wanted to go to the movies. There was to be a "big party in the back of the house." Meschnarz then picked out 10 of those who said they would go and handed them over to a work commando.

On **November 14, 1942,** the transport rolled to the railroad junction in SURDON (20 km southeast of ARGENTAN, north of SEES). There the trains remained standing on the tracks with the loaded vehicles while other units of the Army, among them SS-Panzergrenadier Division "Das Reich," departed for a trouble-free march into unoccupied France over the line of demarcation.

The companies standing still on the transport wagons were lucky that there were no Allied air attacks during this time.

Hans Behrend remembers this day:

> We primarily spent the night in the vehicles on the train. We built a ramp to practice the loading and unloading of vehicles from the train into the field – just for a change of pace.
>
> The days at the train station in Surdon went on and on.
>
> In the barracks next to the train station administration, the scene at the front-theater brought some change. Actress Ethel Rescke performed for an audience there and had great success.
>
> Otherwise the extent of the change included observing the many passenger trains that passed through.
>
> After experiencing an initial mistrust with the French railwaymen at the train station, they "initiated" us with their wine supply in such a simple way, a way that these railwaymen must have practiced for generations. They used the very large wooden barrels which sat on top of wagons and were used for transporting wine. The barrels were drilled from the underside and a can was held under the hole to catch the wine that poured out. After the can was filled, the hole was closed once again with a wooden stopper. We attentively observed them at work and noticed that this ritual, which had been carried on for generations, had put many holes in the barrels. Our large coffee cans made of aluminum were greeted by the railway men with hearty applause, and they gave us enough wine to fill our cans.

These days are also among the best memories of Heinz Freiberg:

> Next to the train station there was a large factory for producing wood railway ties. We had a run there every morning to take a shower. The main attraction was a little train station store where there were two nice girls.

Afterwards, on **December 1, 1942**, the march alert was raised and a transport to LISIEUX followed on **December 2, 1942**. The company took quarter again on **December 3, 1942,** in ORBEC.

The light platoon with three Panzer IIs was removed from the company and transferred to the Regiment, and Untersturmführer Kurt Fröhlich departed the 3. Panzerkompanie as well.

The six Panzer IVs with 7.5 cm short barrels were given to a Police division in southern France. Before that, however, the Panzers were used for a large shooting exercise in the vicinity of our quarters. All of the crews took part so as to reduce the old supply of ammunition.

Due to a divisional order the 3. Panzerkompanie was given a fitness test for tropical weather on **December 8, 1942**. From then on the main theme of discussion was "Africa" and the American advance in North Africa.

From **December 21, 1942,** on the preparations for the Christmas festival and the New Year continued.

Heinz Freiberg remembers the Christmas party in ORBEC:

> The days of the festival took place in a festive setting. Every member of the company received a picture folder of the LAH and of course a Christmas fruit cake sent from the Führer himself.

The days of the festival were overshadowed by the message about the situation in STALINGRAD and the desperate fight of the 6th Army. With that news the mood for the coming New Year's Eve party was ruined.

To that Heinz Freiberg notes:

> Preparations were made for the coming change in the year. Franz Faustmann was doing finger exercises for music to be played in the background. There was no need to exercise the muscles used for swallowing.
>
> During the New Year's party we all – as if it was an evil forewarning – tied one on. Something similar went on with the officers on the second floor.

On **December 30, 1942**, a day before New Year's Eve, the order arrived that the company should acquire a complete supply of winter equipment and that the vehicles were to be prepared for a winter action in the East.

After that it was forbidden to go on leave. All soldiers already on leave had to report back to the company by **January 5, 1943,** at the latest. (See the Operations Order of the Supreme Command of the Army No. 2 from **December 28, 1942,** and its addendum from **December 31, 1942,** in Appendix 2 for more information).

Hans Behrend remembers the transport departing from ORBEC:

> Due the sudden order to leave France, we had to quickly take care of some financial problems. The crews took care of the drinks. The remaining money was collected by the Company and Furier[2] Kurt Briesemeister bought two oxen. The Company then left for the transport train with these supplies. Briesemeister had no problems putting these supplemental rations to good use after reaching our destination.

1943
Kharkov, Bjelgorod (Operation "Zitadelle"), Italy (Disarmament of the Italian Army), Korosten, Berditschev

KHARKOV

After **January 5, 1943,** the transports of the IInd Panzer Battalion rolled in the direction of the Reich.

The train transport departed from LISIEUX and traveled through Namur, Brussels, Aachen, Düsseldorf, Paderborn, Hameln, Hildesheim to BURG near Magdeburg.

On **January 11, 1943,** the 7. Panzerkompanie took quarters in a school in BURG.

On **January 12, 1943,** six new Panzer IVs with white winter paint and 7.5cm 48 (long barreled) guns were received from an army armor depot and given to the Company's commander, the staff company and the 2nd Platoon. A shooting exercise at the troop training grounds in ALTENGRABOW was carried out immediately after picking up the new Panzers.

The driver training, which still had yet to be completed, was brought to a conclusion in the winter conditions.

Hans Behrend reports on these days in Burg:

> The crews took the time to equip the Panzer motors with pre-warmers (the so-called "fox-equipment") for the coming winter actions while located in the vehicle halls of a concern in Burg. Due to the difficult work in the engine compartments, several unavoidable incidents occurred and fire extinguishers had to be used several times.

On **February 2, 1943,** everything was loaded up at the freight train station in BURG.

The transport rolled through Berlin, Dirschau, Elbing, Königsberg, Insterburg, Gumbinnen, Vilna, Kovno, Minsk and Gomel and arrived in LYUBOTIN (west of Kharkov).

A field post letter from Ralf Tiemann paints a picture of the mood of the Transport:

> ... the night lasted for hours while traveling over the vast, snowy Russian landscape.

The candles threw a cozy shine into the corners of the small crowded wagon.

... the train continued again. Whenever I looked through the darkness in the windows, I could see a pale black-gray in which the white snow carpet retreated into the unending distance and then onwards into the unknown. The creaking steps of the guards could be heard outside. The winds from the Russian Steppe swept along the train and pushed into the compartment.

I had my fur jacket on and my felt boots covering my feet. In spite of this, you could feel the cold if you didn't move.

... then it was already night again. The day before the transport had to make a long stop. Partisans had blown the tracks.

The Russian winter came at us with its ice coldness with every Kilometer we traveled.

It was interesting for me to see this part of Russia, since until that day I had only been able to see the endless Steppes of the Ukraine.

But in the middle of the night we changed our direction.

In the morning we were suddenly in MINSK. According to the train official, it was here that the partisan area began. Until this day our train had no acquaintance with these oddballs. Some transports of our Regiment, whom we saw at the locomotive switch-over train stations, had experienced small attacks. I am still unaware of any larger attacks during our transport.

Yesterday morning we passed GOMEL.

Here on the train my life is running an almost regular course.

In the morning "King Kong" brings me water to wash with. The first two days I was bold enough to wash up on the platform of the train. But I gave up this rugged day's beginning as the water began to freeze in the bowl and then freeze on my fingers.

With every kilometer we travel, we penetrate deeper into the wide flatlands of the Ukraine. We can feel the exceptional closeness of the front. It is easily recognizable that the communications zone attendants live with the stress caused by the latest occurrences here and at the front. Our rolling transports give them reassurance.

Today a railway man said to me: "it's all happening where you all are going."

Even if what the good man said to me was a bit naïve, it did however manage to move us when we listened to the way these simple men spoke with such trust and confidence to our divisions here on the front.

It almost gave us a lift to once again to hear the voice of the front after the days of peace and quiet in France, and after experiencing the daily frustrations of having to deal with the communication zone officials there who were completely naïve and arrogant. The men on the front, who had experienced both the difficult and successful days with us, were excited about our appearance and it brought them some new courage.

This lightning transport took five days to get across Russia. Tracks lay behind us which we had estimated would have taken ten days to cross. Other transports had to remain at the switchyards for 34 hours just to let us through. Without taking a break, our division rolls into the new operational area. Tonight we are going to pass KHARKOV. Where we're going after that we don't know.

In LJUBOLIN the 7. Panzerkompanie unloaded under enemy artillery fire and marched through KHARKOV to MEREFA (south of Kharkov).

After the calm time during formation and the basic training, the 7. Panzerkompanie went into its first action with complete confidence, an action which would demand all the Company had to offer.

Hans Behrend remembers the arrival in Russia:

> After unloading in Kharkov we were supplied with supplemental rations – butter, cookies, chocolate, oil sardines, cigarettes and vodka – at an army supply-camp. During the march to Merefa we met Italian soldiers along the way who were on their way back. They made a completely demoralizing impression on us. They didn't even have any winter clothing and dragged their belongings along with sleds.
>
> During the late afternoon our Panzer 717 ripped its right steering brake's brake pad[3] on an ice covered street and the wagon slipped half-way into the ditch along the road. We thought to ourselves: "that's as far as we're going!"
>
> The company continued on and promised to send help. At sunset a Tiger from the 13. Kompanie came. Lucky for us the driver was a former company comrade, Walter Poewe, who was transferred to the 13. Kompanie while we were in Orbec. Without hesitation the two ropes from both wagons were set up and the Tiger pulled us back onto the flat street.
>
> It became dark and started to snow. We hung the straw mats that were given out in Burg over the cannon itself and then hung up a small petroleum lamp underneath. Under the poor lighting conditions we started disassembling the ripped brake pad and waited for the arrival of the comrades from the maintenance battalion.
>
> Everything went pretty shitty for us, five men all alone in this winter night. We also set up defensive positions all-around us just in case. The side-

car motorcycle finally came and the men from the repair unit completed the repair. It wasn't until later that morning that we caught up with the rest of the Company in Merefa. We slept there until the next day.

At this time the desperate fight of the 6th Army in Stalingrad had come to an end.

A later historical writing determined that with this loss the German Reich went step by step into an unavoidable defeat.

But as the 7. Panzerkompanie rolled into combat, it knew and assumed nothing of such a defeat.

Since **January 28, 1943,** the transports of the Panzer Grenadier regiments, the reconnaissance battalion, parts of the combat engineers, the Panzerjäger (tank hunters), the FLAK (anti-aircraft) and parts of the artillery continued to arrive in the area of KHARKOV-TSCHUGUJEV and go straight from unloading immediately into defensive positions on the west bank of the DONEX – an area spreading out 45 km on both sides of TSCHUDGEUJEV, where the left flank (south of SSALTOV) comes into contact with the "DEUTSCHLAND" regiment of the "Das Reich" division, while the right flank (IInd Battalion of Panzer-Grenadier Regiment 2 of the LAH) "hung in the air."

During the time between **February 3-9, 1943,** the attacks by the 69th and 3rd Soviet Armies steadily increased. All of these attacks were successfully beaten off after mopping up local break-ins.

Badly beaten remnants of the 298th Army Infantry Division, fighting along the way on their retreat from Stalingrad, reached the main fighting line of the LAH and were taken in and cared for.

On **February 10, 1943,** the Soviet attacks shifted to the north and to the south and threatened to outflank the "Das Reich" division nearby ZIRKUNY in the direction of KHARKOV. The LAH, which was in the vicinity of SMIJEV began to move in the direction to BORKIZU.

Therefore the SS-Panzer Korps decided to pull back the front to KHARKOV, and to collect the newly freed forces in MEREFA at the positions of the LAH. From there the collected units were to advance in two directions to the south onto NOVOJA VODOLAGA – PARASKOVEJA and onto TARNOVKA – ALEXEJEVKA to cut off the leading attack units of the 3rd Soviet Army. (See map 1).

The attack on NOVOJA VODOLAGA and BULACHI – GORKI that took place on **February 10, 1943,** by the closed Panzer Regiment together with the Reconnaissance Battalion got bogged down in the snow drifts and swamp areas near MEREFA. (See map 2).

During the march to combat the Panzer 718 received its baptism of fire. Karl Müller reports:

Our Panzer 718 with crew members Hans Schubbe (Kommandant), Rolf Weingarten (no. 1 gunner), Walter Schmidt (driver), Richard Bendfeld (loader) and Karl Müller (radioman) rolled together with the rest of the 7. Panzerkompanie in the direction of the enemy. We still hadn't prepared yet for action, the hatches on the turret were still open. Suddenly an armed attack began. A grenade launcher round flew through the open hatch door and exploded in the Panzer. After that there was a deadly quiet and our Panzer was filled with smoke. Three comrades lost their lives there. Only Richard moaned to himself. He was badly wounded. I had a leg wound. A fragment between the knee joint and the knee cap, but I was able to crawl out of the emergency escape hatch and drop off in the deep tread marks carved out by the panzer. During the escape I was shot through the left heel by a Russian sharp shooter. – During a pause in the battle I was found by a crew of medics. They also retrieved Richard out of the Panzer. We were given emergency care and in the end we were transferred with the last train from Kharkov to the next field hospital.

Six months later the two survivors of Panzer 718 were once again in contact. On September 9, 1943 Richard Bendfeld wrote to Karl Müller: (shortened)

Dear Karl,

Where exactly are you hiding? How has you wound healed?

I laid in the Regensburg hospital until July 30. My right eye had to be removed because I had a fragment in it. They also had to remove other fragments from my hide, some of which are still in me. But I feel pretty good. I received the Silver Wound Badge and also the approval from the Kompanie for the Iron Cross IInd Class.

At the moment I am at home on recovery leave. On the 22nd I went to Beneschau near Prague to the Convalescence Company. There I met some old acquaintances: Hermani, Egger, Killat, Schrubel, Kurt Müller, Homann, Freiberg, Bunke, Kardauke. All of them asked about you, they didn't know anything about how it turned out for you.

Did you actually get your personal belongings back from the Kompanie? Our Panzer was eventually pulled out. I didn't get any of my things back.

What became of the comrades of our crew, well, you already know about that. They are laying in graves in Merefa. Obersturmführer Alt was mauled by the Russians, Untersturmführer Stollmayer was killed, Untersturmführer Janke was badly wounded. Yesterday I saw in the newspaper here that he was engaged.

Do you still have contact with the old Kompanie? Ja, there really is barely any of the old comrades still around... The best have almost all been killed.

For today that will have to be it. I hope to here from you soon, so that the two remaining members of the 718 will stay in contact with each other.

Hearty greetings from your old comrade and fellow barber,

Richard

For Hans Behrend the attack on the 1st day remains a lasting memory:

Finally the companies received the order to attack. The goal of the attack was to capture a piece of land in the vicinity of Merefa. The landscape was covered with snow and had not been reconnoitered. There were no hints that would tip us off to the swamp. It was our luck, good or bad, that we suddenly had problems with the steering. The wagon would only turn at its current position. Sternebeck was close to having a heart attack, but fleeing or screaming would have done nothing to help the situation. We had to watch helplessly while Panzer 727 sunk up in the swamp up to its turret. While the crew was escaping, Oberscharführer Eichholz was shot down from the motor area. The wagon 718 got hit and burned out. We could fight from a great distance against a few recognizable Panzerbüchsen.[4]

Balance sheet: 7 comrades killed, 8 wounded, 2 Panzers totaled, and one Panzer in the work station for weeks after its retrieval. I transferred to Stollmayer's Panzer as no. 1 gunner. – This first fight was a shock for our comrades.

Heinz Freiberg from the 1st Platoon of the 7. Panzerkompanie wrote in his diary:

The attack finally started in the afternoon. A swamp area which lay below the deep snow was not noticed. Three Panzers fell in. We had casualties from Panzerbüchsen and anti-tank gun fire – 7 dead and 8 wounded. A Panzer IV, which had sunk down to its turret, was pulled out in the night.

The charred bodies of the fallen comrades were "buried" in MEREFA.
A Russian counter attack was beaten off.

As a result of these losses, the Division decided that in the future the Panzer Battalion should be put into action split up rather than grouped together. They should then be subordinated to the regimental battle groups, which now and then had to advance along streets.

Ist Panzer Battalion (with the 6th Company) is subordinated to the Reconnaissance Battalion under the leadership of Sturmbannführer Kurt Meyer, and is to advance through NOVOJA VODOLAGA – PARASKOVEJA to ALEXEJEVKA.

IInd Panzer Battalion (without the 6th company) is subordinated to Panzer Grenadier Regiment 1 LAH, (with parts of Regiment "Der Führer"), under the leadership of Standartenführer Witt, and is to advance through BORKI on to OCHOTSCHAJE and through TARANOVKA to BEREKA.

The "Battle Group SS-Panzer Korps," initiated its attack on **February 12, 1943,** and took part in eventful battles along the previously mentioned path of advance until February 15, 1943, when all sides of ALEXEJEVKA were taken. (See map 3). Meanwhile, the defensive struggle for KHARKOV developed into a non-stop battle. Parts of the LAH were fighting in this battle, namely SS-Panzer Grenadier Regiment 2, parts of SS-Panzer Grenadier Regiment 1 and the Combat Engineer Battalion.

The Soviet units continued to advance on by the northern sector of KHARKOV (and partly managed to penetrate the city). Their units in the south, which had advanced towards the city after passing through LOSSEVO, threatened to encircle our units.

In this situation the commanding general of the SS-Panzer Korps, Obergruppenführer Hausser, decided (against numerous orders from the Führer) to order the breakthrough to the south and give up KHARKOV.

With that decision he saved the existence of various regiments. His decision also freed up forces for the defense south of KHARKOV, as well as for a later counter-attack.

The "KHARKOV-GROUP" completed its withdrawal on **February 20, 1943,** and integrated itself into a defensive front built up by SS-Panzer Grenadier Regiment 1 LAH on the UDY river. The Soviet attacks directed from KHARKOV were concentrated in this area and continued to increase in strength until **February 24, 1943**.

Hans Behrend reports on the defensive battles on **February 23, 1943**:

At the positions south of ORDIVKA held by the IInd Battalion of SS-Panzer Grenadier Regiment 1 (led by Sturmbannführer Max Hansen), the Soviets had successfully managed a local break-through.

The Battalion's command post was in BULACHI.

From NOVAJA VODOLAGA the Panzers of the 7. Panzerkompanie drove through BULACHI to the position of the breakthrough and were able to effectively support the grenadiers of the IInd Battalion during the annihilation of the enemy forces that had successfully broken in. The enemy troops consisted of Soviet infantry without heavy weapons.

At a distance of 3000 to 4000 meters we could observe Soviet horse-drawn sleds and tanks.

During the attack I successfully positioned my Panzer III in a small depression and was able to kill 48 Russians with machine gun fire.

Since the men of the Maintenance Battalion were interested in the barrels of captured Soviet machine pistols, we searched the bodies of the killed Soviets. During our search we determined that the Russians had German underwear, canned rations and other equipment. They wore German bread bags on German belts as well as German gas masks carrying cases. I was able to supplement my personal stocks with four brand new pairs of Wehrmacht socks and a wad of handkerchiefs.

After mopping up the break-in we drove back to BULACHI. There we tanked up, replenished our supply of ammunition and spent the night freezing in our Panzers. During the night Untersturmführer Stollmayer – my Panzer commander – was with company commander Obersturmführer Alt in the battalion command post of the IInd Battalion in BULACHI.

On **February 24, 1943,** the Soviet attacks reached their peak. Our forces were partially successful in mopping up several deep Soviet penetrations. Above all, the villages of OCHOTSCHAJE, BERESTOVOJE and BULACHI had become focal points.

Heinz Freiberg wrote about this situation:

February 24, 1943. Soviet attack in Bulachi in the early morning. The village was brightly illuminated by a burning gas tanker truck. The Soviets came with their PAKs (anti-tank guns) and positioned them in front of our company command post. There were considerable casualties. Our company commander, Obersturmführer Alt, was shot in the head and killed while trying to flee. It wasn't until the morning that the splintered parts of the company were once again able to collect themselves in the village of NOVOJA VODOLAGA.

This day is also clear in the memory of Hans Behrend:

The night in the cold Panzers did not want to end . Between 0400 and 0500 hours we were awakened by the commander of our Panzer, Untersturmführer Stollmayer. "Alarm – get ready – Soviet breakthrough on the same position as yesterday. Panzers march!"

It was still pitch-black. A figure suddenly appeared next to my open no. 1 gunner hatch and spoke to me. I recognized Sturmbannführer Max Hansen, commander of the IInd Panzer Grenadier Battalion. He climbed on our wagon and sat on my side next to the turret. With Untersturmführer Stollmayer in the turret he discussed the situation and gave the order to drive as quickly as possible to where the Soviets had broken through our lines. In the meantime we had prepared our Panzer for action, turned towards the snow flats (about 30 cm deep) and drove onto the street that would lead us in the direction of the infantry fire. Behind us we could only recognize a single Panzer IV.

Sturmbannführer Hansen spoke with us through the hatch and was of the opinion that this was surely only a local infantry break-in without any heavy weapons. We were not of the same opinion, since we had seen a Soviet tank the day before. Because of the darkness, Untersturmführer Stollmayer held a flare gun ready. I told my loader that he should have a tank round of type "red" ready to fire. We only had five "red" rounds on board.

After a long drive on the street without any sign of the enemy, our driver began to drive in a jerky fashion. He called over the on-board radio: "there's something ahead of us!" He had a better view of the horizon from his position in his seat than we had from the turret. Nothing could be recognized by looking through the gun's optics. I called: "Flare – Load Panzer round!" Untersturmführer Stollmayer fired the flare and the loader called that we were ready to fire our main gun. Before the flare reached its peak I could already see a tank at a distance of about 40 meters. At first glance it appeared to be an American Mark III. The tank stood directly in front of us and was positioned on its side. At this distance my shot was a direct hit. As soon as the flare burnt out there was an explosion in our Panzer.

It was the first tank round of type "red" that I had shot in combat and it had an unusual side-effect. The shell was caught in the barrel and was on fire!

There was a short second of shock, and then a quick look at the knocked-out American tank from the open hatch. No enemy fire. Canon barrel down, evacuate, set up the barrel support and start to work. After numerous tries we were able to dislodge the shell from the gun's breach.

While the crew prepared the canon once again to fire, we hadn't noticed that a motorcycle messenger had reported to Sturmbannführer Hansen. He was noticeably very upset and said: "Turn around immediately, the Soviets have overrun the command post in Bulachi! The attack here appears to have only been a decoy!"

We jumped in the wagon and turned on to the street. We floored it and drove back in the direction of Bulachi. It was still dark and Sturmbannführer Hansen sat next to my open hatch again. In the direction of Bulachi we could already see some light from fire. After turning off the road and toward the village we could see a burning gas tanker wagon standing before the village. The fire lit up the field located in front of the village. The light enabled me to easily recognize the command Panzer "705" of Obersturmführer Alt, which the Soviets were busy messing around with. I scared them away with my turret machine gun.

Sturmbannführer Hansen continually repeated the order to advance into the village. He raised no objection as a result of the Soviet tank.

So we drove alone like a gigantic target over the brightly lit field of snow until we were about sixty meters away from the village of Bulachi. We saw no further signs of the enemy and our second Panzer (with its Kommandant Gerd Killat) and no. 1 gunner Horst Borgsmüller were behind us in the street. Suddenly a bang. A hit in the right chassis section. Filled with shrapnel in the right side of my body, I flew out of my open hatch and into the snow. Untersturmführer Stollmayer flew out of the turret onto the rear of the Panzer and then fell onto the ground behind the Panzer. There sat Sturmbannführer Hansen as well. Neither man had any big scratches. During my attempt to look for the rest of the crew in the Panzer, the Soviets shot at me from the tank's side shields and down. The shot went right through my left upper arm.

My radioman Hugo Hengl then shot the Soviets from the rear of the Panzer down, as he straightened himself up there.

Now the Panzer started to burn. Sturmbannführer Hansen called to me: "Run away boy!" Under infantry fire I trotted back along the tracks left by our Panzer in the direction of the street and crawled over the bow onto the tank's side shields of the protected side of the Panzer that had picked me up. It was the Panzer of comrade Gerd Killat. The wagon then drove me a few hundred meters further on toward the street in the direction of NOVAJA VODOLAGA, where some of our company was already located. Among them were both our company medics, Berger and Szeimies. These guys took care of my wounds right away and then bandaged them up. A healthy sip from the bottle reawakened my spirit.

It was there that I heard about the death of our company commander (Obersturmführer Alt) from the no. 1 gunner of Command Panzer 705, Rottenführer Ritz Eismann (who was later killed as an Unterscharführer in 3rd Company/SS-Panzer Regiment 12). He had stayed in the command post of the IInd Battalion in Bulachi, as Sturmbannführer Hansen was on the way to mop up the Soviet break- through with our Panzer III. Obersturmführer Alt was killed immediately by a shot through the head at about 0500 hours.

I hitched a ride in the direction of Novaja Vodolaga in the side car of one of the medic's motorcycles. On the way we met Untersturmführer von Ribbentrop and a few of his Panzers which were on the march to Bulachi. I told him about what had happened there, especially about the loss of our company commander. During a counter-attack conducted by von Ribbentrop's Panzers, Bulachi was taken and three further Mark IIIs and 2 T-34s were knocked out.

After strong Soviet forces passed north of MEREFA in a wide advance towards the west had threatened to surround NOVOJA VODOLAGA, the Division decided to pull back the Regimenter to a defensive line north and east of KRASNOGRAD. (See map 5).

This line was reached on **February 25-26, 1943,** and the damaged battle wagons were taken to the Panzer work station to be overhauled.

Heinz Freiberg reports:

At about 1800 hours we marched off in the direction of Krasnograd. There the Panzers and other vehicles were overhauled.

The bodies of a few of our comrades were buried in the work station. The order was issued that in the future all fallen comrades were to be buried at the first opportunity.

Untersturmführer Rolf Janke took over the leadership of the 7. Panzerkompanie for Obersturmführer Alt.

On **February 26, 1943,** Soviet attacks all along the defensive front were renewed immediately, but all of them were beaten off.

On **February 27, 1943,** a group of Soviet tanks managed to break through the seam between the 320th (Army) Infantry Division and SS-Panzer-Grenadier Regiment 1 LAH and advance from BLAGODATNOJE to OLCHOVATKA.

A battle group was formed with recently repaired Panzers of the 7. Panzerkompanie and sent from KRASNOGRAD through KARLOVKA and BELUCHOVKA and was set directly against the Soviet attack group in order to seal off the break-in in OLCHOVATKA. (See map 5).

An excerpt from the war diary of the LAH from **February 27, 1943** states:

> At 0800 hours the 1st SS-Panzer-Grenadier Regiment announced that the 320th (Army) Infantry Division reported that the intended withdrawal from Blagodatnoje had just been accomplished. They explained that the enemy had penetrated the gap (that had been created by the withdrawal) with infantry and tanks and was quickly advancing on to Olchovatka.
>
> The 1st SS-Panzer-Grenadier Regiment, strengthened by Panzers of the IInd Battalion of the SS-Panzer Regiment LAH had, for the time being, closed the gap and had established contact with the 320th (Army) Infantry Division in Krutaja Balka.
>
> During the battle two T-34s and eight anti-tank guns were annihilated.
>
> The Ia alarmed the repaired Panzers located in Karlovka and ordered them to gather under the leadership of the regimental adjutant of the Panzer regiment, Obersturmführer Tiemann. This group received the task of preventing the enemy forces (that had broken through the lines in the direction of Olchovatka) from breaking through to the Army supply line between Poltava and Krasnograd, and if possible, to destroy them.
>
> The commander of the 1st SS-Panzer-Grenadier Regiment was instructed of these measures by the Ia and received the order to annihilate the enemy n Olchovatka. The attack was to be launched from the east towards Olchovatka after the mopping up of the enemy break-through south of Staroverovka. The attack was to have the support of Sturmgeschütze (assault guns) and take place in conjunction with the armored group "Tiemann."

Obersturmführer Tiemann explained in an after battle report on March 1, 1943: (excerpt)

> The battle group took off at 0900 hours in the direction of Olchovatka with a light platoon in the lead. For the time being only two of the Panzer battle wagons from the 7th Company could depart. One of the two battle wagons fell out due to brake problems after traveling only half the distance. With

that the battle group consisted of four Panzer IIs, three Panzer IIIs and a Panzer IV. The light platoon advanced until reaching Popovka and secured it in the direction of Varvarovka. Here Hauptsturmführer Schürer of the 1st SS-Panzer-Grenadier Regiment reported with 60 replacements and subordinated himself and his men to me.

On February 28, 1943 at 0400 hours the results of continuous reconnaissance determined that enemy tanks were departing Beluchovka in the direction of Olchovatka. At 0445 hours the battle group began the attack. Platoon Janke attacked the southwest edge of the village head-on, while Platoon Stollmayer attacked the southeastern edge of Beluchovka (along the road between Chalfurino and Beluchovka) with infantry. The village was free of the enemy for the most part. The battle group pushed through the village with the infantrymen sitting on the Panzers until reaching the northern edge of the village. Platoon Stollmayer overtook security on the northeastern exit of the village, Platoon Janke was assigned to reconnoiter in the direction of Olchovatka at 0630 hours and establish contact with the Sturmgeschütz Battery Wiesemann (2nd Battery of Sturmgeschütz Battalion 1 LAH) in Krassnosnamenka. On the southern edge of Olchovatka the reconnaissance troops received strong enemy anti-tank and tank fire. A Panzer IV was knocked out and burned. Both the no. 1 gunner and the loader were killed. The remaining crew members disembarked with bad burns. Platoon Stollmayer opened fire on recognized muzzle flashes and annihilated an enemy tank and an enemy anti-tank gun. Under the protection of our fire the remainder of Platoon Janke pulled back, during which they eliminated an enemy anti-tank gun. Janke's Panzer received four hits from an anti-tank gun and was knocked out. After Janke left the battle on the eastern edge of the village, Platoon Stollmayer opened fire on recognized targets on the western edge of the village and annihilated another enemy anti-tank gun.

At 1200 hours the battle group (under the command of Standartenführer Witt) was briefed by radio about the situation. Staraji Olchovatka was in our hands. The 2nd Battery of the Sturmgeschütz Battalion (under the leadership of Wiesemann) had penetrated into the southwestern part of Novo Olchovatka. The 5th Company of SS-Panzer Regiment 1 LAH was to be pulled from the east to attack Olchovatka with the Ist Battalion of SS-Panzer-Grenadier Regiment 1 LAH after a preliminary artillery barrage. The battle group received the order to lay the western edge of Olchovatka with fire as the battle started and later to join in the battle in Olchovatka from Beluchovka. After the conclusion of the artillery bombardment at 1400 hours the battle group saw its infantry and Sturmgeschütze penetrate the southern edge of OLCHOVATKA.

The battle group opened fire on the western edge with Platoon Janke and set Platoon Stollmayer to the right to attack the southwestern edge in a sweeping manner. At 1430 hours it was recognized that the Soviet tanks and infantry in the strength of two companies were searching to escape from Olchovatka over the swamp and onto Nagornaja. Two tanks stuck in the swamp were discovered and subsequently knocked out. The battle group broke off the attack and brought up the 7th Company of SS-Panzer Regiment LAH as instructed by the IInd Panzer Battalion. The infantry was sent to Jegorjeva and subordinated to the SS-Panzer-Grenadier Regiment 1 LAH on the order of Standartenführer Witt (which was given by Hauptsturmführer Schürer). The light platoon of the Panzer Regiment staff drove back to their quarters in Beluchovka.

Ralf Tiemann described his impressions of the first weeks of the battles for KHARKOV in a letter written in the field:

> It is often painful for me to sit in the command post and not be able to take part in the battles.
>
> I'm thinking of my company as well. My old Panzer 705 hasn't been alive for a long time. Eight days ago the company commander, my replacement, was killed. Many of my best previous enlisted men and NCOs are no longer alive.
>
> But three days ago fate called me to lead my old company in a decisive battle once again. The Russians had broken through the lines in the vicinity of our neighboring division and were close to closing off our supply road. I received the task from the Division to form a battle group and to ward off an attack under all conditions. It was even more of an act of fate that the 7. Panzerkompanie had been freshening up for the last two days in the work station. Unfortunately I lost my light platoon leader (Oberscharführer Scharna) during this battle. He was definitely the best NCO that I have come across in my lifetime. The Russians knocked out his tank and then dragged it away and buried it in a pile of hay. As we took the village the day before yesterday, we found him.... Now I sadly have the duty of burying him. How often have I now had to bury my best comrades under the earth!! How many are there yet to be???

As the IIIrd (armored) Battalion of SS-Panzer Grenadier Regiment 2 LAH (Sturmbannführer Peiper) advanced from ZIGLEROVKA to JEREMEJEVKA on the right flank of the Division, the Ist Battalion of the SS-Panzer-Grenadier Regiment 1 LAH advanced from ALEXANDROVKA to BELUCHOVKA. The Division was able to establish contact with SS-Division "Das Reich," which was advancing from the wide front from the area of LOSOVAJA to the north. This contact had the effect of stabilizing the situation. (See map 6).

On **March 3, 1943,** Untersturmführer von Ribbentrop took over the leadership of the 7. Panzerkompanie and transferred with it to KRISTITSCHE where SS-Panzer-Grenadier Regiment 1 LAH was situated. The 5th and 6th Panzer Companies had just been deployed there as well.

After the SS-Panzer Grenadier Division "Totenkopf" took up contact with the left flank of the LAH (Ist Battalion/SS-Panzer-Grenadier Regiment 1) in the hills of BLAGODATNOJE, it had also established contact with the (Army) Panzer-Grenadier Division "Großdeutschland" on the left flank of the Totenkopf Division on March 5, 1943. The SS-Panzer Korps then began to attack to the North with four divisions to take back KHARKOV.

On **March 3, 1943,** the three strengthened attack groups of the LAH (the strengthened SS-Panzer-Grenadier Regiment 2 LAH, the strengthened SS-Panzer -Grenadier Regiment 1 LAH – with the IInd Panzer Battalion – and the strengthened Reconnaissance Battalion – with the Ist Panzer Battalion) stepped forward to re-conquer KHARKOV by first going around the western part of the city and then attacking from the north.

The 7. Panzerkompanie together with IInd Battalion of SS-Panzer-Grenadier Regiment 1 (under the leadership of Sturmbannführer Hansen) attacked VOJANAJA BALIKA within the framework of the IInd Panzer Battalion advancing from the village of KRISTITSCHE.

On **March 8, 1943,** the attack group shortly veered off to the west in order to advance to VLAKI after taking BOBROVKA. BOBROVKA had just been taken by the Reconnaissance Battalion.

Heinz Freiberg noted in his diary:

> Advance in the direction of Kharkov. We spent the night in Valki between the Soviets. As the lead company we took over the night guard and security duties.

Early in the morning on **March 9, 1943,** the advance continued together with the IInd Battalion of SS-Panzer Grenadier Regiment 1 LAH to take LJUBOTIN in an attack. After silencing enemy resistance in the village, the 7. Panzerkompanie advanced within the framework of Battle Group Hansen until reaching the UDY-section and remained there.

Heinz Freiberg remembers:

On this day we advanced 37 km in the direction of KHARKOV. Stukas and "Nebelwerfer"[5] rocket launchers served us well.

On the gray morning of **March 10, 1943,** the Battle Group Hansen, together with the IInd Panzer Battalion, was once again ready to go. This time, they would advance to TSHERKOSKOJE by passing through PERESSETSCHNAJA and DERGATSCHI, and then on to take the highway running between BJELGOROD and KHARKOV.

After reaching the highway the units paused to prepare for the attack on KHARKOV, which was to take place the next morning.

The commander of the 7. Panzerkompanie reports about the battles on this day:

We were to attack together with the Battalion Hansen (IInd Battalion/SS-Panzer-Grenadier Regiment 1).

After a talk that went back and forth between Sturmbannführer Hansen and our Battalion Commander, Sturmbannführer Martin Groß, Groß decided to order the penetration of the village by advancing with Panzers on the village's main street, which we had already come across following the swampy landscape. I drove the lead Panzer and we were able to hold-off the strong Soviet infantry due to Untersturmführer Stollmayer who was the Kommandant in the Panzer behind us. He shot the Soviets with anti-personnel rounds from behind my Panzer. Despite this situation, we successfully fought our way through the village and advanced easily to TSCHERKASKOJE in the middle of retreating Soviets.

In the early morning of **March 3, 1943,** the 7. Panzerkompanie continued the advance in the framework of Battle Group Hansen along the highway between BJELGOROD and KHARKOV in order to attack KHARKOV. On **March 13, 1943,** the battle group had fought its way through to "Red Square" in continuous dogged street fighting. (See map 7).

Heinz Freiberg confided in his diary about the battles which occurred on this day:

Our battle group forced its way past the airport in Kharkov along the road between Bjelgorod and Kharkov.

The Soviet anti-tank guns at the airport cost us two Panzers.

The crosses at the soldier's cemetery had been destroyed by the Soviet soldiers.

A Tiger which was driving at the lead during the approach to "Red Square" was knocked out by a KW II with a shot to the gun's optics. The no. 1 gunner was dead and the commander was badly wounded.

But then we were able to knock out six T-34s in about ten minutes. Our Panzer IVs would not have done so well without the support of the Tigers.

After the final taking of Kharkov we re-christened the "Red Square" to "Square of the Leibstandarte."

This day of battle has remained in the memory of Heinrich Burk as well:

On March 11, 1943 we fought from the north down into Kharkov. It was always a long, straight road.

The 6th Panzer Company lead the attack, during which they lost some Panzers.

After a Tiger advanced to the front, our unit was able to knock out six T-34s. Then the road was free.

Stollmayer sat at the lead and we in the Panzer 728 covered from behind.

With the words: "On to Red Square" we advanced into the coming dawn. At the entrance to the "Red Square," Stollmayer received a direct hit at a short distance. The Panzer burned immediately. The turret crew with Stollmayer, Ray and the loader were killed.

On the next morning we took the "Red Square."

During this attack, Killat, the commander of our old 728, was killed.

After the street battles of the final mopping up action in the city were brought to an end on **March 14, 1943**, the Reconnaissance Battalion advanced further to the east along the road leading in the direction of TSHUGUJEV and was able to mop up the situation in the tractor factory in LOSEVO.

On **March 15, 1943,** the II. Panzerabteilung collected in the northern sector of KHARKOV underneath the "DYNAMO" Stadium and waited for further orders.

On March 16, 1943 the Soviets strengthened their counterattacks north of KHARKOV and occupied MAL.POCHODY and later DEMENTSEVKA. Parts of SS-Panzer-Grenadier Regiment 2 LAH and the 5. Panzerkompanie (which was subordinated to this unit) were successful in winning back both villages early that evening.

Renewed attacks by strong enemy groups further north to KRESZOVO and DOLBINO forced the Division to prepare for an armored advance to BJELGOROD which was to take place the next day. Parts of the divisions "Das Reich" and "Totenkopf" were to accompany the attack from the right while the Division "Großdeutschland" was to accompany our Division LAH to the left.

At around noon on **March 17, 1943,** the strengthened IIIrd (armored) Battalion of SS-Panzer-Grenadier Regiment 2 LAH (together with its subordinated 7. Panzerkompanie) under the leadership of Sturmbannführer Peiper, began to advance to the north along the main road to BJELGOROD. The units experienced poor road conditions (mud and slush), but by sunset had reached the village of NECHOTEJEVKA. After fighting against tough enemy resistance, the village was taken.

Heinz Freiberg wrote about this battle in his diary:

> We abandoned Kharkov ready for action with all hatches closed and advanced in the direction of Bjelgorod.
>
> After traveling about 3 km the lead Panzer of the second platoon was knocked out. We then proceeded to continue our attack in a spread out formation.
>
> Just before the village of Nechotejevka, which we were to pass, we drove in a wide front and gave the attacking platoon fire protection.
>
> After the Soviet soldiers had disengaged, we floored it and drove into the village and then on through it.

On **March 18, 1943**, Kampfgruppe Peiper advanced their attack with support from Stukas and mopped up the village of OFRADNY. They then continued to advance along the train tracks. At 1000 hours KRASSNOJE was taken and with that the day's attack goal had already been surpassed.

At this time Sturmbannführer Peiper was very close to BJELGOROD and did not want to stop the momentum of his attack. He therefore decided to attack BJELGOROD without receiving any orders as such from the Division.

At 1135 hours he was able to report to the Division:

> Bjelgorod has been taken in hand-to-hand combat. Eight enemy tanks have been knocked out.

Heinz Freiberg reports about the attack on BJELGOROD:

Bjelgorod was taken after a short but difficult attack.

Since we were able to take the city so surprisingly and so quickly, and since the Luftwaffe still had received no notice thereabouts, they flew a "beautiful" bombing run on our positions.

The units of the Division "Das Reich," who were at this time engaged in an attack to the right of us, had to suffer heavy casualties as a result of this attack.

The Panzer Group Peiper received orders from the Division to hold up in BJELGOROD and to secure the northern and western edge of the city, while the approaching parts of the division "Das Reich" were to take-over the securing of the eastern edge. (See map 8).

On **March 19, 1943,** the strengthened III.(armored) Battalion of SS-Panzergrenadier Regiment 2 LAH (along with the 7. Panzerkompanie, which was subordinated to this unit) received the task to advance to TOMAROVKA and to meet up with the advancing parts of the division "Großdeutschland."

After overtaking unexpected tough enemy resistance, above all in and around STRELEZKOJE, the units were successful in meeting up on **March 21, 1943,** in GLINKA (west of Strelezkoje).

Heinz Freiberg noted:

> The attack is to continue in a westerly direction. Enemy resistance and a very complicated terrain cost us three Panzer IVs.

On **March 22, 1943,** the Division ordered all of the units of SS-Panzergrenadier Regiment 2 (under Standartenführer Wisch), which arrived in the meantime in the area of BJELGOROD, to hold the line from JATSCHNEV KOLODES over OSKOTSCHNOJE to KASAZKOJE. There the unit was to remain in direct contact with the neighboring division "Großdeutschland."

On **March 26, 1943,** all of the units of the LAH were relieved from their security positions by a regiment of the division "Totenkopf." The Panzergruppe Peiper was transferred back to KHARKOV.

The 7. Panzerkompanie returned to the II. Panzerabteilung and took quarters in the northwest sector of the city.

Heinz Freiberg reports:

> The Panzer combat group was transferred to the rear to Kharkov. The Horch driver[6] of our commander became wounded. I had to take his place for short time.

In the meantime a disagreement took place between the regimental commander, Obersturmbannführer Schönberger, and the regimental adjutant, Hauptsturmführer Tiemann. The result was that Hauptsturmführer Tiemann was transferred back to the II. Panzerabteilung where he took over the leadership of his old 7. Panzerkompanie.

The company's commander, Obersturmführer von Ribbentrop, became regimental adjutant.

Heinz Freiberg recollected these events in his diary:

> March 27, 1943. Our quarters in Kharkov lie in the vicinity of the opera.
>
> Hauptsturmführer Tiemann took over the 7. Panzerkompanie again. Obersturmführer von Ribbentrop became regimental adjutant. Since I am his driver, I am going with. I have to take over the cleaning duties as well.
>
> R.v.R. (and his dog) always receive beautiful packages of food from Berlin, which I always have to go and pick up from the airport.

Hauptsturmführer Tiemann, who was to return to his old company, wrote in a letter:

> ...every day is completely filled now that I lead my old company again.
>
> At 0530 hours, when the first glimmers of the spring sunshine fall on the moist streets of mud and slush, I wrestle with the Panzers for two hours across Kharkov into the country. There are still knocked out tanks and cannons, as well as burned out houses and destroyed roads which bear witness to the battles which took place here. It is completely unreal and everything looks like monuments from the old times.
>
> The sun shines on this scene, while the supplies roll in long columns over the ruined landscape and on to the east. Under the leadership of a few old men the replacements grow into their new tasks.
>
> During midday I sit with the leader of my 1st Platoon behind a house and try to get a tan in the spring sun.
>
> Yesterday we visited a collective farm which was hotly contested only fourteen days ago. Today we want to train and perform shooting exercises there! – there, where hard reality faced my company just a few days ago.
>
> Everywhere we collected Soviet tanks and PAKs (anti-tank guns) which had already been knocked out by us once before. Now our new recruits are to try out their shooting skills on them.
>
> ...Soon I am in finished with the independent training. Then we perform unit exercises under heavy pressure..

It won't be much longer. I once again have a battle strong, well-trained and well-equipped company. The Panzers and other vehicles have been overhauled and repainted for the summer.

We close the chapter on KHARKOV with a memory from Ulrich Felden. His thoughts bear the characteristic humor of the men of the 7. Panzerkompanie:

Our little Franz from Vienna.

As a long serving Rottenführer and dyed-in-the-wool Wiener (guy from Vienna) our little Franz Faustmann was surely no model soldier in the classic sense. With that it can be said that Franz sometimes annoyed his superiors.

Unbeknownst to them, Franz was a good Panzer Kommandant and especially good for any special operation.

Shortly before Kharkov, that was back in March 1943, as little Franz stood close to the right of us, his Panzer was knocked out by a Soviet PAK. The entire crew evacuated the Panzer and quickly jumped off.

The effectiveness of the direct hit was documented by the small clouds of smoke that climbed to the sky through the turret hatches. But suddenly I saw from my Panzer our good Franz jump off our Panzer, turn around and in long leaps and bounds he made for his smoking Panzer. With an ape-like speed he disappeared into the Panzer and shortly thereafter he reappeared with a white sack in his hand. He then quickly turned back and ran from the Panzer. As he once again sat on the back of our Panzer, I called to him: "Are you crazy, why did you climb back into that smoking crate?" Franz responded with his most beautiful grin and said in his strange Viennese dialect:

"Oh my, do you think I would be so stupid as to let my cigarettes burn?"

OPERATION "ZITADELLE"

On **March 28, 1943,** a long period of refreshing and an organizational realignment began for all units after the gathering of our units in Kharkov concluded.

According to the plan, the 7. Panzerkompanie was to conduct the Panzer driving school and radio school for leading the unit.

Heinrich Burk recalled this period of the refreshing.

Tiemann, our old Kompanie Chef, is once again here. The company now has four platoons with five Panzer IVs. I am to be the driver for the commander of the 3rd Platoon, von Husen.

On **April 26, 1943,** the formation of the 12. SS-Panzer Division "Hiltlerjugend" was ordered. Their officers and NCOs were to be almost exclusively supplied by the LAH.

With this order the following commanders are transferred from the LAH:

The divisional commander, Obergruppenführer Sepp Dietrich, as future commanding general of the I. SS-Panzer Korps.

The commander of SS-Panzer-Grenadier Regiment 1, Standartenführer Witt, as future commander of the 12. SS-Panzer-Division "Hitlerjugend."

The commander of the Reconnaissance Battalion, Obersturmbannführer Kurt Meyer, as future commander of a Panzer-Grenadier Regiment within the 12. SS-Panzer-Division.

The commander of the I. Panzer Battalion, Sturmbannführer Max Wünsche, as future commander of the Panzer regiment of the 12. SS-Panzer Division.

With him went the complete I. Battalion of the Panzer Regiment LAH.

...And many other officers and NCOs.

Newcomers were to replace the departing commanders.

As commander of the Division LAH: Standartenführer Wisch, until then commander of the SS-Panzer-Grenadier-Regiment 2.

As commander of SS-Panzer-Grenadier Regiment 1: Obersturmbannführer Frey, until then commander of the Ist Battalion, SS-Panzer Grenadier Regiment 1.

As commander of SS-Panzer-Grenadier Regiment 1: Obersturmbannführer Kraas, until then commander of the Ist Battalion, SS-Panzer Grenadier Regiment 2.

For the time being the Ist Panzer Battalion was not to be replaced.

The Panzer Regiment LAH had at its disposal for the planned offensive only the IInd Panzer Battalion and the 13. (Tiger) Kompanie.

On **May 30, 1943,** the 7. Panzerkompanie transferred to a section of forest east of BLJSCHNY, where it took quarters behind the front and was deemed a reserve unit of the 4th Panzer Army.

Hauptsturmführer Tiemann wrote about this time in a letter:

...Tonight I have to remain behind the current main fighting line with my company as a reserve counterattack unit so that another unit can be relieved.

The night march has once again returned to us.

...After a two night march we reached the front and took quarter in the preparation areas.

We lied in a small crippled section of forest on the slope of an erosion ditch.

Outside the breadth of the Ukrainian area extends in the direction of the enemy. On the half of the slope there is a small clearing where my company built me a small block house covered with straw. A bed made of branches, a table, benches, etc. were also constructed. It could be wildly romantic, if it didn't remind us daily of the raw reality.

In spite of the wind, the god of weather smiled upon us. The sun shined and the life in the bivouac with all of its peculiarities was refreshing. On the first day I arranged a competition to see which platoon could erect the nicest quarters.

Every platoon lay spread out, separated and hidden in the forest. The shelters were decorated and painted. Signs were made. Under the trees small huts made of leaves were built along with stools and tables for the inside. Every platoon had something special.

We naturally brought our shower equipment with us and built it into the scheme of things.

As a token of my company we built a sport field right on the edge of the forest.

Right in the middle of our forest quarters "culture" has appeared. Now I have a radio in my "hut," wire contact with my platoons and electric light.

The vacationers have built me a small table lamp made out of birchwood as "ransom."

In front of my bungalow, under a young oak, a terrace is thrown together and a small fence placed around it. In good weather King Kong has to "serve breakfast on the terrace."

...I already wrote you that I have to prepare an NCO training company. As far as the relations here at the front allow it, the company has been put together as of yesterday and is located in my company's small forest down in a tent bivouac in the ravine.

Training plans, organizing materials, instruction, duty roster and training are once again my activities.

If it only wasn't so cold. During the last few days a storm peculiar to the Steppes swept over the land, such that I thought my straw roof would fly through the air. The wind pushed itself through the erosion ditches and the rain dripped from the straw roof onto the table and the orders, exactly like it is dripping on the pages of this letter. King Kong is here to prepare one hot tea after another.

...To the front on the horizon climb mushroom clouds of smoke to the sky, the result of incoming rounds, then the thunder of guns being fired and rounds landing in our forest.

When the wind turns its course, the sound of rattling of machine gun fire comes back to us. During the night flares of all colors stand on the horizon and flashes of red can be seen when guns are fired and rounds hit their targets. In the air is an endless rumble.

As we sat before the entrances to our trenches, we observed the usual squadrons of Stukas roaring on by over the forest. Four times a day we would hear their blubbering motors as they set out on their reconnaissance missions.

Even Ivan came on a regular basis to unload his eggs on anything he noticed. Then we would stand under protection and watch from our FLAK guns as the sky was dabbed with clouds of smoke and streaks of fire from the smaller caliber guns.

There is a hearty "hello" when suddenly an Ivan shows his blast of flames and runs away.

...Whenever the noise of fighting to the front of us increases, then we get up and stand ready to jump into action, ready to beat back enemy breakthrough points and to close any gap in the front with a counterattack.

But it hasn't come to that.

...By the way, last night I had a visit from Obersturmführer von Ribbentrop, who informed me with a big grin, that after two months in his new position as regimental adjutant he was commended with the comment "you are starting out exactly like Tiemann."

The weeks of serving as a reserve unit ended on **June 16, 1943**.

The company received the order to abandon its position and to transfer back to the quarters in the village of PETROPAVLOVKA. In another letter Hauptsturmführer Tiemann wrote:

Outside the sun of the Russian Steppes burns on our village. It took us a few days of marching and several breaks to reach our destination. We have been in this old village with its large chestnut trees and forested valley for two days now.

Since yesterday the sandbox is once again under the chestnut tree and the shower has once again been set up in its old place. A "work commando" is mowing the sport field right now. This evening there is going to be an NCO party. The NCOs of my company are really looking forward to it. Tomorrow there will be a sport festival for our battalion at the sport field.

On **June 20, 1943,** a Panzer radio exercise took place in a large sandbox under the leadership of the Ia of the division, Sturmbannführer Lehmann. The divisional commander, Standartenführer Wisch, and the commanding general of the II. SS-Panzer Korps, Obergruppenführer Hausser, were in attendance.

The exercise was to break through Soviet positions with a Panzer group in the course of the Kursk Offensive. The situation was such that a Panzer company had to overtake the leadership of the Panzer group with improvised radio contact after the fall out of the Panzer group's leader.

The 7. Panzerkompanie had been chosen for this exercise. The leaders of the 5. and 6. Panzerkompanie, Hauptsturmführer Schmidt and Obersturmführer von Ribbentrop, were to be platoon leaders. Obersturmführer Hoffmann and Untersturmführer Mülbert were also chosen as platoon leaders.

The conduct of this Panzer radio exercise was deemed such a "complete success" that Obergruppenführer Hausser remarked to the commander of the Panzer Regiment, Obersturmbannführer Schönberger, "Herr Schönberger, my congratulations to you and your company!"

On **July 1, 1943,** came the order to "get ready for action!" Load up on ammo, fill up the gas tanks, pack and load.

The 7. Panzerkompanie marched off in a "northeast" direction during the night.

After an extremely massive artillery barrage and after heavy Stuka attacks on the enemy positions, the strengthened Panzer-Grenadier Regiments of the LAH attacked along the road to BYKOVKA in the early morning of **July 5, 1943**.

With SS-Panzer-Grenadier Regiment 1 LAH to the right and SS-Panzer Grenadier Regiment 2 LAH to the left, the quadruple Soviet system of positions was broken through and BYKOVKA was won, but only after heavy battles which lasted the entire day.

During the night BYKOVKA was secured to the north and to the east.

The attacking unit to the right of SS-Panzer Grenadier Regiment 1, SS-Division "Das Reich," fought up to the forward point of the line secured by the LAH. (See map 9).

The 7. Panzerkompanie, in conjunction with the IInd Panzer Battalion, drove in toward the preparation zone southeast of STRELEZKOJE until **July 3, 1943**.

They pulled in behind the main fighting line of the Panzer-Grenadier Regiment on the morning of July 6, 1943 in the marshaling zone northeast of BYKOVKA.

The SS-Panzer-Grenadier Regiment 1 continued their advance in the morning hours of **July 6, 1943**. They broke through the Soviet lines east of KOSMA DEMJANOVSKA and with that accomplished the prerequisite for the attack of the Panzer Group.

On **July 6, 1943,** at 1330 hours the Panzer Group received the order from the Division to attack LUTSCHKI-NORTH and TETEROVINO.

Ralf Tiemann, commander of the 7. Panzerkompanie remembers:

> The Ia (Rudi Lehmann) appeared at the lead of the attack and informed us that the battalion commander (Martin Groß) drove over a mine and was out of action. The 7. Panzerkompanie received the order to launch the advance and lead the attack of the Panzer Group in "battalion wedge" formation.
>
> The Panzer Group was also given the task to "drag along" the other subordinated units (Reconnaissance Battalion, IIIrd (armored) Battalion, SS-Panzer Grenadier Regiment 2 LAH).

The 7. Panzerkompanie won the first wave of the attack and recognized that, so far as one could see, a grand march of the Panzers of Panzer regiments from the SS-Divisions "LAH," "Das Reich" and "Totenkopf." The 7. Panzerkompanie also observed the deeply stacked and widely spread out Soviet tank units, which were rolling in from the north.

Without regard for mines, heavy anti-tank gun fire (coming from the direction of JAKOLEVO) and the attack of a few Soviet tanks from LUTSCHKI (which were beat off), the Panzer Group deployed itself for the attack on LUTSCHKI NORTH.

Heinrich Burk recalls:

> Large attack on July 6, 1943. The 3rd Platoon drove at the lead on the right.
>
> As driver I looked at the beaten down grass in front of me and assumed correctly: "mines."
>
> Then Kompanie Chef Tiemann called to us over the radio: "Georg, Georg (code name for the 3rd Platoon), why are you driving so hesitantly, drive faster!" I said to my self, "here goes!" and I gave it some gas so that I could shift up a gear. The next moment was followed by a heavy detonation. I could feel the pressure of the blast come from below. That meant mines.

As I looked down and see a hole on the floor pan on the left side, I thanked God that I was shifting gears when the detonation went off.

With a few fragments and after little bleeding I was allowed to remain with the company after being attended to by the medics.

In further quick breakthroughs the company reached the village LUTSCHKI-NORTH and advanced further to the north.

While passing the village, the 6. Panzerkompanie got involved in one-on-one battles with a few formations of T-34s which came out of the village and rammed into the flank of the Panzer Group.

Without regard for the threat to the flank (the company leader of the 7. Panzerkompanie had his barrel shot off here and the village of TETEROVINO was taken. After overcoming a Soviet position with steep tank trenches north of the village the advance onto JVANOVSKI VYSSELOK was continued.

With the coming darkness the 7. Panzerkompanie, along with the 6. Panzerkompanie, were positioned in the rear to the right. The 5. Panzerkompanie was positioned in the rear to the left and took a position on the back of a slope above a tank trench.

The Spieß[7] (Brandstätter) and the Schirrmeister[8] (Fischer) brought fuel, munitions and food to the front. They also brought the news that during the afternoon the enemy had temporarily stopped the further advance of the Panzer Grenadier Regiments with a counterattack in LUTSCHKI NORD. The Panzer Group was therefore cut off.

The SPW Battalion[9] (IIIrd (armored) Battalion, SS-Panzer-Grenadier Regiment 2 LAH) under the leadership of Sturmbannführer Peiper went over the line of Panzers to the front and took position on a front slope. (See map 10).

At dawn on **July 7, 1943,** the call of "enemy tanks" woke the company. Just as the platoons were ready for action, the first wave of T-34s came out of the morning fog. Further waves followed closely behind. Loud T-34s decked with infantrymen. And then began the dance! What wasn't knocked out by Soviet tanks at very short distances continued to drive on right between the Panzers of the 7. Panzerkompanie and was taken care of with "turret 0600." The company counted 43 knocked out T-34s that night. Shortly before noon came the second Soviet tank attack. The attack was initiated on the other side of the railroad tracks to go around the Panzer Gruppe. Here lay the 6. Panzerkompanie. "They threw a similar shooting party."

The companies remained in firing position for the rest of the night.

Again on **July 8, 1943** the companies remained in firing position on the back of the same slope above the tank trench. The Soviet tank attacks began again in the morning gray, but they were beaten back from concealed firing positions from great distances. The positions of the IIIrd (armored) Battalion of SS-Panzer-Grenadier Regiment 2 were overrun, however.

To the relief of the SPW-Battalion a few Tigers of the 13. Panzerkompanie partook in a counterattack. A platoon of Panzer IVs had to accompany them for protection.

This action has especially remained in the memory of Rolf Ehrhardt:

> The 7. Panzerkompanie (or, better said, the remains of which were again ready for action after the mine dilemma from July 6) stood in wide formation on the hill; somewhere is the village of TETEROVINO. Behind us there were the smoking wrecks of the first wave of Soviet tanks. Before us was a wall which could not be penetrated. There stood dozens of T-34s from the main wave which we had taken care of in a heavy and dogged battle.
>
> It was a wall of steel and fire. In the middle of everything was the infantry: our Panzer Grenadiers, which were overrun, Soviet soldiers, who were sitting on the T-34s or were pushed forward between the tanks during the attack.
>
> Platoon Leader Untersturmführer Weiser, whose Panzer was still at the repair station, had climbed into my Panzer IV the day before. He came from leave in the homeland and was wearing his dress uniform as he still hadn't had any opportunity to change into his field uniform. We checked out his wedding pictures, everyone tried to find some contact with home.
>
> The previous day didn't bring anything earth-shattering. The tank trenches cost us much time, and until evening we would have gladly given the night watch to the IIIrd Battalion of 2nd Panzer Grenadier Regiment which was not far from our current position. We removed ourselves from the back slope to spend the night with the calm feeling of laying under the protection of 24 tons of steel in the foxholes underneath the Panzers. After a very early waking we heard a call, then orders and commands: "Start your engines – get up – get ready for action!" As we stowed away our cover, Untersturmführer Weiser came from the direction of the command post in long strides and called "hurry, enemy tanks!" Then it cracked, the first T-34 was burning, barely 200 meters away. A Panzer from the staff wiped him out with its 5 cm gun. Now no more long orders were needed. We rolled away and a few minutes later four T-34s were knocked out, some at very short distances. The other Panzers of the 7. Kompanie experienced something similar. Slowly the situation became more organized. The radio calls became normal orders.

The monotony of the orders from the many changes in position was suddenly interrupted: "Georg" to "Irene" we hear. We knew that "Georg" was the leader of the 1st Platoon, Obersturmführer Hoffmann, and that "Irene" is the company commander of the 7. Panzerkompanie, Hauptsturmführer Tiemann. After a few seconds of talking the following was the result: an infantry messenger reported that Sturmbannführer Peiper, commander of the IIIrd (armored) Battalion of Panzer-Grenadier Regiment 2 was wounded, surrounded by the enemy and had to be retrieved. The wall of fire and smoke was a border for both friend and enemy. We observed every movement. A T-34 breaking through the line couldn't even drive 50 m. How deep was this smoke zone? Would it be possible to remain covered and go to Peiper's command post? I wondered how bad Hauptsturmführer Tiemann had to feel at that moment, since he was to be the one to decide whom to give the order for the retrieval. Then came the message over the radio: "Irene" to "Walter" – that was us – "you are in the best position. Take the messenger with you in your wagon and try to get Peiper. Drive 'karacho,' it is your only chance." When he used the word "karacho," I definitely knew what the situation really was. This Landser lingo is not even in the commander's dictionary and made me realize that even he was really worked up. Untersturmführer Weiser confirmed the order, gave the corresponding orders to the Panzers of our platoon and took in the messenger. "Driver march!" was his order to me. After a few moments I was surrounded by smoke. I had to drive slower so as not to drive off in the wrong direction. The sights before my view slot were like scenes from a silent film: wrecks, flames, twisted and unreal figures wearing Soviet helmets. Crater upon crater. Suddenly there was a heavy hit somewhere. I asked myself if I should correct my course.

How could one find a command post in this chaos? The messenger had no possibility of finding his way, especially since he was sitting in a closed turret and therefore couldn't see a thing. Weiser was constantly on the radio and was requesting stronger fire protection. He ordered the vehicles of our Group to stay back, then reported a hit. He then reported that he would drive on with our lead vehicle. Then the last call: "we received Panzerbüchsen and light PAK hits, figuring out where we're going is now impossible, despite this we will drive on." During this hectic time it never occurred to us that no confirmation, no order came from outside. When had the antenna given up? There was no more contact to us – no orders. This entire episode took less time than is required to read it. The on-board radio was intact. We were still driving in the direction of the enemy, in the middle of the enemy. Was there even a German SPW? German helmets? Keep going! Again and again we

> came upon Soviet soldiers. Suddenly there was an alarming order: "T-34 at 0200, load and fire at will!" – "The turret is blocked!" reported the no. 1 gunner. Then it was serious. "Driver – drive to the right!" came the order. I turned, drove in third gear, had to shift and knew that I didn't have any time. I ripped the wagon around. Suddenly a crack, then everything was still. I looked at the tach, it said that the motor wasn't running – did it die or was it hit? Start it! The motor was suddenly running again. I asked, "What should I do?" The radioman ripped his head set off and roared at me: "The no. 1 gunner is dead – the on-board radio is out." I screamed back: "Ask the loader to ask the commander what I should do!" Answer: "The commander is dead too!" "Driver, it is now up to you," went through my head. In the seconds since the hit I saw Soviet soldiers storm the wagon on the no. 1 gunner's side, I drove on, then suddenly I saw our opponent, a T-34, at a distance of 100 meters at the most. I asked myself, "Can our gun move?" I ripped the wagon around 90°, then I heard another crack. But this time I was a second faster. With my sixth sense I was successful in getting behind a wrecked tank just in time. One more time I executed a 90° turn – that had to be the way home. The messenger got out of the Panzer right in the middle of the enemy, the loader was wounded. But I was still not out of it yet. I came out of the smoke and saw the half-platoon leader Unterscharführer Harald Stein and his wagon. My sight block[10] was shot blind. I stuck my head out of the hatch and Stein gave me directions with his hands. Hauptsturmführer Tiemann instructed me to drive back while Stein covered me with his gun at 0600. After we reached the tank trenches, the radioman got out of our Panzer together with the wounded loader and left for the wound station. I was alone.
>
> Later someone counted the hits on my Panzer. My sight block went from hand to hand. My comrades counted 17 hits by rifle bullets and 3 hits from tank rounds.

In the evening the company was relieved from the Battalion and collected in the area south of TETEROVINO.

In the meantime the Soviet tank units advanced into the section of our left neighbor, the "Totenkopf" Division, which still had not advanced as far as the LAH. The enemy's advance had enabled them to attack our open flanks.

In the morning hours of **July 9, 1943,** the 7. Panzerkompanie was put on alarm and was to attack to the west with the rest of the Panzer Battalion to shut down the threat to our flanks and to cut off the lead units of the Soviet attack.

The first attack goal was to reach the southern quarter of the village MAL

MAJATSCHKI and then to advance to VESSELY and make contact with the SS-Division "Das Reich." (See map 11).

Company commander Ralf Tiemann remembers this attack:

> During the early morning we marched to the south and then turned to the west after reaching Lutschki-North.
>
> The "Totenkopf" Division was to stay right where it was.
>
> We were to take a shot in the eastern flank of Ivan and open the way to freedom.
>
> After reaching a long basin in the landscape the battalion spread out in a wide wedge formation and began to drive along the back side of the basin. After reaching a hill at in the direction of 1200 we discovered a wide area of forest. A few T-34s disappeared into the forest as we appeared.
>
> We went right for them at high speed and began to attack.
>
> As we paused before the forest we received strong fire on our right flank. We had landed right in front of a row of PAKs.
>
> My wagon received a hit in the chassis.
>
> Immediately we got out due to the danger of an explosion.
>
> The radioman was wounded.
>
> I changed into the company-troop Panzer.
>
> I barely had the throat mike and headset on and we received a hit in the turret. The loader was dead.
>
> I immediately got out.
>
> I stood stunned under a firing Panzer gun and looked for a new lead Panzer.
>
> Finally the leader of the 2nd Platoon realized this and got out so that I could get in.
>
> In the meantime the 5. Panzerkompanie attacked from the right and rolled over the row of PAK guns.
>
> A few Panzer Spähwagen from the "Totenkopf" Division approached the small forest from the south.

During the evening hours the Panzer Battalion was held up and pulled back to the disembarking position south of TETEROVINO.

On **July 11, 1943** the strengthened Panzer-Grenadier Regiments resumed their attack and came upon strong enemy resistance. The battles went back and forth on both sides of the railway to PROCHOROVKA.

The 7. Panzerkompanie stayed with the Battalion in the area south of TETEROVINO and remained ready to follow SS-Panzer-Grenadier Regiment 2.

At 1000 hours the Panzer Group received a divisional order to advance over the line of SS-Panzer-Grenadier Regiment 2 and to attack and take Hill 252.2 (which was currently being doggedly defended by the Soviets).

At 1300 hours the hill was secured in the hands of the Panzer Group and the Group continued on to the village of OKTJABRSKI.

An immediate heavy Soviet tank counterattack was beaten off.

Since both of our neighbors, SS-Division "Das Reich" to the right and the "Totenkopf" Division to the left hadn't caught up yet, the Panzer Group received the order to hold up half way in PROCHOROVKA and to remain there due to the open flanks and the superior enemy.

On **July 12, 1943,** the Soviets attacked the lead attack units of the Division from the east, north and west, this time with new, stronger forces.

This attack strengthened during the course of the day and there were numerous tank battles.

From this developed the largest tank battle of the Second World War.

Heinrich Burk remembers this day:

> On July 12, 1943, the day of the big tank battle, I sat once again in some Panzer IV. After we knocked out four or five T-34s, a T-34 wiped us out itself. The hit ripped off the cover of the transmission and the brakes were out. The driver and the radio man were lightly wounded by shrapnel. That was the end of "Zitadelle" for me.

At 0900 hours the 6. Panzerkompanie fended off a massive enemy tank attack in OKTJABRSKI and knocked out twelve T-34s. The T-34s swarmed between the battle wagons of the Panzer Group and were knocked out at a distance of 30 meters. After this action 62 knocked out T-70s and T-34s were counted.

After joining up with the Division "Das Reich," the attacks decreased.

Company Commander Ralf Tiemann put together his impressions of this day in a letter written in the field:

> Then began the heated defensive battles. It was a battle for existence from all sides, we were often cut off the entire day without rations.
>
> The enemy tried to cut off our Panzer wedge from east and west with masses of tanks. Day and night in a Panzer. Four battles a day. Then we were pulled back. With half of my Panzers, part of them limping along, I arrived back at the disembarking position in the dark during a heavy rain.

I had never experienced this kind of battle against a tank enemy with a ten-to-one advantage. It was an enraging struggle. On this day our regiment knocked out 62 enemy tanks. My company alone, which took part in the first strike, knocked out 20.

Until today my company knocked out 43 enemy tanks, during which I only had a single complete loss of one Panzer.

One time my Panzer was shot to pieces, but I was able to get out in time, only the radioman was wounded.

Now my good 'ole 705 is once again in the garage.

...I am writing you this letter shortly before a new battle.

We are standing waiting behind a hill. In front of us an artillery and infantry battle is cooking.

Around us is the breadth of the Steppes with the treacherous erosion ditches.

A wind always blows the clouds away so that the sun can shine between the rain showers for a few seconds. The battle is distancing itself from us.

In a few seconds we will be plowing forward over the infantry lines.

On **July 14, 1943,** the Panzer Group accomplished limited local advances (the 6. Panzerkompanie reached OKTJABSKI to the north and the 7. Panzerkompanie reached MICHAILOVKA to the west) which were held back by surprisingly strong enemy fire. On **July 15, 1943,** the Panzer Group prepared itself for an attack on JANJKI to east. The purpose of this was to relieve the SS-Division "Das Reich" from the strong enemy threat to their flanks.

The attack proceeded after navigating through roads of deep mud. After advancing very hesitantly the Generalkommando of the II. SS-Panzer Korps stopped at midday.

The Division pulled back the Panzer Group and directed it to a collecting area nearby Swch.KOMSOMLEZ.

On **July 16, 1943** the strengthened SS-Panzer-Grenadier Regiment 1 was pulled back to the train tracks in VASSILJEVKA where it had contact with the SS-Division "Das Reich" on the right and the "Totenkopf" Division on the left. The remainder of the Division was pulled back behind this line and brought together.

The Panzer Group transferred during the course of these movements to the area west of TETEROVINO.

Even though the enemy didn't pursue our forces, the SS-Panzer-Grenadier Regiment 1 departed for the rear in the evening.

On this day the commander of the 7. Panzerkompanie, Ralf Tiemann, wrote the following letter in the field:

...Hard weeks lie behind my company. So hard, like I never experienced before in this war.

There were two unheard of Panzer battles, then days full of bitter flank and security battles. For days we were on the edge in enemy fire from every weapon. For four days and four nights we didn't leave the confines of our Panzers. We had to be awake the whole time.

I was able to achieve proud results with my company. In total my company annihilated 79 enemy tanks in twelve days of battle. That is four times the strength of my company. To add to that I only had two complete Panzer losses.

...Surprisingly I attacked an airport with my company and annihilated six airplanes.

Despite heavy casualties and over-exertion there is a real excitement amongst my troops. Everyone, even the last loader, has grown close to my heart.

...Now we have been lying here on our battlefield in foxholes under the Panzers since last evening. Around us rages an artillery battle. Mörser batteries and Howitzer batteries. A cannon battery makes me wince every time I go outside. – We have never heard a battle simmering so loud and clear. Even in a Panzer with a closed hatch, humming motor and a headset, it is quieter than being in the middle of incoming enemy artillery.

A day-long break on **July 16, 1943** did the Panzer Regiment good.

Panzer status: 9 action-ready Panzer IVs, 42 Panzer IVs, 5 Panzer IIIs, 4 Panzer IIs.

On **July 17, 1943,** all of the Division reached the collecting area and erected field quarters.

On **July 18, 1943,** the entire II. SS-Panzer Korps was pulled out, removed from the area of the 4. Panzer Armee and was transferred to the area south of KHARKOV. It remained there at the disposal of the Army Group "South" and was to be subordinated to the AOK 6.

The tracked portions of the IInd Panzer Battalion LAH marched to BJELGOROD and loaded up there. The trip went to the south. The Division was to mop up Soviet penetrations on the Donez Front near ISJUM in the area of the SS-Division "Wiking."

Company Commander Ralf Tiemann wrote about this in a letter from the field:

> In two hours the few days of calm will be over already.
>
> We don't know where and on which section of the front we will be deployed. Surely to where the front is burning.
>
> For me these past three days have not been calm.
>
> I had to award medals and promotions.
>
> It was a sad and painful duty to write to the families of my fallen comrades.
>
> I know how much such personal letters from the unit leader mean to the parents and other members of the family.
>
> I want to write personally and full of heart in each and every case.
>
> Although I wrote every letter with great effort, it was somehow unavoidable that in twenty cases a cliché came up.
>
> I lost three platoon leaders. There were moments in action where I had to lead every single platoon.
>
> The death of the young platoon leader Untersturmführer Weiser especially struck me deeply. He came back two days before the beginning of the offensive from vacation, from his honeymoon.

Operation "Zitadelle" had ended for the LAH – and with that – for the 7. Panzerkompanie as well.

A feeling of dissatisfaction remained due to having to depart from the theater of the war before a decision could be reached.

On **July 23, 1943** the Kompanie transport arrived in the area between BARVENKOV and SSLAVIANSK (south of ISJUM) and the company commander took up contact with the leader of the Panzer Group, Sturmbannführer Peiper, to inquire about the unloading station and the preparation area.

He found out that the original foreseen action had quickly blown over and that the tracked portions of the Division were to continue on to the area directly north of STALINO.

On **July 24, 1943** the transport continued to roll on to the ordered area where it was unloaded on July 25, 1943.

On **July 26, 1943** the 7. Panzerkompanie received the order to hand over all its Panzer IVs to the "Totenkopf" Division and to report for a "lightning quick transport."

On **July 27, 1943**, the 7. Panzerkompanie handed over its Panzer IVs to a commando force of the "Totenkopf" Division assigned to receive them. With that they departed from their battle wagons which were their loyal companions through the battles around KHARKOV and the difficult Panzer battles in the BJELGOROD Offensive.

A rumor made its rounds: On to Italy, where new Panzers waited ready to be picked up.

But due to the upcoming action it remained a puzzle for the time being.

ITALY (Disarming of the Italian Army)

On the evening of **July 29, 1943** the 7. Panzerkompanie was made aware of details concerning the greater situation and their further use.

The order was issued for loading up on the following day at the freight train station in STALINO for a "lightning-fast transport" to ITALY.

The war diary of the Supreme Commando of the Wehrmacht gives the background to this world renown speedy transfer (extracts).

> The political upheaval which arrived in Italy on July 27 immediately triggered German countermeasures. The first were issued on July 27 to carry out operation "Case 'Alarich'" on the "Cold Way" (disarmament of the Italian Army in Upper Italy) and to immediately prepare the special operations "Copenhagen" (securing the crossing at the Mont Cenis Pass) and "Siegfried" (occupation of the French southern coast in the area of the 4th Italian Army).
>
> The General Staff of the Army received the order to transfer the command of the IInd SS-Panzer Korps with the SS-Panzer-Grenadier Division "Adolf Hitler" and "Das Reich" to Army Group B from the East.
>
> General Field Marshall Rommel, who had just taken over command in Saloniki, would be called back and would take over the command of the still secret Army Group B in Upper Italy.
>
> Summarization of the condition of the preparations made by the Wehrmacht Leadership Staff (excerpt):
>
> A. Initial Assembly and Forces
>
> 1. 4th and 305th Divisions depart on July 27 and arrive with combat squadrons in the area of Nizza – St. Raphael – Fréjus and Innsbruck – Wörgl
> 2. The following are to be ready for a transport within 36 hours:
>   76th Division (on A + 5 Day northwest of Mont Cenis)
>   389th Division (on A + 5 Day with 1/2 of their battle squadrons on the southern coast of France)

3. The 65th and 94th Division still lack transport material
4. The SS-Division "LAH" is to depart on July 28 and arrive with battle and replacement squadrons until August 8 in the area Innsbruck – Wörgle as well as Rosenheim – Innsbruck.

On **July 7, 1943** everything was loaded up and the company rolled to the west.

The company commander wrote about the troop transport in a letter from the field:

> The day before yesterday the ban on letter writing was lifted once again. Where should I begin? It seems like everything was years ago. Correct – we were on the march to the preparation position in Issium. The other morning (it was the middle of July) there was to be an attack against a Russian break-through on the Mius. The columns were once again standing on the long dusty roads of Russia. The sun burned hotly in the midday sky. Then came the call: company commanders to the commander. – And then the unbelievable. The Division was to pull out and prepare for a loading for a transport by train. Now you can only imagine that only the worst rumors were floating around. I assumed we were going to Orel. Then, when we had taken up our new accommodations, came the next order: prepare the Panzers to be given up.
>
> And then everything went blow by blow. Without weapons, with bundles of clothing under our arms, we drove our Panzer men to Stalino.
>
> On the way we heard about Mussolini's resignation.
>
> Then we went right on to the de-lousing station. And then we were sitting on the troop transport.
>
> My commander had flown to Berlin. I had to lead the entire Battalion for the time being. Therefore I didn't ride with my company, but with the Battalion Staff. Passenger cars are seldom to be seen or experienced in this war. I spent this memorable ride in the battalion doctor, Dr. von Guelfenburg's Sanka.
>
> Once again a week on the train. A week of sun and nothing to do. We stood in the cars in shorts and watched old and new landscapes go by.
>
> We once again reminisced about the names of the train stations from the battles of 1941. Everything was deeply peaceful, Summer – it is barely believable for us after the past few days. Then we arrived in Poland, it almost looked like the homeland to us. And then on to Germany.
>
> People stood along the way and waved to us.
>
> Through Silesia – Sachsen – Fichtelgebirge – Fanken – Rosenheim it went. On the 6th of August we unloaded in Innsbruck.

After unloading, the march of the 7. Panzerkompanie began on **August 8, 1943**. Loaded on trucks, the company traveled through the ETSCHTAL, through BOZEN – TRIENT – VERONA into the PO FLATS (flatlands bordering the PO river), crossed over the PO near MANTUA and on further to the VIA EMILIA until reaching PARMA.

The company took field quarters in wine hills near the hamlet CAVRIAGO-CAPE.

An excerpt describing these movements from the war diary of the Supreme Commando of the Army (OKH):

> Troop movements to Italy:
>
> The Wehrmacht Leadership Staff sent the following message to the Supreme Commander "South" about conditions of the forces early on August 7th : 23 platoons of the 76th Division arrived in Genoa in the area of Nizza, 12 platoons of the 94th Division have unloaded into a temporary rest area. The 44th Division remains in the area of Brenner as before.
>
> The SS-Leibstandarte "A.H." joined up with the other units in the area of Parma – Reggio – Manua; 29 platoons from the 26th Panzer Division departed from the area of Garmisch – Bozen.

Rolf Ehrhardt reports on the march through the Po Flats to the field quarters which took place on **August 8, 1943**:

> The reception by the southern Tyrol population during the ride to Reggio is worth noting. Again and again the trucks were stopped so that they could hand us delicious fruit, wine and other home-grown specialties. Otherwise the ride would have only been broken up by a short stop.

On **August 9, 1943** the everyday life of the field camp began, but only after the Company received its armament of 22 Panzer IVs in MODENA.

The company commander commented about this day in a letter from the field:

> In our field quarters we found our Panzers. They were brand-new! Now the company is on the foot of the Appenin in wine gardens. The sun burns the entire day. From 11 to 4 in the afternoon it is simply impossible to take care of our duties.

Johann Wohninsland remarked about these days in his diary as well:

We went by carriage to the area of Reggio. There we received 22 new Panzer IVs. The usual freshening up and training began once again.

Rolf Ehrhardt especially enjoys remembering the quality of the field quarters:

We only came upon barren land in our village quarters. The lack of sheltered quarters and blankets were accommodated for by beautiful weather. The nights were so warm that they were comfortable as well.

During the day it was so hot, however, that after a few days several cases of heat exhaustion were grounds for a regimental order that forbid doing any duty from 11 to 4 o'clock in the afternoon. During this time we were only allowed to work in the shade cleaning and patching our uniforms and cleaning our weapons.

The new Panzer IVs were picked up by the drivers at the train station in MODENA, but only after they were unloaded by the men of the repair company.

During the course of the security operation of protecting the strategically important buildings (in consideration of the expected treason of the leadership of the Italian Army), the 7. Panzerkompanie had to guard the bridge over the ENZA near ST. ILARIO, which lay within the area of their field quarters.

Rolf Ehrhardt reports about the bridge guard arrangements:

The job of guarding the bridge crossing the Enza near St. Ilario d'Enza (which led to Parma) was one of our duties. The guard commando consisted of about 16 EMs, 2 NCOs and a platoon leader. This commando changed every 24 hours.

On **August 15, 1943**, Kompanie Chef Hauptsturmführer Ralf Tiemann left the 7. Panzerkompanie to take a general staff training position in the staff of the Division as 1st Ordnance Officer (01). The previous leader of the 1st Platoon, Obersturmführer Kurt Hoffman, took over the leadership of the company.

This is how Ralf Tiemann remembers his departure from the company:

Ja, for six days I have been in the General Staff. Leaving the company was really hard for me.

But the new tasks have helped me not miss my men so much.

Immediately it was "full speed ahead" with my work. The 1st General Staff Officer, Sturmbannführer Lehmann, went on a business trip and I had to take over for him while he was gone! So then again I must stand over the map table, wait for reports and write orders.

The days from **August 10** until **August 28** passed by without anything happening that is worth mentioning. The troops spent their time doing monotonous duties, training and reconnoitering the road system for the expected action for the disarmament action.

On **August 28, 1943** came the order to prepare for "be ready for the alarm," which meant that the troops would have to be ready to march within two hours at any given time.

On **September 7, 1943,** the first incidents occurred as a proclamation of the coming betrayal of the Italian Army. Rolf Ehrhard reports about one of these events which happened while he was guarding the bridge in St. Ilario:

> At that time I was with the guard commando with Oberscharführer Inmann (Platoon Leader, IIIrd Platoon). Since I could speak some Italian, the behavior of the Italian civilians made me suspicious. They declared to me, partly drunk, that the war was over and all soldiers should go home.
>
> I went with Oberscharführer Inmann along the bed of the Enza river to the train bridge (which was parallel to our bridge) which was guarded by 60 Italians. We carefully stalked up on the guards. To our surprise the commando there had been greatly reduced in strength. Obviously the officers and NCOs had taken off, even some of the soldiers were gone. The rest slept soundly, as if they had been drinking. We took the locks of their guns out and threw them into the river. We then went back to our bridge with a queasy feeling in our stomachs. We had no further orders.
>
> Our bridge was secured at both ends with MG 34s behind some sandbags. Italian military trucks passed the bridge. One time a few unaimed shots from a machine pistol went off. Under the gray sky of the morning we were picked up and brought back to the company, which was in the alarm phase.

On **September 9, 1943,** there was another confrontation with the bridge command of the 7. Panzerkompanie near St. Ilario.

Heinrich Burk, the driver of the lead platoon Panzer for Unterscharführer Inmann, remembers this event:

> We were assigned to bridge guard duties with about twelve men a few kilometers from our quarters in the wine gardens.

> Approaching evening we were in a bar and the radio there was playing music. Suddenly the music stopped and there was a speech by Marshall Badoglio, the Italian head of the government. (September 8, 1943 – between 6 and 8 p.m.).
>
> Suddenly the Italians jumped on the tables and yelled: "Viva, Viva – Badoglio!" We slowly realized that the war was over for the Italians. A messenger came from the company and was all worked up. He brought the alarm message and some men. The Italian soldiers on the bridge were disarmed and sent home. In the morning gray a few rounds from a cannon were heard firing from the direction of Parma.

On **September 8, 1943,** came the expected Italian betrayal by the Italian Marshall BADOGLIO who agreed on a special surrender with the Allies.

An order followed for immediate preparations for the alarm case – code name "North Wind."

At 2315 hours the 7. Panzerkompanie received the order to occupy the airport in REGGIO/EMILIA with the rest of the IInd Panzer Battalion.

Heinrich Burk reports on the preparations:

> We drove full throttle with two Panzer IVs and a jeep full of grenadiers to the administration building of the airport. Oberscharführer Inmann fired a salvo out of his MP into the air. Eight Italian officers came out of the building and handed over the airport. The soldiers in the surrounding buildings were disarmed and sent home. We collected a large heap of weapons. At the end we became somewhat uneasy as we noticed two batteries of 8.8 cm anti-aircraft guns.

On **September 9, 1943,** the Division issued the order establishing disarmament areas along with assignments for the tasks to be performed by the regiments and battalions.

Among the orders were the instructions that the IInd Battalion was to march in the direction of MILAN after mopping up difficulties with local disarmament actions. This action was to be conducted in conjunction with SS-Panzer-Grenadier Regiment 1, parts of SS-Artillery Regiment 1, the SS-Panzerjäger Battalion 1 and the anti-aircraft units. The area was to be occupied and disarmed.

In preparation of this march, the 7. Panzerkompanie transferred to the area around the villages of PARMA and PIACENZA.

Rolf Ehrhardt recalls this transfer:

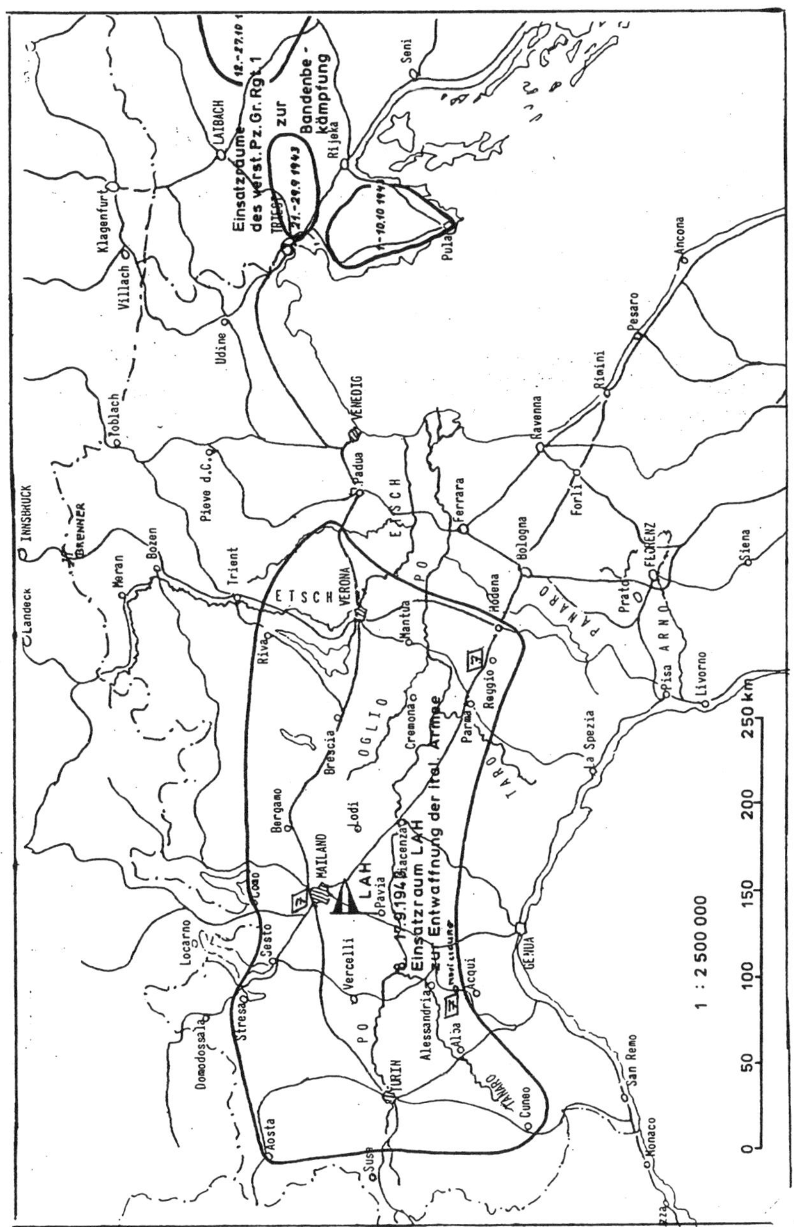

Area of action of the LAH for the disarmament of the Italian Army.
Area of action for anti-partisan operations conducted by the strengthened SS-Panzer-Grenadier Regiment 1, ***September 21-29, 1943.***

We spent the night of September 12 in Melegnano. Everything proceeded very uncalmly. We drove to a small village. The residents were bewildered, intimidated and scared. There was nervousness everywhere. Grenadiers came and drove on. Partisans and enemy activity were discussed. One of the company's platoons ordered to support the grenadiers, then later half-platoons. For the actual march the company didn't have their ten Panzers anymore.

The march group of SS-Panzer-Grenadier Regiment 1, together with the subordinated heavy weapons reached the edge of the city of MILAN from the three march roads.

The Italians had built up field positions on both sides of the approach roads.

In order to avoid the unnecessary flow of blood, the commander of SS-Panzer-Grenadier Regiment 1, Obersturmbannführer Frey, made contact with the Italian Commanding General RUGGERO to negotiate a disarmament. General Ruggero proved himself to be a sensible officer and agreed with the disarmament under certain conditions. The fact that the Italian King fled and abandoned his soldiers helped influence his decision. General Ruggero called over a loudspeaker for the population to remain calm and ordered.

On **September 12, 1943** the Panzer Grenadiers advanced to the inner city of MILAN and occupied the military concerns.

In the mean time, the IInd Panzer Battalion joined up with the others and marched into MILAN.

Rolf Ehrhardt, our untiring reporter, wrote about this:

Rumors spread about 7,000 Communists with 8.8 cm guns in Milan. Luckily these were all just rumors, or better said, the heroes got cold feet. In any case there wasn't any serious resistance found anywhere. During the next few days the Company took part in security operations in different places in Milan. For about two days we camped out in the zoo, then for three days outside a school with a bell tower, then for about two days in a fruit garden in Villa le Monza. The city was secured with platoons or half-platoons, among others the "Commando Varese."

The company leaders, equipment, supplies and about eight to ten Panzers were located in the "Scoulo Elementario" in the Villa Settembrini. In the vicinity was a bicycle race-track. A special occurrence, Red Cross packages for English prisoners were illegally given out and brought a change of pace for the kitchen crew.

During the disarmament of the Italian units there were no problems.

Heinrich Burk remembers the days of the occupation of Milan as well and wrote about them:

> During the afternoon (September 12) we rolled in the great heat to Milan. Approaching evening we arrived in the suburbs. There the cannons were turned down and impeccably cleaned. The civilians who ran around the Panzers had been told that we were to attack the next day. The IIIrd Platoon was to occupy the train stations in Porta Romano and Porta Victoria and then guard them. The Platoon was split up. Whenever platoon leader Inmann had the desire and was in the mood, we would roar through the city in our Panzer to control the half platoon in Porta Victoria. It really was a "funny" war.
>
> So it went for the next two to three weeks.

The disarmament of the garrison in MILAN was conducted without any great incident.

The company remained there until October in different parts of the city of MILAN under the subordination of the Battalion in order to fulfill their security tasks. They also had to take over other security operations since the strengthened SS-Panzer Grenadier Regiment 1 was pulled out to fight against partisans in Croatia.

Until **October 10, 1943**, the days of the security operations in MILAN passed by without any noticeable incident, while other units of the Division were still disarming parts of the Italian Army in areas by the edge of the Alps and on the coast of the Mediterranean Sea.

On **November 11, 1943,** the Division was brought together in the area of VOGHERA, TORTONA, ALESSANDRIA, and ASTI.

The 7. Panzerkompanie marched from MILAN through PAVIA, TORTONA, ASTI and arrived in its new village accommodations in NOVI LIGURE.

Heinrich Burk wrote about the quarters in this city:

> One day in Novi Ligure an alarm was called and we marched in the direction of the Swiss border. The Italians had opened the prisoner of war camp and the prisoners streamed in the direction of Switzerland. In order to prevent this the Swiss were to close their borders. From our side the march was more like a threatening gesture, since a halt was called way before we reached the border.

The days of calm and refreshment came to an end when the order to prepare for a transport to Russia arrived on **October 20, 1943**.

For a glimpse into the development of this order, below is an excerpt from the war diary of the Supreme Command of the Army (OKH) from **October 20, 1943**:

> The Wehrmacht Leadership Staff recommended on October 18 that more forces should be made available for the east, since the eastern front cannot be secured with the forces on hand after the pull-back of Army Group "North."
>
> After that, on October 19, the Wehrmacht Leadership Staff checked out the possibility of relieving the 384th Division, the 1st and 25th Panzer Division, as well as the SS-Division "LAH" from their current action.
>
> At this stage an order was issued by the Führer for the following units to be transferred to the east:
>
> 1. Immediately: 1st and 25th Panzer Division, 384th Infantry Division.
> 2. After being relieved: 76th Infantry Division.
> 3. Upon special order: SS-Division "Leibstandarte Adolf Hitler."

In the meantime Obersturmführer Herbert Sprunk took over the leadership of the 7. Panzerkompanie.

In the east, where the battlefields were once again to become the home of the company, the situation had worsened considerably.

In the area of Army Group "South," where the Division was to go, the 6th Army was up until this time indeed able to defend off Soviet attacks, during which the Soviets successfully broke through to KIEV in the north.

The war diary of the Supreme Command of Army reported on the transfer of the LAH on **October 23, 1943** (excerpts):

> The Supreme Command of the German Armed Forces (OKW) communicated to all of its offices today that the Führer is reserving the SS-L.A.H. for a departure to the east. The motorized portions of the Division are to be transferred to the area of Laibach to assist SS-Panzer Grenadier Battalion 1 in combating partisans. The tracked portions of the Division are to remain in the previous area. On October 24 the order will be revised to the effect that the Division will be transferred to the area of Vienna.
>
> The reason for this measure is that the Division can be quickly transferred from this area either to the east or again to the west, which is also considered a threatened area.

On October 24, 1943 the 7. Panzerkompanie marched to PARMA to load up.

The entraining followed on October 25, 1943, about which Heinrich Burk reports:

While loading up the trains a staff Panzer slid from the Wagon and this held up things for a few hours. For the departure and for our amusement we drank a few bottles of sweet Malage-Creme. Suddenly I had to report to company commander Obersturmführer Sprunk.

He ordered me to load up the entire company with two older Panzer drivers. Oh no! Despite or because of the sweet Malaga there were no mishaps.

The trip went over the PO, through ETSCHTAL, over BRENNER and on to ST. PÖLTEN.

The previously foreseen rendezvous stop for picking up the winter equipment was shortened and the transports rolled on into a new Russian winter.

EASTERN FRONT/UKRAINE – November–December 1943

In the meantime, the state of affairs in the east had developed into a threatening situation.

In the section of Army Group "South," the Soviets, spurred on by their defensive success in BJELGOROD, pushed their counterattack and advanced from the DONEZ to the DNJEPR in barely five months. That meant that they had won an area of 350 km to the west. They crossed the DNJEPR in KREMENTSCHUG and DNJEPROPETROVSK and were pushing on both sides of KIEV to the west in their advance towards SHITOMIR.

At the same time strong units swung around to the southwest to take the industrial area around KIRIVOI ROG into their possession.

The Soviets owed their success to an earth-shaking superiority in regards to their quantity of people, weapons and equipment.

In order to stop the Soviet advance to KIRIVOI ROG, the 1. SS-Panzer Division "LAH," which was at that time just rolling out of Italy in widely spread-out transports, was to attack FASTOV. For this the XXXXVIII. Panzer Corps ordered the course of action for single companies from platoon down, without even being able to wait for the Division to completely collect itself. The transports had to be unloaded within enemy activity and even right in the midst of the enemy.

As the wheeled portions of the 7. Panzerkompanie were unloaded in the area of KIROVOGRAD, the tracked portions of the company were still on their way, so that the planned action for the company to advance to FASTOV was still not possible.

After **November 9, 1943** the Ist Battalion (Panzer Vs) arrived and was subordinated to the SS-Panzer-Grenadier Regiment 1 and joined in the attack on FASTOV on the march.

On **November 12, 1943** the Soviet attack spearheads had penetrated so far to the west on both sides of the highway that a battle broke out on the edge of the city of SHITOMIR

The Corps feared that they would be out-flanked in the north and that there would be a flank attack from the north against the units fighting in FASTOV. Therefore they ordered the "LAH" to turn with all its masses to the north and prevent the opponent from reaching the highway by attacking KORNIN and BRUSSILOV.

For this the attack units were to prepare themselves in the area southwest of FASTOV in the area between DUNJAKA, KOZANKA and STOVIZE, south of the IRPEN.

From this area the SS-Panzer-Grenadier Regiment 1, along with the subordinated Ist Panzer Battalion (Panzer Vs), advanced to KORNIN on **November 14, 1943**.

The attack of the highway between KIEV and SHITOMIR was ordered for **November 15, 1943**, which also approached SOLOVJEVKA. (See map 13).

In the meantime the tracked portions of the 7. Panzerkompanie had unloaded in the area of BERDITSCHEV and rolled forward over KONIN to SOLOJEVKA, where they arrived on **November 16, 1943**.

On **November 17, 1943,** the 7. Panzerkompanie departed for the attack on the area between ULSCHKA and CHOMOTEZ from SOLOVJEVKA within the formation of the IInd Panzer Battalion.

Heinrich Burk noticed the following:

> In the beginning of November 1943, we were once again on our way to Russia.
>
> November 17, 1943 was the first day of battle, hard battles which were conducted with bitterness.

The large scale attack was prepared for BRUSSILOV on **November 18, 1943**. The II. Panzer Battalion, in conjunction with both of the Grenadier Regimenter and the Reconnaissance Battalion, was to take the city in a night attack.

The attack ran over MOROSOVSKA, which was taken at midday. Soviet counterattacks on MOROSOVSKA and DIVIN prevented the planned attack on BRUSSILOV.

The 7. Panzerkompanie switched over to the defense with the rest of the battle group.

The continuance of the advance onto BRUSSILOV was ordered for **November 20, 1943**. The attack continued somewhat sluggishly, hindered by a tank trench (which was located before the city) and swampy attack landscape. The progress of the attack was stymied after the Soviets counterattacked from DIVIN.

At around noon Obersturmbannführer Schönberger, the commander of SS-Panzer Regiment 1, was killed by an artillery round which landed in the regimental command post in the trenches in SOLOJEVKA.

Sturmbannführer Peiper, the commander of the IIIrd (armored) Battalion/SS-Panzer-Grenadier Regiment 2, overtook the leadership of the Panzer Regiment.

On **November 22, 1943,** the attack of BRUSSILOV was renewed after the 7. Panzerkompanie took and mopped up DIVIN on **November 21**. The advance pulled to the east to BRUSSILOV and continued on to the north where the troops reached JASTREBENKA.

Heinrich Burk reports:

> On November 22 a large-scale attack was launched by the entire SS-Panzer Korps, supported by divisions of the Wehrmacht. I have never seen so many Panzers driving to the attack in a wide front. In spite of this we advanced only slowly. There were many fall-outs, even in the Panzer Battalion.
>
> We were then barraged by heavy Russian artillery for the entire night.
>
> In the morning gray a grenadier came and climbed onto our Panzer and asked if whether we wanted to knock out another Russian tank. We wanted to!!!
>
> He guided us around some corners and then behind a house. Our commander Inmann, no. 1 gunner Gläsner and I climbed out and carefully looked around the corner of the house. There stood a T-34 at about a distance of 120 m. It was in a trough surrounded by fog with its cannon pointed crosswise to us.
>
> The plan was firm, we would drive quickly around the corner and ..... but if we were a hair off, it would be over.
>
> As I drove around the corner, the T-34 pointed its cannon at us and my no. 1 gunner Gläsner screamed: "I can't seen anything!" The view through the optics was blocked by a small tree.
>
> I then popped the clutch and our Panzer jumped with a leap about one meter forward. At the same time our shot went off. I saw the hole in the T-34 that our round had ripped open with my naked eyes. We all breathed a sigh of relief.
>
> During that same morning we knocked out another T-34 and two others fled the village.

On **November 23, 1943** the Panzer Group Peiper (IInd Battalion/SS-Panzer Regiment 1 and IIIrd (armored) Battalion/ SS-Panzer-Grenadier Regiment 2) advanced from JASTREBENKA to DUBROVKA, took the village and continued on to CASAROVKA. From there the attack was resumed in the direction of MESTETSCHKO, where the SDVISH River was an immediate obstacle.

Heinrich Burk remembers this day:

> On November 23 the company attacked out of a forest and drove full power down a decline in the landscape. Wherever you looked the Russians could be seen fleeing, but suddenly we received a direct hit. The Panzer burned, the loader was dead. No. 1 gunner Gläsner lost a leg. Inmann, Vorpahl and I had burns. Obersturmführer Rümmler was dead as well. During this attack we lost at least six Panzers. This was the first day that Peiper led the Regiment. The company commander at this time was Sprunk.
>
> It was here that the Shitomir-Action came to an end for me.

After erecting a command bridge over the SDVISH on **November 24, 1943**, the Panzer Group was ready to go and advanced to STARIZKAJA. A strong PAK-Front on the edge of the village and a Soviet counterattack from MAL KARASCHIN stopped the Panzer Group, which was forced to remain in STARIZKAJA.

The continually increasing attack strength of the Soviets forced the SS-Panzer Korps to order the units to switch over to the defense.

With that the battle for BRUSSILOV concluded.

Due to the continually increasing strength of the enemy forces north of the highway, there was a danger that the SS-Panzer Korps would be outflanked. Because of this the LAH had to regroup on **November 26, 1943** so that it would be ready for further attacks to the east, north of the highway.

The LAH was then transferred to the preparations area between NEGEBOVKA and SABELOTSCHE, so that it could then attack RADOMISCHEL. (See Map 14).

On **November 28,** the Panzer Group set out and advanced to a point just before RADOMISCHEL and then turned from there to the southeast on to GARDOV, so that the Division could intercept a Soviet flank attack that was initiated there.

The disengagement and the relief of the "LAH" by the 2nd Fallschirmjäger Division was foreseen for **December 2, 1943**, so that the Division could attack the railway between TETEREV and KOROSTEN from the area between the villages of STUDENIZA and VAZKOV.

After a successful reorganization, the Panzer Group Peiper attacked on **December 6, 1943** and took the villages of MOKRENSCHTSCHINA and ANDREV. It then continued to advance until reaching STYRTY.

On **December 7, 1943,** the Panzer Group continued its advance, taking TORTSCHIN and then advancing on to TSCHAIKOVKA.

Company commander Obersturmführer Herbert Sprunk was killed during the attack on SABOLOT on **December 8, 1943**.

Untersturmführer Sternebeck took over the leadership of the company.

On **December 14, 1943,** the Panzer Group reached the line between FEDOROVKA and VERIN due south of the railway after engaging in a number of bitter local combats for almost every village. There the Group received the orders to disengage and collect in the area between SABOLOT and LJACHOVAJA. With that the battle for RADOMISCHL ended.

Then there was the intent to engage the LAH together with two army Panzer divisions further in the north to destroy recently recognized enemy troops collecting in the area northeast of MALIN (from the area southeast of KOROSTEN).

On **December 19, 1943,** the Panzer Group set-out for and reached the railway and took the train station in TSCHEPOVITSCHI.

The constantly increasing strength of the enemy resistance and the continual Soviet attacks on the flanks from MELENI forced the Panzer Group to switch over to the defense.

Our loss of Panzers was very high. That forced the Division to put together all of the battle worthy Panzer Vs and Panzer IVs into a Battalion under the leadership of Sturmbannführer Kuhlmann on **December 21, 1943**, so that an attack to relieve units could be undertaken. This attack was to be conducted in a southerly direction against the threat from the rear from MELENI. (See map 14).

On **December 24, 1943,** strong enemy forces southeast of SHITOMIR attacked and reached the area of KOTSCHEROVO. The LAH was pulled out and transferred during the evening to the area south of SHITOMIR by order of the XXXXVIII. Panzer Korps.

With that the battles in the area of KOROSTEN found their end as well. The disengagement movements were executed according to plan. Nothing special was reported about the drive through the heavily crowded village of SHITOMIR in the heavy snow during Christmas Eve.

After **December 25, 1943**, the march groups of the LAH met in the collecting area between VOLIZA, IVNIZA and KOTELNAJA. They immediately prepared themselves for defensive battle.

In the night between the **27th and the 28th of December, 1943**, the Panzer Group (along with infantry from SS-Panzer-Grenadier Regiment 1, which rode along on top of the Panzers) embarked on an advance to ANDRUSCHEVKA The attack was fended off by a superior enemy on the edge of the village, however.

From then on the Soviet advances began to strengthen on all sections of the front. In the area of the LAH, the Soviets intended to advance past the local LAH defensive strongpoints to the north and to the south in order to cut off the Division. This forced the Division to decide on December 31, 1943 to pull back the line of defense to the line connecting the villages of BERDITSCHEV, KATERINIVKA and TRAJANOFF.

1944
Vinniza, Tscherkassy, Tarnopol, Lemberg, Hasselt, Caen, Mortain, Falaise, Rahden, Ardennes, Breakthrough to Lüttich, Bastogne

VINNIZA – TSCHERKASSY – TARNOPOL

With the defensive battles for BERDITSCHEV, the war in Russia stepped into the final phase of constant retreat over the deeply snowed-in Steppes and over mucky and deeply muddy streets following the seasonal period of thaw.

Constantly located on a flank or surrounded on both sides of the advancing divisions of the Red Army, the Division was always in the danger of being cut off and surrounded.

With an indescribable self-sacrifice the increasingly shrinking battle groups of the Division managed to conduct an orderly and continuous defense against the Soviet storm. Their defense continued despite a restless exhaustion, a lack of rations and no replacements of men or weapons.

– In the framework of the German counterattack east of VINNIZA at the end of January 1944, the Division fought on the northern flank of Army Group "South." There the Division conducted counterattacks to the west in order to hold up the Red Army and stop them from outflanking the army group along the highway connecting SHITOMIR and ROVNO.
– February 1944 was characterized by constant attacks against the Tscherkassay Pocket by increasingly small attack groups. They tried to make a breakout possible for the two German army corps and seven divisions (among them the SS-Panzer Division "Wiking") which were surrounded there.
– Increasingly pushed to the west, the LAH (now reduced to the size of battle group) found itself in defensive battle in the first half of March in Galicia, in the area between PROSKUROFF and TARNOPOL. The battle group, now encircled itself, spent the end of March through the beginning of April 1944 in the "Wandering Pocket" and managed to box its way through to LEMBERG.

During the flank battles east of VINNIZA in the beginning of January, the remaining Panzers (4 Tigers, 8 Panthers and 10 Panzer IVs) were already formed into a battle group under the leadership of Sturmbannführer Kuhlmann.

During the last days of January the number of Panzers had been reduced to 3 Tigers, 6 Panthers and 8 Panzer IVs and from then on formed the "Panzer Pack Sternebeck."

On **February 2, 1944,** the Division reported the following number of Panzers as ready for action: 2 Tigers, 4 Panthers and 1 Panzer IV.

At the end of the battles for the TSCHERKASSY Pocket there were only 1 Tiger and 2 Panthers left which were capable of fighting in battle.

With the arrival of the "battle of mud" in Galicia, there were no more Panzer IVs in action.

Shortly thereafter the remaining Panzers were formed into the "Panzer Pack Sternebeck," and the 7. Panzerkompanie ceased to exist as a battle ready unit.

Enlisted men and vehicles were transferred to BALKOVZY under the leadership of Untersturmführer Werner Sternebeck. They were to form the basis of a field training company.

Manfred Thorn supplied a very detailed report about a special action conducted by the 7. Panzerkompanie in BALKOVZY:

> The 7. Kompanie was pulled out of the front lines on January 20, 1944 near Kirijevka and collected in the village of Balkovzy, a small village on the road between Proskuroff and Tarnopol. It was days until all of the members of the company had arrived. Again and again came single men, partly by foot, until the rest of the company was present on February 10, 1944.
>
> No one really knew what we were to do in this village with its 25 straw covered houses.
>
> The company commander was Untersturmführer Sternebeck. The Spieß was Oberscharführer Engelhardt. We had about 40 men, three old Panzer IVs, an old Panzer III (former commander-Panzer, with a crew of six men) and a few supply vehicles; that was all that was left.
>
> The village itself was surrounded by a lake which covered half of its length. At the higher end of the village the landscape rose slightly. About 150 m further stood a collective farm which was converted into a garage and provided shelter for our four Panzers.
>
> Unterscharführer Kurt Sametreiter arrived at the 7. Panzerkompanie on January 29, 1944. Eight days later he was promoted to Untersturmführer.
>
> About 60 replacements arrived. They had all been transferred from the infantry. Most of them were young boys, but a few of them were battle proven men. Among them was Rottenführer Kliewa.
>
> Duty began little by little with cleaning hour, mending hour, inspections, instruction and exercises with rifles, machine guns and Panzer cannons.
>
> In Balkovay, the 7. Kompanie became a training company. While their duties started to get the old Panzer men down, they were also very happy to be about 80 km behind the front.

During this time, I often drove with my quick horse-drawn sled to a village located about 3 km away in order to "organize" a few things for us.

After five weeks the training came to an end. On the evening of March 5 there was supposed to be a party. Untersturmführer Sternebeck gave me the task of decorating the area the next morning. In order to see to the well-being of the men, I drove once again to the neighboring village to fetch eggs, milk and meal. As usual I left my sled standing and snuck around the corner of a house. There I saw a T-34 standing at a distance of about 60 m. I was so shocked that the Russians could have crossed so surprisingly into our vicinity. I didn't figure on such a possibility.

I rushed back to Balkovzy. All worked up, I reported the occurrence to the company commander. He didn't want to believe me, but despite that he put the company on alarm. The men packed their belongings up. The armorers Unterscharführer Kuhnke and Rottenführer Wölfel split up the rifles between the men and loaded the rest on a sled. We abandoned the village together with the field kitchen. The crews for the four Panzers were quickly put together.

My friend Heinrich Theye was chosen to be the driver for the Panzer III. I didn't want to leave him alone, so I climbed into the Panzer III as a replacement driver. Suddenly I heard a crack, and it got very hot in the Panzer. I thought we had received a hit that strafed the side of our Panzer. Someone screamed "get out!"

I climbed through the turret and through the no. 1 gunner's hatch and out. What happened? Heinrich Theye hung in the loader's hatch. His face and hands were burned. He didn't see the loaded flare gun and had accidentally set it off. Somewhat later he departed with a bandaged head and hands. He was the first wounded in Balkovzy.

Now I overtook the position of driver for the Panzer, although I was originally to leave the village with my sled.

The commander of the Panzer III was Unterscharführer Haan, radioman was Henne, the no. 1 gunner was Kotyrbe, the loader was Mäusel.

The "chicken crew" was together once again.

In the meantime it was 1400 hours and we still were at the collective farm.

The crew was busy loading up the tank with ammunition as Sternebeck wanted to convince himself that my report was valid. He rode to the hill on his high horse, and then suddenly we heard the rattling of MGs. We looked on as our company commander fell off his horse and ran back to us.

Now the men were really starting to move, all available men took position before the hill. Without any real entrenching tools they dug themselves into the hard ground.

Two Panzer IVs took position on the collective farm. We then drove into a ravine, on the right flank of the defensive position.

It was later determined that we didn't have an open shooting field to the left. The third Panzer drove back to the houses.

By now we had been waiting for hours. Nothing moved. During the middle of the night, two comrades came to us and reported that they could hear the quiet squeaking of tank tracks. Supposedly the Russians were moving up as close as possible to the reverse slope of the hill with their tanks.

We really couldn't imagine how our hurriedly trained Panzer men were supposed to bring the quickly advancing Soviet tank attack to a halt acting as infantry men, armed only with carbines.

At exactly 0100 hours on March 6, 1944, all hell broke loose. The enemy fire was strong. In just a few minutes our people were overrun by various T-34s, decked with infantry. No one came up against us. Even more we saw how the Russian tanks rolled on by us above the ravine. I turned at that point and drove back to the starting place, where our flag still fluttered on its mast. Someone forgot all about it in the excitement.

Now there was time to fix a shooting position behind the village fountain. While the first two T-34s came up behind the houses, the Russian infantry (as well as our people) ran next to the Russian tanks. They tried to run back to the village after they were overrun, so that they wouldn't get caught behind the enemy lines. This mess was perfect, and as the first close combats developed before our eyes, we still couldn't join in. This scene was illuminated in a phantom-like way by the burning houses.

At a distance of only 40 meters two T-34s turned to the left and offered us their broadside. We knocked each of them out, one right after the other.

We didn't have any radio contact with our other Panzers because the radios were defective.

We received orders from foot messengers to drive back to the command post, so that we could protect it. I drove in reverse until reaching the garden fence of the command post while scanning the scene in front. Suddenly, a T-34 broke through a shed and stood right in the middle of the yard of the command post, not even six meters behind us. Unterscharführer Haan observed everything from the turret and called to us "tank from the rear!" Everyone thought that the end had arrived for us. Oddly, nothing of the sort happened! Without hesitation I ripped the wagon around and no. 1 gunner Kotyrbe only needed to press the button.

I had never seen an enemy tank standing so close. We saw, so to say, how their hatches opened and the crew got out. On the T-34 were the smashed remains of the shed laying all over. The debris probably blocked the sight of this Ivan. That was our luck!

An Ivan of the crew crawled on all fours until reaching the door of the command post. Behind the door stood Rottenführer Herbert Junge with his machine pistol. As he pressed the trigger it made a click, the magazine must not have been fully engaged. The Russian must have heard the sound, because he turned around and crawled back to the shed.

Unterscharführer Haan climbed out of the Panzer. None of us knew why. After a while he stood in front of the wagon and directed me to go backwards. I didn't understand his instructions at first as taking off in the direction of the lake would have disastrous results once we reached the shore. On the hill where the command post was located there would still be a possibility to escape the situation – at least it would be easier at the other end of the village.

The foot messenger who came from the company commander brought us a last message: one Panzer IV had been knocked out and two others took off over the bridge. One of those two remaining Panzers had broken down. Only we were still in the village, cut off from the others. He then said: "You all have acted bravely," and then he disappeared into the darkness.

Our Panzer Kommandant, still outside of the wagon, waved me further back. What was he planning, did he want to sink us all in this Panzer? It still remains a mystery to me.

Only a few meters before the lake our Panzer received a hit in the tracks, which finally put an end to our drive in the wrong direction.

After feeling a certain sense of relief I made sure that my bones had remained healthy.

In a Panzer III it is only possible for the driver to get out after going through the turret, so it took me longer to get out.

What would await me outside? Were we possibly surrounded by the Russians? Where are my comrades and how am I going to get over the lake, as a former "non-swimmer?" Everything went through my head at once. I was full of fear.

Luckily the Russians were not yet in my vicinity.

Four dark figures ran into the water, and were already a few meters past the shoreline. Everyone of them had a rifle in their hands. I couldn't imagine, how my crew had gotten the rifles. At the last moment I saw a carbine laying on the turret, which, as I then determined, was also loaded. My comrades hadn't forgotten me.

Now I only thought about being quick. With a gun in my hand I jumped from the Panzer and into the ice cold water. At first I tried to wade in the weedy coast to the bridge, where I saw my crew running on the ice, that would be my savior. Even if I had to stand in the water up to my chest, I had to at least manage to get to the ice. Like a seal I climbed onto the thin sheet of ice, which immediately broke. A second try was finally successful. It was high time to distance myself further from the shore, because Ivan stood there and was firing at us with rifles and MPs. Tracer bullets zinged by us. Just as I caught up to my crew, Unterscharführer Haan got hit and fell onto the ice. He was dead. We ran for our lives in a criss-cross pattern for some 600 meters until we reached the life-saving other side of the lake.

With that a one and a half hour close combat, which had been a somewhat confusing situation, came to an end. We had to leave our dead, wounded and captured comrades behind.

Approaching 0300 hours we reported to Untersturmführer Sternebeck's command post in a neighboring village.

In the village we found the remains of the 7. Panzerkompanie, which had been fighting along with the men of Obersturmführer Armberger's 8. Panzerkompanie in houses and trenches since 0145 hours.

In the early morning, at about 0500 hours, twenty men under the leadership of Untersturmführer Sametreiter took position in a small village about one kilometer away.

The remains of my crew dug into a house with borrowed shovels. As it became light we saw our knocked out Panzer standing on the other side of the coast, where a few Russians were busy sitting on the turret with our possessions. A bit further to the left there was a dark spot on the ice. It was a pitiful sight for us! We wanted to fetch our dead comrade Haan from the ice in the coming night and then bury him. It didn't matter anymore, because the Russians attacked with their infantry from the railway. In heavy defensive fighting we drove Ivan back. During the fighting a prisoner was taken.

On another day, following the warm, thawing weather which had been going on for days, the ice broke and our dead Panzer commander fell into the water. During the afternoon of March 7 our Panzer men were fighting as infantry, about 40 meters behind the houses. They were nailed shut inside their trenches. No one could go and get them since Russian sharpshooters ruled the hill. Within an hour we had seven casualties, all shot in the head.

Untersturmführer Sametreiter gathered everyone in the middle of the houses and asked for two volunteers to get the men out of the holes. Another comrade and I volunteered. We both went silently up the edge of the hill. I never knew his name, but one thing I knew, he was ready to fetch a wounded comrade, for whom he was willing to risk his own life.

We crept up to the trench and saw a comrade with a shot through the head collapsed in the corner. His head lay in his helmet. He was still alive and was moaning heavily. We didn't dare get up even a little. While lying on the ground we tried to grab his left and right arms and pull him back out of the trench. With our last bit of strength we were able to pull him out a few meters from edge. From there we brought him to the field-dressing station.

During the evening of March 7 we broke out of the ring of surrounding enemy forces past the sugar factory.

Due to the fact that the front was being pulled back, the 7. Panzerkompanie was transferred:

to KOROSTOVA on March 9, 1944
to FRIEDRICHOVKA on March 11, 1944
until reaching STANISLAU on **March 17, 1944** with the rest of the "Wandering Pocket."

Johann Wohninsland reports on his experiences with the field replacement company:

In February 1944 we were located near Tarnopol with the training company. Sternebeck was the company commander.

From there I had to bring an Untersturmführer with a wagon to the battalion at the front. As we arrived there, the TFK[11] wouldn't let me go back, since wagons were few and far between...

During the ride I broke a universal joint. I stood there alone on the road with the TFK for two days. The Russians were coming closer. Finally, after three days, they towed me away. By this time my feet had frozen.

The next day I looked for my wagon and determined that it had been stolen. The TFK and I looked for the wagon. Unfortunately it had disappeared without a trace. I then broke through and back to my company, because the Russians had broken through at various places.

While located in the village we were jumped by partisans.

There I was once again a "stolen soldier" and I had to stay and fight as an infantryman in Stanislau.

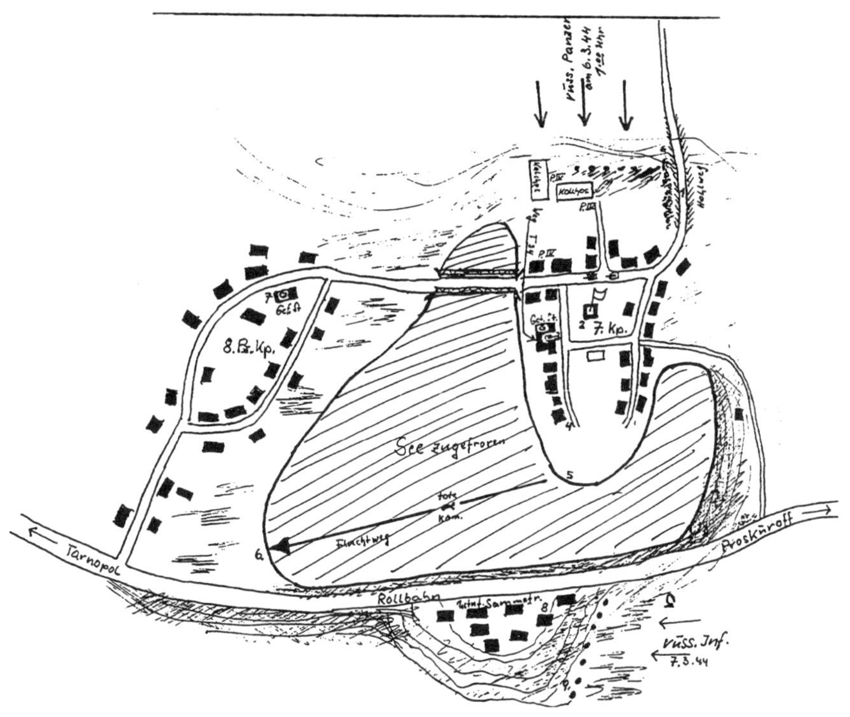

Action of the 7. Panzerkompanie (training company)
on ***March 6 and 7, 1944*** *in BALKOVZY*

1. *Ravine*
2. *Assembly Place*
3. *Command Post Sternebeck*
4. *End of the Village*
5. *Firing Position of Panzer III*
6. *Escape Path*
7. *Command Post Ster.-Arm6.*
8. *Position of Untersturmführer Sametreiter*
9. *5 dead and two wounded comrades*

The company then marched to the troop training grounds in DEBICA, Poland. From there they were transported by train to GENK in FLANDERS.

THE BATTLE IN NORMANDY (INVASION)

On **April 14, 1944,** the OKH (Supreme Command of the German Army) ordered the remains of the 1. SS-Panzer Division LAH (which had collected in the area of LEMBERG) to be transported to the area of the OB West (Supreme Commander West). There they were to be deployed (after a suitable refreshing) along the coast of the canal for the defense against the expected Allied landing.

The first transport departed on **April 18, 1944.** The entire transport concluded on **April 25, 1944.**

Unloading followed in the area of TURNHOUT, in northern Flanders, where the General Commando of the I. SS-Panzer Korps, Obergruppenführer Sepp Dietrich, was located.

The 7. Panzerkompanie took village quarters in GENK near HASSELT. The reorganization of the beat-up units commenced after the arrival. New weapons, equipment, vehicles and Panzers were supplied. There were replacements as well.

Gerhard Stiller, platoon leader in the 7. Panzerkompanie wrote about this time:

> The entire company was quartered in a larger boarding school. The numerical strength of officers, NCOs and enlisted men was way under what it should have been.
>
> The weapons we had were like a pile of junk since everyone had brought back their side-arms from the Eastern Front. Everything else was absent. I had to get used to this situation and then figure out what to do with the associated duty plans. The leader of the company was Obersturmführer Werner Wolff. Full of energy and a desire to perform, he tried to form the company and strengthen its readiness for action on a daily basis, despite the unfavorable situation. The remains of the troops were trained as infantry and performed drills for defending against landings from the air.
>
> In the beginning of May the company started to fill out. Former members of the company, who had been assigned to other battle groups on the Eastern Front, were transferred back to the unit for "freshening up." They were all "alte Panzerhasen."
>
> Soon the company was 2/3 up to strength.
>
> Extreme problems resulted from the continuous fighter plane attacks on the train bridge in Hasselt and also on the railways. The activities of the "White

Brigade" are associated with this. Night actions in platoon and company strength, as well as a double shuttle post on the main street in the garden house quarter at night, were the preventive measures of the company. These measures avoided great anger, except for a couple of cases of meaningless fire raids. Despite this, Kurt Sametreiter and I always had hand-grenades and machine pistols in hand at night, especially after we heard a few suspicious noises in our vicinity. Also, people who had no business being around would appear in the vicinity of the garden houses on occasion.

The increasing rattling finally concluded with all of the officers residing in a single house. At the end of May we received enlisted men replacements for the entire regiment. The men came on a train transport until reaching the edge of Turnhout. From Turnhout they had to be picked up. I clattered off with a dozen wood gassers. One man per transport train was given a carbine or MP. We reached the unloading train station unmolested. The transport train arrived late. It was the highest order of alarm due to the "White Brigade." A transport train rolling in with factory-new Panzer IVs was not allowed to continue for security reasons. The train was supposedly for the 2. Panzer Division and was to be driven on to Lille. We put together some temporary crews for the Panzers. This task was difficult since there was a lack of trained Panzer commanders.

Approaching 0300 hours the alarm was lifted. The enlisted men received their wood gassers and were marched off in the direction of Hasselt. I was happy to deliver the transport without incident.

Now even our company was filled with men and up to battle strength. Panzers and other vehicles arrived a few days later. An NCO's evening and a handball tournament in Swartberg, a Sunday before the invasion (!) brought some change.

For the company itself a small sensation paved the way. Obersturmführer Wolff prepared his marriage for the 8th of June, 1944. Since leave for this purpose was not even thinkable, the young lady had to be brought over the border with a few tricks. The invasion exploded right in the middle of the preparations for the wedding.

For the last appointment of the company, we had to receive our equipment, vehicles and Panzers. Lack of fuel, unfavorable terrain and security problems hindered the Panzers from being driven. This occurrence was to bring the young drivers a considerable amount of anger in just a few days.

On **June 6, 1944,** the Allied landing, during which the American and British/ Canadian landing corps were supported by 5,339 warships and 11,510 planes, began between the mouth of both the ORNE and VIRE rivers.

On the side of the OKH (Supreme Command of the German Army) it was determined that the Allied landing would take placc at the PAS DE CALAIS, for which the LAH was transferred on **June 9, 1944** to the area between BRUGES and GHENT as a reserve unit.

The 7. Panzerkompanie marched within the framework of the Division to their new accommodations, the village of URSEL.

Johann Wohninsland remembers the transfer to URSEL:

> On June 10, 1944 we were transferred to Ursel.
>
> Due to the fighter plane attacks we could only drive at night, because the invasion was already in full swing. We had received many young Panzer drivers and the heat made it difficult for the drivers.

After reaching the preparation area the Division received the assignment to prevent a break through of the coastal front at the mouth of the SCHELDE river by conducting an immediate counter attack in the event of an Allied landing.

Gerhard Stiller reports on the march of the 7. Panzerkompanie to the preparation area:

> June 6, 1944. In the early morning hours the company set out in a march. The goal of the march was the area Bruges-Ghent. The Battalion set out just beyond Genk. It didn't go so easily with the new horses. A few young Panzer drivers, who were often trained only with a full chassis as opposed to an entire tank, couldn't get used to the barrels and after a while became weak in the knees. Since they weren't used to the heat next to the transmission and the narrow view of the slit made for them to see out of, they became exhausted after a few hours. Therefore, Panzer Kommandanten who were experienced drivers had to jump in. The march went from Hasselt through St. Truiden, Tienen, Leuven and in the late hours of the evening went on by Brussels; the street crossing with the sign for "Waterloo" didn't bring forth any predictions. We rolled further in the night in a westerly direction. From time to time there were technical problems that required a pause in the march, during which the dozing crews would crawl under their vehicles. In the light cast by pocket flashlights, bolts and pins were repaired and the totally exhausted drivers had a short rest.
>
> The continuing drive became increasingly difficult for the men on the steering mechanism. They squatted on their seats for over twelve hours.

Then the drive continued into the night. The men's view was fixed spellbound on the night march equipment of the man in front of him.

The good and often longer roads which ran straight ahead made it easy for the experienced drivers to operate the clutch, steering mechanism and brakes in such a way to save gas and their own energy.

Approaching 0400 hours we rolled onto a large national street in Ghent. The lanes were large. The lead of the company stopped. Since there were no signs, a guide had to be brought to the front. The guy who didn't stop was my driver. The crew was dozing behind him. All the yelling in microphone proved to be useless. There was only one thing left to do, get out of the turret and rip open the driver's hatch, but it was sealed shut. Another twenty meters we banged into the guy in front of us. Like a crazy man I jumped all over the driver's hatch. That seemed to do the trick in the nick of time and with a slight jolt the Panzer stood still. From then on a man of the crew sat at the front on the open driver's hatch every time we had a night march.

Ghent was soon behind us. The drive went on side streets. Tight curves and exhausted drivers (who had had to sit at the steering wheel uninterrupted for the previous 24 hours) don't go well together. Because of this the Panzers ripped up pavement and scraped the sides of houses in the smaller villages. It couldn't go on much longer, because the drivers really couldn't drive any more. The Battalion guide piloted us finally into the little village of Ursel. The platoons received their quarters spread out from each other.

Due to the danger from fighter planes the enlisted men had to remain at the wagons, which were pulled into the shadows of trees and houses so that they would be camouflaged from sight.

An air-raid warning commando occupied the windmill on the southwestern flank of the village. The mayor and village police warned us about communist sympathizers believed to be in the village. The mayor told us that we could do without any great amount of camouflage. At the latest, London would be informed of their presence by the evening. The warning meant for us that we had to increase guard duty with double posts in the area of the platoons, as well as change posts in the village. There were no recognized actions of the "White Brigade" or other units of this type during the entire stop-over in Ursel.

The first few days of rest in Ursel were marked with extensive work on the Panzers, which also received their camouflage paint.

The first platoon consisted now of only four wagons, since the second wagon of this group (Oberscharführer Clotten) was in the workshop due to problems with the steering. The crew switched between technical and guard duty.

A rare change during the days in Ursel was the marriage of our company leader Wolff. The "invasion marriage" was set up by the Regiment.

The Division's judge and the young pair went to a festively decorated little chateau. The party was surrounded by a string quartet, which later took care of the table music as well.

The rare marriage round table was a gentlemen's party completely in gray or black uniform with the exception of the bride. The regimental toast was held by Obersturmbannführer Peiper, while the company's best wishes were expressed by me, during which Jochen Peiper couldn't help but recommend that the still unmarried officers follow the example of Werner Wolff. It was somewhat curious as he brought to our attention that the oldest amongst them men, the Division's judge, was still single.

The OB West (Supreme Commander "West") realized at last on **June 16, 1944,** that the expected second landing of the allies was a decoy movement. An immediate transfer of the LAH to the front south of CAEN for the rondévous with the 12. SS-Panzer Division HJ under the leadership of the I. SS-Panzer Korps was then ordered by the OKH.

The loading up of parts of the Division began on **June 17, 1944**.

Gerhard Stiller reports about the loading up of the 7. Panzerkompanie:

The company was only allowed a few days in Ursel. The expected Allied landing in the Calais Pass didn't take place. The Division was urgently needed in Normandy. For transport and camouflage reasons the Company's 1st Platoon remained for about a day and a half longer in Ursel, after which the entire company took off during the night and loaded up in Eeklo. The immediate vicinity of the canal coast (a 30 km air line), which led us to expect constant dive bomber visits, forced the entrainment to take place at night.

We were the last Panzers to be loaded with the transport of the 6. Panzerkompanie (Obersturmführer Junker). We were to have reached Maldegem at about 2100 hours after passing through Kneselar. The train had barely reached the tracks in the open land and we already saw bomber squadrons fly in. We took off with the gas floored. The four wagons pulled out, as quick they could, but the dust gave us away. "If they see us, it is over," thought every one of us. Mushroom clouds of smoke and detonations between Oedelem and Maldegem were our savior. Luckily, the unloading ran without disturbance. At the same time, we expected a visit from the air at any minute from the west during every moment that it got lighter. But we had luck.

And finally our transport rolled to a new destination and into a dark future as well.

With the beginning of the Invasion the Allied air forces had systematically destroyed all of the railway junctions with continuous bombing runs. Once the Allied supreme command realized that the 1. SS-Panzer Division was to be transferred from Belgium, they strengthened their attacks and extended them onto the entire train system in western France. They attacked railway junctions and freight train stations. They also attacked the transports with dive bombers.

The casualties during the transports were heavy.

Therefore, the Division had to decide to unload the entire transport movement in the east, which partly passed through Paris, right where the trains were located. The transports were then to continue separately in long land marches to bring the Regiments to the front.

Single units arrived very late in the preparation areas around BRETTEVILLE SUR LAIZE/ FORET DE CINGLAIS, while the tracked units, among them the 7. Panzerkompanie, took the most time. This resulted in the conclusion of the march on **July 6, 1944**.

This train transport stuck in the mind of Gerhard Stiller:

> First we rolled in an easterly direction. The sky and the edge of the railway were constantly observed, because we had to figure on visits not only from dive bombers, but also from the "White Brigade."
>
> We drove around Brussels to the north. Then our trip went on through Leuven and Tirlemont, then Namur and Dinant. As the evening sun appeared we disappeared into an area in the Ardennes rich with tunnels, which would have been more comfortable for us during the day. Here we were safe from planes, but the danger from the "White Brigade" was considerably greater.
>
> Only three men can sleep under our wagon, one is in the turret with a machine gun, the second has the commander's machine pistol. So it went, hour after hour.
>
> The new day greeted us in the vicinity of Longuyon in Lorraine. We stood at the switching yards in Mars-la-Tour, and got ready for a long wait and... then it was already nighttime.
>
> The sun climbed and the leader of the transport slowly grew nervous. He should have already been in the Paris area by then. We were the last battalion.
>
> After an hour the anger was gone and a locomotive that was to pull us on arrived. It was already evening before the train departed. We reached the Mosel

River under the evening skies and in Pont-á-Mousson we had to stop again. But just before dawn the train started up again. We departed from Moseltal near Toul, traveled for a short stretch through the Maas-Tal and curved off behind Commercy and set out once again to the west. We drove through Bar-le-Duc. Before reaching Vitry-le-Francious we were held up for a long time. The locomotive driver and it's heater had been driving transports continuously and that meant dive-bombers, danger of carpet bombing, Maquisards and foreign tracks with left turns. We provided the locomotive personnel with a sense of calmness, but we wanted to finally get off this train. We knew we would feel much better after we were once again on our own tracks.

At the switching yard in Vaires-sur Marne all hell had broken loose. The main tracks had been hit, which meant we would have to wait again.

The jolt of the train starting startled us out of our sleep. It was dawn already. We asked ourselves if we would see anything of Paris.

We crossed the Seine and we drove along the soft view of the large city. Suddenly a familiar name, "Versailles."

The switching yard and the large locomotive huts in St. Cyr-l'Ecole offered a picture of destruction. A crater field of many dozens of locomotives of all different sizes lay criss-crossed all over between bomb craters and ripped up tracks. Finally the transport stopped. We were told to get ready to unload. The transport train was shoved up against a little ramp and the wire shears went into action.

Away from the railway is the Devise. Past Millemont we reached the Fôret des Quatre Piliers. Parts of the Battalion took quarter on the southwestern edge of the forest.

After unloading, the march of the 7. Panzerkompanie continued in the early evening within the framework of the Battalion and went over National Street 12 to DREUX and through NONANCOURT to TILLIERS SUR AVE.

The next night's march continued on the National Street 12 through AIGLE into a forested section behind NONANT.

During the following night the trip traveled on National Street 24 through the burning village of ARGENTAN. After crossing through this village the units spent the day in fruit gardens north of the city. During the next night the march went onto National Street 158 through FALAISE until reaching the FÔRET DE CINGLAIS. In the northwest section of this town, the 7. Panzerkompanie reached its preparation area.

Gerhard Stiller remembers the arrival at the Fôret de Cinglais:

As we began to recognize the guide standing at the beginning of the forest, we lightened up. But it was getting to be high time, since it became active in the air just as the last Panzer was loaded from the street.

Obersturmführer Wolff made it clear to his platoon- and group leaders and the Panzer commanders that they could count on constant Allied air reconnaissance. After grabbing some coffee the crews went to work. Pick, shovel and entrenching tools became active. To bring an entire Panzer into the earth is hard work. The necessity of this work was also realized, however, because the heavy bombs, which indeed fell far in the distance, shook the entire earth.

We also knew then where we actually were. The 7. Panzerkompanie took quarter in the northwest point of the "Fôret de Cinglais." Entire divisions could disappear here, and therefore that had to be assumed by others.

Everyone knew that this area was in danger of being carpet bombed. That inspired the men who were still extremely tired from the trip. Soon the Panzers disappeared into deep walls of earth.

It had then been ten days since our original departure from Belgium. We left Usel on June 21 (Tuesday) and arrived in Paris on the 26th or 27th. The arrival in the "Fôret de Cinglais" must have been on the 2nd of July, 1944.

Since June 6, 1944 the 12.SS-Panzer Division HJ stood northwest of Caen in bitter defensive fighting against the British and Canadian landing troops.

The following three weeks were characterized by earth-shattering superiority in material and in the air. In tough fighting the enemy was able to push back the Division step by step to the edge of the city.

On **June 14, 1944,** the commander of the 12.SS-Panzer Division, Brigadeführer Fritz Witt, was killed at his command post in Venoix. The arriving portions of the LAH, SS-Panzer-Grenadier Regiment 1, arrived in their preparation zone south of CAEN on **June 28, 1944**. They were assigned to strengthen the defensive fighting and were subordinated to the HJ Division.

As the masses of the LAH arrived in the Fôret de Cinglais on **July 6, 1944**, the northern edge of the city of CAEN had just fallen into the hands of the allies.

The German troops mopped up CAEN until **July 10, 1944,** and set up a new defensive line south and southwest of the city. At this point in time the regiments of the LAH were transferred to the front and overtook the main fighting line between CAEN and MALTOT southwest of CAEN and to the right of the 9. SS-Panzer Division.

The Panzer Regiment transferred to the area around ST. ANDRE SUR ORNE. The 7. Panzerkompanie received the order to advance to BULLY.

Gerhard Stiller wrote about this:

On the night of the 11th of July we left the Fôret de Cinglais. The lightning on the horizon from the fighting on the front accompanied us during our drive to the north. Le Pont du Coudray lay under light fire. Just after reaching the first houses we turned to the right and pulled into a large fruit garden, which had trees sparsely spread out. We spread out amongst the trees. Immediately we were told to dig in. Dig in, but how? There wasn't but 30 cm of topsoil, then came chopped up rock. The crews desperately reached for their pick axes. The hacking lasted for the entire day. The crews then had blisters on their hands. Whenever we got tired, the bomb attacks in the area of Maltot – Hill 112 – Esquay – Notre Dame, reminded us of the necessity of digging in. We needed more than two days to finally get into the ground.

Just behind our bivouac the riverbank fell sharply to the Orne. It was bout a 35 meter drop. This sharp angle made the narrow riverbank into an artillery-safe sunbathing beach. If a barrage came, you were safe from the falling rocks in the deep water.

Johann Wohninsland remembers the time in BULLY as well:

In Bully almost the entire maintenance squadron was hit. There was between six and seven wounded. Erwin Klopp was killed, Ludwig Kühn was badly wounded. He died later.

As the units of the LAH arrived at the preparation area, the heavy defensive fighting continued in the section of SS-Panzer Grenadier Regiment 1 from **July 11-14, 1944**. (See map 20).

After putting all the weapons into action, the Canadian advance was beat off, however.

On **July 12, 1944** the mass of the HJ Division was temporarily taken out of action and the LAH had to take over the LAH sections with other units.

On **July 15, 1944** the units of the LAH in action on the main fighting line were relieved by the 272. Infanterie Division (Army) and pulled back to the preparation area. From there the units took over the former section of the main fighting line previously occupied by the HJ Division along the line between the villages of GAGNY and BRAS.

On **July 18, 1944** a large attack, code named "GOODWOOD" was undertaken by the British and the Canadians in this section.

The Panzer Regiment LAH, including the IInd Battalion, were transferred as attack reserve into the area between GARCELLES and SECQUEVILLE where the 7. Panzerkompanie set up in the village of TILLY LA CAMPAGNE.

Gerhard Stiller remembers this transfer:

In the night of July 18/19 we were once again told to pull out. Instead of going forward, we were to travel over the still intact bridge onto the other side of the Orne. From there we were to go to Percouville. Under the lightning showers of the front we reached Clinchamps sur Orne. We then pulled into a fruit garden before Laize la Ville.

The company leaders went to the command post to receive instructions and orders. We then found out that the Panzer of Hauptsturmführer Streipart, the company commander of the 5. Panzerkompanie, had a break-down on the ramp of the Orne bridge.

After waiting for a few hours we continued our trek to the east.

We rolled on – decked out as a "rolling fruit garden" (Boccages) – at about noon. There was loud noise from action to the north. Wolff finally came back during the early afternoon. We came upon action in the area of Caen, where the "Tommy" was pushing forward along National Street 158. That is all that we experienced of him. We rolled through Fontenay le Marmion. Before reaching Rocquancourt we veered off to the north and soon we reached the National Street 158. We crossed over the road and then rolled directly upon a smaller village. A look at the map says we were in "TILLY LA CAMPAGNE."

Rudolf Ehrhardt can easily remember this transfer as well:

As the men of the 7. Panzerkompanie climbed out of their Panzers along a street next to a railroad embankment between wheat fields and grazing land, they had no idea what stood before them.

Until then the action had hardly been overlooked. Preparations, transfers, night marches, dive bomber attacks, casualties. We stood around our Panzers the entire night. The village in the background was barely noticeable due to the dust in the air. It was like all the other villages that we happened upon: evacuated. There was no life in this ghost town except for an occasional dog, a cat or perhaps a few chickens and rabbits. Did someone see the town's name plate? Suddenly the name was there. TILLY LA CAMPAGNE.

Before us was the sound of battle. Now and then a vehicle, a Sanka, an infantry man. The situation was like the fog. "Secure the village – in the form of a half-circle – to the North – prepare for a counterattack" is the first order. Sight becomes better. The field in front of us is even, ideal for Panzers. Somewhere on the horizon you can imagine more than you can see – "Caen."

Greetings from the sea came more often than desired. The minute-long rumbling ripped at our nerves. It became even more uncomfortable as the air cleared and it became easier to see the fire from the incoming artillery.

In the preparation area, which soon became a part of the main fighting line, the 7. Panzerkompanie pulled down into defensive position.

The task of the company was to:

Perfect camouflage along the rows hedges.
Maintain absolute radio silence, communication by messenger, and flare signals for an enemy attack
No opening fire without express orders from a company leader.

With a good firing area to the north and easily viewed terrain until the next village, the much needed position had been found. While taking the position there was light fire landing on the field in front of us. Heavy fire from the battleship artillery went over the village and behind us.

On **July 19, 1944,** three British armored divisions stepped up for the attack in wide formation, during which the advance of the 11th British Armored Division was aimed at BRAS and HUBERT – FOLIE.

The Ist and IInd Battalions of SS-Panzer-Grenadier Regiment 1 were able to hold all attacks and then beat them off.

On **July 20, 1944,** the Britons and the Canadians attacked the entire area of the section held by the Division with strong air support. A few break-throughs were mopped up by the 6. And 7. Panzerkompanien.

On **July 22, 1944,** an uninterrupted artillery barrage was laid on all positions of the Division. Enemy tanks could be seen gathering everywhere. An attack by the Canadians on BOURGUEBUS advanced to a distance of 1 km away from the positions of the 7. Panzerkompanie in TILLY LA CAMPAGNE.

During the **23rd and 24th of July 1944**, the focal point of the Britons and the Canadians were the villages of TROTEVAL and FRENOVILLE. During this time, the attack on the village of TILLY LA CAMPAGNE by the 7. Panzerkompanie, which the men of the company had been waiting for a long time, began on **July 25, 1944**.

Gerhard Stiller wrote about the battle for TILLY LA CAMPAGNE:

The Tommy's tank preparation area in Hubert-Folie left no doubt that hell would break loose on the morning of the 25th at the latest. The midnight magic of the German Luftwaffe developed into fireworks over the village of Hubert-Folie. The warning signals from the planes didn't tell us anything new.

During the night of the 25th it had already broken loose.

There were no more artillery barrages onto our section. Tilly was then being shot ripe. The infantry squatted in their foxholes, the Panzer crews under their wagons.

Then morning broke. We were lucky that the sun sat so deep, since the Tommy-tanks, which then rolled out of the northwest, had to aim into the sun.

"Let them come nearer" was the idea. Finally, flare signal white. "FEUER FREI!" (FIRE AT WILL!) The Panzers lurking in their hidden position swept streams of fire forward. Shot after shot came out of the barrels while the other Panzers in the row of hedges cut in. The magic didn't last for more than five minutes and the Tommy's attack was at a standstill. When will the second wave come that will push forward the stopped opponent? There was nothing behind us but rumbling. There were heavy grenade launchers and 500 meters in front of us all hell was breaking loose. Like rabbits, the Tommies mopped up this section of land. A Panzer must have received a direct hit, because it was no longer there. The others one stayed back, smoking.

What wasn't successful from the front, wasn't desired from the west. No one noticed the dozens of Tommies on Carretes and went unknowing to Tilly. Unterscharführer Hohmann, who got out of his Panzer because he wanted to direct it back to the starting position, was jumped by a big Brit who sprang from a hedge. Hohmann didn't have a chance. But his no. 1 gunner was a fraction of a second quicker and he saved his commander with his MG. More Tommies were flushed out of the houses that they had hid themselves in after they abandoned their tanks.

The situation was unknown on the west side of Tilly. The IVth Platoon, under the leadership of Untersturmführer Kothmann, went behind the row of trees in position. The southwest exit secured the company's other vehicles. A few infantry men stood around, available. Along the National Street 158 the Tommies won some area. How far they advanced, we don't know.

Manfred Thorn remembers this fateful day well:

It was during the night of July 25th in Tilly la Campagne, time to get something to eat. From time to time a man from a Panzer crew made his way to Panzer 702 with his mess tin.

Loader Peiper and I armed ourselves with mess tins and took off with mixed feelings towards the field kitchen. It was an evil undertaking to leave a Panzer in a battle position without a driver and a loader.

The English Carretcs, which we used along with Heinz Wölfel to bring food to Tilly, stood at Panzer 702. The noise from the motor invited grenade launcher fire and the first incoming landed in the vicinity. The fire thickened, and it looked like a Tommy attack.

We filled our mess tins and then ran through the bomb craters right across Tilly to our Panzers. Our instincts didn't let us down. Our Kommandant, Rottenführer Rattke, yelled to out to us from the turret: "where have you been, three Canadian tanks are thirty meters away in the field!"

Our Panzer stood well camouflaged right next to the wall of a house, and in front of it was a 1.5 meter high stone wall. The three Canadian tanks hadn't noticed us yet. A shot from our main gun would surely have brought us our deaths. The loader and I took our positions immediately. The radioman called a message to the company leader: "Enemy tanks, coming from Bourguébus towards our position."

I immediately started up the engine and shifted it into reverse. The Panzer moved backwards in the protection of the wall, out on to the farmstead and then onto a ravine in back of it. We wanted to knock out the three tanks which were still standing in the same position: backwards.

We drove in the ravine in an easterly direction coming from Tilly. After traveling 200 meters we turned to the north in the direction of Bourguébus, and after traveling a further 200 meters we tottered once again in a southerly direction towards Tilly. With extreme care we drove upon the three enemy tanks, which we could already see. We observed sharply the entire area for enemy infantry, at least as far as we could see during the night. At a distance of about 20 meters the no. 1 gunner opened fire on the first tank. It burned immediately. The second and third tank each received a hit. The crews got out. During this action we didn't feel too good, because we were positioned right in the middle of the Tommies.

Suddenly there was clattering on the turret.. I roared: "Don't open up your hatches, the Tommies are on the wagon!" – There was more clattering and we heard: "It's Obersturmführer Wolff, open up!" We were shocked at the unexpected visit of our company leader. Now it hit us, we had driven away from our position near the house without orders.

The no. 1 gunner opened the turret hatch and Wolff handed us a bottle of Cognac and said: "Well done, keep it up!"

In the days from **July 26-29, 1944,** there were local battles with isolated British and Canadian attacks on all positions of the division with little success.

> During a Canadian attack on Tilly our company was able to capture a Carette, which we used to bring food to the front from then on.
>
> One time I drove a tank drive from Tilly back to Bretteville. During this drive we slipped into a bomb crater and the motor died. In order to start it back up, we had to use the inertia starter. Since the front of the Panzer was stuck in the crater, the back end stuck up rather high in the air, which forced us to have to shovel some dirt, in order to use the inertia starter. We finally made it to our parsonage in the morning gray.

On **July 30, 1944,** the 2nd British Army attacked after the resulting reformation of the 21st British Army Group. During this attack three tank divisions were deployed along National Street 158, and their goal was to advance directly to TILLY LA CAMPAGNE.

Gerhard Stiller reports about the course of this attack:

> On July 31st the hour of truth revealed its dark shadow.
>
> The Ist Platoon, which drove into Tilly with four wagons, only had Panzer 711 and 712 still available for action.
>
> Panzers 713 and 715 (Panzer 714 reached the area of Falaise on August 2 after lengthy repairs in Paris) were shot up by artillery rounds. They were due for a visit to the repair station and were sent to the workshop in Bretteville sur Laize.
>
> Panzer 712 had been excellently camouflaged days ago behind a row of hedges, and the camouflage fit the northwest side of our defensive position well. This was the wagon that was positioned next to the hill 72, where the Tommies had positioned some troublesome infantry cannons. The forward observer of the grenade launcher unit (the unit which turned the area before Bourgués into a "clean ship"), wanted to order the bombing of the hill 72 from Panzer 712. Leutnant Weiß from the grenade launcher unit wasn't a novice here on the Normandy front. Everywhere, be it the situation to the left of or the right of the National Street, he could become a decisive element of the battle, as long as munition was available. A forward observer can't work without a radio, however. Even for Panzer 712, located in a corner, a few short radio directions were needed,. That must have been enough for the Tommies.
>
> Leutnant Weiß didn't signal anymore after a few minutes, since a flat of about 300 square meters was turned into a burning hell after only the wave of

a hand. The enemy on hill 72 not only defended himself, be he defended himself with everything that had a barrel. The mass of the incoming hit its mark. The effect on morale was unimaginable. The highly sensitive fuses caused the rounds to burst on every branch. A hit near the Panzer blew away its lighter parts and the camouflage flew through the air.

The crew, at this time squatting beneath the Panzer, counted the seconds left in their lives with their fingers. The thick incoming took the air from the men under the Panzer. During a short pause in the fire, the men ran in a 100 meter sprint back into the craters in Mairie.

Shortly thereafter Oberscharführer Siptrott took his badly shot up and damaged 712 out of position. The wagon stumbled back to the middle of the village and took full cover behind the ruins of some houses. Now wagon 711 was alone in the position in the hedges. Obersturmführer Wolff decided to pull it back into the Mairie garden, where a more active battle was more of a possibility. It would already be shown early the next day that Wolff had made the correct decision. For the men of the 711 it meant that they had to once again dig in, which due to the soft earth in the garden was accomplished in just a few hours.

Calmness then ruled, as if the dismantling of the 712 had softened the evil spirits on hill 72.

The night of **July 31/August 1** brought hot battles full of casualties which lasted into the next day. But during the evening, the much longed for relieving of the company followed.

Gerhard Stiller wrote in his report:

But right after 0200 hours the situation changed drastically. The barely felt nightly light artillery fire was relieved by a full-bore barrage. A wall of fire slowly made itself over the road and the west side of Tilly went up in an inferno. The men in their fox holes in the northern sector of the village were somewhat used to it, but it was never this violent in Tilly. The barrage lasted for over two hours. Incoming after incoming touched almost every square meter of the landscape. The men in the foxholes and under the Panzers almost suffocated in the smoke of the exploding middle and heavy caliber bombs. Now and then it shook even worse. Even the Panzers jumped up and down a little. Smoke from smoke-bombs waltzed over Tilly where the music from the incoming was playing. The Kommandant of Panzer 711, Untersturmführer Stiller, became suspicious. Something didn't seem right. He climbed into the turret from the hole in the ground, but couldn't recognize anything due to the smoke. The incoming were now landing some 30 meters behind the wagon in the middle of the village. In the smoke, Stiller recognized men with flat helmets already past the infantry positions in the area of the railway crossing. No doubt, Tommy had broken through there.

For the moment the crew of the 711 was at the battle and the radioman gave the order to get ready for action to all battle wagons.

Out of the wall of smoke on the road crossing, there was a group of Canadians in the strength of about a company. The men in the wagon had no idea what was going on. The man in the turret was indecisive. Sturmmann Pager, the no. 1 gunner, was just able to break the turret free before the group was noticeable. The Canadians advanced in a funeral tempo past the Mairie. It appeared as if they feared mines and paused at the village street, which didn't pass wagon 711 which was 30 meters away. Stiller's assumption was correct. The first enemy tank came diagonally across from the right. It approached to a distance of about 30 meters, and a Panzer round hunted its way into the side of the turret. As it began to pull back a second round hit the upper part of the chassis. The disembarking crew was driven away by a bunch of machine guns. This situation was barely taken care of and a second enemy tank rumbled in. "Enemy tank 11 o'clock – fire at will!" The streak of light bored itself between the turret and the chassis and this tank gave up as well. A hail of machine gun bullets mopped up the vicinity of the tank and scared away the accompanying men on the road crossing. More enemy tanks were recognizable. A look to the rear showed the Kommandant, that the group of Canadians was coming back. The knock out of their accompanying tanks and the fact that the other infantry didn't follow through didn't seem to have fit into the Canadian plans.

Since opening fire on the group of Canadians would result in the Canadians retreating to the shot up Mairie, the men waited until the majority of them were located between 10 and 12 o'clock. Grenades and machine gun fire forced the opponent to quickly retreat and leave their dead and wounded behind.

Obersturmführer Wolff wanted to drive up to us with his wagon from the Marie yard. But his turret was stuck and he couldn't get it pointed in the right direction as the second enemy tank came over the road crossing and aimed at his turret. Not a second too early Pager shot a round from the 711. Turning the entire Panzer, the 701 gave the motionless enemy tank on the road crossing a coup de grâce, so that its munition would blow and give the Canadians a fireworks display.

As Obersturmführer Wolff recognized that parts of the fleeing enemy infantry wanted to set themselves up on the road, he pushed on with his stuck turret, so that even these brave ones would be forced to rush back to their starting positions.

The attack seemed to be blunted. Weapons, wounded and dead enemy soldiers lay in the area of the street. Our infantry was not to be seen.

Stiller and his radioman got out of their wagon as the other three men from the 711 – driver Schäfer, no. 1 gunner Pager and loader Graupne – kept the battle wagon ready for action.

Cries of "help, help!" come from the two Canadians lying on the street next to machine pistols and pistols. Teichert first threw all their weapons out of their reach, since no fist-fight could be expected from these poor young men.

Two more men jumped out of Wolff's wagon, and they went to retrieve more wounded Canadians from the field around the road crossing. A badly wounded Canadian captain informed the men that he was the battalion adjutant. The opponent was at best in the strength of a company, however.

The wounded Canadians were gathered in a wasted area of land in the Mairie.

Finally a few men from the infantry appeared. They had left the recently re-captured positions before us in the direction of Hill 72 and sent out a few men to transport the wounded enemy soldiers out of the area. The light artillery fire required us to once again be alert. The noise of action coming from the west forced us to conclude that ongoing battles were taking place on the other side of National Street 158. But the situation in Tilly remained stable.

The knocked out Canadian tanks in the front of the Mairie garden proved to contain booty for the men of the wagon 711. Cigarettes, chocolate, cookies and other rations then switched into the 711. For the most part they were spread out in the stern of the wagon after a heavy grenade launcher hit. But the stern side armor was ripped open and only the repair station could help this situation.

It was midnight when the 711 was relieved. We then traveled on the roads until reaching Garcelles-Secqueville. Wide reaching artillery fire blew over us. The village before us was under fire. So we turned off into the open field. Tank and Carette tracks showed us the way. Finally we reached the National Street 158. On the la Jalousie crossing (point 115) heavy bombs landed. We waited out the situation, then we continued on.

At about 0200 hours we reached Bretteville sur Laize. In the rectory we stretched out in feather beds. Bretteville was still in good shape.

The chronicler of the "Calgary Highlanders" wrote about the defensive battles of the 7. Panzerkompanie in TILLY LA CAMPAGNE.:

> The 1.SS-Panzer Division continued to give evidence of their unshakable will to prove their courage.

Still under the pressure of the inferno of the two six-day defensive battles, Untersturmführer Gerhard Stiller, platoon leader in the 7. Panzerkompanie rode the Pegasus:

"We named it 'the Tilly of the field operation,'
unnecessarily run over by a higher power.
A tower of fire, it never came to rest.
People and walls covered her,
everything smashed, trees and bushes alike,
barely a crop still lived, around us only terror.
We the defenders, a small group of soldiers,
in the fifth year of war, sold and betrayed.
The grenadiers squat in their foxholes,
patches of steel splinters instead of grass,
a clump of people often searching for cover,
gritting their teeth they hold out, only fleet for them;
the sweat under their helmets is the only moisture,
their lips swelled up, their faces pale yellow,
smoke being coughed out of their lungs,
breathing heavy, the old and the young.
Here and there is still a Panzer, cut into the earth.
Just a few more, paired up with five men,
twisted steel skirts, shot up extra parts
shackled in cover, like a deployed anti-tank gun,
as a support made of steel for the infantry,
the target of the enemy artillery.
Marks of direct hits all over the chassis and turret,
burnt all around from firestorms of steel splinters;
the men within as living beings,
fear the end and hope for luck,
close to each other and pressed to the ground,
they hope that Mars is rolling the dice for them.

The earth shook too hard back then,
and many didn't survive.
Today the wind blows over the village, the graves and the field,
unforgotten Tilly, may you be a memorial of freedom to the world"

On **August 3, 1944,** the entire LAH was ordered to be relieved by the 89. Infanteriedivision.

In the meantime, the American invasion troops broke through the German coastal defense and advanced past ST. LO to AVRANCHES. In ongoing advancing attacks they wanted to cut off BRETAGNE.

In just this way, they turned their units to the east. These units were to threaten the flanks of the German units located in front of the British/Canadian landing section and then surround them.

In order to run into the flank attack, prevent the encirclement and then further cut off the American advance to the south, the German leadership deployed the XXXXVII. Panzerkorps. The 116. Panzer Division, the 1. SS-Panzer Division, the 2. SS-Panzer Division and the 17. Panzer Division were subordinated to this corps for the attack.

Up until **August 6, 1944**, the action-ready portions of the LAH were to advance from the area north of MORTAIN to ST. BARTHELMY – BELLEFONTAINE between the 2. Panzer Division and 2. SS-Panzer Division. The 7. Panzerkompanie departed late, since urgent and necessary overhauls of weapons, equipment and vehicles were required after the exhausting battles in TILLY LA CAMPAGNE. Gerhard Stiller reports about the trip to the West, where the 7. Panzerkompanie traveled to its new battle section:

> On the evening of August 7 we were to roll on once again. We were to go the area of St. Lô, where the Americans were supposed to have broken in. In the dark of night the rumbling of Panzer motors, the rassling of our tank tracks and the flapping of the chassis skirts once again accompanied us on the roads. This time we were well-rested and the trip ran smoothly.
>
> Department Street 23 ran through Barbery-Bois Halbout and St. Clair to Pont-d'Ouilly. Since the bridge over the Orne was no longer capable of supporting Panzers, we traveled on to Pont des Vers and from there through a U-turn from the valley of the Orne and on out. Our goal for the night march was to reach a large forest, the Fôret d'Andaine. We drove our jalopies as fast as they would permit. In la Carnaille the skirts on the side of our Panzers, which were set up so beautifully, were left hanging within the narrow confines of the

gates to the village, but there was no damage to our wagons. We noticed that the drivers were tired. Dusk arrived quickly and the large forest was still far away. As we reached la Ferriere, the 8th of August had already arrived and life was in the air. We reached the Fôret d'Andaine spread far apart from each other. After a few minutes all of the crews were asleep. Only a carpet bombing could shake us up here. And then we were told to wait, wait, wait. We waited for an entire day.

A straight street running in a west-east direction went right through the Fôret d'Andaine. It seemed as if everything drove through this forest and we experienced extreme difficulties with the arrangements. This street ran to Domfront, which had already experienced a carpet bombing raid which caused a traffic jam on the D 908. Stressed-out columns of soldiers came upon us or were in our way. We drove around the Domfront just as it became light out. We took quarter in a fruit garden in Rouelle.

The situation appeared to be confused. Wolff went to the regimental command post. We stayed put for the entire day. As darkness fell, we went on. We rolled through Barenton and turned off once more in the direction of the north. In the Fôret de Lande-Pourrie we took up quarters.

In the meantime the 7th German Army (under Oberstgruppenführer Hausser), to which the LAH was subordinated, was deployed for an attack. They met up with the units of the 1st U.S. Army which were attacking to the west. This occurred on **August 6, 1944**. On **August 7, 1944,** this German army advanced over the line between SOUR-DEVAL and MORTAIN with Reconnaissance Battalion 1 (with parts of the 2. Panzer Division) and took MESNIL-TOVE. On **August 8, 1944,** they took MESNIL – ADELEE, while Panzer Group Peiper reached ROMAGNY from LA TOURNERIE. (See map 22).

Continuous dive bomber attacks (Typhoons) on the lead attack units, massive artillery barrages and carpet bombings stopped the German advance on **August 9, 1944,** along the entire width of the attack and required that the Division switch over to the defense along the main fighting line.

During a dive bomber attack Obersturmbannführer Peiper suffered a serious heart attack and had to be taken back to a field hospital.

On **August 10, 1944,** the allies began to encircle the 7th German Army from three sides with:

The 1st Canadian and 2nd British Army in the north (south of Caen)
The 1st US Army in the west
and the 3rd US Army in the south.

On **August 11, 1944**, under the pressure of the looming encirclement, the 7th German Army decided to pull back its battered divisions to the line between the villages of FLERS and DOMFRONT. On **August 12, 1944**, the LAH reached the area around FERTE and MACE as part of this retreat.

The 7. Panzerkompanie, which at this time had just reached the Panzer Group LAH and was ready for action, had to withdraw along with the Panzer Group once again to the east through BARENTON, DOMFRONT, FERTE – MACE. They reached JOLIE DU BOIS on **August 14, 1944.**

During the defensive battles the 7. Panzerkompanie was deployed near LA CHAUX on **August 15, 1944,** in ST. GEORGES D'ANNEBEC on **August 16, 1944** and in FAVEROLLES on **August 17, 1944** during the retreats to the north.

In the meantime the British and the Canadians executed a full-scale attack on FALAISE into the back of the Division in the section of the HJ Division. The Americans reached ARGENTAN from the south and approached the British and Canadian advance to within 18 km. In order to escape the encirclement the badly beat up German troops, now in the form of battle groups, retreated further to the north and managed continuous defensive fighting in strong points along the road D 19.

During this fighting, the 7. Panzerkompanie formed a strong point on both sides of ST. LEONARD.

After **August 17, 1944,** the DIVISION ordered a further retreat to the north-east. The 7. Panzerkompanie formed a new strong point with its last Panzers in ST. ANDRE DE BRIONZE. FALAIS had just fallen, which forced the 7. Panzerkompanie to retreat further to the south of FALAIS, traveling through FROMENTEL, PULANGE and across the ORNE.

To cut off the German retreat, the Canadians attacked TRUN to the south along the DIVES River. In the meantime, the Americans advanced from the south towards CHAMBOIS.

Only the road from ST. LAMBERT to CHAMBOIS remained open for the destroyed German units to retreat further to the east.

On **August 18, 1944,** the remains of the 7. Panzerkompanie, together with other parts of the Panzer Regiment, reached the area between TOURNAI and QUANTITE. Approaching evening on this day the Canadians took the wide front which spanned from TRUN through MAGNY and on to MONFORMEL. There they met up with the pressuring American forces coming from the south in CHAMBOIS. This situation threatened to close the pocket.

In order to free up the surrounded units of the 7th German Army, the 9. SS-Panzer Division "Hohenstaufen" and the 2. SS-Panzer Division "Das Reich" were deployed from the 5. Panzer Armee (under Oberstgruppenführer Dietrich) and advanced toward MOUNT ORMEL and SURDEVAL. (See map 23).

On **August 20, 1944,** the breakout of the surrounded units began. During this time, the remains of the 7. Panzerkompanie – together with parts of the Panzer Regiment LAH and other parts of the Division – attacked from TOURNAY onto CHAMBOIS. Their goal was to break through to the advancing attack leads of the 2. SS-Panzer Division, which was advancing to MONT ORMEL and SURDEVAL.

Gerhard Stiller, who was at that time the company commander leading the marching portions of the 5. Panzerkompanie during the break-out, reports about theses battles:

> We laid on the edge of a fruit garden a few kilometers south of Tournai (probably between Montmilcent and Méguillaume). It was midnight. We were supposed to depart at dawn.
>
> Password: Breakthrough to the east. – The situation was unknown.
>
> We laid dead tired and hungry under the wagon. Approaching 0200 hours a messenger came. We were to report our readiness to receive wire messages. It didn't take long to carry out the orders, but that was enough for our opponent to find us, and immediately it rained fire as thick as hail on our wagon. Then everything broke loose. We rolled into the dawn towards the east. On a hill of the farm group Aubry-en-Exmes we could see in front of us our group of Panzers rolling forward along the D 113. To the left we caught up to a few of the wagons. A group of infantrymen stumbled on behind us. Then the tank rounds began to sweep by our ears. According to the direction of the shots, the rounds had to be coming from the south. The distance was about 2,000 meters in front of the forest lying in the background between St. Eugenée and Fougy. We shot back, despite the fact that it was useless from this distance.
>
> A medic column with Red Cross flags flying all about came from the direction of Aubry-en-Exmes. It was immediately decked with tank rounds. Round after round blew the column in the air. We shot off our last smoke bombs to take the Ami's view away, but it was already too late. The wagons with Red Cross flags were burning in an inferno.
>
> We rolled on because the breakthrough was continuing. Our Panzers to the front of us were already in action. We knew that we would come upon the opponent at any minute. A bush bordered meadow before us buzzed with soldiers of all branches of service. We had to move forward slowly so that we didn't run over these men that waved at us doubtingly. From behind us Ami tank rounds exploded around us. It couldn't last much longer, or we would be tightly encircled.

We were standing as well. Twenty meters before us was a row of hedges. Everywhere men were squatting in their holes. Directly in front of us next to a hedge stood an abandoned troop carrier – but we moved forward to the hedges. 150 meters behind it was a group of farms. Obviously occupied. Then you could also recognize the enemy infantry. A retreat to the left seemed barely possible.

The right attack wedge, still hanging before Chambois, didn't allow us to go through between there. The enemy artillery, the mass of which was landing behind us, became stronger. Every hesitation cost valuable time. Therefore, before we were slowed to a stop from behind, we had to go forward and through. "Get up and get through" was the decision. – "Panzer March!" – Hopefully the other two Panzers would follow, as well as the infantry here. The driver gave it some gas. Artillery rounds fell all around us. Onward – through. In front of us the enemy infantry was spraying us.

Even the radio man Jupp Steinbüchel, from the remains of the Reconnaissance Battalion (a part of the breakout group) can remember the breakout:

On our road between Villedieu and Tournai sur Dives the enemy artillery shot directly at us. I don't need to describe this feeling. Shells were landing a short distance to the front of, next to or behind the wagon.

We flew over the road as fast as we could.

Then we came into a village (St. Lambert sur Dives). Everywhere it was crowded with horse-drawn wagons, Panzers, autos, etc. Now enemy tanks shot into everything with anti-personnel rounds. It was barely possible to understand the confusion. Cannons without crews, Panzers without crews. Everyone and everything on the run. Many ran around and didn't find a way out. Fire came from all sides. Our retreat slowed up a bit, since the enemy forces were too strong. A new path was found. It went on. We were shot at without success by anti-tank guns at a distance of about 600 meters. The Canadians stood at their guns in white sport pants.

The number of the abandoned or burning vehicles became increasingly large. It was barely possible to get through on the road. Once again across the field. It was good that we had tracked vehicles, otherwise it would have been over.

Then came the last leg of the march, the so-called street of death. Here was the most dreadful part of the entire trek. What we saw and experienced here cannot be described. I can only pause now in a moment of silence for the comrades who fell there. After passing this last leg we were out of the pocket. Then came the planes. The entire road was a smoking heap of craters.

Although it could not be determined from reports, the rest of the 7. Panzerkompanie was to have traveled through VIMOUTIERS, ORBEC and NEUBURD and have crossed the SEINE near ELBEUF. From there it was to marched on to CAMBRAIS where a few of the vehicles of the 7. Panzerkompanie were loaded up. This march was supposed to be by foot, with parts of the company traveling with captured vehicles. Another splinter group was said to have reached SIEGBURG in the middle of **September, 1944** after marching throughout HASSELT.

Heinz Wölfel reports about those last movements of the invasion battle:

On August 20, 1944 we broke out of the Falaise Pocket together with the infantry. Wohninsland and I had a tracked vehicle, an English Carette, which we captured in Tilly after the Tommies abandoned it to take some defensive fire from our company. We were a colorful group, 7. Panzerkompanie, 8. Panzerkompanie, Fallschirmjäger and the HJ Division, as well as some men from the Wehrmacht.

On the way to Elbeuf we took some vehicles which had been abandoned. In the meantime, Rolf Ehrhardt had broken through to us. That is how we all reached Elbeuf where we crossed the Seine. From there we went to Cambrais where Untersturmführer Sametreiter broke through to us. At this time we were still a group of about 25 men. In Cambrais a few of the vehicles of our company were loaded up. The resumption of the drive continued on to Hasselt/ Genk. Gas from the Luftwaffe and the Army was organized without any difficulties, because when we were organized we weren't to be beat. We also had to deal with partisans on the way. But it was only small skirmishes.

After arriving in Genk our old school had been turned into a field hospital which later evacuated.

After driving on through Maastricht/Aachen we went to the area of Siegburg. Here we still only had one Panzer, which Suttner and Thorn had brought back from Normandy.

Johann Wohninsland also remembers some of the events in the area of Siegburg:

At the end of August we had pulled out of France. The collecting point was in the area of Siegburg. Our company collected itself in Geber. We brought our Panzer back from the invasion. We were in Geber for about three weeks. Otto Thoma was killed there while driving to get rations. A comrade, whose name I have now forgotten, shot himself in Geber in a barn.

After the time in Siegburg, the company was ordered to transfer at the beginning of October to the refreshening zone between RAHDEN and OPPENWEHE.

ARDENNES OFFENSIVE

In about the middle of **October, 1944**, the Panzer Regiment finished collecting itself in the area of RHADEN.

The 7. Panzerkompanie took village quarters in OPENWEHE.

The refreshening time began with the arrival of personnel and material. During the course of the refreshing, a battle strength of approximately 75% was reached.

Four weeks remained for the short training of replacements. The supplying of Panzers dragged on, such that the company had received 60% of the required Panzers by the beginning of November.

Due to the situation with the available weapons, the 1., 2., 6., and 7. Panzerkompanien were put together to form the I. Panzer Battalion (under the leadership of Sturmbannführer Poetschke) in order to be able to put together a battle ready Panzer Battalion.

A portion of the young crews had never sat in a Panzer – and had never received any training with on-board radio equipment or firing training. The burden of the training and the strengthening of the battle morale of the troops lay completely on the shoulders of the "alte Hasen."

On **November 9, 1944,** the order to transfer to the west side of the Rhine in the area directly southwest of COLOGNE was issued.

While the company took quarters with the rest of the Battalion in the area of WEILERSWIST, the other companies (which still had not been equipped with Panzers) remained in the area of RHADEN under the subordination of a FEB.

On **December 14, 1944,** the divisional order arrived for the attack in the framework of the operation "Wacht am Rhein" (awakening on the Rhine). The focal point of the attack was to be LÜTTICH.

For the purpose of a quick advance, the LAH formed an armored battle group under the leadership of the commander of the Panzer Regiment, Obersturmbannführer Peiper.

The task for the Panzer Battle Group was the following:

Panzer Battle Group Peiper was to advance along the street D into the depths of the area after the breakthrough of the 12. Volksgrenadier Division through the American positions around LOSHEIM. The Panzer Battle Group was not to take threats to its flanks into consideration while advancing through TROIS-PONTS and WERBOMONT and then on to the Maas between LÜTTICH and HUY. There it was to build bridgeheads and prepare for a further advance onto ANTWERP.

Rolf Ehrhard, the driver of the command Panzer of the 7. Panzerkompanie remembers the day that the unit prepared for the battle:

> After the march from Bliesheim we pulled our Panzers into the preparation area in the Schmidtheimer Forest. We covered up the tracks they had made and camouflaged them so that they couldn't be seen by planes.
>
> The night camp and protection against the wind were well set up.
>
> We spent our time freezing and exchanged thoughts on the coming battle. No one knew anything! And from where anyway? Everything about this action was held in complete secrecy.
>
> After the officers had returned from their meeting in a close-by building, Hauptsturmführer Klingelhöfer called the platoon leaders into the map wagon and gave them orders to pass on to the platoons.
>
> While the platoon leaders informed their crews, the commander of the company troop (Panzers 701 and 702) explained the orders for the action. During his speech we felt a certain optimism that would have otherwise not been present in this man.
>
> The length of the war had left marks on him as well.

In the night from the 15th to the 16th of December 1944 came the drive to the starting position.

The day of December 16, 1944 began with gloomy, foggy winter weather, then snow and rain came – all requirements not to fear the Allied air dominance.

At 0535 hours came the artillery attack. The fire didn't manage to accomplish its intended effect. Our artillery maintained fire on recognized observation posts and enemy battery positions. The men of the Battle Group Peiper and today's historians have different opinions about the effect of our fire.

> During the night from the 15th to the 16th of December we all didn't sleep very much. As we awakened before "hour X," it didn't take much effort

ORDER OF BATTLE FOR THE PANZER BATTLE GROUP PEIPER FOR THE ADVANCE ON DECEMBER 16, 1944.

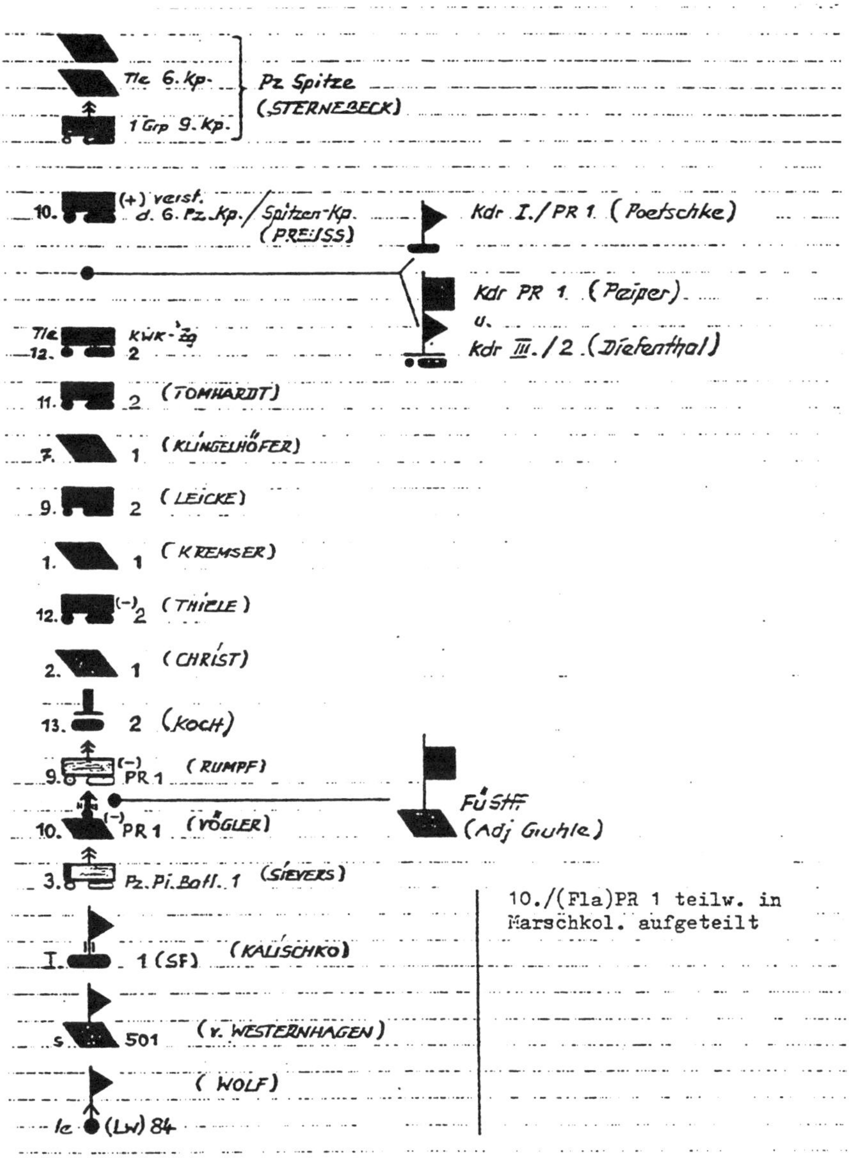

Tle 6. Kp. | Pz Spitze (STERNEBECK)
1 Grp 9. Kp.

10. (+) verst. d. 6. Pz. Kp. / Spitzen-Kp. (PREUSS)

Kdr I./PR 1 (Poetschke)

Kdr PR 1 (Peiper) u. Kdr III./2 (Diefenthal)

Tle 12. KwK-Zg 2

11. 2 (TOMHARDT)

7. 1 (KLINGELHÖFER)

9. 2 (LEICKE)

1. 1 (KREMSER)

12. (–) 2 (THIELE)

2. 1 (CHRIST)

13. 2 (KOCH)

9. (–) PR 1 (RUMPF)

10. (–) PR 1 (VÖGLER)

Fü Stff (Adj Guhle)

3. Pz. Pi. Batl. 1 (SIEVERS)

10./(Fla)PR 1 teilw. in Marschkol. aufgeteilt

I. 1 (SF) (KALISCHKO)

s 501 (v. WESTERNHAGEN)

(WOLF)

le (Lw) 84

to get up. The general excitement, combined with the cold made it much easier to get up.

We looked at the time and waited for the artillery barrage to begin. The minutes came and went, everything remained calm. After a few minutes a single cannon, positioned at about a distance of one kilometer, suddenly began to fire a few shots.

With this artillery barrage came the beginning of the Ardennes Offensive.

The infantry divisions in the front of the line began their attack.

At 1600 hours the Panzer Group accomplished the order of the I. SS-Panzer Korps to pull up to LOSHEIM, and from there to send out reconnaissance troops to scope out the situation for the possibility of joining in the attacks to take LOSHEIMERGRABEN.

After reaching the railway viaduct, one kilometer west of SCHEID, Peiper realized that the bridging column of the Pionier battalion of the 12. Volks-Grenadier Division could not reconstruct the blown bridge there.

The Panzer Group abandoned the road and slid down the slope to the railroad, crossed the tracks and then got back on the road. There it managed to advance and reach the entrance to Reich Street 421, and then continue its advance in the direction of LOSHEIMERGRABEN.

At approximately noon the Panzer Group Peiper reached LANZERATH.

On **December 17,** the vanguard of the Panzer Group set out from LANERATH to break through the reported American positions in the forest of LANZERATH, and from there to set out on an advance in the direction of BÜLLINGEN.

The lead company pushed its way into BÜLLINGEN. They received heavy fire from houses on both sides of the streets while driving through the village.

After the breakthrough of the lead company, American artillery fire on BÜLLINGEN increased.

With the lead company in the front, the vanguard continued its march. They turned off to the southwest in BÜLLINGEN and then won the street to AMEL. From there the group turned down a country road to SCHOPPEN at the street crossing at point 616.

Rolf Ehrhardt reports on how the 7. Panzerkompanie experienced the road through BÜLLINGEN as a main troop of the vanguard:

> It went further in the direction of BÜLLINGEN. Before reaching the village we passed an American airport where various mono-planes, obviously reconnaissance planes, were burning!

Drive on! A crossing in the village. Hold up!

The commander got out, inspected the ranks of the platoons, spoke with the platoon leaders and tried to figure out where he was.

As he inspected the drivetrain of our wagon, the rest of my crew reconnoitered the next area.

It was between night and day and we were sitting at our places. Radio communication was in order.

Suddenly, a completely clueless American Sanka came toward us at a quick pace from the direction of BÜTGENBACH. I jumped out of my driver's seat and got hung up on the wire. I forgot to take off my throat microphones. With a jerk I set myself free and ran towards the Sanka, which in the meantime had come to a stop. The driver and his passenger raised their hands, flabbergasted, and I made it clear to them with one hand on the skirt of our Panzer, that they should drive in the direction of Honsfeld.

These heroes were barely gone and a six wheeled OMC coming from the direction of Büllingen appeared. This time the driver grasped the situation faster, pulled back immediately and disappeared.

On the right side of the curve there was an apothecary. At the window in one of the floors above I saw an older gentleman. He was wearing a sleeping cap, as I knew them from Wilhelm Busch pictures. He made a sign to me that I should be careful, during which he pointed down in the direction of the house door. First I saw an olive green tent between the large pine trees before the garden. I felt quite different as I looked in and saw three dozing Americans getting out of their sleeping bags. Luckily my loader Peter Mühlbacher followed after me. At the same moment I noticed a pile of gas canisters in the small camp. We made it clear to the Americans with hands and feet that that they were to bring the canisters to the road. While being watched by Peter Mühlbacher they began their new jobs with our transport in the "work commando."

I reported to the commander and drove forward with my wagon. We were successful in gassing up with a few of the canisters of gasoline, and a few are loaded up for later. The other Panzers of our company did the same.

On **December 17, 1944,** at about 1200 hours the lead Panzers of the Panzer Group Peiper drove through the village of THIRIMONT and marched on north to the road coming from WAIMES. This road fed into the road from MALMÉDY to ENGELSDORF, N 23, further down the road about 800 meters near the hamlet of BAUGNEZ.

The 7th U.S. Armored Division had been marching on the N23 since the early morning of **December 17, 1944** to join in the battle near ST. VITH. The CCR (battle commando "Reserve") passed the entrance to the N 32 as the last march group.

The observation battery of the 285. Feldartilleriebeobachtungsbataillon (285th Field Artillery Observation Battalion) penetrated this road and reached the crossing at about 1230 hours.

At this time the lead Panzers of the Panzer Group approached the entrance to the N 32 and were at a distance of about 800 meters. There they recognized the American column of the American observation battery at a distance of about 1000 meters to the west. The American column was driving to the south on the N 23, which ran almost parallel to the road the Panzer Group was on. The lead German Panzers opened fire with anti-personnel rounds after the column reached a point about 200 meters south of the crossing. Immediately a portion of the trucks began to burn. In confusion the Americans jumped from their vehicles and searched for cover in the field and the ravine next to the road.

The lead Panzers used this confusion to pull up quickly to the entrance to the road near the village of BAUGNEZ, where they were received with American machine gun and rifle fire from the observation battery which had managed to situate itself there.

The Panzers attacked the American column with machine gun fire while on the run, as a result of which about twenty American soldiers were killed.

As the lead Panzers reached a point at a distance of about sixty to seventy meters, the Americans stood above the trenches and surrendered. The main leader of the lead Panzers, Obersturmführer Sternebeck, made hand signals to the Americans signifying that they should retreat to the back as prisoners.

Obersturmbannführer Peiper drove immediately to the lead due to the noise of the battle. As he recognized that that battle was virtually over, he gave Obersturmführer Sternebeck the order to continue the advance towards ENGELSDORF.

He pushed American vehicles which were blocking the street out of the way and continued with his troops of the lead Panzers in the direction of ENGELSDORF. (See map 25).

The captured American soldiers took the opportunity to use the calmness for the most part to surrender their weapons and then flee in the direction of the houses in BAUGNEZ, or better said, to flee to the edge of the forest which was at a distance of about sixty meters.

Then the other parts of the 7. Panzerkompanie which were arriving late to the scene saw the fleeing American soldiers, took them for enemy infantry and opened fire. As a result, several more Americans were killed. The rest of the American observation battery surrendered again and collected themselves under the leadership of Lieutenant Lary in the meadow between the street café and the crossing.

After that the 7. Panzerkompanie turned off to the south, turned onto the N 23 (in a sharp wedge formation and while experiencing difficulties) and then continued the march in the direction of ENGELSDORF.

As the Panzers turned onto the N 23, one of the Panzers of the 7. Panzerkompanie slid into the ravine next to the road. This was an unfortunate incident which was to happen to a few other vehicles in the lead group as well. While the column of the Panzer Group rolled to the south on N 23, the crews of the vehicles that slid into the trenches tried to get them back afloat, so that the march to ENGELSDORF could proceed as quickly as possible.

The stalled Panzers at the crossing caused a gap in the column of the Panzers. The Americans used this opportunity to renew their attempt to flee.

During the American attempt to flee, another shoot-out developed, during which another portion of Americans fell victim. Another group surrendered again, only to continue their attempts to flee later.

The subject of what caused this shoot-out has brought forth many statements and varying opinions, all of which are vastly different. Surely and understandably the Panzer men acted with nervousness. At the same time the Americans acted wrongly with their continuous and unclever attempts to flee (during which a portion of them attempted to recover their weapons).

On **December 18, 1944,** the weather was cloudy and gloomy, which was at first favorable for the attack groups of the Division. (See map 26).

Before reaching STAVELOT Obersturmbannführer Peiper rearranged his Panzer Group in the early morning for an attack on the village.

For the lead of the attack the Panthers of the 1. Kompanie under Obersturmführer Kremser and the 2. Kompanie under Obersturmführer Christ, together with the lead Panzer Grenadier company, 10.(armored)/SS-Panzer-Grenadier Regiment 2 with Hauptsturmführer Preuß and under the leadership of Sturmbannführer Poetschke.

The 6. and 7. Panzerkompanien received the order to surround and attack TROIS – PONTS in an encircling movement after passing through WANNE. The companies were also to also to take and secure the bridges in TROIS – PONTS as early as possible in the event that the lead Panzers became involved in a lasting battle.

Without hesitation Obersturmbannführer Peiper continued the march to TROIS – PONTS after his lead units quickly broke through STAVELOT. As his lead Panzers approached the village, they received fire from anti-tank guns. Peiper recognized that all of the bridges over the AMBLEVE and the SALM had been blown up. This had forced his quickly advancing Panzers to halt again, this time on the road leading in the direction of MAAS. He then decided to retreat to the north through the AMBLEVE valley. Passing the COO River the Panzer Group's lead Panzers reached the village of LA GLEIZE without any disturbances from the enemy shortly before 1300 hours.

The lead group turned off to the southwest and won the road leading to CHENEUX after crossing the bridge in AMBLEVE. Traveling along this road the Panzer Group passed through RAHIER and then reached the road planned for the advance, the road between TROIS – PONTS and WERBOMONT.

At approximately 1800 hours, after passing through RAHIER, the lead Panzers reached the point where the main road between TROIS – PONTS and WERBOMONT increases in size. The group remained there to let the parts of the III.(armored)/SS-Panzer-Grenadier Regiment 2 to catch up. At 2000 hours and upon reaching a branch in the road in CHAUVEHEID, the LIENNE bridge, located in the direct vicinity of the lead Panzers, blew up.

Obersturmbannführer Peiper decided to pull his Panzer Group back to LA GLEIZE, so that he could later attempt to open the street passing through STOUMONT which led to the west.

A flank attack conducted by the 6. And 7. Panzerkompanien accompanied by Fallschirmjäger from Regiment 9 began at 0800 from STAVELOT. WANNE was reached at 1200 hours after passing through HENUMONT and BOUEN. Just before reaching the entrance to the village the 9. (engineer)/SS-Panzer Regiment 1 had to clear a mine field. While passing through the village the battle group was shot at from houses with infantry weapons.

The Pioniere (engineers) and a few Panzer IVs reached the lead of the Panzer Group in the late afternoon in the SALM section after advancing through AISMONT. They reported that the SALM bridge crossing near TROIS -PONTS had been blown up.

While the mass of the battlegroup passed through WANNE, they received a message from the Panzer Regiment: "Back to the starting point and follow the lead."

Due to lack of fuel, both of the Panzer companies (6th and 7th) could only partially attempt to carry out the order. Fueled with the remaining gas, both company commanders reached the village of LA GLEIZE in the evening hours with a few Panzers.

On **December 19, 1944,** the attack of STOUMONT by the Panzer Group began. There was massive defensive fire from anti-tank guns and tanks. This put a stop to the attack. In the meantime, the Panzer group received fire on its flanks from enemy positions on the edge of the forest to the right of the street. Only Sturmbannführer Poetschke, through a display of courage, was able to bring the attack back in full-swing. (See map 27).

The commander of the 7. Panzerkompanie, Hauptsturmführer Klingelhöfer, had in the meantime arrived in LA GLEIZE. He received the order to abandon the portions of the 6. and 7. Panzerkompanien located east of STAVELOT. The plan was to meet up with the attack of the Panzer Reconnaissance Battalion 1 to win the road passing through STAVELOT and then to travel back towards LA GLEIZE and meet up with the rest of the Panzer Group.

Rolf Ehrhard reports about this:

> We reached both the lead and the commander before noon of the next day during the heavy battles for Stoumont.
>
> A knocked out Panther, numerous burning vehicles, a heavy 9.2 cm American anti-tank gun, noise, smoke and dead comrades formed the scenery of a meeting at the entrance to the village of Stoumont.
>
> Obersturmbannführer Pieper's order, as I remember it: "Lay your head down for a few hours and go fetch the 7. Panzerkompanie tomorrow morning."

The remains of the 6. And 7. Panzerkompanie were left behind in WANNE on **December 18th** due to a lack of fuel. In the meantime they had met up with the supply wagons and fueled up. In an effort to catch up with the rest of the Panzers in LA GLEIZE, the Panzer companies turned off to the north to force the breakthrough from the south over the AMBLEVE Bridge (after forcing their way through WANNERANVAL STAVELOT). However, after experiencing newly and heavily strengthened American resistance, their advance was not successful. A Tiger – which had joined the company after being repaired from damage in battle while fighting with the 2./SS-schwere Panzer Abteilung 501 (SS-Heavy Tank Battalion 501) – was knocked out during the approach to the bridge. Roman Clotten wrote about this incident:

> On the morning of December 19 we launched an attack on Stavelot together with the remaining Panzers of the 6. Panzerkompanie (Obersturmführer Sternebeck). We were also supported by a company of Fallschirmjäger who fought as infantry. As we approached with our Panzers we came upon the

eastern sector of the village of Stavelot. No enemy activity was noticed. The portion of the village on the other side of the river was occupied by strong enemy forces, however. As we approached the village we were immediately barraged with heavy anti-tank and mortar fire, and infantry fire as well. It proved to be impossible to win the bridge crossing despite numerous attempts.

On **December 20,** the secure positions of Panzer Group Peiper in the area of LA GLEIZE were attacked from all sides. In the north the Americans tried to break the German barricade on the western edge of the village of STOUMONT from the rear. An American attack on the flank of the Ist Battalion/SS-Panzer Regiment 1 was beat off with heavy casualties for the Americans. A Major McCown, commander of the IInd Battalion/U.S. Infantry Regiment 117 was taken prisoner.

Rolf Ehrhardt, who at that time was on the way with his company commander to pick up the rest of the 6. And 7. Panzerkompanie, reports:

> We drove off at the first sight of dawn. Before reaching the viaduct along the road to Coo we came upon an SPW (Schützenpanzerwagen) with an ordinance officer of the divisional staff. He reported that the street was blocked by the Americans. We set off for the mill and overtook the security position on the road to Coo.
>
> A King Tiger under the command of Untersturmführer Hantusch, as well as a small unit of the Reconnaissance Battalion – which was in the possession of a Panzerspähwagen (armored reconnaissance wagon), an eight-wheeled Puma, and a Panzerschreck (German bazooka) – formed the "Security Group 'Mill'" during the course of the day.
>
> Our Panzer IV stood behind the garden of trees. The King Tiger stood in a shed in the yard, while the Puma stood between the trees on the road. All barrels pointed at the bend in the road, where the attackers would first become visible.
>
> Suddenly we received fire from (supposedly) a 16 mm MG. An American patrol troop had worked its way up to the creek unnoticed and then further to a point within the vicinity of the house. Six or eight other comrades and I threw ourselves under the window because the massive natural wall of rock offered us protection.
>
> Then the fire broke off as suddenly as it had begun. The Puma had put an end to the spooky machine gun. What a wonder, no dead or wounded. One comrade had a mild shrapnel wound. The good wall and the cover in the dead angle were our savior.

The situation became worse as evening continued to approach.

The artillery fire on the villages of STOUMONT, CHENEUS and LA GLEIZE did not lose its force throughout the entire day.

The American patrol troop attacks did not let up either. One remembers especially the battles on the edge of the villages of CHENEUX and STOUMONT which were carried out with growing bitterness.

Some of the battles were carried out in the houses, in man-to-man combat with pistols and knives.

Because of this Obersturmbannführer Peiper ordered the mop up of the villages of STOUMONT and CHENEUX and the pull back of positions to the east edge of LA GLEIZE. With that the small village of about thirty houses became a fort of all-around defense.

With the pulling back of the front, the security north of PETIT COO was given up and the crew defending the eastern edge of LA GLEIZE was called back.

Rolf Ehrhardt remembers this day:

> We abandoned the mill and came back in the village to the Ferme Verimont unscathed. It was there that Hauptsturmführer Klingelhöfer took over the command of section "East."
>
> Our command post was set up in a basement of a neighboring building of the Ferme. The basement was constructed from large rocks and was therefore very secure against artillery fire.
>
> Here there were also signals men and medics who had to share the burden. We constantly had other guests in the basement, especially the Panzer crews, who wanted to stretch out their tired muscles.
>
> I was assigned as a signaler within Peiper's command post, or within the other units of the section.
>
> During the evening we fetched another Tiger from Untersturmführer Hantusch from the mill. There remained a patrol troop from the Reconnaissance Battalion which retained contact with us by wire.
>
> At the Ferme there were the Tigers of Untersturmführer Hantusch and Obersturmführer Bollinger, a Panther of Unterscharführer Friedrichs, another Panther and a few other armored vehicles.
>
> During this day I made my way to Peiper's command post about twenty to thirty times.
>
> An American anti-tank gun shot its way up to the deepest point on the road approaching the village. This shooting sent me into the dirt more often than I so desired it.

Since the 13th of December we hadn't had any more warm rations. We only received rations for three days. For days none of us ever had our fill. Many hadn't eaten anything for days.

It was similar with our sleep. We couldn't even think about that.

I believe that since the attack began I had only slept for more than an hour two or three times.

For the most part all of the comrades, whether simple soldier or commander, were no different concerning their condition. We were well beyond the border of our performance capabilities and well overburdened. Our faces were unshaven and dirty. Our eyes burned and we all had a cold. Many were wounded.

On **December 22,** the Americans launched an attack with many masses of tanks mounted with infantry.

The forcefully led advances were beat off by the Panzer men in their positions on the edge of the village and partly in the houses. A few tanks that had pushed their way into the village turned into harmless heaps by Panzer counter attacks. These attacks were conducted using the last few drops of fuel and the last rounds, and partly with Panzerfäusten as well.

The accompanying infantry was taken prisoner.

Our casualties were heavy.

Rolf Ehrhardt experienced a tank attack on the east edge of the road to ROANNE:

A number of American Shermans approached on the road on the other side of a ravine. The cannons of our Panzer IVs were ineffective due to the distance. The Shermans would be easy game for the too-long 8.8 cm cannons of the King Tigers and the 7.5 cm cannons of the Panthers, which were superior at this distance.

The American unit was recognized early enough and we let it approach to a favorable position. After the first miss of one of our Tigers, the Shermans unexpectedly formed a front and opened quick fire. This forced me to flee to the basement of the house where I had an observation post on the second floor. From there we pursued the battle.

The rounds coming from our Tigers were noticeably different than the incoming. Every shot fired by an 8.8 cm was a hit in our thoughts.

Suddenly the Tiger commander, Untersturmführer Hantusch, collapsed in the basement, both hands pressed to his head. His Tiger had received numerous hits which shook up its weapon system, and the electrical power was knocked out. After another round to the turret he was wounded on the head and had to abandon the smoking Panzer which could catch on fire at any minute.

Minutes later the second Tiger Kommandant, Obersturmführer Dollinger, came back and was bleeding heavily from his head and was silent. After his wound had been dressed he reported that the smoke from the rounds made it impossible to see through the gun's optics. It was impossible for him to see his targets. The thick response of enemy hits ruined the possibility of hitting another Sherman.

The numerical superiority of the approximately fifteen Shermans turned our superiority in weaponry into nothing. The Tiger of Obersturmführer Dollinger then received another hit which "amputated" the first third of its cannon.

This caused us to realize that we had been literally crushed, which had never before been so obvious.

The day's casualties and the lack of everything needed; what would the next day bring?

As darkness set in at about 1700 hours, the battle strongly receded.

A clear sky full of stars sparkled in the sky, which meant that air attacks could be expected for the following day.

On **December 23, 1944,** Obersturmbannführer Peiper prepared the breakout from LA GLEIZE for the night of **December 24**. He issued all necessary instructions during a commander's meeting on the afternoon of **December 23** from his command post, which was located in the basement of a farmer's house.

Rolf Ehrhardt gave a description of the atmosphere in the command post:

In the last days of the action in La Gleize I acted as an order receiver or messenger in this basement.

Things ran like a pigeonry there. Messengers came and went uninterrupted.

Everyone's faces weren't just characterized by fatigue, but were also very serious and hard looking. Obersturmbannführer Peiper was a model of calmness. He barely ever displayed a trace of emotion. He asked questions in a business-like manner and gave orders. No outbursts, no cursing, not a single loud word.

That was Peiper, the man who gave even the last of his men so much support and a strong sense of security.

I came across another personality while in this basement. I just happened to be there as the American Major Mc Cown, staff officer of the 30th U.S. Infantry Division, was brought forward as a prisoner of Obersturmbannführer Peiper by Oberscharführer Max Bergmann. This very large officer had to stand bent over under the top of the door frame to this small basement, and he introduced himself with a very non-chalant salute. I didn't understand the conversation that followed.

During the last commander's meeting in LA GLEIZE, Obersturmbannführer Peiper was most concerned about the care of his wounded, who would have to be left behind and would fall into American hands.

In order to secure a bearable fate for these men, he depended on the captured American Major Mc Cown, with whom he came to the agreement that:

> all American prisoners were to be freed and handed over to the American troops after the Panzer Group pulled out, in exchange for the release of the wounded Germans of the 1. SS-Panzer Division, who were to be handed over by the Americans.

Now the chance to hear about this meeting from Rolf Ehrhardt:

> The last orders issued in La Glieze were in the evening hours of the 23rd of December 1944.
>
> I can't bring together all of the names of those present.
>
> Besides Obersturmbannführer Peiper, officers Hauptsturmführer Diefenthal and Sturmbannführer Poetschke were present.
>
> The map lay on the heavy stone table.
>
> All officers present expressed their views of the situation. Then followed the order for the break-out:
>
> Along the road between Basse and Bodeux through Trois – Ponts to the south.
>
> During the conclusion of the meeting the time of the breakout and the code word were decided upon:
>
> 24th of December – 0200 hours – password: Merry Christmas!

In the early morning hours of **December 24, 1944,** the rest of the Panzer Group Peiper departed for the long and difficult foot march to the main fighting line of Battle Group Hansen. The Panzer Battle Group had consisted of approximately 3000 men in the beginning of the offensive. Today only 800 men were betting on breaking out of the American encirclement.

On **December 25, 1944,** after an exhausting march through snow covered hilly forests and constantly fleeing American forces, the last forces of the remains of the Panzer Battle Group reached the SALM between TROIS – PONTS and GRAND HALLEUX. (See map 28).

Some of the group found fjords along the riverbank, others simply waded through the river where they were. The steep opposite side of the riverbank had to be overcome under a heavy barrage of American artillery fire, after which the main fighting line of Battle Group Hansen (strengthened SS-Panzer-Grenadier Regiment 1) was reached.

During the morning of **December 25, 1944,** the following order was issued by the Supreme Commander West, General Field Marshal von Runstedt: (excerpts)

> 1. It is of decisive importance that the enemy attack wedge in the area of Bastogne is smashed very quickly and with sufficient and sweeping forces and means.
> 2. For this I am in agreement that the 1. SS-Panzer Division is to be quickly led into the area of Bastogne in order to add force to a concentrated attack of the 3. Panzer-Grenadier Division and the 167. Volks-Grenadier division against the deep flanks of the American units. The units of the 1. SS-Panzer Division are to apply their forces in local strongpoints where necessary.

On **December 27th,** the relief of the 1. SS-Panzer Division by the LXVIth Army Corps was in progress. At this time the Division was located between STAVELOT and TROIS – PONTS and was engaged in defensive battle.

Movements in regards to the pull-out could only be carried out at night, since the air was ruled during the day in the clear weather by the Allied air force. The relieved portions of the Division collected in an elongated forested area east of VIELSALM.

On **December 28, 1944,** the gathering of the Division concluded with the majority of the Division being located east of VIELSAM while the tracked units were located west of ST. VITH.

The General Kommando of the I. SS-Panzer Korps received the order to transfer the Division to the area east of Bastogne during the night of **December 29th**, after which they would be subordinated to the 5. Panzer Armee.

Due to a lack of fuel the last parts of the Division could not set out on their march until midday on **December 29th**.

Rolf Ehrhardt remembers this day:

Yesterday, on the 27th of December, we transferred from our chassis to our new camp in Hindenhausen west of St. Vith. I had spent the last 48 hours sleeping in this chassis. The march was difficult since my feet, which were frozen in my wool boots, made it difficult to drive. I could only just follow the man in front of me.

During midday today, the 28th of December, my loader, Peter Mühlbach, awakened me. He then gave me the order: "Go to the command post for a report immediately!"

My uniform hadn't been cleaned for the last two weeks since we were in Bleisheim. Despite the camouflage coveralls the uniform was in a horrible condition. And I had to present myself in front of Sturmbannführer Poetschke. Six comrades took care of my rags and I brought myself into a somewhat presentable condition. So there I was after a short time in somewhat better shape and on my way to the command post which was located in a forester's house. There I received the Iron Cross 1st Class and a promotion to Unterscharführer.

A big hello and best wishes. Dr. Neumeyer, who indeed knew me from LA GLEIZE, said to me: "Bring it home in good health!" Later that evening we transferred further in the direction of the Belgium-Luxembourg border in the area of Niederwampach.

Manfred Thorn recalled his memories of this day, short and sweet:

On December 28th, at about 1600 hours, I took off with the 7. Panzerkompanie in march. The road lead us through St. Vith to Trois, Vierges, and then onto Oberwampach. The company had melted away due to the many heavy casualties in the area of La Gleize. It still had 10 Panzer IVs.

The Division organized its action ready units on the BASTOGNE corridor into two battle groups for the attack which was to take place on **December 30, 1944**:

Group 1: A northern group from the remains of SS-Panzer Regiment 1 (6. and 7. Panzerkompanie), strengthened by a single Panzer V of the Ist Battalion coupled with action ready portions of the IInd Battalion of SS-Panzer-Grenadier Regiment 1 and Ist Battalion of SS-Panzer Grenadier Regiment 2.

The Regiment's Panzer strength consisted exclusively of Panzers which where were out of commission before the attack on STAVELOT and LA GLEIZE or for some reason had never made it to the pocket but had escaped destruction. The battle group was led by Sturmbannführer Poetschke.

Group 2: A southern group built from the rest of the SS-Panzer Grenadier Regiments 1 and 2 (without the IInd Battalion of Regiment 1), a recon platoon from SS-Panzer Reconnaissance Battalion 1 and a company of Panzer Pioniers (tank combat engineers). This battle group was led by Obersturmbannführer Hansen.

The northern group had the task to reach the road between BASTOGNE and MARTELANGE in the area between SAIWET and REMONFOSSE, after a quick advance which was to begin in the area of TAUCHAMPS and advance through LUTREBOIS. In the meantime, the southern group was to take VILLERS LA – BONNE – EAU, and then to win the road between BASTOGNE and MARTELANGE (after initially embarking from the same preparation area in LUTREMANGE).

Cloudy and misty weather with poor visibility impaired the action of enemy fighter bombers on **December 30, 1944**.

The attack of both battle groups began at 0625 hours.

At 0625 hours the attack units of the 1. SS-Panzer Division advanced from LUTERMANGE with the northern battle group through the western part of BOIS DE JEAN COLLIN on the road to LUTREBOIS in a northwesterly direction. During this time, they encountered only light enemy resistance.

Leaving LUTREBOIS to the left, the 6. Panzerkompanie turned to the west, advanced to REMONFOSSE and reached the road between MARTELANGE and BASTOGNE directly north of hill 535. There they met up with heavy artillery fire and were halted by a counter attack by portions of the 4th U.S. Armored Division. (See map 29).

During the advance to SAIWET, the 7. Panzerkompanie happened upon heavy fire on its flanks coming from units of the 4th U.S. Armored Division. This unit had in the meantime occupied LUTREBOIS and the edge of the forest northwest of there. After experiencing heavy casualties the company had to take cover in BOIS DE JEAN COLLIN.

Manfred Thorn reports about the attack:

At about 0630 hours we were on our way to Lutremange with the task of breaking in to the American "Assenois Corridor" from the east. The sky was cloudy and we weren't bothered by fighter planes. Lutremange was lightly bombarded by American artillery; one could assume that the main fighting line wasn't far away.

At about 0930 hours we arrived at the hill of Lutrebois. Here the road bent off to the right and after a short distance ran into the forest. The lead Panzer of the 7. Panzerkompanie, 701, suddenly stopped twenty meters before the forest; single German infantry men, presumably from the 26. Volks-Grenadier Division, appeared from the forest and ran over the meadow to the first Panzer to search for cover. Some of them collapsed before the Panzers, so there must have been Americans in the forest shooting at the fleeing infantry.

Our ten Panzers of the 7. Panzerkompanie still remained on the narrow path of the march column for between fifteen and twenty minutes, one right behind the other.

Communication with the 6. Panzerkompanie, which was advancing on the left, broke down.

I drove Panzer 734 of the IIIrd Platoon in the column as the seventh Panzer. The Panzer in front of me was that of my platoon leader, Panzer 713, Hans Siptrott. The order from the company commander: "IIIrd Platoon – take over the lead!" got the company going forward once again.

My Panzer received the order from the platoon leader to drive in the lead. I drove along past the still unmoving column and into the forest, which reached to the left and right of the road.

Now we came upon the first enemy activity. American infantry lay strewn across the left part of the forest and close to the road. The forest bordered the road for about one hundred meters, then you could see the first farm house of Lutrebois.

At the end of the forest to the right stood a Panther. I could not tell to which unit it belonged. I drove quickly through the forest and on past the farmhouse. Then came the sights of open and lightly climbing landscape. On the horizon to the west I saw the last Panzers of the 6. Panzerkompanie disappear behind a small hill. They drove in the direction of Remonfosse. I drove in this direction anyway. The landscape was open, the ground frozen. Therefore I could drive my Panzer at high speed on the open flats.

I received the message by radio that I should drive more to the north in the direction of Marvie.

Now the 7. Panzerkompanie drove in a wide wedge formation on the hill four kilometers before Bastogne. To the right of us was the forest, to the left the free landscape, and in the back of us was the village of Lutrebois. We didn't know if this village was occupied by the Americans.

From my position forward I was able to take care of an anti-tank gun positioned in front of a barn.

What we didn't know at this time was that the Battle Group A of the 4th U.S. Armored Division had attacked from Hompré – Salvacourt. We ran into this the lead infantry unit of this battle group in the previously mentioned forest.

As we stood on the road from Remonfosse to Villers La Bonne Eau, we assumed that there were American tanks in the forest which would take us under fire in the open land.

Just before 1515 hours we noticed from there that some of the Panzers behind us had already been knocked out and were on fire. In this episode, an episode which only lasted about ten minutes, eight Panzers of the 7. Panzerkompanie had been taken care of.

I turned around at my position, drove back as quickly as possible and went right on by the burning vehicles.

Now the entire American firepower concentrated on us.

We were lucky. I drove into cover behind a haystack in the vicinity of the farm. It was about 150 meters to the forest where the Panther stood. We didn't dare leave our cover until sundown. Our situation was very unpleasant. Cut off from the remaining companies of the Panzer Regiment without knowing where the American tanks stood, we waited behind the pile of hay for two hours. The radioman couldn't make contact. In the meantime the Panther disappeared from the forest's edge. We didn't know if the Americans were in the village. There were no shots. We only saw the burning Panzers to the right of us. The knocked out crews had fled into the forest to the right and took cover on the road to Bra.

At about 1730 hours we drove to a road leading northeast and then back into the forest. We immediately received artillery fire.

We stood on the edge of the forest for about an hour, and it hadn't stirred one bit in Lutrebois, as far as we could see.

Suddenly a tank came from the behind and was approaching us. The no. 1 gunner turned the cannon, but then we recognized that it was a Panzer from our company. We took off with the other Panzer through the three kilometer wide forest toward the northeast.

We reached the road connecting Bastogne and Bras near the on-ramp in Wardin. We drove on this road further in the direction of the east and reached the village of Bras. There we met up with the crews whose Panzers had been knocked out. We received an order from the company commander to once again drive to Lutremange on the night of December 31st. We weren't really into that idea. We waited the night out in a house behind the village of Watrange instead.

Rolf Ehrhardt remembers the fire of the American tanks from the left flank and its devastating effect:

Early in the morning on December 30th we drove to the preparation position. I believe it was in the small village of Watrange. There our orders were made known to us. At this time the 7. Panzerkompanie still had an entire seven Panzer IVs! It was to be a break-through attack, with which we were to cut off an American convoy on its way to Bastogne. Our attack was only to cross over a few kilometers, where we would meet up with units of the Army coming in the opposite direction.

We lay in a farm house together with infantry men of a Volks-Grenadier Division. Peter Mühlbach came at dawn with the question of whether we should make some Bratkartoffeln. I told him that he should only use the best butter, otherwise everything would burn in the Panzers. You got that kind of a feeling!

After the Bratkartoffeln and a dive bomber attack (which was unsuccessful), we departed for the attack at about 0930 hours. Lutremange and Lutrebois are names of villages which have remained in my memory.

The atmosphere on this day was spooky. It was wet and cold, foggy and unreal.

We were to pass by a piece of road on which artillery fire was falling. The Americans concentrated their fire in typical wasteful fashion on a curve. Numerous supply vehicles burned at that time, one of them was loaded with munitions which blew bits of unknown objects in all directions in the sky.

Especially shocking was yet another scene. Not far from our road, which lay a bit beyond the meadow landscape, we saw between sixty and eighty of our infantry men laying on the ground. Obviously they had all been killed there. Suddenly one in the group lifted out his upper body and called to us noticeably with his hand waving. A machine gun began to fire from the nearby edge of the forest and the poor devil was hit many times. A storm of bullets from the machine gun hit our Panzer as well. As soon as we moved to the front to beat out the guns that had been firing on us, there was a tense stillness in the air. The left edge of the forest was probably occupied by strong American infantry forces.

On the last bit of the road there were various fall-outs due to mechanical damage, but also from artillery. At some point during this episode the commander of the Panzer Battalion, Sturmbannführer Poetschke, was knocked out of action.

The 6. Panzerkompanie, which was advancing independent of us, found itself at a distance of about one kilometer to the left along the front to the west.

We left the center of the village alone and drove a few hundred meters straight ahead into the open field toward the front in the northwest. On our right lay a tall forest which we didn't recognize, perhaps it hid something.

After the experience with the infantry man we could no longer tell which direction was forward or which direction was backwards. We had no idea where the front was or in which direction it ran. Suddenly, as another two American observation planes flew over us at a low altitude and made their circles very calmly, a bad feeling swept over us which we had learned from previous experiences.

Suddenly there was a knocking on the driver's hatch. I opened it and didn't believe my own eyes. Sturmbannführer Poetschke stood there with his adjutant, Untersturmführer Rolf Reiser. Due to the broken down command Panzer they had both come by foot to find out how everything up here looked and – if needed – to join into the fight.

In the meantime the American artillery did not go to sleep. We could have hit the observation planes if we threw rocks at them, they were that close, and the incoming artillery shells followed every move we made. As we were watched by unseen and seen eyes, we made only small changes in position with increasing nervousness. It was like we were sitting on a serving tray.

Every attempt to make contact by radio, even to the 6. Panzerkompanie (from which six to eight Panzers were within our sights), remained unsuccessful. Suddenly we observed a movement in the vicinity of the 6. Panzerkompanie. The Panzers moved more to the left and one of the wagons fired with its cannon. One also had the feeling that the artillery fire was getting stronger. Then there was a new tone within the scale of explosions. The hard, dry crack of a whip! "What was that?" asked the commander over the on-board radio. "That was an anti-tank gun," I said, "and it's shooting at us!" The fire was coming directly from the west. The American anti-tank gun must have been located still further to the left of the 6. Panzerkompanie. Two rounds plowed down into the earth in front of our wagon but flashes of fire from its barrel were not noticeable. Flooring it in reverse was our only chance. The tall forest formed a dead angle which could save us. The things that go through one's head in such moments! I opened the lock to the hatch. Were we driving in the right direction? How many meters could it still be? "Damned crate, drive faster! Hopefully the motor will be able to hold out at these RPMs," I thought to myself. "If we get hit, stop immediately so that you don't run over any comrades that get thrown out by the blast."

In front of me an anti-tank gun knocked out a wagon. Once again I heard a bang that was very close. "Where did it hit?" I asked myself. It was almost a relief when we finally got hit. The motor was still running. I killed it with the brakes. As the smoke started to clear I saw that my hatch was already gone. What I couldn't see, however, was that our cannon had been ripped right off the turret. Now that the motor had fallen silent I could easily recognize the sound of machine-gun bullets hitting our wagon. Now I had to get out, whether I wanted to or not, and I had to go in the direction of the enemy. For the driver there is no other possibility. I couldn't hesitate. The next anti-tank gun round was certainly on its way. I thought to myself: "Pull up your legs, squat on the driver's seat, get up quickly, get out and immediately, let yourself fall down next to the tracks." Somewhere along the line I got snagged. My clothes ripped. I fell hard on the ground. There were machine-gun bullets everywhere. I looked for the first cover under the Panzer and I found three men of my crew who were standing there in shock. But where was Hauptsturmführer Klingelhöfer? I pulled myself up on the back of the Panzer at the same time he climbed out of the loader's hatch. I jumped over to him and asked him whether he was wounded or not. As he told me that he wasn't, I ran in the direction of the forest. We stayed in the dead angle of our Panzer. On the edge of the tall forest there was a wall made of earth and stone. Behind that wall there were some deep holes where we were going to take a breather! There we determined that the commander was missing. Once again back to the edge of the forest, but nothing was to be seen of him. With the assumption that he went a different way, I ran back to the crew. Peter Mühlbach was wounded in the head. Engelbert, Bock and Helmut Rentsch were still all right. Mühlbach could still walk. We took off in the direction of the east without knowing whether or not the forest had already been occupied by the enemy.

After a short time we met up with two German Landsers who were dragging one of their dead comrades in a shelter quarter. Upon questioning them they didn't give us any answer. They just looked us as if they were destroyed and dragged their lifeless payload on.

After a relatively long time we met up with a unit of the Panzer Lehr Division. At least we knew at last that we are on the right side of the front line.

On a road we found a bandaging station where Peter Mühlbach was cared for. There we met up with other members of our company, among them our commander. He had lots of shrapnel on his chest and burns on his face.

After getting out of our Panzer he hooked up with the crew of Oberscharführer Siptrott and company troop leader Schrader.

Six of the seven Panzers of our group had been knocked out. There was only one Panzer IV left which had stood the furthest forward. Obviously it had driven with full power right through the area where the Americans had been firing. The frozen ground and the light foliage had certainly helped them.

With that the Ardennes Offensive had ended for me and my crew.

Reinhold Kyriss, loader in the Panzer of Unterscharführer Clotten, experienced the black day of the 7. Panzerkompanie as follows:

The attack was to take place on the morning of December 30th after only having arrived in the preparation area on December 29th. We were to take off at dawn, but, as it happened so often, we got held up.

A nervousness crept its way into the crew, mainly due to the fact that the first Jabos were already in the air and we still didn't have any contact with our neighboring units. We didn't know who we were supposed to attack. The only thing that we found out was that we could figure that the enemy was about three kilometers away. At approximately 0930 hours the seven Panzer IVs of the 7. Panzerkompanie rolled out of a piece of forest from an attack, completely independent. Just a few meters away our Panzer had to stop because one of our tracks had jumped off the rollers after driving over a tree stump. The other Panzers rolled on while we tried to get the track back on the wheels as quickly as possible. Once we finally did it and rolled on we heard on the radio: "Achtung Panzerfeind!" That was thc last we heard of our comrades.

Unterscharführer Clotten tried as quickly as possible to establish communication with our company. We had one clue, the tracks which ran off and disappeared in the forest. Clotten stopped our Panzer on a path between two pieces of forest. We turned off the motor to cut the noise so that we could better orient ourselves. The result: everywhere was the sound of battle! – so drive on and search, but the motor didn't start – so get the hand crank! Next we started to crank the motor by hand. Then came an American Jabo which flew upon us from the rear. We let the crank fall and jumped into cover in front of the Panzer. The shots went right over us. The Jabo then tried it from the front side, but to no avail. We breathed a sigh of relief and he flew on.

With much effort we were able to get our crate running again. On with it! Now we came upon a large patch of forest which was being bombarded by heavy artillery. The wood all over the forest floor was so thick that we had to pull back from it.

Suddenly we saw our Battalion Commander, Sturmbannführer Poetschke, racing through the artillery fire. He noticed us and climbed in our Panzer. He was shocked to find us here alone and asked where the Panther was. How should we know where his Panther was, when we didn't even know where our 7. Panzerkompanie was!

We then had to drive back with him to his command post and wait for further orders.

Then evening fell upon us. During the night Unterscharführer Clotten received the order to drive away and to look for the Panzers. The night was calm. Not a shot fell from the sky. We drove on a narrow road to a crossing. Here the Kommandant ordered his Panzer to halt and for the motor to be turned off. We listened to the night, but nothing was to be heard. It was later determined that the Americans were only a shot's distance away from us. It lasted about 45 minutes until Clotten decided to go back. His report was crushing: all six Panzers IVs of the 7. Panzerkompanie stood burned out in a row on an open field. With this sad message we drove back to the command post.

It was only the Panzer Grenadiers (remains of the Ist Battalion/SS-Panzer-Grenadier Regiment 2 under Untersturmführer Pfeifer and parts of the IInd Battalion/SS-Panzer-Grenadier Regiment 2) that were successful in mopping up the enemy in LUTREBOIS in the evening. During the morning of **December 31, 1944** they were able to take the American anti-tank gun which was dug in there. With that they relieved the units from the threat to its flank.

Sturmbannführer Poetschke prepared his remaining Panzers for an attack on the road between MARTELANGE and BASTOGNE on the morning of **December 31, 1944**.

Reinhold Kyriss reports on this attack:

Already on December 30th, the cracking began once again. Heavy American artillery fire fell on a small village. We were instructed that the command post would be given up the following dawn. We had to clean up the house before that, because the house was to be burned to the ground. Therefore we drove back with a heavily damaged Panzer IV to the next village. There the rest of the 7. Panzerkompanie had collected itself in a basement. There we determined, to our amazement, that only two comrades had been killed during the knock out of the six Panzers. Our company leader, Hauptsturmführer Klingelhöfer, who had gotten out of his Panzer too late, had been burned.

Approaching noon on December 31, 1944, Sturmbannführer Poetschke gave Unterscharführer Clotten the order to drive forward again.

This time a Lieutenant of the artillery came along as an observer, but he was killed during the first reconnaissance action.

Lost in the forest, no one know which way was forward and which was backwards, and then our Panzer was knocked out too. An American anti-tank gun had hit us from a short distance to the rear. The driver was killed instantly. Clotten still wanted to pull him from the Panzer, but then he was shot in his upper arm. Thanks to the wood on the ground the rest of the crew was able to beat a path back to the command post.

An intact Panther had arrived at the command post. Now we were to gain contact with the men in front of us with this Panzer. The crew didn't know the area however. Then Unterscharführer Clotten decided to drive with the crew, despite his wound. Unfortunately they didn't come back.

Rolf Ehrhard reports about the rest of the remains of the company:

After the seven Panzer IVs of the company had been knocked out near Lutrebois on December 30th, the survivors departed towards Rodt near St. Vith. The supply wagons were located there, along with a field kitchen and parts of the repair squadron.

We celebrated a not so special New Year's Eve with Hauptsturmführer Klingelhöfer, who was lightly wounded, and Untersturmführer Münkemer. Obersturmführer Wolff took part in this celebration as well. Untersturmführer Rehagel had remained with the action-ready Panzers and a part of the repair squadron in the area of Lutrebois.

Manfred Thorn reflected on the course of the battles of the day.

During the evening hours of January 3rd, we received the order to renew the attack in the direction of Lutrebois and to break through to the road to Bastogne.

Finally, we had a task, as well as close contact to the infantry which lay in front of us. The infantry helped us to determine the exact location of the Americans. This time we wanted to have more success, as we had four days before in Lutrebois.

In the meantime we had become well acquainted with the landscape. Our Panzers drove from their position onto the street in the direction of Lutrebois. Before reaching the only house, we first turned to the left into the open landscape. We fully utilized the unevenness of the ground. Unseen by the enemy, we turned off wide to the right for an advance directly against the forest.

Both of our messengers sat on top of the Panzer behind the turret.

We drove with the pedal to the floor and shot anti-personnel rounds and our machine guns into the forest. It was an annihilating fire for the Americans, and two American soldiers – a medic and a sergeant – appeared at the edge of the forest with raised hands. We held our fire and motioned them both to come to us. The medic reported that two companies of the 134th Regiment of the 35th U.S. Infantry Division lay in the forest. They had heavy casualties and they would surrender. After the medic went back in the forest 150 Americans surrendered. A few German Grenadiers were called up to take the prisoners.

During the afternoon we were able to penetrate the village, but during the evening we once again had to pull back to Lutremange.

On **January 10, 1945,** the Army Group decided to pull back the positions of the 9., 26., and 167. Volks-Grenadier Divisions, as well as the 5. Fallschirmjäger Division, to the line between BIZORY, WARDIN and WINSELER under the pressure of the threatening encirclement of the forward units southeast of BASTOGNE. At the same time the 1. SS-Panzer Division was to be completely pulled out.

In the early morning hours, the Division began to pull out the battle groups engaged in forward positions and lead them back through DONCOLS, GRÜMELSCHEID and DERENBACK. The transfer was conducted with a formal march until they reached the area east of ST. VITH.

January 15–24, 1945. At this time, following the relief of the last portions of the 1. SS-Panzer Division from their positions at the front, the Divisions of the 1. SS-Panzer Korps were transferred to the area west and north of Cologne to load up.

Johann Wohninsland recalls a special experience during the relief:

In the middle of January we were on the road near St. Vith on our way to Luxembourg with three or four Panzers. The Panzer crews were split up amongst two houses. Wölfel and I didn't get a place. We then found quarters in a house about a hundred meters to the rear. At dawn there was once again a shoot out. The Amis had broken through and had taken about ten of us prisoner. Rehagel was able to hide himself in a basement. One of us was killed during the shoot-out.

During the march into captivity the comrades were able to free themselves. They took away a rifle from one of the Americans, after which the other one took off.

Our kitchen wagon drove into a crater during a bomb attack. Luckily we were able to repair it.

Rolf Ehrhardt reports from the area of RAHDEN, where the as yet unprepared portions of the Battalion remained during the beginning of the Ardennes Offensive:

A freshening-up program for the remains of our company was run under the leadership of Hauptsturmführer Klingelhöfer in the aspen camp. We had returned after being released from the field hospital.

Untersturmführer Münkemer was also there.

The company had a strength of about seventy to eighty men.

1945
Gran Bridgehead, Lake Balaton, retreat battles through Hungary, Battles in lower Austria and in the Vienna Forest, Capitulation, Malmédy Trial

In the meantime, the situation on the Eastern Front had become critical.

The Soviet troops stood before Berlin and Breslau was surrounded.

At the end of **January 1945,** the majority of the regiments of the LAH collected in the area between BONN and SIEGBURG.

The assumption was that the 6. Panzerarmee was to be put into action for the freeing of Breslau, an assumption also made by the Soviets.

However, the Supreme Command of the Army (OKH) planned to transfer the recently relieved 6. Panzerarmee to Hungary, where it was to free up the last oil area in the wedge of land between the DRAU and the DANUBE.

In order to camouflage this transfer, all of the Divisions of the 6. Panzerarmee had to take off their cuff-titles and remove the tactical markings from their vehicles. For that they received other harmless markings.

After the load up, the LAH was called the "replacement squadron 'Totenkopf.'"

The gathering in the collection area was brief, since every troop movement was noticed by the Allied Air Force and was immediately shot at from the sky.

Therefore, the Panzer companies were already on the transport by **January 20, 1945** and received an improvised freshening-up during the ride.

Johann Wohninsland experienced a disrupted transport to Hungary:

> In the middle of January we were pulled out of the Ardennes Offensive. We had between three and four Panzers which were not lost during the advance. The other wagons were knocked out or blown up by our troops. We then pulled into our old quarters in Bliesheim.
>
> At the end of January, we were loaded up as a battle group for a transfer to Hungary. The rest of the company was transferred to Rahden.
>
> Wölfel, Dommel and I got out in Pilsen and went to a house to wash ourselves. As we came back the transport was gone. No one could say where it had gone. Papers and Soldbuchs were in the wagon. We had nothing other than our toiletries. We drove with a passenger train to Vienna and there we went to the SS commander. We received new Soldbuchs and were sent back to Rahden.

The unloading of the Panzer companies followed in the beginning of **February 1945** in RAAB, from where they were transferred to the collecting are on the SCHÜTT ISLAND.

GRAN BRIDGEHEAD (Operation "South Wind")

In the southern section of the Eastern Front, the 2nd Ukrainian Front (Army Group) with parts of the 3rd Ukrainian Front overran the entire eastern and middle portions of Hungary. This area crossed over the DANUBE on both sides of BUDAPEST. From there it extended north of the DANUBE where a bridgehead was built over the GRAN, near the oil area of FIVE CHURCHES (FÜNFKIRCHEN), until reaching the LAKE BALATON. BUDAPEST was also occupied and surrounded.

During the time period between **January 2 until January 19, 1945**, the IV. SS-Panzer Korps, along with the 3. SS-Panzer Division "Totenkopf," the 5. SS-Panzer Division "Wiking" and the 2. Panzer Division, conducted four attacks to free Budapest. The attacks were unsuccessful.

Before the beginning of the Lake Balaton-Offensive (Operation FRÜHLINGSERWACHEN – SPRING AWAKENING), Army Group South was of the opinion that the elimination of the Soviet threat to our flanks from the GRAN Bridgehead was necessary.

For this the following units were prepared:

The I. SS-Panzer Korps (with all portions that had arrived in the meantime)
Panzerkorps "Feldherrenhalle" (Army)
The LAH (together with the HJ Division in the I. SS-Panzer Korps) had only
  21 Panzer Vs of the earlier 1. and 2. Panzer Kompanien
  25 Panzer IVs of the earlier 6. and 7. Panzer Kompanien
due to the casualties during the Ardennes Offensive, and despite the continual meager freshening-up the units had received until this time.

On **February 11, 1945** the Panzer Regiment formed one battalion from these Panzers with:

a group of Panzer Vs from the still action-ready Panzers of the former Ist Battalion and
a group of Panzer IVs from the still action-ready Panzers of the former IInd Battalion under the leadership of Sturmbannführer Poetschke.

Along with this came a Battalion from the remains of the heavy Panzer Battalion 501 (Tigers) with 16 Panzer VIs (Tigers) under the leadership of Sturmbannführer von Westernhagen. With the III. (armored) Battalion of SS-Panzer-Grenadier Regiment 2 under the leadership of Sturmbannführer Diefenthal, the battalions formed a "Panzer Group" under the leadership of Standartenführer Peiper.

On **February 2, 1945,** the Panzer Group transferred into its preparation area for the attack on the Soviet GRAN Bridgehead southeast of FARNAD. Due to the arriving warm weather the resulting thaw (and along with it the constant rain), the streets turned to mush and made the march movements difficult.

On **February 15, 1945,** the new Divisional Commander, Brigadeführer Otto Kumm, arrived in the preparation area.

Despite bad weather and street conditions Operation South Wind started on **February 17, 1945** with an attack by the 46. Infanterie Division on the Soviet positions before NEM SELDIN. After overcoming the outward-most positions by the Panzer Group, the attack was stalled before a strong row of anti-tank guns. (See map 30).

Untersturmführer Reiser from the Panzer V group reports about this attack:

> In the morning dawn it was time for us as well and we followed the army infantry division, which stepped up for the attack to break the Soviet main fighting line. The street and land conditions were bad. Acres and meadows stood under water and the Panzers driving from the preparation zones waded through the deep layers of muck.
>
> The 1. Kompanie overtook the lead, and after that the right wing along with the security of the flank, for the attack formation.
>
> We still drove on the street and we advanced quickly. Then we came upon the former main fighting line. We passed on by and stopped in a basin. In the meantime, grenade launcher fire started to set in, but the incoming were falling far behind us.
>
> After a short discussion about the situation (Peiper – Poetschke – Diefenthal), the Battalion went on. The Battalion readied itself for an attack. We started out in a deep and wide wedge formation left of the street that led to Nem. Seldin. I took over the security of the flank while driving with my platoon on the right wing and hanging somewhat back.
>
> Anti-tank gun fire set in from Nem. Seldin. Since we were supposed to push by the village, we accelerated the drive (deep farmland) and avoided the fire by putting the wavy landscape to good use. We stopped and prepared for an attack in the cover of a hill which lay before us. Here we received heavy fire from mortars and Stalin's Organs. The Ivan must have noticed that we

were collecting on this far side of the hill. After the Schützenpanzer of the III.(armored)/SS-Panzer-Grenadier Regiment 2 and the Panzergrenadiers from the 1. Regiment hooked up with us, the battle group departed in a decisive attack on the Perizsky Canal (which was our goal of the day).

With the Panthers and the Tigers in the front followed by the Panzer IVs and the Schützenpanzer, we rolled over the hill and immediately answered the massive fire of the Russian anti-tank guns. Due to our concentrated fire and the quickly executed attack we were successful in destroying the row of anti-tank guns and throwing the Russians from their positions. Ivan fled in the rage of our attack. As dawn broke our lead units reached the canal near Gyva. The bridge had been blown up, however.

Reinhold Kyriss remembers this day as well:

Towards noon I prepared the entire Panzer Group for an attack on the far side of the hill. The task was clear: a strong row of anti-tank guns was to be broken through. Standartenführer Peiper allowed enough time. He wanted to do things by the book, which turned out in the end to be the right decision.

Peiper let five King Tigers drive up the hill. What a picture!

They stood on the hill as if they were on a serving platter and were immediately shot at by the Russian anti-tank guns. You could clearly see how the anti-tank rounds slid off the front side of the King Tigers. What a shock that must have been for the Russians as the King Tigers knocked out one anti-tank gun after the other. The fire from the anti-tank guns died down and then Peiper immediately gave the order: "Panzer marsch!"

As the battle group drove over the hill in tight formation, a magic fire was let loose – in the truest sense of the word. The Panzers, driving at full power with the armored reconnaissance cars, shot from all barrels. In the slowly approaching dawn one could see even better the streaks of fire along with the grenades. It was an impressive picture.

During this Panzer attack, conducted like a cavalry attack, there was only one thing the Russians could do: take off. After overrunning the front of anti-tank guns we stopped to collect ourselves. To our surprise the Russians took the majority of their anti-tank guns away in the protection of the darkness. Kampfgruppe Peiper had no casualties to report for this attack.

On **February 18, 1945,** the "Infantry Group" of the LAH under Standartenführer Hansen, together with the 46. Infanteriedivision, crossed the PARIZSKY canal on both sides of SARKAN.

The Panzer Group was pulled back to conduct an attack on BELI.
Reihnold Kyriss reports about a mishap during the crossing:

We reorganized along a street that led to the canal bridge: the 7. Panzerkompanie to the left of the street, the Panther Kompanie to the right of the street. In darkness, the Panzer march was only possible at a slow pace, with each driver following the other by sight. Just after driving 200 meters we heard a crack of fire near our radio man. While getting out of the Panzer someone called: "Don't jump, mines!"

Then we saw the salad – everywhere there were wood-crate mines, and another Panzer IV was coming already. One of us jumped through the wood-crates which were easily visible and climbed from behind the Panzer to warn the Kommandant. Too late! The right front track tensioner blew away. Then another Schützenpanzerwagen drove into the mines and one of its front wheels flew in the air.

On our Panzer, it didn't just blow the track tensioner away, it also blew open the chassis. The radioman lost his right foot.

The Battle Group rolled on. We took care of our radioman and he was taken away by car the next morning. One of us who knew mines really well disarmed the wood-crates by taking out the triggers: 175 of them. During the afternoon we received a visit from Soviet fighter planes, which surely intended on getting us. We stood there so beautifully on the open land. They flew in formation, unloaded their bombs in an open field about 150 meters behind us and then flew on. Luckily for us they must have been beginners.

During the evening two 18-ton tow trucks arrived to bring us back to the work shop in Raab.

The Panzer Group continued to attack and went by SARKANYFALVA, through the high hills near BELI, until reaching the road between KÖBÖLKUT and PARKANY. After the last Panzer caught up both sides of the road were secured for the night.

On **February 19, 1945,** the Panzer Group advanced through MUZSLA for an attack on PARKANY. They took the village in a tough battle with the enemy, who retreated to the other side of the river. Quarters were set up for the night in a position northwest of the train station.

After the IIIrd (armored) Battalion/SS-Panzer-Grenadier Regiment 2 took NANA northwest of PARKANY at the same time we took PARKANY, the southern portion of the Soviet bridgehead was considered cleared up.

In further attacks to the north along the road from PARKANY to KEMEND, the Panzer Group attacked KAMDAROTY (KÖHID GYARMA) with its Panzer IV group on **February 20, 1945**. However, they were held up due to annihilating Soviet artillery fire, coming from the other side of the river, which was landing before the village.

On **February 21, 1945,** the Panzer Group, together with the partially Panzer mounted Infantry Group, renewed the attack and pushed to the center. Once again, they were stalled by a massive barrage of artillery fire.

As dusk approached, Sturmbannführer Peiper decided that the Panzer IV Group would lead the continued attack.

Late in the evening, the Panzer Group was able to completely take the village.

On **February 22, 1945,** the Panzer Group, together with parts of the infantry, advanced until reaching the fork in the road south of KEMENT. With that the Soviet bridgehead had been pushed back to the village of BENY and KEMENT.

After heavy and difficult battles, during which the units engaged in house-to-house combat, KEMENT was taken on **February 23, 1945**.

With that the battle for the destruction of the Soviet GRAN-bridgehead was concluded.

LAKE BALATON – OFFENSIVE (Operation "Spring Awakening")

After the units that had been engaged in the battle for the GRAN-bridgehead were freed up, Army Group South was able to prepare the focal point operation – operation "Spring Awakening."

The 6. Panzer Armee (Sepp Dietrich) with seven divisions was ready for the advance between the LAKE BALATON and the VELENZSEE to the south into the DRAU – DANUBE angle.

After **March 1, 1945** the divisions were to march to their collecting areas.

This march proved to be very difficult and time consuming due to the poor conditions of the streets. The thaw period and the heavy rains had turned the dirt roads into muck.

The LAH marched very slowly and in a widely spread out formation on completely muddy streets. They reached the collecting area around VESZPREM – ZIRÇ, where the first groups arrived on **March 2, 1945**.

A doubting Panzer Kommandant moaned:

Muck, wherever one looks, muck, wherever one steps.
Muck, wherever one drives, – muck, muck, muck!

On **March 4, 1945,** the greater part of the LAH had arrived in the collecting area. Large parts of other divisions were still on the march.

Because of this situation, the Panzer Armee Ober Kommando 6 (Panzer AOK 6) delayed the planned day of the attack to **March 6, 1945**. But the OKH (Supreme Command of the Army) turned them down!!!

The Ia of the Panzer AOK 6 wrote:

> In the trust of the battle spirit of her divisions, the 6th Panzer Army was in any case ready to attack without waiting for all of the units to complete their preparations.

During the night of **March 5, 1945,** the Panzer Group Peiper marched to its preparation area southwest of POLGARDI.

Due to the casualties during the battles for the GRAN-bridgehead, the Panzer IV Group had only 14 Panzers left. In the future they were to be a part of the 3. Panzerkompanie, a company which would consist of all remaining Panzer IVs (including those of the former 7. Panzerkompanie).

On the morning of **March 3, 1945,** the 3. Panzerkompanie initiated an attack on KALOZ.

After annihilating a front of anti-tank guns, the advance led the company to Hill 149. During this advance the company got bogged down and stuck during a drive through a depression of mud. The attack on KALOZ could only be continued with much effort. In the end the company was successful in penetrating KALOZ. The Soviets retreated and left behind equipment and vehicles. Only then was there an opportunity to pull out the stuck Panzers from the mud – a task which took tremendous effort. (See map 31).

On **March 7, 1945,** the Panzer Group, along with the 3. Panzerkompanie, turned north to initiate an attack on SOPONIA – which would eliminate the Soviet threat on the rear of the German troops. SOPONIA was taken after a short but difficult battle.

Once again the unit turned back to the south within the framework of the Panzer Group and advanced further to PUSZTA EGRES (NAGY) on March 8, 1945. During the advance the Panzer Group came upon a row of anti-tank guns. One of the Panzers was knocked out while over-running it. The attack then continued on in the direction of the road between IGAR and CZECZE. Once again the Panzer Group came upon a strong row of anti-tank guns, which made the continuance of the attack on SIMON – TORNYA no longer possible for this day.

On **March 9, 1945,** the attack on the row of anti-tank guns before SAREGES was continued. During the attack, the Soviets returned massive defensive fire which brought the attack to a standstill and cost the units some casualties. Enemy counterattacks had to be fended off.

During the afternoon the attack extended into the river and the units were able to reach the hilly land north of SIMONTRNYA. It was here that the 3. Panzerkompanie, along with the rest of the Panzer Group, switched over to the defense for the night.

On **March 10, 1945,** the attack on SIMONTORNYA developed very slowly. Due to the strong Soviet defense in addition to a terrain which was difficult for Panzers to negotiate, the attack was beaten back.

In order to strengthen the LAH, the 23. Panzer Division (Army) was pulled into its sector by the Panzer AOK 6.

The commander of the 3. Panzerkompanie, Obersturmführer Sternebeck, remembers both of these days:

> On both days we had to beat off tank and infantry attacks. Our freedom of movement was constrained by these attacks. Results from reconnaissance missions revealed that Simontornya lay in a depression. A protected approach to the village was not possible. Besides that the village was set up with rows of anti-tank and anti-aircraft guns for a very strong defense.
>
> We had an open declining plane with a length of about between 500 and 700 meters to the south, which would need to be overcome in order to approach the village. To halt in order to fire during the advance across the plane would be impossible.
>
> We tried many times to approach the village by traveling through ravines to the northeast and northwest of Simontornya. We were not successful in this since the lead Panzer, which in the meantime stepped out of the ravine, was knocked out. The same happened to me when I tried.

On **March 11, 1945,** a spell of frost and wind for the most part caused the streets and the landscape to once again be driveable. The row of anti-tank guns west of SAREGES was broken open and the advance was carried directly into the northern part of SVOMONTORNYA.

During the night the Soviets doubled their artillery on the southern riverbank of the SIO and laid massive artillery fire on the lead units of the attack. With that came non-stop fighter plane attacks. As night fell, the attack had to be halted.

Finally on **March 12, 1945,** the Panzer Group was able to force its way into the northern part of SIMONTORNYA and continue the advance through house-to-house combat.

Werner Sternebeck wrote about this advance:

Attack on Simontornya. After initiating the attack from the backside of a hill, we overcame the declining plain in a hellish drive over the open and unprotected landscape. We reached the west edge of the village without pausing to fire our cannons. From here we attacked to the east and south through the village. The village battle was heavy and short. Simontornya was secure in our hands. During this attack we lost three Panzers on the open plane and another two in the village.

The enemy did not have any time to dismantle his row of anti-tank and anti-aircraft guns before his retreat. This enabled us to destroy some of the guns and capture the rest.

On **March 13, 1945,** the infantry continued the street battles during the remaining mopping-up operations. They then built a bridgehead on the bank of the SIO, after which the Pioniers blasted together a command bridge over the river.

It was here that the Soviets immediately concentrated their counterattacks, which increased continuously until that evening.

On **March 14, 1945,** the battles for the SIO bridgehead continued.

The infantry led these battles. The rest of Panzer Group Peiper was pulled out and collected in the area of DEG.

After **March 15, 1945,** a continuous and incredibly strengthening Soviet troop movement was noticeable on all sections of the front. Reconnaissance spotted masses of Soviet troops south of the SIO, south of the VELENCE LAKE and east of the VERTES MOUNTAINS in the section of the IV. SS-Panzer Korps ("Wiking" and "Totenkopf").

After exact approximations of the strength of the Soviet troops in this section, it was determined that the Soviets had reached a 4:1 advantage.

Therefore, it was assumed that a massive Soviet attack would take place in a relatively short period of time.

Above all it was feared that the German Division, which had advanced between the LAKE BALATON and the VELENCESEE on to the SIO, would be cut off and encircled.

Under this impression, the 6. Panzer Armee relieved the I. SS-Panzer Korps ("LAH," "Das Reich" and "Hitlerjugend") and issued the order for a transfer to the area west of STUHLWEISSENBURG for the defense of a possible Soviet breakthrough near the IV. SS-Panzer Korps.

With that, Operation "Spring Awakening" ended after ten days.

RETREAT THROUGH WESTERN HUNGARY

To fulfill the ordered task to transfer to the north as battle reserve behind the IV. SS-Panzer Korps, the Panzer Group (now totaling 16 Panzers) received an order on **March 18, 1945** to march to the preparation area between VARPALOTA and INOTA.

Rolf Reiser:

> In the night of March 18, 1945, we were transferred to the foreseen preparation area east of Inota. We marched on the roads through Küngös, Berhida, Petfürdö, Várpalota and Inota.
>
> The march was especially difficult to organize because the roads were not only used by and stuffed with refugees, but they were also used by retreating supply units and their vehicles. In addition, the road running north and south on our side of the Sárviz Canal (near Szabadbattyán) was no longer passable since the bridge had been destroyed by bombers. On March 19 at about 1300 hours the highway south of Várpalota was finally reached. There were once again difficulties in Panzer trenches east of Várpalota. The refugees streaming from the area of Stuhlweißenberg blocked our path and the roads could only be held open with force.

During the afternoon of **March 19, 1945,** the lead units of the Panzer Group reached INOTA.

Since the Soviet lead attack units had just advanced through STUHLWEISSENBURG and had managed to go around INOTA with strong forces to the north, a preparation was no longer possible.

The arriving Panzers had to take a defensive position as soon as they arrive.

Obersturmführer Werner Wolff was badly wounded and died in a field hospital in Austria.

Rolf Reiser reports on the action of the Panzer V company:

> At approximately 1600 hours Inota was reached and the battalion command post was set up. The enemy situation and our situation were completely indeterminable. There was loud battle noise, coming from a northerly direction (Bakonykúti) and from the east from Csór, which led us to determine that the enemy had reached our foreseen preparation area.
>
> The forested hills east and north of the highway between Inota and Csór were to be taken during the coming day.
>
> A preparation was definitely no longer possible, because our march unit

was ripped apart. The Panzers continued to arrive and took security positions during the night.

The Soviet units advancing to the north and south outflanked the security position of the Panzer Group and pushed their way into INOTA during the evening.

Werner Sternebeck wrote about the action of the Panzer IV Group (3. (7.) Panzerkompanie) on **March 20, 1945** in the security position east of INOTA:

> The 3. Panzerkompanie (6-7 Panzer IVs) and 2 King Tigers (Obersturmführer Wessel) had the task of going over to the defense east of Inota and preventing an enemy advance to the road between Stuhlweißenburg, Varpalota and Veszprem. We were able to fend-off the Soviet advance on both sides of the street and finally to stop it. During the late afternoon (March 20) we recognized that we were encircled by infantry and by strong tank forces in the south along a an erosion ditch. We were bound in the front. There was no contact with the battalion or regiment. A retreat without orders wasn't even considered by any of us. After night fell we recognized fires in Inota and heard fighting. During the late evening our artillery fired upon the village with Haubitzer and rocket launchers. Now it was clear to us that Inota was occupied by the enemy.

In the meantime, the Panzer V Group and the rest of the Panzer Group (remains of III.(armored)/SS-Panzer Grenadier Regiment 2) were pushed out of their positions north of INOTA and pulled back to the edge of the village of VARPALOTA.

During the evening Obersturmführer Sternebeck noticed that he and his Panzer IV group were cut off.

He reports:

> Before midnight we decided to break through Inota.
>
> Formation: 1 King Tiger, followed by 6 Panzer IVs and another King Tiger at the end.
>
> By using the darkness and a further barrage of fire we reached the edge of the village. At first the Russians assumed that we were their troops. Once the enemy recognized us, the darkness and the angling street saved us. (With full-power we stormed through the village).
>
> At a point almost on the west edge of the village our lead Tiger had to knock out a few more T-34s so that we could abandon Inota without damage.

As we reached Varpalota, where we ran into the rest of the Panzer Group, it was almost a tragic ending. Our units in Varpalota expected the enemy – not us – to be coming from an easterly direction. We only saved ourselves from being knocked out by our comrades with flares.

During the night Poetschke confirmed to me that the rest of the 3. Panzerkompanie and the two King Tigers would have had to be given up in the case that there was no more radio contact and the enemy had taken Inota.

At the last second we once again had luck on our side.

Obersturmführer Malkomes, commander of the Panzer V company, was killed as he looked out of the turret of his Panzer by a shot to the head fired by a sniper in Varpalota.

On the morning of **March 21, 1945**, the battles for VARPALOTA continued with increasing hardness. The Panzer V group, along with the rest of the Infantry Group Hansen, was able to bring the advancing enemy to a silent halt.

Rolf Reiser reports about the battle of the Panzer V group:

In the morning hours the opponent attacked. This time, they came from the northeast with infantry forces and five tanks. They were able to push their way into the landscape surrounding the factory. During a counter attack three enemy tanks were knocked out. A further attack was warded off.

The enemy then brought up new tanks and with increasing hardness were able to penetrate the landscape surrounding the train station.

In a battle of tank against tank the enemy was finally prevented from continuing the advance into the southern portion of the city. They were stopped at a point just before the road passing through the village. Seven enemy tanks were destroyed. We had three casualties of our own.

In the northern sector of the city the enemy infantry, with superior tank support, was successful in working its way through the houses and streets up to the main road. It was cracking from all corners, Ivan was suddenly everywhere. It appeared hopeless to fight against this overpowering force in close combat and house-to-house combat.

The Soviet attacks were supported by uninterrupted dive bomber and fighter planes that attacked the German positions from nearby.

Reinhold Kyriss (from the Panzer IV Group), who at the time was searching for the Panzer workstation in VESZPREM, remembers such a bomber attack:

On March 21, we were with our Panzer IV in the work station on the edge of the village of Veszprem. A comrade and I, together with the brickyard master and a Hungarian major, crept to a house in a nearby brickyard. I was awakened at 0400 hours and heard a noise that sounded like airplanes. I then watched as both the men ran out of the house. Before I could tell what was going on the cracking had already started. My comrade stayed in the house. I ran out and saw that the brickyard building was half collapsed. The chimney still stood and the residence was only slightly damaged. I saw the two men lying before the building. The major was dead, the brickyard owner was still alive. The light of day was shining through the pine tree that the planes had just shredded. Suddenly I noticed that they were flying in for a second run. In front of me was a large bomb crater and I jumped into it lightning fast. I could still feel the warmth of the ground from the bomb that had just exploded there and then it began to crack again. As the spitting fire had passed by, I saw that the brickyard building was completely destroyed – the residence still stood.

I found my comrade who had escaped unscathed. Together we carried the owner into the house. My comrade looked after him and I went outside again. The planes had obviously flown away, but it was still bright. While I was outside I noticed a woman and two children coming towards me. She made it clear to me that three comrades of ours were buried in the brickyard. The woman showed me a brick drying-chamber in which she hid with her children. The three comrades were in such a chamber. I began to work, which was naturally useless. The towering stack of bricks slid down immediately. In this hopelessness it occurred to me that the 3. Panzerkompanie was not far away. I reported to Untersturmführer Münkemer, who led the company immediately to the brickyard. After a short discussion of the situation, it was clear that the comrades could only be reached from the outside. I was issued the order to remain in the chamber. The buried comrades gave regular signs by knocking which were answered by me. After two hours the first ones wanted to give up, but they continued knocking. With bare hands the men cleared away the rubble. Everyone did his best. At 1000 hours I heard the last knock, and at 1100 we finally found them.

The 3. Panzerkompanie battled to complete exhaustion for the lives of those three Grenadiers of the LAH, but it was all for nothing. Death beat us to it.

During the course of the afternoon the attack on VARPALOTA was renewed from three sides by a superior enemy with packs of tanks. After 46 enemy tanks were knocked out, the Panzer Group definitely had to give up.

The group departed for the west and erected a new collecting point before ÖSKÜ.

On **March 22, 1945,** the Soviet attack units aimed all of their strength on this position. During the course of the morning the position was ripped open and the Panzer Group in ÖSKÜ was surrounded.

The divisional commander, Brigadeführer Otto Kumm, found himself with the Panzer Group and ordered the break-out through LITER and then on to reach the eastern edge of the village of VESZPREM.

Werner Sternebeck reports about the "Battle of LITER," which developed from this break-out:

> Enemy tank forces went around us once again. The road between Varpalota and Veszprem, near the fork in the road northwest of Liter and east of Veszprem, was completely shut off. The portions of the Division continuing to battle – from a southeasterly direction – were now no longer able to retreat to the west. The available area quickly became tight, so we had to get some space and quick. Two Sturmgeschütze, which were immediately available, started to battle at the fork in the road. They were at such a disadvantage, however, that they were not able to bring any relief.
>
> We, the rest of the Panzer Group under Sturmbannführer Poetschke, received the task to retreat along the highway and to immediately attack the enemy tanks east of Veszprem. The fork in the road was not to be opened from the front. The enemy tanks had such favorable positions that we couldn't get into the battle. From there we attacked, swinging in from the south to reach Veszprem through Liter. We surprisingly came upon a group of enemy tanks ready for the defense just north of Liter. We fell into this situation and suddenly stood across from the enemy tanks at a distance of between three and four hundred meters. A murderous tank battle began. We lost various Panzer IVs and Panzer Vs in a short time. Defeated Panzer crews were running everywhere and glittering fires could be seen all around on the battlefield. We had no chance to annihilate the enemy and take the fork in the road. We broke off the battle and were able to retreat from the enemy behind a massive wall of smoke (from smoke bombs). Even though we had to suffer incredible losses of men and tanks and were completely shredded, we had inflicted heavy casualties on the enemy as well.

The Panzer Group reached VESZPREM from the south late in the evening without coming across the enemy.

In the early morning hours the enemy attacked with massive infantry and tank forces.

They crossed over the road from ZIRC to RAAB after the situation in VESZPREM. Rolf Reiser reports about the battles of the Panzer Group and their tragic course:

> It was morning, shortly after 0600 hours. We were on the march to Veszprém with nine Panzers, one armored radio car and two Schwimmwagen. We were going to take position on the northern edge of the village.
>
> It was a clear day and already in these morning hours it was warm. We stopped the vehicles so that we could get a view of the landscape in front of us. Through our binoculars we noticed a column of tanks coming from Kádára. There had to be between thirty and forty of them, and they were driving to the south and approaching Veszprém. Our Panzers came up and Poetschke called in all the Panzer Kommandanten as quickly as possible so that he could give them orders in person.
>
> Standing next to a shack the Panzer Group collected around Poetschke. Suddenly there was a massive grenade attack, right in the middle of the group!
>
> The results: Poetschke was badly wounded – he died hours later – Untersturmführer Münkemer, Untersturmführer Gerdes, Untersturmführer Heubeck were all wounded. There were three further Panzer Kommandanten, more or less, who were also badly wounded.
>
> None of them were ready for action. We made efforts to care for the wounded. Despite his bad wounds, Sturmbannführer Poetschke recognized the desperate situation and called to the signals officer, Untersturmführer Pönisch: "Give a message per radio to Peiper about what happened here."
>
> He asked me for a pistol. We carried him away on a door.
>
> In the meantime, the opponent had advanced on by Veszprém in the north to close off the highway near Márko 8 km behind us. In this situation the Panzers, without their Panzer Kommandanten, were ordered to pull out to Márko.
>
> This was the blackest day of our Panzer regiment. The last battle had begun, the end was in sight.

After these exhausting battles the regiments and battalions of the LAH had little better than a fraction of their intended strength in men, equipment and weapons. The Division "Leibstandarte" consisted of only a few thrown together battle groups.

Even the Panzer Group was just a handful of men.

Rolf Reiser reports:

> After the fall out of Poetschke, Malkomes and Wolff in the "catastrophe of Veszprém" (where another eight Panzer Kommandanten were wounded), the remains of the Panzers were collected. Obersturmführer Sternebeck led the Panzer IVs, Hauptsturmführer Birnschein the few Tigers and Panthers.
>
> The leadership of the Panzer Group ceased to exist with the death of Poetschke.

On **March 24, 1945,** the large Soviet offensive had completely developed after overcoming a mountainous and lake filled landscape. They had entered the western Hungarian flatland. (See map 32).

The battle weary, beaten and thrown-together groups of the LAH were indeed successful at bringing the Soviet attacks to a stand still again and again at certain points of the line. However, these strong points were immediately outflanked, attacked from the flanks and then in danger of being surrounded.

The Panzer Group, or better said, what was left of it, suffered in this way. Completely exhausted, the group made its way back to the border of the Reich from **March 24 - March 30, 1945**. They crossed the border on **March 31, 1945** near Sopron.

Werner Sternebeck reports about these retreat battles:

> From Veszprém through Marko, Herend, Varoslöd, Kislöd, Ajkarendek, Noslop until Merseva we managed a continuous defense with our few Panzers against the Soviet tank and infantry attacks and prevented the Division from being overrun.
>
> After a short barrage we retreated from the enemy on the evening of March 31 and reached the area east of Vienna Neustadt (Pöttsching – Sauerbrunn) in one movement.

Rolf Ehrhardt, the Schirrmeister (in charge of all vehicles), wrote about the 7. Panzerkompanie's border crossing:

> At the border crossing in Klingenbach, supply troops of the 7. Panzerkompanie – mixed with comrades of other troops – collected and formed the Group "Klingelhöfer." Still present were Untersturmführer Rehagel, Werner Koch as Spieß, Kurt Mai as Repair Troop leader, Heinz Wölfel as weapons

attendant, Hans Kuhnke as radio attendant. There was still a desk and an administration leader. We still had our old Feldpostnummer 31 820.

BATTLES IN LOWER AUSTRIA/VIENNA FOREST

After crossing the borders of the Reich and passing the so-called "Reich Protection Position," the 3. (7.) Panzerkompanie reached the area between PÖTTSCHING and SAUERBRUNN during the evening of **March 31, 1945**.

Kompanietruppführer (responsible for the welfare and personal affairs of the troops) and Obersturmführer Sternebeck remembers:

> The rest of the 3. Panzerkompanie (4 Panzer IVs) arrived in the area east of Vienna Neustadt (between Pöttsching and Sauerbrunn) and were able to get a real night's sleep.

On **April 1, 1945,** the defensive battles in Austria began. The Soviet armies had crossed the "Reich Protection Position" uncontested and now stood in the area of the German Reich.

The 3rd Ukrainian Front was tottering west of the NEUSIEDLERSEES to the north in the direction of VIENNA.

The 2nd Ukrainian Front went along both sides of the DANUBE to the West and attacked VIENNA from the northeast.

The remainders of the LAH had arrived in the area of VIENNA NEUSTADT and MATTERSBURG south of VIENNA and turned towards this line to defend themselves to the south.

Werner Sternebeck reports:

> On Easter Sunday, April 1, 1945, the 3. Panzerkompanie was supplied with 10 new Panzer IVs with crews which arrived from Linz. The Kompanie was temporarily subordinated to a platoon of Panzer Vs and a company of mountain troopers from an Army division. I reported to the battle commander of Vienna Neustadt with this battle group. He had his command post in a war academy. In the command post there was an atmosphere of defeat, a certain doubt, because the troops that were intended to defend the city were weak and without artillery support. The impression was really bleak, the issuing of orders barely convincing. Orders were sloppy and inconsistent. I had the impression that the we were only there to slow the impending collapse of Vienna Neustadt to the last battle with our 17 – 22 Panzer IVs and Vs, the only Panzers

which were available for the defense of Vienna Neustadt. The battle group received the task "to block all roads leading to Vienna Neustadt from the direction of Neuenkirchen, Aspang and from the direction of Sopron and Eisenstadt and to prevent an advance of all enemy tank and infantry forces."

This was the first and last order that I received for the defense of Vienna Neustadt.

With the orders issued by the battle commander to the subordinated troops, the "cooperation" had ended and we were now dependent on ourselves.

We occupied our ordered defensive position with the platoon of Panzer Vs of the Army, namely the four to five streets on the city's edge with the strong point to the southeast in the direction of Eisenstadt and Sopron. The mountain troopers positioned themselves between the Panzer platoons so that there was contact between left and right. During the course of the afternoon and also after sunset, the enemy probed Vienna Neustadt with tanks and infantry. We were able to successfully fend off the attacks and avoid a penetration into the city.

On **April 2, 1945,** the Soviet attack leads went around Vienna Neustadt and turned in a further advance to the west.

The entrances to the valleys in the VIENNA FOREST were defended by the rest of the I. SS-Panzer Korps, which was spread out in local strong points.

West of VIENNA NEUSTADT in the area of the LAH were the entrances to PISTINTAL and THE TRIESTING VALLEY

North of there the HJ Division battled, while to the south a few thrown-together battle groups fought.

The previously deployed portions of the Panzer Regiment 1 LAH had to battle through VIENNA NEUSTADT, which in the meantime was occupied by the enemy. Just before evening they were able to reach a position in PIESTINGTAL near WÖLLERSDORF.

Werner Sternebeck remembers these battles:

In the early morning hours of Easter Monday, the mountain troopers pulled out without reason. Our Panzers now stood on the streets like islands, abandoned by the mountain troopers, and had no contact to left or the right except for radio.

The enemy pressure from the southeast became stronger during the late morning hours. The radio contact to the left platoon (Panzer Vs of the Army) suddenly broke off and the battle noise became stronger. There was also an attack from the south. We were still able to hold our positions, but for how much longer?

There was no more contact with the battle commander in the war academy. An NCO from the 3. Panzerkompanie rode a bicycle (we had no motorcycles or vehicles) to the academy to get some information about the enemy situation because we wanted to know how it looked on the eastern edge of the city.

He came back with clear results: the academy was occupied by the enemy. We still stood on the southern edge of the city and the enemy had penetrated the city to the north of us. Later I found out that the platoon of Panzer Vs on the eastern edge of the city couldn't hold out under the pressure of the enemy. They had ran out of ammunition and shortly thereafter the Panzers had been given up. The enemy then managed to penetrate the city there from east.

We he had to get out of this miserable situation but there still weren't any enemy tanks in front of us. We were then finally successful in getting the remaining eight Panzers onto a single driveable street which ran from south to north. In a hellish drive through Vienna Neustadt we drove by the surprised enemy and reached the north edge of the city. At the fire station the Russians had almost erected a blockade and we drove at it at full speed. We were successful and broke out to the north.

On the northern edge of Theresienfeld, north of Vienna Neustadt, we managed to get some air as an anti-tank company with six guns was brought into position south of Felixdorf. We began to fire at the anti-tank guns as we stood there and we managed to annihilate them and all of their supplies before they could fire a single shot.

The bridge directly south of Sollenau, which crossed the Piesting river seven kilometers north of Vienna Neustadt, had been blown up. We turned off to the road crossing northeast of Wöllersdorf to find out where we were.

There wasn't much time left for us. The lead tanks of the Red Army were on their way. They were coming from Vienna Neustadt and were now on the hill in Felixdorf. We had such a good flank position that we were able to knock out the entire lead group of tanks, some ten to twelve T-34s, without suffering any casualties. We were then recognized and took off for the eastern edge of Wöllersdorf. Numerous attack-planes gave us some breathing space by attacking the pursuing enemy tanks, so we took a break.

On **April 3, 1945,** the Soviets continued their attacks toward the entrances to the mountains and were able to push back the defensive unit of the LAH. OBERDIESTING was lost.

The leader of the Panzer IV group, Obersturmführer Sternebeck, reports:

> During the battles in and around Wöllersdorf the remains of the armored car battalions under Hauptsturmführer Preuss were still deployed.
>
> The local Volkssturm units were not ready to defend their own village due to fear of reprisals.
>
> During the next day the Soviets were successful in breaking into the Vienna forest near Wöllersdorf. The defensive battle was now led along the streets and into the valleys. There was no possibility to bring the weapons into action.

In order to re-establish a link to the HJ Division, the rest of the Panzer Group had to transfer to the north on **April 5, 1945** and take over the section of the TRIESTING VALLEY.

For the Panzer Group, the battles in this mountainous valley took place on a single valley road. The battle for single villages went back and forth.

The focal points of these battles included the villages of BERNDORF and POTTENSTEIN in particular.

The Panzers of the Panzer Group LAH were only able to be put in action in small defensive groups due to the narrowness of the area.

The leader of such a defensive group, Untersturmführer Borchers, reports:

> The Russians broke through north of Berndorf. I overtook a battle group with four Panzer IVs, four Sturmgeschütze and fifty infantry men. A machine gun, twenty rifles and a few pistols werc all we had for weapons. The rest had fat clubs. I let a few Panzers stand at the fork in the road. The infantry overtook the Panzer security. We waited through the night in this manner.
>
> In the early morning I reconnoitered the landscape, during which Russian machine gun fire held me down. The Russians were laying on the fields. A 3.7 cm anti-aircraft gun, which managed to break through to us, drove the Russians out from their sunken-in position. The T-34 didn't wait for long. Already two Panzer IVs had been knocked out, but they could be dragged away.

Battles of this type recurred daily at all the previously named focal points. The battles for BERNDORF and POTTENSTEIN increased in size until **April 18, 1945**.

Werner Sternebeck noted about these battles:

> For the next battles two villages stood in the background again and again, Pottenstein and Weißenbach. Here the advance of the enemy in the Triesting Valley was held up for several days by defense and counterattacks by our Panzer blocking group. Together with our Grenadiers, our Panzer blocking group circled in the north again and again.

On **April 10, 1945,** the Red Army's expected large-scale attack on ST. PÖLTEN began along the road between BADEN and ST. PÖLTEN.

In consideration of the danger of an out-flanking of the I. SS-Panzer-Korps during a Soviet break-through in ST. PÖLTEN, the General Kommando of the Korps demanded the provisional security of the left flank to the north on both sides of the road between ST. PÖLTEN and LILIENFELD in the TRAISEN VALLEY near the village of WILHELMSBURG. For this provisional security, a mixed battle group was formed from parts of the rest of Panzer Regiment 1 LAH, parts of the infantry of the HJ Division and from the rest of the Korps Tiger Battalion under the leadership of Standartenführer Peiper.

As the remaining parts of the 3. (7.) Panzerkompanie, together with the last Panzer Vs and Panzer IVs, were taken up as Panzer Group Kling with Group Peiper, the other part remained with the security group in the TRIESTING VALLEY under the leadership of Obersturmführer Sternebeck.

With that the rest of the former 7. Panzerkompanie was split up again and fought on two fronts.

Unterscharführer Rolf Ehrhardt, the Schirrmeister of the company, reports on the supply difficulties in this situation:

> The Panzer Group tried for days to secure the Triesting valley in the area of Berndorf and Pottenstein. Besides the few Panzer IVs we had various Sturmgeschütze and tank hunters. We also had some infantry and Fallschirmjäger, as well as some soldiers who had lost contact with their units who were happy to have found an intact group. We did our best to look after the troops.
>
> While I was on a "night and fog" drive in a sidecar, an old Landsturmmann (corporal from the Volksgrenadiers) stopped me: "Herr Unteroffizier, do you know anyone who needs some fuel?" How good that he didn't recognize the dumb look I gave him.
>
> The good man guarded various tanker wagons on side track which had about 60 tons of the stuff, which we handed out in liters. At neck breaking

speed I raced to the regimental command post to make a report. It was worth it, we were able to fill our tanks, which were as good as empty.

On **April 15, 1945,** ST. PÖLTEN was in Soviet hands and a few units of the Red Army advanced from the TRIESTING VALLEY to the south.

The Panzer Group Kling was set against these lead attack units and won ST. GEORGEN. They were able to beat back the Soviets to the north.

The day of **April 16, 1945** brought a renewed advanced towards ST. GEORGEN, which had to be given up by the Panzer Group Kling shortly before midday.

During the evening the Soviets attacked from ST. GEORGEN to WILHELMSBURG, but were stopped by the Panzer Group on the edge of the village.

In the TRIESTING VALLEY the high and lows of the battles went on with continued ferocity as the units fought for single villages. In a counterattack, the Panzer Group Sternebeck was about to win back the lost hamlet of STEINHOF.

While the defensive battles for WILHELMSBURG were continued by Panzer Group Kling on **April 17, 1945**, portions of the Red Army won ground east of the TRAISEN road, continued through FAHRFELD and advanced to the south.

On **April 18, 1945** these attack groups went around WILHELMSBURG and continued on to secure the TRAISEN road.

The Panzer Group Kling was indeed able to hold WILHELMSBURG, but was then encircled in the southern portion of the city.

The Panzer Group Sternebeck, located in the TRIESTING VALLEY, had to give up WEISSENBACH in bitter battle with continuous resistance and retreated to the entrance to the GÖLSEN VALLEY near HAINFELD.

The Soviet attacks taking place on **April 19, 1945** on both sides of WILHELMSBURG reached the area around ROTHEAU, where they were brought to a standstill by parts of the Group Peiper.

The Panzer Group Sternebeck had to retreat from the flank attack of the Soviets coming from the north out of the area of SCHWARZENBACH to the entrance of the GÖLSEN VALLEY. They retreated from HAINFELD through KLEINZELL to the south.

Werner Sternebeck wrote about this:

> Northeast of Hainfeld, in the area of Rohrbach, we conducted our last Panzer battle with some success, but then had to retreat through Hainfeld to the south, to get out of it alive.

April 20, 1945 brought a renewed Soviet Advance east of WILHELMSBURG. They took PLAMBACH and threatened ST. VEITH and the GÖLSEN VALLEY ROAD. With an advance to the south conducted from STOLLBERG the Soviets took HAINFELD and secured the TRIESTING VALLEY – GÖLSEN VALLEY ROAD.

A counter attack by Battle Group Peiper on **April 21, 1945** was led by Panzers of the 3. (7.) Panzerkompanie, together with portions of the 9. Panzerpionier-kompanie (Panzer engineer company). The counter-attack was led from the west into the GÖLSEN VALLEY to win back HAINFELD and open the valley road but was unsuccessful.

The group then had to switch over to the defense in the hills of ÖDHOFEN.

The Panzer Group Kling, along with further portions of the 3. (7.) Panzerkompanie, broke out of WILHELMSBURG in the morning and collected in the area of ROTHEAU and GÖBLASBRUCK.

The driver of the a Panzer IV in the 3. (7.) Panzerkompanie, Manfred Thorn, reports about this breakout:

> Approaching 0900 hours we fled from Wilhelmsburg until reaching Göblasbruck, because the Russians threatened to infiltrate us and cut us off left and right on the mountain climb and on by Wilhelmsburg. We received heavy infantry fire from the front and a hit from a Russian bazooka during the retreat. We had to cross over a wooden bridge in order to once again be able to get onto the B20, which lay to the right of the river Traisen. During the morning we lay in this position and got some sun in the grass.
>
> My crew and I tried to imagine how such a bridge would hold if it was crossed by a Panzer. Driving fast we approached the bridge. I quickly thought of what we did during the morning and whether it was good or bad luck that I hadn't tested the bridge for strength myself. I down-shifted and drove over the bridge in second gear. I immediately noticed how the bridge sunk where I was driving. With a bit of gas I tried to get to the first bridge post. From there it went up, and with a bit more gas I got the second bridge post. The last bit I drove with a bit of elegance. A Panther driving behind me collapsed the bridge.
>
> In Göblasbruck we took quarter in a house and began to camouflage our Panzer as if it were a house by surrounding it with a garden fence and bushes. We called it a village "with heart."

In the meantime, the remains of the Panzer Group Sternebeck had continuously retreated in the direction of KLEINZELL while battling the pursuing Soviets.

Wildflecken Company Quarters

Driving school

Cleaning duty

HAUSTENBECK April through June 1942

Cover from airplanes

A break from battle

Repairs

Inspection by the divisional commander

HAUSTENBECK April through June 1942

I. Platoon - Rudolf von Ribbentrop

II. Platoon - Rolf Janke

HAUSTENBECK April through June 1942

Maneuver critique

Company commander, platoon leader and half platoon leader

HAUSTENBECK April through June 1942

Loaded up, direction: Taganrog

Field parade in Paris July 1942

Company starting point

Field parade in Paris July 1942

Through Melun

Ist Platoon before Paris

Field parade in Paris July 1942

Through Champs Elysée

Marching by General Field Marshal von Runstedt

Field parade in Paris July 1942

Drive around the Arc de Triumph

EVREUX - August through October 1942

Panzer parking place on the concern

EVREUX - August through October 1942

In front of the firing range

Work during the waiting period

EVREUX - August through October 1942

Left: Radio simulated battle exercises in Gravigny

Below: Chow time

Left: I-Staffel (Repair Squadron) is ready

Battalion Sport Festival

3. Panzer-kompanie passing the baton

Taking a break

EVREUX - August through October 1942

Company sharp shooting with important visitors

Field trip to Paris

EVREUX - August through October 1942

The Ist Platoon on a hunt for partridges.

ORBEC - November 1942 through January 1943

Company quarters in the Chateau Mervilly

ORBEC - November 1942 through January 1943

Improvising a "command ramp"

Railroad tie factory in Surdon - our bathing establishment

MEREFA - February 11, 1943

MEREFA - February 11, 1943

KHARKOV - March 10 - 14, 1943

KHARKOV - March 10 - 14, 1943

KHARKOV - March 10 - 14, 1943

Panzer Stollmayer

Graves of fallen comrades in Kharkov

Graves of fallen comrades in Merefa

Kompanie instruction in Petropavlovka

Offensive exercises in sand boxes

OPERATION "ZITADELLE" July, 1943

Ready to load up

Russian tank counterattack in Tomarovka

UKRAINE - November 1943 through April 1944

The new regimental commander issues his first orders in Ssolojevka

Attack on Jastrebenka on November 23, 1943

UKRAINE - November 1943 through April 1944

Attack on the train station in Tschepovitschi on December 20, 1943

NORMANDY - July and August 1944

Ready for the attack in Bois de Cinglais

NORMANDY - July and August 1944

Tilly la Campagne - knocked out Sherman tank

NORMANDY - July and August 1944

Before Faverolles on August 16, 1944

Breakout out of the Falais Pocket on August 20, 1944

NORMANDY - July and August 1944

Breakout out of the Falais Pocket on August 20, 1944

ARDENNES OFFENSIVE - December 1944/January 1945

Craterfield La Gleize

ARDENNES OFFENSIVE - December 1944/January 1945

Lutrebois: the grave of the 7. Panzerkompanie

MALMÉDY TRIAL - Dachau, May 16 - July 17, 1946

The accused

Joachim Peiper with his defenders

Werner Sternebeck wrote:

> We were increasingly pushed into the narrow valley. Only one Panzer had a round and we were more and more at a disadvantage to the enemy infantry. It was a doubtful, punishing and hopeless battle with no success in sight.

On **April 22, 1945,** the Soviets reached the GÖLSEN VALLEY – TRIESTING VALLEY ROAD in a wide front and completely secured it. On **April 23, 1945,** the retreat over the mountains and the mountainous valleys continued in full swing with retreating battles.

The new defensive line of the LAH and the HJ Division ran from GUTENSTEIN in PIESTING VALLEY over the UNTERBERG (Unter Mountain) – (1341 meters high) and the REISALPE (1398 meters high) to LILIENFELD in the TRAISEN VALLEY until reaching RABENSTEIN in the PIELACH VALLEY. (See map 33).

On **April 24, 1945,** the new line was almost occupied.

On **April 25, 1945,** the rest of the Panzer Group Sternebeck fought back with continuous resistance from KLEINZELL through the HALBACH VALLEY until reaching the fork in the road in FISCHERMÜHLE. Together with splinter infantry groups, they secured the hills south of the GÜTENBACH VALLEY until the KLEINZELLER FELS.

Günther Borchers from the Panzer Group remembers:

> We occupied the next mountain again. In the middle of the night the Russians attacked over a meadow. Our machine guns and Sturmgewehre brought in a good harvest. Suddenly in the morning gray came ten unknowing Russians who marched onto the street. We wanted to capture them, but in his excitedness one of our men shot too early and they disappeared once again. Ivan then shot his heavy grenade launchers at us.
>
> On the mountain next to us the Russians were already there, but we still had time. They attacked us once again.
>
> Untersturmführer Fischer, who lay next to me, had a few wounds. The Russians didn't get through here.

On **April 26, 1945,** the construction of the new security line was completely finished. During the day there was light reconnaissance activity on both sides and in all sections of the front.

On **April 27, 1945,** the Soviets began their attacks on the defensive positions of the I. SS-Panzer Korps on all roads and in all valleys.

Already during the defensive battles on the right flank in FISCHER-MÜHLE the supply of fuel and munitions to the Panzer Group Sternebeck had just about ceased to exist. Since there was no further possibility of effective Panzer actions in the mountainous landscape, the last four Panzers of the Group were pulled out. The Group transferred to the collecting area SCHWARZENBACH on the PIELACH river.

Manfred Thorn noted the following about the Panzer Group Kling in TRAISEN VALLEY on this day:

> At approximately 0600 hours, I freed myself from cover in my Panzer and opened the blind covering the bullet-proof glass covered viewing port. I looked in the direction of Wilhelmsburg over green meadows and a few rows of bushes in the Traisen valley. Suddenly there was a flash from one of the bushes at about a distance of eight hundred meters. At the same instant a round hit the driver's side. One time before I had seen the shot and hit of a round, but I was still able to see the retreating T-34. Camouflage was once again everything. The guy with the other Feldpost number probably recognized us as an anti-tank gun and shot with an anti-personnel round, – that was our luck. The anti-personnel mine ripped off our replacement track guide, and in the track there was a hole. The track was held together only by a short dowel pin. During the evening we were to stop an enemy infiltration to left of the road on a mountain decline. We now stood on the mountain summit in the forest without an open shooting field. It was nighttime. We were without infantry support as well. I called for infantry support which I knew was not possible, but after a while, three infantrymen showed up. To my great surprise and happiness I saw loader Karras once again.
>
> I didn't see any more of our other Panzers of the 7. Kompanie. They were probably pulled out, and sent to other focal points.
>
> The night was calm. On our high position the Russians were not allowed to attack. They would have taken care of us up here.

On **April 28, 1945,** the war at the focal points in the mountains was conducted with bitterness and extreme hardship.

The last remaining men of the security group were able to deal with the suddenly very cold winter temperatures even though they had already grown used to the beautiful spring weather.

The mood was especially depressed because of the uncertainty of the future.

On **April 29, 1945,** the defensive battles at all security positions continued with unrelenting hardness.

Manfred Thorn reports about the battle of the rest of the 3. (7.) Panzerkompanie in the area of TRAISEN:

> As it became bright we looked down the side valley west of Wilhelmsburg which led to Bösendorf. It was swarming with Russians and T-34s down there. We couldn't lower our cannon down far enough to shoot into the valley. I drove the Panzer down a slope and prayed that the brakes would hold after a shot. We were able to knock out a T-34, another took cover behind a house, but we were still able to knock it out.
>
> In the meantime a messenger came to us with an order to retreat.
>
> It was an calming feeling for us to know that despite the apparent mess, no one was forgotten.
>
> We drove back to Traisen. I didn't see any of the other Panzers of the 7. Kompanie.
>
> During the evening we were just south of Traisen on the B 20 for security.
>
> In the meantime we heard that the Fallschirmjäger that had fought with us before were now encircled in a factory in Traisen. They were supposed to be the "green devils" from Monte Casino.
>
> In front of us, on the street in no-man's land, a soldier in a black uniform moved toward us. We couldn't believe our eyes when we recognized our Kommandant Staudegger. He had been with Ivan for two days.
>
> In the evening, we curved around further with our Panzer and its four man crew and took off for Marktl. There they were building up a new defensive front. In the houses were the Fallschirmjäger who had covered themselves during the retreat and had taken position. Our infantry, which partly consisted of crews from knocked out Panzers, secured to the left of the street.
>
> I stood with my Panzer IV and a Panther in the middle of the village of Marktl on the only road in this small village.
>
> The command post was in the last house on the other end of the village in a southerly direction. There wasn't much more – it was all that was left-over of our unit in these last days of this horrible war. One noticed in general that it couldn't last much longer; despite everything everyone fought according to his soldierly duty until the bitter end.

On **May 1, 1945,** the news about the death of Adolf Hitler reached the men in the Panzers on their security position on the radio. It was now clear to everyone that the war had found its end. Despite this, the battles on the focal points went on, as well as depressing thoughts about how everything would go on, and how one would manage get through it all.

Despite this the Landser's humor was not defeated. Manfred Thorn reports:

> During the night of May 1, 1945 a messenger brought me the order to drive back to the command post with my Panzer to take over the security there.
>
> I traveled in reverse gear the entire way back. As I arrived at the house of the command post, I noticed how the turret of the Panzer went up and then went down again. I drove forward and got out, when I saw that I had run over a VW whose driver was in the command post. We had to grin about the little pack of sheet metal.
>
> In the meantime the driver of the VW stepped out of the house. In the dark night he looked for his wagon. He inquired with us about his VW. We showed him the heap of sheet metal. He was noticeably sad and almost started to cry – not about the wagon – but about the rations that were squished inside.
>
> As it got light out, I drove thirty meters to a house to find better cover. There we stood for a few days. Everyone knew where we were to be found. If it got hot anywhere, the message would come from the main fighting line to the rear to the command post. From there a messenger would run to us and then we would be into action once again.

In the time from **May 2 to May 6, 1945,** all surviving vehicles, heavy weapons in need of repair, rear area services, medical services, supply troops and signals troops were pulled out of the vicinity of the front and pulled together in the area of JESSNITZ VALLEY and TÜRNITZ VALLEY.

The main fighting-line remained occupied at certain strong points by small battle groups. In the security position in the TRAISEN VALLEY humor had not abandoned our Panzer men.

Manfred Thorn reports about an uncommon episode:

> On May 3, 1945, a messenger came and asked me whether I could drive a T-34. He reported: "The Russians attacked Marktl in the morning hours with three T-34s and the Fallschirmjäger knocked out the last two tanks with a Panzerfaust. The crew of the first T-34 got out of their tank since the other two blocked the way back. The Panzer has to be removed since the Fallschirmjäger don't have any shooting field to the houses on the other sides, in which the Russian infantry is already located."

I made my way to the front. I reached the middle of the village and everything was still peaceful. The houses were not damaged, the population evacuated. In this way I reached the Panther before our lines. I informed the crew that I would come back with a T-34.

It really scared me when I thought that I could be knocked out in the last days of the war by my own people. Therefore I informed every soldier whom I came across on my path of my intentions.

After a short discussion with the Panther crew about where our infantry was, they informed me that they were to the left of the street. They added, however, that I should abandon the street here since the Russians could see it from the mountains.

After coming through the house I came upon a guard in a small garden behind it.

I inquired with the guard about the Fallschirmjäger. This comrade showed me a way over a potato field which I had to cross over on hands and knees, since the Russians shot at everything that moved and it was still about fifty meters to the next guard. Having arrived there the guard informed me that the Fallschirmjäger were waiting for me and that I should go along the trenches in order to get into the house from the rear. I traveled the last part of the trip in this way into the forward most line without incident.

Arriving in the house I saw an unusual scene. In the residences were all the pieces of furniture, closets were full of clothes, food and the tables were set. The evacuation of the population must have happened suddenly. It was a startling to see this abandoned German village, through which the main fighting line now ran between the right and left rows of houses.

In the area along the street were the Fallschirmjäger who were armed to the hilt. Under the window there was a machine gun, various Panzerfausts and hand grenades. Through the shattered window I saw the T-34 standing on the street in close proximity. I sat squatted with two Fallschirmjägers behind the window while they explained the situation to me. The Russians were in the three houses across from us, not even thirty meters away. In the middle of the street stood the T-34, about four meters in front of the house, which took away our field of vision.

The Fallschirmjägers covered me with fire and the operation began.

I ran out of the door on the side of the house and along the stone pallets in the garden in the direction of the street. I reached the forefront of the house and there were three steps which led down to the deeper lying street. These steps were visible to the enemy and I could only slide down them lying on my stomach. With my head in front I went off the steps onto the street. It was still about three more meters to the T-34.

I then laid on the space between the tracks and was happy that the Russians had probably not noticed me on my way here since everything was still calm.

My heart beat like a drum. For the first time in my experience as a soldier I lay before a T-34 (between the German and Russian lines, which were only forty meters apart) and didn't know if it was really empty. It was clear to me that the tank was being observed by them and I imagined that climbing into the open driver's hatch would be very dangerous.

I pulled myself up under constant observation of the right houses and took a quick look in the inside of the tank. Except for a few bundles of uniforms, there was nothing inside.

The ventilator was still running and I looked over to the house once more. There I saw a Russian officer step out. He went up to the foot bridge which ran over the Traisen. Therefore he had to go in the direction of the tank. I thought, either he is very brave or tired of life, since the Fallschirmjäger that cowered behind me would shoot him at any moment. Nothing happened. He went on towards me. He stood just twenty meters in front of me. I pulled out my pistol, laid it with my outstretched arm on the side skirts and aimed. My pistol was secured with its holster on my shoulder strap. It stretched and got caught so that the hammer couldn't release so that my gun couldn't fire. There must have been a sound, since the Russian saw me and turned around and went back into the house faster than he had come out.

I used this situation to my advantage and crawled through the open driver's hatch into the inside of the tank. The noise of the still running ventilator made me nervous, so the first thing I did was turn it off and then I closed all of the hatches. Slowly the tenseness eased in me since the greatest difficulties had been overcome. It was apparent that I was still worked up, because I couldn't get the motor to run. The Fallschirmjäger were observing attentively because they reacted promptly as I called through the reopened hatch: "send me the Panther to drag me away!" – the Panther stood about a hundred meters away in the middle of the village. They were gone for barely fifteen minutes as I heard the noise of the Panther's motor and saw the canon with the turret at six o'clock come around a corner and shove itself in my direction.

Then everything went seemingly fast. The Panther stopped in front of me, two men got out and secured the already prepared hitch of the T-34. Just as quick both of the men disappeared again into their Panzer and drove away.

After a few meters the motor of the T-34 started up. After that they dragged me behind the bend in the road and loosened the tow rope. With that the action had ended without an exchange of fire. I thanked the Fallschirmjägers and drove at a quick pace back to my post.

My crew received me joyously. With special attentiveness we tried to make ourselves at home in the enemy tank. We determined that it had just been re-fueled and loaded up with ammunition. Therefore we didn't have to be sparing with our ammunition.

Now I stood with two Panzers and a total crew of four men for special purposes.

At sundown two women come to us. I was startled to see two such pretty women since the village had been evacuated for days. They asked us: "can we fight along with you? We want do defend our hometown!" I explained the situation to them and said that Ivan was already in the village and asked them to go back. I noticed that the both of them were not pleased with this "Wehrmacht Report" and they stuck to their plans and told us that they would stay.

On the one hand I would have definitely liked to "freshen up" my crew, but on the other hand, what would the Kommandeur say when he found two women in the Panzers? But as a soldier, one shouldn't be confronted with the toughness of a woman. Therefore I gave in and told them that if they came back within fifteen minutes with a Panzer uniform on, they could stay. I didn't believe, however, that they would be able to fulfill this task and assumed I would be able to send them back. But I hadn't consider the excitedness of my crew, which quickly pulled out uniforms and hats from the compartment in the Panzer. As I saw the two women in uniform with their hair stuck up and shoved under their hats, I knew that I couldn't tell the difference between them and a normal Panzer man if it was night out. I took the risk and let the both of them climb into the Panzer so that no one else would see them.

In the meantime we learned their names and ages (18/21 years). I took the larger of the two ladies in the T-34 and put her on the radioman's machine gun. I explained to her how to use it. We couldn't radio with this equipment anyway, so no one would be suspicious that something here wasn't right.

On the next day came the message that the Russians had pulled up crates of munition to a barn about 1000 meters in front of Marktl. We assumed that they were preparing a new artillery position. We definitely had our choice. So I drove into action with the "second wagon," the T-34, to approach without raising any suspicions. We were a four man crew, with an old radio man –

Willi Richter – as loader. The loader served as the no. 1 gunner. The new crew member "Inge" worked the radioman's machine-gun and I, Manfred Thorn, served as driver. Then we advanced to the Fallschirmjäger who informed us of the situation. The farm was called "Wiegenhof." The Russians still hadn't notice anything of our plans. They dragged more crates into the building. We closed in on the farm, driving on the B 20. Distance 600 meters, cannon, anti-personnel round, finished! – Fire! – Hit!

After four shots the barn was burning. In a wild run the Russians ran here and there. Radioman, fire at will! – Shoot! – the machine-gun rattled and Inge sprayed the entire landscape. She didn't stop and shot the entire magazine empty. Then the girl screamed, "the MG doesn't work anymore!" I pulled up to her and screamed: "Pull the hammer back!" It was glowing. "PUT IN A NEW MAGAZINE!" Then Inge: "Where are the MAGAZINES???" "Willi come down here and help her!" Willi reported: "MG again ready to fire!" – Inge started to let the machine gun loose again and Willi pulled back once again into the upper area of the tank with the words: "is that a Flintenweib!"[12]

No one could tell what was going on in our Panzer because the fire attack was effective – despite Inge's lack of knowledge of her weapon. Suddenly grenade launchers and artillery fire drove us from our position. I turned around and drove back to Marktl. Inge didn't notice the change in direction and said: "Are we going to drive further forward?"

CAPITULATION/WAR PRISON

On **May 7, 1945** the capitulation documents were signed in Reims.

Together with the announcement of the capitulation, the divisional order was issued to cross over the ENNS near STEYR with the rest of the Division and go into American prison.

It was now up to the LAH to relieve the battle groups in action in the security positions and to lead them (together with the units that collected in the area of PUCHENSTUBEN SCHEIBBS) to the ENNS river.

This relief of the battle groups had to be conducted in such a way that would only allow the Soviets to pursue slowly, because no one wanted to end up in Soviet prison.

The relief efforts ran surprisingly good in most of the security positions.

From the security position in TRAISEN Manfred Thorn has another humorous, but also sad memory:

During the afternoon of May 7, 1945, we received the order to pick up four new Panzer IVs in Kirchberg on the Pielach. We had to leave our T-34 in Marktl. Approaching evening we arrived at the station that was issuing us the new Panzers. An Unterscharführer took care of the transfer of the Panzers and inquired if we were going to drive to the front that evening. I told him that we would spend the night there in the house and that we would leave early in the morning. The Unterscharführer asked me who he could order to serve as guard that evening, to which I answered: "Order the radio men to serve guard!" He went from Panzer to Panzer to find out the names of the radiomen; as he came to my wagon and called "radio man", the radio man's hatch opened and there stood in the dark a figure with a cap on. "Your Name?" – "Inge" – He looked at me with amazement and disbelief. I had to laugh at the expression on his face and told him that that was one of my radio men. I didn't really figure that Inge would dare come out. I was of the opinion that radio man Willi Richter would report for guard duty – but who wants to do that? We spent the night in the house and early the next morning we were awakened by large amounts of screaming. We looked out on to the street and saw Landsers of all branches of service streaming back. At first look we thought it was a Russian breakthrough, but then we heard the soldiers call: "The war is over! – The war is over!"

We readied ourselves quickly for the march. The two women wished us well and went back to the place where we fought the previous day, to Marktl.

During the early morning of **May 8, 1945** the first portions of the division, which were located in the furthest westerly area of SCHEIBBS – PUCHENSTUBEN, departed in march for the ENNS.

The crossing over the ENNS proved to be difficult, since the Americans first had to be dealt with.

On **May 9, 1945,** the Soviets were still advancing behind our units and we began to have doubts as to whether a crossing of the ENNS could still prove successful. Since no soldier of the Panzerkorps wanted to fall into Soviet hands, the unit leaders searched other methods to get across to the other side.

Therefore the previous Panzer IV Group, now once again put together under the leadership of Obersturmführer Sternebeck, marched from WEYER to ALTENMARKT on the ENNS.

Werner Sternebeck wrote about this:

The battle group of the 3. (7.) Kompanie and other portions of the Division reached the Enns in Steyr during the course of May 9. There we wrecked the remaining Panzer IVs and drove them into the Enns and then marched on with our other vehicles.

Since Ivan had supposedly advanced from the North to Steyr, we turned east of the Enns to the south to finally go into American prison across the Enns in Altenmarkt, some fifty to sixty kilometers away.

This depressing day also remained clear in the memory of Manfred Thorn:

With our loyal Panzer IVs we drove to the line of demarcation near Altenmarkt. There I sunk my Panzer in the Enns.

A long trying path into prison began.

Rolf Reiser, leader of the Panzer Group, described the course of the trip to prison exactly:

The continuation of the march in the direction of STYER was at first not possible. There was no movement. The bridge in Steyer had supposedly been blocked by the Americans, or the Soviets. The Soviets, coming from Amstetten, had reached Steyer and had secured the bridge.

Due to this situation and the directions to surrender to the Americans on May 9th at 0001 hours. At a house west of the Enns, we decided upon another march path. The last four Panzers were driven into the Enns and sunk. The 3. (7.) Kompanie, about sixty men strong, drove in the opposite direction to the south into the mountains, in the direction of Altenmarkt. In oncoming traffic, everything was indeed traveling in the direction of Steyr, our trip was only able to proceed slowly. First the road was narrow and there was a 17% incline. Beyond Altenmarkt we took the street to the west and went over the Hengst Pass, and reached the village of Winischgarten 1,050 meters high. Here was our first contact with the U.S. Army. A young American Lieutenant handled himself in a correct manner. Disarmament, all arms had to be turned over. Officers were allowed to keep their pistols.

On **May 10, 1945,** began the long and depressing march into war prison.

The 3. (7.) Panzerkompanie followed its own path together with other splinter groups of the Division.

Werner Sternebeck tells his story:

With very few exceptions the remains of the battle group (3. (7.) Kompanie) stayed together after the disarmament and marched with the still available vehicles, including the field kitchen, into the camp in Mauerkirchen (southeast of Braunau), which was reached on May 12.

The march into prison proceeded without incident; despite the fact that we had no weapons and remained in close formation, no one stepped up to beat us or plunder us, (meant are: US Soldiers, former concentration camp inmates, Austrian soldiers with red-white armbands or other resistance fighters).

Almost the entire division and our vehicles were kept in the "open" prison camp, in the meadows around Mauerkirchen. Since the old unit still remained intact, the relationship with superiors remained intact. As far as I remember there was no loss of discipline and no cases of disobedience or mutiny.

Memories from the camp in Mauerkirchen still remain with Rolf Reiser:

Outside of the village was our collecting camp. In the Auland landscape of the Mattig we were collected in the open field and in the meadows. We camped out there. During the following days there were supposedly 300,000 soldiers that arrived there. None of the Americans really looked after the "prisoners."

The field camp time in Mauerkirchen lasted until **May 20, 1945**. From then on the Americans shipped out groups to be "dismissed" on a daily basis.

This was nothing other than a camouflaged transfer to the village of ALTHEIM, later notoriously known as the "hunger camp."

Werner Sternebeck expresses his opinion about the situation:

Due to the transfer to the "hunger camp" Altheim and the supposed dismissal of our former units, we were mixed in with Army units which automatically caused loss of discipline. This was what the Americans wanted. A certain calm could only be maintained with hardness and the threat of the use of weapons in the camp in Altheim. After about five to six weeks, Altheim was evacuated and the Division was transferred to Ebensee and split into two camps while maintaining the leadership of the old units.

Rolf Reiser can't rid himself of memories of ALTHEIM either:

After about ten days the supposed "dismissal" was to begin! Starting with the lowest enlisted man, ranks groups of soldiers were called out and transported off.

After about four weeks the leaders and the officers stood in the waiting line too. Men were marched by foot through Mauerkirchen, Moosbach to ALTHEIM.

Here on the edge of the village we reached our first "camp." In the closest quarters, secured on one side by a creek and on the other side bordered by American tanks, the former SS members were to be found in the area of Uttendorf. Sanitary conditions and the situation in general was very bad. There were shovels for digging latrines, as well as lime-wash, and very few rations. The name "hunger camp" was correct.

Groups of prisoners from the former 1. SS-Panzer Division "LAH" arrived in the camps EBENSEE I and II until the middle of **August 1945**. Gradually the men began to come to terms with their irreversible fate.

The daily life of the prisoner of war camp became routine.

Werner Sternebeck confirms this with satisfaction:

Bearable conditions developed once again in Ebensee, even though new rules of conduct had to be observed due to the isolation of the prison.

Johann Wohninsland remembers his special trip to the prisoner of war camp:

We were happy to get over the Enns. There we took off once again, to Passau. There the Amis caught up to us for the sixth time. Unfortunately we couldn't take off again, because they put us in a former RAD (Reichsarbeitsdienst – German Work Service) camp which was guarded heavily.

Fourteen days later one thousand of us were loaded in trucks and handed over to the Russians in Budweiss (Czech Republic). We were then marched for the next fourteen days and arrived in Austria in a prison camp. First the Russians removed our last possessions and gave us crew-cuts. From there we were shipped off to Russia. Once they realized that I had been with the Waffen-SS, they shipped me off to the coal works in Stalinogorsk.

In 1949, I was released from the prisoner of war camp. I was then transferred to the Americans in Ulm, released from the Americans and then shipped to the French in Tuttlingen. There I was finally fully released on December 24, 1949.

In the beginning of 1946, the transfer of members of the Waffen-SS who were citizens of the German Reich began. They were sent from American camps to West Germany, where they were put in the so-called internment camps.

On **November 1, 1946,** the soldiers of the Waffen-SS were officially released from active duty and given "automatic arrest" status as civilians.

The long awaited releases began in the spring of 1947.

THE MALMÉDY TRIAL

The fate of a group of our old Panzer Kompanie was still to travel a bitter path, however.

In the prisoner of war camps the men of the Panzer Group Peiper who had fought in the Ardennes Offensive heard that the short and definitely irrelevant combat incident with the American observation battery at the fork in the road from BAUGNEZ was fashioned as brutal slaughter and was called the "Malmédy Massacre" by the American public. The Americans called for revenge and retribution.

Right after the capitulation, the commander in chief combed through the camp for former members of the Panzer Group in order to find out about the supposed execution of 73 American prisoners through continuous interrogations.

Rolf Ehrhard, the Schirrmeister of the 7. Panzerkompanie, reports about these first interrogations:

> In the camp in Regensburg (DEFC 22) the first inquiries were carried out. All of the members of the LAH had to be interrogated.
>
> A former member of my 7. Panzerkompanie said to me that he heard the Americans say something about a dirty trick at a crossing. This was really the first information that I heard about this business.
>
> ... One day around October 30, 1945 came the big list for the transfer to the camp in Zuffenhausen. It turned out to be a positive change. Strong compound buildings, which were well heated and had sanitary conditions – which was like luxury for us. There was also a reunion with comrades who hadn't been seen in a long time. Comrades returning from their interrogation arrived on a daily basis. However, not all of them came back. They were isolated in cell rooms in another building. Many, including me, didn't suspect anything. The entire complex was surrounded with double barbed wire. The single buildings were then separated by more barbed wire fences.

All of the members of the Panzer Group Peiper who were separated in this way were transferred to the penitentiary SCHWÄBISCH HALL in **November 1945**.

Here began the actual course of suffering of our comrades. With interrogations (whose methods of torture came from the shadows of the middle ages), the interrogating officials – among whom a Lieutenant Perl distinguished himself through his extreme cruelty – the men of the Panzer Group were forced to confessions.

It is not the task of our company chronicle to report on the course of the "Malmédy Show," with all its interrogations in SCHWÄBISCH HALL, the so-called "proceedings" in DACHAU and the confinement in the penitentiary LANDSBERG where our comrades suffered mental and physical torture.

In the meantime their detailed and truthful documentation has come forth.

But since a large group of men of the 7. Panzerkompanie had to suffer throughout the fate of the "Battle Group" and the 7. Panzerkompanie was pulled into the middle of the claimed events for a time, a few members of the company should be allowed to tell their stories.

Rolf Ehrhardt reports on the first interrogations in SCHWÄBISCH HALL:

> Without any warning we were transported to Schwäbisch Hall on December 7, 1945, in a large convoy that was heavily guarded. The fact that it was a large prison was unmistakable, and was a shock.
>
> The rude tone of the Amis, who removed us from the seats in our vehicles and split us up into cells with billy clubs, was our first taste of what was to come.
>
> I was put into a single cell on the first floor in a typical prison building with three other comrades. None of us knew each other. We introduced ourselves – with a certain mistrust, however, which had already begun to spread during the time in Zuffenhausen.
>
> We spent a few hum-drum days in our four-man cell, which was so small that it got on one's nerves. There were two straw sacks for four men, we all had a blanket. The only thing in the cell was a toilet. We weren't allowed to lay down during the day. Therefore we had to sit or stand around. The guards always got bored. Every 15 minutes the mirror-window was opened. The guard would then scream: "Open the window!" If we acted dumb, then the yelling would get crazy.
>
> The guards would especially like to disturb the peace at night in short intervals on a regular basis -through loud whistling, conversation at a yelling

volume, or orders like "stand up" and the sort. The guards especially liked to run along the steel prison bars with their billy clubs. This noise could have awoken the dead.

The little news (we could hear some things) let us know that some people were picked up from the building at various times throughout the day. This always happened with a lot of "lets go" and "Mak snell snell" (bad German for "go fast fast"). As one of us four was picked up, we saw for the first time the later well known "hoods."

One day I was on the row. They put a hood over my head, then I had to put my hands on someone's shoulder's in front of me. We were given directions from the guard assigned to us: "Spreken verboden!" (again, bad German for "speaking forbidden"), and then we had to take off in a goose step.

If anyone tried to get some air in the hood, then came a voice in the best German: "Du Schwein, willst Du die Pfoten weglassen!" (You pig, take your hands away from the hood!). Then there was a thud, surely from a hit with a billy club, followed by light moaning.

Everyone had now learned his lesson. We stood. The air under the hood escaped and became bad. The call of ones name was like a deliverance. A door was opened. They led us into a room and the hood was taken off. Due to the sudden bright flashes of light I recognized a larger cell. In the middle there was a table and behind it two Americans. There was a Mr. Morris Ellowitz. He began the interrogation in a bad German, and then let the second American take over, who could speak an accent free High German and had to act as a translator.

They then laid out the pictures from Baugnez, which I couldn't even begin to believe. The large ones were either completely fake or from somewhere else, perhaps wrongly interpreted. These pictures disturbed me greatly. I couldn't understand how something such as this was even possible.

In order to get the urgently needed statements for the trial, the so-called "interrogations-officers" used every gangster method.

The main point here was the burden on the camaraderie and how the comrades had to act towards each other and think of one another.

Rolf Ehrhardt has still another report about an interrogation:

The next two weeks were filled with continuous interrogations. First Lieutenant William R. Perl and Mr. Harry Thon tried to outdo each other by carrying out as many brutal abuses as they possibly could.

The most shocking interrogation that I experienced was when they sat me across from a certain Rottenführer (whose name I don't remember), who was the first to tell me about the supposed incident in Baugnez while in the camp Regensburg. In the firm belief that we would receive fair treatment I had named him during an interrogation.

I was led into a cell in which he sat on a stool bare-chested. He had quite obviously been beat up and mistreated. I will never forget his accusing eye.

"Is that the X, that told you in Regensburg about the incident at the crossing?" was the question. I feverishly tried to think of how I could still help him. How could I make him understand that I did not directly accuse him? The realization that we had been sent into an evil system was paralyzing. I couldn't come up with anything better than to look into his eyes and ask for forgiveness. I hoped that he understood me. But the Amis recognized it immediately, screamed at me and ripped me out of the cell.

A further encounter with such a situation happened as follows.

Perl fetched me from my cell and led me a few doors further to a one-way cell mirror. "Do you know this man?" I looked through the mirror and I was shocked. Hauptsturmführer Klingelhöfer, my old commander? I saw a man who could be Hauptsturmführer Klingelhöfer at first glance. Same size, same figure, hair and face similar too. At the second glance I was sure that it was not him. So then I said to Perl: "You think this man is Klingelhöfer, but it is not him!" Perl answered: "It is Klingelhöfer!" Me: "But not Oskar Klingelhöfer!" Perl: "You'll see, but don't speak a word!" He opened the cell, in the middle stood the man in an "eight-thirty" position. Perl asked him: "Wie heißen Sie?" (what is your name). Answer: "Klingelhöfer." Perl: "Dienstgrad?" (rank?). Answer "Hauptsturmführer." Perl: "Which company did you lead?" Answer: "The seventh." Perl: "Then shake your driver's hand!" I was only left to communicate with my eyes. Did he understand me? The hand remained down. After the cell was closed again Perl said: "That is definitely him!" Then I said to him that Oskar Klingelhöfer had a large scar from a wound on his stomach. I hoped that that would help the wrong Klingelhöfer. At this time I thought the right Klingelhöfer was dead. Untersturmführer Fischer told me in Zuffenhausen that Klingelhöfer had been shot by a Russian while trying to cross the Enns in Austria and was washed away.

Equipped with statements obtained in this way the military court opened its trial on **May 16, 1946,** in Dachau.

With disregard for all the very basic international principles of law, the sentence was then pronounced.

The following members of the 7. Panzerkompanie were among the 73 convicted:

Oberscharführer Roman Clotten	10 years
Sturmmann Georg Fleps	death
Hauptsturmführer Oskar Klingelhöfer	death
Untersturmführer Erich Münkemer	death
Untersturmführer Heinz Rehagel	death
Hauptscharführer Hans Siptrott	death
Obersturmführer Werner Sternebeck	death

Now began the punishing years of imprisonment in LANDSBERG.

Here the convicted found peace and quiet and time to think over the consequences of their forced confessions. With support from the example set by self-sacrificing lawyers who worked very hard, all of the so-called "statements" were reproached.

Even Roman Clotten made a statutory declaration:

> On June 10, 1948, Oberscharführer Roman Clotten made the following state under oath:
>
> With regard to and in addition to my request for an additional investigation dated November 8, 1947, I would like to make the following statutory declaration:
>
> I state herewith, that my statement from January 1946, having to do with my part in the incident on the street crossing south of Malmédy did not reflect the real facts. The reasons which led me to write this statement and the methods that forced me do to so are described below.
>
> On November 1, 1945, I, along with three other members of my regiment, was transferred from the POW Camp in Ebensee-Austria to Zuffenhausen. Upon my arrival I was split from my comrades and put in solitary confinement in a basement without light, a toilet or a sink. The reasons for this treatment were not given. Four weeks long I was help prisoner in this basement, and I only received the opportunity to wash my face and my hands three times. On the fourth day of my stay I was given a bucket without a cover, so that I could relieve myself. Until this time I had to do that in the room in which I stayed, since my request to be led to the toilet was refused. The bucket with the excrement remained in the room and was only emptied three times per day. I received neither books nor writing paper, nor was I ever

listened to. The reasons for this inhumane, disgraceful treatment were not given.

On December 4, 1945, I was transferred over to Schwäbisch Hall. After all my personal belongings were taken from me (which I never saw again), I was locked in a cell with four comrades from my regiment.

After a course of about four more weeks, on December 19, 1945, I was put in front of an interrogation officer (Mr. Thon). He posed a few questions to me, insulted me in the worst way and then threw me in a barred cell. On January 4, 1946 I was heard by Herrn Perl, who mentioned, that I was to be quartered in a death cell. During the evening of the same day, at about 2000 hours, Herr Perl came into my cell again and swore at me in the most disgusting way. He hit me with his fists a number of times in the face and the stomach and demanded that I immediately write a statement about my part in the incident at the stated street crossing. He told me that only an immediate complete confession could spare me from an immediate hanging. Bullied and bluffed by this treatment and the threat, I wrote a report that very evening in full detail about the events of the incident, as far as I knew and could remember. This report did not appear to satisfy the interrogation officer. He continued to insult me in the most dirty and mean way, and threatened that I would not leave the cell alive if I didn't write a confession. He also said that he would only stop punching me if Mr. Thon appeared. Mr. Thon was then very friendly to me. He asked me where I was from, where my family lived, etc. He told me that he had come from the same area as me and that he would find out how things were going for my family, from whom I hadn't heard for almost a whole year.

A few days later (in the meantime no one had spoken to me) Herr Perl visited me again and said that he was informed that my wife and my children were killed during the last days of the war. I had to accept this as the truth, since I knew that several heavy battles had taken place in my home town. During the afternoon of these tortures I was once again brought to Herrn Perl, who said to me that I would now have to write my statement once again; he would dictate it to me.

As the result of this ordeal, which I had to suffer through during the previous weeks, and because of the message of the death of my family (it was only months afterwards the I found out that it was a lie for the purpose of breaking me down) I was in such a mental condition, completely indifferent and apathetic, that I wrote everything that Herr Perl dictated, without any fundamental objections. I remained in this so-called death cell until January 14. After that I was put up in a better cell.

During the entire time that I spent in Schwäbisch Hall, I had – with the exception of a few days – no bed and had to sleep on the bare floor. The majority of the time I was kept in solitary confinement. I was not allowed to read and didn't have any possibility of doing anything else. I was never given the opportunity to wash myself, or to even move for a few minutes. During the first days of my stay in Schwäbisch Hall I caught a skin ailment (scratches), which was caused by the dirty clothes which I received to replace my clothes. Despite my almost daily request to be brought to a doctor, I was finally treated after six weeks. During this time I slept only three hours a night due to a nerve-grating horrible itch.

Due to this hard-pressed physical and mental situation, I wrote the statement which formed the basis of the judgment against me. This statement is the only form of proof that was used against me during the entire trial. It was not confirmed by other facts or statements from other witness or other accused persons.

Due to the above reasons I declare that this questionable statement was made under pressure and coercion and that it does not reflect the true facts. The statement is therefore null and void.

I swear that the details of the above statement are true to the best of my inner knowledge and conscience.

Roman Clotten

After carrying out various inquisitions about the course of the trial by the American commission, after pardons of the then American supreme commander and the findings of the "Parole-Proceedings," again and again all of the convictions were overturned and the convicted released.

On **December 22, 1956,** our highly esteemed regimental commander, Standartenführer Joachim Peiper, was released into freedom.

We close the chronicle of the 7. Panzerkompanie with a thoughtful word from Joachim Peiper:

> In war our proud Division was known as secure in every crisis. In prison we became well-known due to our steadfastness. May our children be able to say in the future that in our misfortune we were not smaller than our fate – and that in our great plight we were still able to make a contribution to reconciliation and European thought.

NOTES TO PART I:

[1] The "Unteroffizier von Dienst" is an NCO that is entrusted with the continuing affairs of the company. The Unteroffizer von Dienst usually holds this position for only a certain period of time, in most cases one night. His responsibilities include for citing soldiers who are late arriving back to the barracks or have unapproved guests in the barracks, and also to wake the soldiers when they are put on alarm in the morning.

[2] The Furier (a French term, spelled "Fourier" in German) is the turm for the NCO in charge of the troop's rations and quarters.

[3] Panzers were steered with brakes. If the driver steered to the left, the left steering brake was activated which would slow or stop the left track while the right one continue. This caused the Panzer to pivot on the left track and hence turn to the left.

[4] A Panzerbüchsen was a Russian gun which was very long and stood like a machine gun on two legs. It was specially designed to combat armor and fired highly explosive ammunition.

[5] Nebelwerfer were guns which launched smoke bombs and other rockets.

[6] Horch was an automobile firm which produced luxury cars. So here "Horch driver" refers to the commander's chauffeur. Sine the word "Horch" means "listen" in German, the name of this firm was later changed to "Audi" which meains "listen" in Latin.

[7] The "Spieß" was the sargeant-major and was considered the "mother" of the troops and the right hand of the company commander.

[8] The Schirrmeister was in charge of the inventory of the company's vehicles and equipment.

[9] SPW = Schützenpanzerwagen (armored infantry vehicle) - the translator.

[10] The sight block was a piece of bullet-proof glass the driver looked through during battle.

[11] TFK = Technischer Führer Kraftfahrzeugwesen. This man was a leader and responsible for maintenance of the unit's vehicles.

[12] A "Flintenweib" was a female Russian soldier. "Flintenweiber" had a very nasty reputation amongst the German Landsers and were especailly well-known for their brutality.

PART II

LISTS AND TABLES

REPORTS FROM MEMBERS OF THE COMPANY

The writing of the actual chronicle text and determining the point in time of the course of the combats, refreshening, transports, etc. became a reality through the reports of experiences from company comrades, and give our chronicle its personal flavor.

The following should receive our best thanks:

Hans Behrend
Richard Bendfeld
Günther Borchers
Heinrich Burk
Roman Clotten
Rolf Ehrhardt
Ulrich Felden
Heinz Freiberg
Reinhold Kyriss
Karl Müller
Rolf Reiser
Rudolf von Ribbentrop
Jupp Steinbüchel
Werner Sternebeck
Gerhard Stiller
Manfred Thorn
Ralf Tiemann
Heinz Wölfel
Johann Wohninsland

AWARDS in the 7. Panzer-Kompanie

KNIGHT'S CROSS TO THE IRON CROSS

	Born	*Awarded On*
Obersturmführer v. Ribbentrop, Rudolf	May 11, 1921	July 15, 1943
Untersturmführer Sametreiter, Kurt	April 9, 1922	July 31, 1943
Obersturmführer Wolff, Werner	Nov. 11, 1922	August 7, 1943

GERMAN CROSS IN GOLD

Hauptsturmführer Tiemann, Ralf	August 6, 1918	October 2, 1943
Obersturmführer Malchow, Walter	Sept. 30, 1921	September 2, 1943
Obersturmführer Astegher, Hans	July 15, 1916	March 28, 1943
Oberscharführer Siptrott, Hans	May 27, 1919	December 30, 1944
Obersturmführer v. Ribbentrop, Rudolf	May 11, 1921	August 25, 1944

HONOR ROLL CLASP

Obersturmführer Wolff, Werner	Nov. 11, 1922	February 5, 1945

IRON CROSS

Untersturmführer Janke, Rolf	Oct. 10, 1919	(IC I) Mar. 20, 1943
Untersturmführer vcn Ribbentrop, Rudolf	May 11, 1921	"
Untersturmführer Eckardt, Hans	May 6, 1922	"
Untersturmführer Stollmayer, Luis	July 28, 1918	"
Unterscharführer Killat, Gerhard	Dec. 17, 1917	(IC II) Mar. 20, 1943
Unterscharführer Schubbe, Hans	July 8, 1921	"
Unterscharführer Siegmüller, Wilhelm	Dec. 15, 1913	"
Rottenführer Wendorff, Ewald	August 10, 1921	"
Rottenführer Rau, Adolf	August 30, 1922	"
Sturmmann Kardauke, Günther	April 5, 1919	"
Sturmmann Hengl, Hugo	Feb. 11, 1924	"
Sturmmann Behrend, Hans	Nov. 24, 1923	"
Sturmmann Höss, Siegfried	May 11, 1923	"
Sturmmann Burk, Heinrich	August 12, 1923	"
Sturmmann Berger, Filip	April 1, 1922	"
Sturmmann Borgsmüller, Horst	June 4, 1923	"
Sturmmann Muthke, Ernst	Dec. 14, 1922	"
Sturmmann Felden, Ulrich	May 23, 1924	"
Schütze Bendig, Erwin	Dec. 3, 1924	"

Obersturmführer Alt, Heinrich	May 20, 1901	(IC II) April 4, 1943
Rottenführer Bührer, August	Feb. 16, 1921	"
Sturmmann Klein, Kurt	April 29, 1924	"
Oberscharführer von Husen, Hans	Sept. 21, 1915	"
Sturmmann Schwarz, Ernst	October 3, 1924	"
Oberschütze Gläsner, Walter	Feb. 23, 1923	"
Obersturmführer Sprunk, Herbert	Feb. 21, 1919	(IC I) July 23, 1943
Oberscharführer Inmann, Ernst	May 22, 1917	(ICII) "
Unterscharführer Stotz, Walter	Dec. 9, 1922	"
Sturmmann Leppin, Gerhard	March 4, 1925	"
Sturmmann Prill, Hans	August 9, 1923	"
Obersturmführer Hoffmann, Kurt	Dec. 31, 1919	(IC I) Sept. 9, 1943
Untersturmführer Wesier, Alfons	Dec. 2, 1921	"
Oberscharführer Siegmüller, Wilhelm	Dec. 5, 1913	"
Oberscharführer Inmann, Ernst	May 22, 1917	"
Unterscharführer Koch, Werner	April 18, 1918	"
Unterscharführer Wenndorf, Ewald	August 10, 1921	"
Unterscharführer Schulze, Werner	January 11, 1917	"
Unterscharführer Stotz, Walter	Dec. 9, 1922	"
Hauptscharführer Fischer, Kurt	Feb. 5, 1911	(IC II) "
Scharführer Bergmann, Ludwig	July 8, 15	"
Unterscharführer Stein, Harald	July 1, 1921	"
Unterscharführer Fischer, Bruno	Feb. 8, 1918	"
Unterscharführer Engel, Walter	April 18, 1920	"
Unterscharführer Koch, Werner	April 18, 1918	"
Unterscharführer Szeimis, Willi	March 4, 1922	"
Unterscharführer Nowack, Rudolf	June 10, 1922	"
Unterscharführer Homann, Eduard	March 4, 1909	"
Unterscharführer von Elling, Heinz	February 5, 1920	"
Unterscharführer Deeg, Arthur	January 29, 1923	"
Unterscharführer Häusler, Alfons	Sept. 20, 1920	"
Rottenführer Litzau, Otto	August 23, 1922	"
Rottenführer Kuhnke, Hans	Dec. 7, 1921	"
Sturmmann Kern, Helmuth	January 30, 1925	"
Sturmmann Koch, Werner	Sept. 6, 1922	"
Sturmmann Reissner, Franz	March 31, 1923	"
Sturmmann Tschreschnigg, Hans	June 24, 1923	"
Sturmmann Brüttel, Helmut	January 10, 1925	"

Sturmmann Rossmann, Heinz	August 30, 1925	"
Sturmmann Isenberg, Heinz	Sept. 21, 1923	"
Schütze Fröhlich, Paul	April 25, 1925	"
Schütze Ehrhardt, Rolf	February 8, 1924	"
Schütze Albrecht, Gerhard	Dec. 4, 1924	"
Schütze Anders Reinhold	June 28, 1925	"
Sturmmann Ludwig, Horst	January 1, 1923	"
Schütze Kotyrba, Reimond	March 1, 1923	"
Obersturmführer Rümmler, Wilhelm	March 6, 1901	(IC II) May 12, 1943
Untersturmführer Witte, Hans Joachim	Dec. 30, 1920	"
Unterscharführer Tribusser, Heinrich	Feb. 10, 1912	"
Rottenführer Gienke, Reinhold	March 15, 1921	"
Rottenführer Rathjen, Günter	July 22, 1921	"
Rottenführer Mai, Kurt	May 25, 1923	"
Unterscharführer Briks, Heinz	April 21, 1919	(IC II) Dec. 24, 1943
Rottenführer Thuma, Otto	May 17, 1922	"
Schütze Sroka, Erhardt	June 26, 1923	"
Schütze Wolff	January 12, 1920	(IC I) Dec. 24, 1943
Oberscharführer Hoffrichter, Rudolf	June 8, 1920	"
Unterscharführer Stein, Harald	March 4, 1921	(IC I) Jan. 30, 1944
Unterscharführer Zander, Karl-Heinz	July 14, 1921	(IC II) Jan. 30, 1944
Schütze Kabisch, Emil	July 6, 1924	"
Schütze Teichert, Gerhard	July 19, 1924	"
Schütze Müller, Andreas	March 22, 1925	"
Rottenführer von Janikowksi, Josef	June 1, 1920	"
Unterscharführer Joch, Werner	Sept. 6, 1922	(IC I) Mar. 15, 1944
Unterscharführer Reissner, Franz	March 31, 1923	"
Oberscharführer Brandstäter, Walter	May 23, 1919	"
Rottenführer Rau, Wilhelm	January 27, 1917	(IC II) Mar. 15, 1944
Rottenführer Wettengel, Oswald	May 10, 1922	(IC II) May 5, 1944
Rottenführer Reincke, Udo	October 8, 1921	"
Sturmmann Elgetz, Josef	Feb. 21, 1923	"
Sturmmann Ihring, Werner	Feb. 11, 1921	"
Sturmmann Raffau, Anton	Feb. 12, 1921	"
Oberschütze Wachtschek, Egon	May 3, 1924	"
Sturmmann Bock, Engelbert	April 26, 1924	"
Oberschütze Jung, Herbert	Sept. 24, 1924	"
Schütze Gasper, Ferdinand	April 5, 1923	"

Schütze Stamer, Karl-Heinz	Dec. 13, 1924	"
Schütze Kahlen, Heinrich	March 19, 1924	"
Untersturmführer Stiller, Gerhard	Dec.15, 1921	(IC I) Sept. 16, 1944
Unterscharführer Schrader, Heinz	May 20, 1923	"
Hauptscharführer Meschnarz, Michael	April 27, 1909	"

KEY STAFF POSITIONS WITHIN THE 7. PANZERKOMPANIE "LAH"

COMPANY COMMANDERS

Obersturmführer	Hans Asteghe r	+	Feb. 7, 1942 – Feb. 22, 1942
Obersturmführer	Ralf Tiemann		Feb. 22, 1942 – Oct. 14, 1942
Obersturmführer	K. W. Schütz		Oct. 14, 1942 – Nov. 11, 1942
Obersturmführer	Heinrich Alt	+	Nov. 11, 1942 – Feb. 24, 1943
Untersturmführer	Rolf Janke		Feb. 24, 1943 – Mar. 13, 1943
Untersturmführer	Rudolf von Ribbentrop		Mar. 13, 1943 – Apr. 26,1943
Hauptsturmführer	Ralf Tiemann		Apr. 26,1943 – Aug. 15, 1943
Obersturmführer	Kurt Hoffman	+	Aug. 15, 1943 – Oct. 17, 1943
Obersturmführer	Herbert Sprunk	+	Oct. 15, 1943 – Dec. 8, 1943
Untersturmführer	Werner Sternebeck	+	Oct. 17, 1943 – Apr. 26, 1944
Obersturmführer	Werner Wolff	+	Apr. 26, 1944 – Oct. 10, 1944
Hauptsturmführer	Oskar Klingelhöfer	+	Oct. 10, 1944 – Dec. 30, 1944
Untersturmführer	Erich Münkemer		Dec. 30, 1944 – Jan. 20, 1945
Hauptsturmführer	Oskar Klingelhöfer	+	Jan. 20, 1945 – Mar. 7, 1945
Obersturmführer	Werner Sternebeck	+	Mar. 7, 1945 – Aug. 5, 1945

PLATOON LEADERS (HALF-PLATOON LEADERS)

Untersturmführer	Hans Berg	+	
Oberscharführer	Ludwig Bergmann	+	
Unterscharführer	Heinrich Burk		
Unterscharführer	Roman Clotten	+	
Untersturmführer	Hans Eckardt	+	
Oberscharführer	Wilhelm Eichholz	+	
Untersturmführer	Frey		
Untersturmführer	Kurt Fröhlich	+	
Obersturmführer	Kurt Hoffman	+	(temporary company commander)
Oberscharführer	Rudolf Hoffrichter		
Oberscharführer	Hans von Husen	+	
Oberscharführer	Ernst Inmann	+	
Untersturmführer	Rolf Janke		(temporary company commander)
Oberscharführer	Werner Koch		
Untersturmführer	Kothmann		
Untersturmführer	Walter Malchow		
Untersturmführer	Mülbert		
Untersturmführer	Erich Münkemer		(temporary company commander)
Untersturmführer	Heinz Rehagel		

Obersturmführer	Horst Rempel	+	
Scharführer	Retz		
Untersturmführer	Rudolf von Ribbentrop		(later company commander)
Obersturmführer	Wilhelm Rümmler	+	
Untersturmführer	Kurt Sametreiter	+	
Hauptscharführer	Hans Siptrott		
Obersturmführer	Herbert Sprunk	+	(later company commander)
Oberscharführer	Karl Scharna	+	
Untersturmführer	Karl Schittenhelm	+	
Untersturmführer	Herman Steininger		
Untersturmführer	Werner Sternebeck	+	(later company commander)
Untersturmführer	Gerhard Stiller		
Untersturmführer	Luis Stollmayer	+	
Untersturmführer	Vockelmann		
Oberscharführer	Otto Weber		
Untersturmführer	Alfons Weiser	+	
Oberscharführer	Alfred Wienke	+	
Untersturmführer	Hans-Joachim Witte		
Untersturmführer	Zeizold		

SERGEANT MAJORS (SPIEß)

Hauptscharführer	Michael Meschnarz	
Oberscharführer	Walter Brandstätter	
Scharführer	Döring	
Hauptscharführer	Engelhardt	
Unterscharführer	Roman Clotten	+
Oberscharführer	Willi Bolze	
Oberscharführer	Werner Koch	

TECHNICAL SERGEANT (SCHIRRMEISTER)

Unterscharführer	Karl Stein	+
Hauptscharführer	Kurt Fischer	
Unterscharführer	Karl Dietrich	
Unterscharführer	Rolf Ehrhardt	

MAINTENANCE SQUADRON LEADER

Unterscharführer	Ludwig Kühn	+
Unterscharführer	Kurt Mai	+

WEAPONRY NCO

Unterscharführer	Walter Engel	
Unterscharführer	Heinz Wölfel	+

OUR DEAD COMRADES

SIE LIEGEN IM WESTEN UND OSTEN.	THEY ARE BURIED IN THE WEST AND IN THE EAST.
SIE LIEGEN IN ALLER WELT.	THEY ARE BURIED ALL OVER THE WORLD.
UND IHRE HELME VERROSTEN.	AND THEIR HELMETS ARE RUSTING.
UND KREUZ UND HÜGEL ZERFÄLLT.	AND THEIR CROSSES ARE CRUMBLING AWAY.
SIE LIEGEN VERSCHARRT UND VERSUNKEN.	THEY ARE BURIED IN TRENCHES.
IM MASSENGRAB UND IM MEER.	IN MASS GRAVES AND IN THE SEA.
ABER ES LEBEN HALUNKEN,	BUT SCOUNDRELS STILL LIVE,
DIE ZIEHEN HOCH ÜBER SIE HER.	THEY TREAD ON THEIR GRAVES.
HEUT TOBT MAN MIT FRECHEM GEBAREN	TODAY PEOPLE BECOME ENRAGED AND DISPLAY AUDACIOUS BEHAVIOUR
DURCH FLITTER UND LÜGE UND GLANZ.	WITH TINSEL AND LIES AND SPARKLE.
SIE FIELEN MIT ACHZEHN JAHREN	THEY WERE KILLED AT JUST EIGHTEEN YEARS
– IN EINEM ANDEREN TANZ.	- IN A DIFFERENT DANCE.
HEUT MACHT MAN MIT FUNKELNDEN WAGEN	TODAY PEOPLE DRIVE FANCY CARS
UND DÜKEL UND MAMMON STAAT....!	IN A DARK AND FILTHY DISPLAY...!
SIE STARBEN AN VIELEN TAGEN	THEY DIED ON MANY DAYS
NOCH HINTER DEM STACHELDRAHT.	AND LATER BEHIND BARBED WIRE.
SIE WAREN NICHT AUSGEZOGEN	THEY WERE NOT RAISED
UM BEUTE UND SCHNÖDEN GEWINN:	TO SWINDEL AND SHAMELESSLY PROFIT FROM OTHERS:
WAS HEUTE VERLACHT UND VERLOGEN,	WHAT IS LAUGHED AT AND LIED ABOUT TODAY,
ES HATTE FÜR SIE EINEN SINN.	FOR THEM IT HAD A MEAINING.
SIE HATTEN IHR JUNGES LEBEN	THEY DIDN'T VALUE THEIR YOUNG
NICHT WENIGER LIEB – ALS DIE	LIVES ANY LESS – AS OTHERS SNEER
HEUT HÖHNEN: ES HINZUGEBEN	TODAY: TO GIVE IT UP
SEI REIN IDIOTE!	WOULD BE COMPLETELY IDIOTIC

SIE KONNTEN NICHT DEMONSTRIEREN: MEHR FREIZEIT BEI HÖHEREM LOHN! SIE MUßTEN INS FELD MARSCHIEREN. DER VATER. DER BRUDER. DER SOHN.	THEY COULDN'T DEMONSTRATE FOR MORE FREETIME AND HIGHER PAY! THEY HAD TO MARCH INTO THE FIELD. THE FATHER. THE BROTHER. THE SON.
SIE GINGEN, DIE HEIMAT ZU SCHÜTZEN – UND HABEN ALLEN ENTSAGT. WAS KANN UNS DER EINSATZ NÜTZEN? HAT KEINER VON IHNEN GEFRAGT!	THEY WENT TO PROTECT THEIR HOME-LAND - AND DIDN'T CARE WHAT ANYBODY SAID. OF WHAT USE IS THE WAR TO US? WAS NOT ASKED BY ANY OF THEM!
SIE HABEN IHR LEBEN UND STERBEN DEM VATERLAND GEWEIHT.	THEY DEDICATED THEIR LIVES AND THEIR DEATHS TO THEIR FATHER-LAND.
UND WUßTEN NICHT, WELCHEN ERBEN – UND WELCHER ERBÄRMLICHKEIT!	AND DIDN'T KNOW WHAT THEY WOULD INHERIT OR HOW MISERABLE IT WOULD BE!

Der Reichsführer-SS
Der Inspekteur für Statistik

50235

Verluste im Kriege

1. a) Name: Rabenau b) Vorname: Heinz
2. a) Allgem. SS-Dienstgrad: b) SS-Nr.:
3. a) SS-Einheit: b) O. A.: Elbe
4. a) Geburtsort: Weißenfels b) Land oder Landesteil: Prov. Sa.
5. a) Geburtstag: 6. 4. 24 b) Alter n. J.: 18 c) Fam.-St.: ledig d) Konf.:
6. a) Zahl der Kinder: / b) Vornamen und Geburtsdaten: 1. 2. 3. 4. 5. 6.
7. a) Letzter Wohnort: Weißenfels b) Land od. Landest.: Prov. Sa.
8. a) Letzter Beruf: Oberschüler b) Soz. Stllg.: Schüler
9. Gefallen / Verwundet / Vermißt / Verunglückt / Erkrankt / Selbstmord — Wann: 28. 2. 43 — Wo: in Charkow (möglichst genaue Bezeichnung) — Land oder Kriegsschauplatz: Rußland
10. a) Todestag: 28. 2. 43 b) Todesort: Charkow
11. Todesart: 12. Lazarett:
13. Schlacht: 14. Auszeichnungen:
15. a) Einheit: 7./SS-Pz. Rgt. 1 / Lbst. SS-„AH" b) Waffengattung: Panzer
16. a) Wehrmachtteil: W-SS b) Dienstgrad: SS-Sturmm.
17. Ist der Vater Kriegsteilnehmer? jetzt i. [illegible], jetzt oder 1914-18, gefallen, an Kriegsleiden gestorben, kriegsversehrt [illegible], Auszeichnungen: [illegible]
18. Zahl der Geschwister: 2 weibl. 2, männl.: /, davon im Wehrdienst: /
Wehrmachtsteil: / Dienstgrad: / gefallen: /
kriegsversehrt: / Auszeichnungen: /

C 1435

Handzeichen des Bearbeiters

OPPOSITE:

Der Reichsführer-SS
The Inspector for Statistics
Casualty in War

1. a.) Name: Rabenau b.) First Name: Heinz
2. a.) General-SS Rank: b.) SS-Nr.:
3. a.) SS-Unit: b.) O.A.: Elbe
4. a.) born in: Weißenfeld b.) State
5. a.) birthday:
6. a.) number of children: 0
7. a.) last residence: Weißenfeld b.) state:
8. a.) last occupation: soldier b.) social standing: student
9. a.) killed when: February 28, 1943
wounded where: in Kharkov
missing in action war theater: Russia
sick
suicide
10. a.) date of death: February 28, 1943 b.) where: Kharkov
11. cause of death: 12. field hospital
13. battle 14. medals:
15. a.) Unit: 7./SS-Pz.Rgt. 1 „Lbs. SS- ‚AH' " b.) Branch of service: Panzers
16. a.) part of Wehrmacht: WSS b.) rank: SS-Mann (private)
17. Is the father taking part in the war as well: Off. in SHA, now or 1914-1918, killed, killed from war wounds, impaired from war wounds _____%, medals: IC II, Wound Badge in Black
18. # of brothers and sisters: 2 female 2 male 0 of whom are in service:
0 part of Wehrmacht rank killed
impaired from war wounds medals

We Mourn For Our Comrades:
– who were killed in action during the battles of the 7. Panzerkompanie/SS-Panzer Regiment 1

February 10, 1943 in Merefa, Russia

Eichold, Wilhelm Oberscharführer
Born: April 15, 1914 in Bochum
Grave:
Honor Cemetery Merefa, 16th Row

Hilbig, Winfried Schütze
Born: November 21, 1923 in Kraftborn, Niederschlesien (Lower Silesia)
Grave:
Honor Cemetery Merefa, 16th Row

Laude, Artur Sturmmann
Born: October 7, 1922 in Heiligenbeil, East Prussia
Grave:
Honor Cemetery Merefa, 16th Row

Schmidt, Walter Rottenführer
Born: January 1, 1923 in Stottmert, Westfalen
Grave:
Honor Cemetery Merefa, 16th Row

Schubbe, Hans Rottenführer
Born: June 8, 1921 in in Reinberg, Kreis Demmin, Pommerania
Grave:
Honor Cemetery Merefa, 16th Row

Schult, Heinz Sturmmann
Born: November 27, 1923 in Stade
Grave:
Honor Cemetery Merefa, 16th Row

Weingarten, Rolf Sturmmann
Born: July 6, 1922 in Cologne
Grave:
Honor Cemetery Merefa, 16th Row

February 24, 1943 in Bulachi, Russia

Alt, Heinrich Obersturmführer
Born: May 20, 1901 in Lich, Oberhessen
Grave:
Soldier's Cemetery Krassnograd, Grave 12

Hengle, Hugo Sturmmann
Born, November 2, 1924 in Viennea
Grave:
Soldier's Cemetery Krassnograd, Grave 11

February 27, 1943 in Laz. Breslau

Gittel, Alfred Sturmmann
Born: July 23, 1920 in Topolno, Kreis Schwetz
Grave:
Community Cemetery Topolinken, Kreis Schwetz

in Bulachi, Russia

Höss, Siegfried Sturmmann
Born: May 11, 1923 in Wangen im Allgäu
Grave:
Soldier's Cemetery Krassnograd
8th Row, Grave 46

in Olchowat, Russia

Scharna, Karl Oberscharführer
Born: January 9, 1922 in Buer-Erle, Gelsenkirchen
Grave:
Soldier's Cemetery Krassnograd
1st Row, 5th Grave to the Right

February 28, 1943 in Beluchovka, Russia

Hannig, Hans Oberschütze
Born: October 26, 1924 in Groß-Ottersleben
Grave:
Soldier's Cemetery Krassnograd
1st Row, 22nd Grave from the Left

in Pelevoje, Russia

Rabenau, Heinz Sturmmann
Born: April 6, 1924 in Weißenfels, Thüringen
Grave:
Soldier's Cemetery Krassnograd
1st Row, 23rd Grave from the Left

March 11, 1943 in Kharkhov

Bendig, Erwin Schütze
Born: December 3, 1924 in Ragnit, East Prussia
Grave:
Honor Cemetery Kharkhov
Row 76, Grave 48

Rau, Adolf Rottenführer
Born August 30, 1922 in Sodau near Karlsbad
Grave:
Honor Cemetery Kharkhov
Comrade's Grave, Row 76, Grave 49

Rückner, Ernst Sturmmann
Born: December 17, 1921 in Heubach, Kreis Hildburghausen
Grave:
Honor Cemetery Kharkhov
Comrade's Grave, Row 76, Grave 22

Stollmayer, Alois Untersturmführer
Born: July 28, 1918 in Brunn, Steiermark, Austria
Grave:
Honor Cemetaty Kharkhov
Comrade's Grave, Row 76, Grave 25

March 13, 1943 in Kharkhov, Russia

Osterwald, Hermann Unterscharführer
Born: June 12, 1920 in Alderswalde, East Prussia
Grave:
Honor Cemetery Kharkhov, Grave 40b

July 6, 1943 in Jakolovo, Russia

Schwarz, Ernst Schütze
Born: October 3, 1924 in Rechnitz
Grave:
Jakolovo, 35 km northwest of Bjelgorod

in Teterovino, Russia

Neiseke, Wilhelm Schütze
Born: September 9, 1924 Kreiensen, Hannover
Grave:
Teterovino, 45 km north of Bjelgorod
Single Grave, No. 4, Row 1

July 12, 1943 in Prochorovka, Russia

Schwarz, Albert Schütze
Born: May 11, 1921 in Lorch, Würrtemberg
Grave:
Teterovino, 45 km north of Bjelgorod
Single Grave, Row 1, Grave 1

Wallenschuß, Heinz-Georg Schütze
Born: January 8, 1923 in Wesermünde
Grave:
Jakovlevo, 35 km northwest of Bjelgorod
Single Grave, 1st Row, Grave 5

Weiser, Alfons Untersturmführer
Born: December 2, 1921 in Vienna
Grave:
Jakovlevo, 35 km northwest of Bjelgorod
Single Grave, 2nd Row, 1st Grave

July 13, 1943 in Prochorovka, Russia

Siegmüller, Wilhelm Oberscharführer
Born: December 15, 1913 in Oldendorf, Hessen
Grave:
Teterovino, 45 km north of Bjelgorod
Single Grave, Row 7, 1st Grave

July 20, 1943 in a Field Hospital, Kharkhov

von Husen, Johannes Oberscharführer
Born: September 21, 1915 in Guderhandviertel, Stade, Hannover
Grave:
Honor Cemetery, Kharkhov, Field B
Single Grave, Row 93, Grave 35

October 2, 1943 in Pavia, Italy

Falckenhagen, Friedrich Schütze

Born: December 25, 1924 in Eutin
Grave:
Soldier's Cemetery Costermano, Italy
Block 7, Grave 1048

November 22, 1943 in Divin, Russia

Pieritz, Kurt Rottenführer
Born: July 29, 1920 in Gnevezin
Grave:
Ssolovjevska, 30 km northwest of Fastoff
Single Grave Nr. 4, Row 3

near Ssolovjevska, Russia

Lenkewitz, Reinhold Schütze
Born: August 28, 1925 in Gudden, Kreis Tilsit, East Prussia
Grave:
Ssolovjevska, 30 km northwest of Fastoff
Row 4, 4th Grave from Left

November 23, 1943 before Dubrovka, Russia

Anders, Reinhold Paul Sturmmann
Born: June 28, 1925 in Berlin-Pankow
Grave:
Ssolovjevska, 30 km northest of Fastoff
Row 6, 7th Grave from Left

von Elling, Heinz Unterscharführer
Born: Februay 5, 1920 in Soltau, Hannover
Grave:
Ssolovjevska, 30 km northest of Fastoff
Row 6, 4th Grave from Left

Fröhlich, Paul Sturmmann
Born: April 25, 1925 in Marburg, Lahn
Grave:
Ssolovjevska, 30 km northest of Fastoff
Row 6, Grave No. 5

Pernkopf, Franz Unterscharführer
Born: September 8, 1919 in Hinterstoder, Steiermark, Austria
Grave:
Ssolovjevska, 30 km northest of Fastoff
Row 6, 2nd Grave from Left

Rümmler, Wilhelm Emil
Obersturmführer
Born: March 6, 1901 in Vienna IX
Grave:
Ssolovjevska, 30 km northest of Fastoff
Row 6, 6th Grave from the Left

before Ultschka

Kals, Hubert Schütze
Born: April 17, 1924 in Neuberg, Steiermark, Austria
Grave:
Ssolovjevska, at the Church

in Divin, Russia

Tschurz, Josef Oberscharführer
Born: January 10, 1915 in Markersdorf
Grave:
Ssolovjevska, 30 km northwest of Fastoff
Row 6, 8th Grave from Left

December 8, 1943 in Sabalot, Russia

Groll, Alfred Schütze
Born: October 4, 1924 in Schoppinitz
Grave:
Heroes's Cemetery Hegewald in Shitomir

Litzau, Otto Unterscharführer
Born: August 23, 1922 in Müggenwinkel-Danzig Hills
Grave:
Tschaikovka, 15 km west of Radomuschl
West Exit, 2nd Grave from the Left

Sprunk, Herbert Obersturmführer
Born: February 21, 1919 in Pohlenz, Sachsen
Grave: unknown, buried by another unit of the Army

Died on December 8, 1943

Schid, Alfons Schütze
Born: May 3, 1923 in Oggelshausen, Württemberg
Grave: Tschaikovka

December 12, 1943 in Sabolot, Russia

Eschrig, Karl-Heinz Unterscharführer
Born: December 26, 1918 in Wilhelmshaven
Grave:
Heroes Cemetery Hegewald bei Shitomir

December 19, 1943 in Tschepovitschi, Russia

Heider, Herbert Sturmmann
Born: May 24, 1922 in Datrinhausen
Grave:
Hero's Cemetery Hegewald near Shitomir

Kannenberg, Erwin Unterscharführer
Born: September 4, 1920 in Frankfurt on the Oder River
Grave:
Hero's Cemetery Hegewald near Shitomir

Schmidt, Günter Sturmmann
Born: May 25, 1923 in Magdeburg
Grave:
Hero's Cemetery Hegewald near Shitomir

December 21, 1943 in Tschepovitschi, Russia

Höhn, Friedrich Sturmmann
Born: November 27, 1924 in Sobernheim
Grave:
Hero's Cemetery Hegewald near Shitomir

Januray 11, 1944 in Lupjatin near Januschpol, Russia

Sroka, Erhard Schütze
Born June 26, 1923 in Reimersdorf/ O.S.
Grave:
Lypjatin near Januschpol,
40 km southwest of Berdischev

January 12, 1944 in Starokonstantinov, Russia

Helmstetter, Heinrich Sturmmann
Born: April 3, 1924 in Frankfurt on the Main River
Grave:
Hero's Cemetery Konstantinov
Row 12, Grave 3

March 5, 1944 in Balkovzi, Russia

Haan, Christel Rottenführer
Born: October 30, 1919 in Nordenham, Oldenburg
Grave: could not be buried

Seifert, Peter Unterscharführer
Born: January 27, 1919 in Liebenseen, Hohenalza
Grave: could not be buried

March 7, 1944 in Korostova, Russia

Henne, Karl Schütze
Born: July 5, 1925 in Harzefeld
Grave:
Soldier's Cemetery Tarnopol
Row 1, 2nd Grave from Left

Niebank, Johann Schütze
Born: January 21, 1923 in Heilsborn
Grave:
Soldier's Cemetery Tarnopol, Single Grave

Wienke, Alfred Oberscharführer
Born: March 24, 1911 in Jena
Grave:
Soldier's Cemetery Tarnopol
Single Grave, 1st Row, 3rd Grave from Left

July 14, 1944 in Bully, Normandy

Koch, Franz Schütze
Born: January 13, 1925
Grave:
La Cambe, Block 22, Row 5, Grave 104

Wossal, Emil Rottenführer
Born: August 9, 1922
Grave:
La Cambe, Block 22, Row 5, Grave 102

July 15, 1944 in a Field Hospital in Sees, Normandy

Giencke, Reinhold Unterscharführer

Born: March 15, 1921
Grave:
Mont de Huisnes, Manche, Tomb 41, Grave Chamber 34

July 21, 1944 in le Hamel near Falaise, Normandy

Griesche, Werner Schütze
Born: April 2, 1925
Grave:
St. Desir de Lisieux, Block 24, Grave 385

July 23, 1944 in le Hamel bei Falaise, Normandy

Wohlfart, Alfred Rottenführer
Born April 10, 1924
Grave:
St. Desir-de-Lisieux, Block 2, Row 36, Grave 856

July 25, 1944 in Tilly la Campagne, Normandy

Fischer, Bruno Unterscharführer
Born: February 8, 1918
Grave:
La Cambe, Block 34, Row 10, Grave 356

Sonnenschein, Fr. Unterscharführer
Born: April 27, 1909 in Essen-Kupferdreh
Grave:
La Cambe, Block 34, Row 9, Grave 344

July 26, 1944 in Tilly la Campagne, Normandy

Schramek, Karl Schütze
Born: November 29, 1924
Grave:
La Cambe, Block 34, Row 10, Grab 357

Warmuth, Erwin Schütze
Born: June 4, 1924
Grave:
La Cambe, Block 34, Row 10, Grave 359

August 16, 1944 in Falaise, Normandy

Knippel, Franz Rottenführer
Born: May 9, 1924
Grave:
Champigny – St. André, Block 13, Row 29, Grave 1711

Koch, Hans-Werner Sturmmann
Born: January 17, 1925 in Eilsleben
Grave:
Soldier's Cemetery Marigny, Dep. Manche Block 3, Row 7, Grave 262

August 20, 1944 in Bernay, Normandy

Wendorff, Ewald Unterscharführer
Born: August 10, 1921
Grave:
La Cambe, Block 18, Grave 106

September 11, 1944 in O.U. Geber

Karsten, Gerhard Schütze
Born: April 27, 1926
Grave:
War Cemetery Birk/Siegkreis
amongst the unknown

October 1, 1944 in Birk/Siegkreis

Thuma, Otto Rottenführer
Born May 17, 1922
Grave:
War Cemetery Birk/Siegkreis
Block 1, Row 1, Grave 1

December 17, 1944 in Losheim

Jaspers, Matthias Oberscharführer
Born: June 1, 1923
Grave:
War Cemetery in Reifferscheid, Kreis Schleiden
B II – 11 – 195

Rapp, Hans
Born: April 10, 1923 in Sönstetten, Württemberg
Grave:
War Cemetery in Reifferscheid, Kreis Schleiden

Comrade's Grave L

December 17, 1944 in Büllingen

Rempel, Horst Scharführer
Born: June 3, 1921 in Heidelberg
Grave:
Soldier's Cemetery Lommel, umong the unknown

December 18, 1944 in Main Dressing Station Blankenheim

Oberhäuser, Heinrich Hauptscharführer
Born December 3, 1915 in Scherpemich
Grave:
Berg – Seelscheid / Siegkreis
Grave 11

December 24, 1944 in Reserve Field Hospital in Gerolstein

Langhammer, Anton Sturmmann
Born: February 23, 1925 in Schönbach/Eger
Grave:
Soldier's Cemetery Gerolstein, Kreis Daun
Grave VI – 2 – 21

December 26, 1944 in Logbieme near Stavelot

Klopp, Erwin Unterscharführer
Born: February 19, 1922 in Garzinger
Grave:
Soldier's Cemetery Lommel, among the unknown

December 30, 1944 in Lutrebois

Theye, Heinrich Rottenführer
Born: July 22, 1923 in Heidhausen, Landesbergen
Grave:
Soldier's Cemetery Recogne – Bastogne, Belgium
Block 9, Grave 114

December 31, 1944 south of Bastogne

Junge, Herbert Rottenführer
Born: October 27, 1920 in Liegnitz
Grave:
Soldier's Cemetery in Sandweiler/Luxemburg
Block D, Reihe 7, Grab 151

January 3, 1945 in Clerf, Luxemburg

Häusler, Alfons Unterscharführer
Born: September 20, 1920 in Wölferdorf
Grave:
Soldier's Cemetery in Sandweiler, Luxemburg
Comrade's Grave

January 2, 1945 in Vallendar

Wettengel, Oswald Rottenführer
Born: May 10, 1922 in Schlagenveld
Badly wounded on December 30, 1944 in Lutrebois
Died on January 2, 1945 in Vallendar
Grave:
War Grave Cemetery Vallendar Kreis Koblenz
at the Catholic Cemetery, Grave 54

January 10, 1945 in Pützchen

Sender, Alfons Sturmmann
Born November 12, 1921 in Holsterhausen
Wounded on December 26, 1944 in St. Vieth
Died on January 10, 1945 in Pützchen
Grave:
Bonn-Beuel, Honory Cemetery, Field 1, Grave 128

March 30, 1945 in Austria
Kern, Helmuth Rottenführer
Born January 30, 1925 in Dresden
Grave:
Cemetery in Ittenbach
Block B – Row 8 – Grave 156

April 4, 1945 in Austria

Schäfer, Gerhard Rottenführer
Born: August 20, 1921 in Elbing
Died on April 4, 1945 while in transit to the field hospital in Whilhelmsburg

Grave:
Cemetery Oberwölbling, Lower Austria
Block 1, Row 19, Grave 786

April 18, 1945 in Austria

Bruttel, Helmut Rottenführer
Born: January 10, 1925
Grave:
Soldier's Cemetery Oberwölbling
Block 1, Grave 848

Their Honor Was Loyalty!

We Mourn For Our Comrades:

From February 1945 until the capitulation on May 8, 1945 WAST did not receive any more reports and hence there are not records for this time period.

Due to this fact we are unfortunately unable to honor the names of the comrades that were killed on the Gran Bridgehead, on the Lake Balaton, in Inota/Varpalote and Vesprem, during the retreat through western Hungary and in the Vienna Forest!

Despite this they will remain in our memory!

MISSING IN ACTION

Behsen, Heinrich Sturmmann
Born: January 31, 1925 in Hamburg
Missing since March 6, 1944 in Balkovzi near Tarnopol
Registry Case (Munich) 405669 -VBL WA 293

Briks, Heinz Hauptscharführer
Born: April 21, 1919 in Königsberg
Last message on April 5, 1945 from I./Pz.Rgt.10,
Field Post No. 27 732, about 100 km before Berlin.
Suppossedly seen in May, 1945 in Prague.

Endres, Adolf Rottenführer
Born: Frebruary 5, 1945 in Planegg, Munich
Missing since December 31, 1944 in Lutremange, Mosel
Stated as dead by the AG Munich on Septermber 21, 1966
VBL WA 293

Englet, Josef Schütze
Born: July 21, 1927 in Diedorf
Lived in Augsburg in 1939
Last message in March 1945 from the Lake Balaton, Hungary
Neither MIA nor KIA message was reported by his unit
Registry Case Munich 138095, VBL WA 293

Erhardt, Georg And. Sturmmann
Born February 25, 1924 in Aufham, Aschau
Lived in Stetten/Obb. in 1939
Last message on August 12, 1944 from St. George, Normandy
Neither MIA nor KIA messege was reported by his unit
VBL WA 293.

Fritsch, Georg Schütze
Born on February 5, 1922 in Arkeden, Romania
Missing since March 6, 1944 in Balkovzi near Tarnopol

Greil, Jakob Schütze
Born: June 19, 1925 in Lengries
Lived in Lengries, Bay in 1939
Last message in March 1945 from Hungary
Neither MIA nor KIA message reported by his unit
VBL WA 293

Haas, Franz Rottenführer
Born: July 24, 1923 in Engelhardszell
Lived in Fürstenstein/Nbdy.
Last message from March 16, 1945 from Fallingbostel
– Camp unit Kuhlmann I (Replacement Unit?)
Neither MIA nor KIA message – VBL WA 293

Herbel, Ludwig Sturmmann
Born: March 19, 1926 in Mannheim

Lived in Mannheim in 1939
Last message from Hungary, suppossedly he was badly wounded.
Neither MIA nor KIA message freported by his unit.

Jaeger, Josef Schütze
Born: March 14, 1925 in Neu St. Anna
According to message from his unit he was missing since March 6, 1944 in Balkovzi near Tarnopol

Jensen, Jens-Nicolei Schütze
Born: December 22, 1924 in Neuer Freiedrichsen-Koog, Denmark
On November 23, 1943 wounded near Dubrovka and went into prison, no other message.

Kania, Günter Schütze
Born: August 26, 1925 in Hannover
Lived in Hannover in 1939
Last message: August 16, 1944 from Normandy
Neither MIA nor KIA message reported by his unit.
VBL WA 293

Kirschbaum, Karl Schütze
Born June 1, 1926 in Gelsenkirchen
Last reported missing in Farverolles, France on August 19, 1944 by a company list of missing soldiers.

Lechl, Paul-Peter Sturmmann
Born June 27, 1926 in Passau
Lived in Passau in 1939
Last message from Hungary, suppossedly seen again on March 13, 1944 near Stuhlweissenburg. VBL WA 286.

Müller, Andreas Sturmmann
Born March 22, 1925 in Stgt.-Hedelfingen
Lived in Schammelsdorf/Ostfr. in 1939
According to company casuatly report he was missing since August 19, 1944 in Faverolles, Fance. VBL WA 293

Mutke, Ernst (named Mufti)
Untersturmführer
Born December 14, 1922 in Magdeburg
After released from American prison he was suppssedly taken prisoner by the Soviets after crossing into the Soviet Zone and mysteriously disappeared.

Rau, Wilhelm no rank given
Born January 21, 1917 in Hüttenhauland
Lived in Posen in 1939
Last message: January 1945 from Siegburg, missing in Hungary, no message from the company.
Registry case Munich 2639545, VBL WA 293

Schmidt, Michael Schütze
Born November 6, 1919 in Wolfs, Hungary
Last message: August 1944 from France, no message from the company, VBL WA 293

Schmidt, Otto Sturmmann
Born June 25, 1926 in Wallhausen
Lived in Renningen, Würrtemburg.
Last message from August 21, 1944 from the area of Caen, no message of the company, VBL WA 293.

Wilhelm, Walter Schütze
Born December 4, 1926 in Heidelberg
Lived in Rülzheim/Rhpf
Last message from February 1945
No report from the company, VBL WA 293

Wolfram, Anton Schütze
Born on March 3, 1924 in Johannisfeld, Banat
Missing since March 6, 1944 in Balkovzi near Tarnopol.
Declared dead on Septermber 22, 1981

Wunnenberg, August Schütze
Born March 9, 1925 in Almsted/Kreis Alfeld
Accoring to single MIA report issued by the company, he was missing since March 6, 1944 in Balkovzi

Zellner, Werner Oberschütze
Born Pril 22, 1924 in Pirmasens
Lived in Pirmasens in 1939
Missing since June 3, 1943

Registry case Munich 633872, VBL WA 288

Gerhard, Hugo Sturmmann
Born September 8, 1926 in Hirschfeld
Wounded on December 26, 1944 in Wanne, last message from February 12, 1945 from a field hospital in Marienbad, since April 30, 1945 no further messages.

The one time members of our company that were killed serving with other units:

Wolff, Werner Obersturmführer
Born: November 28, 1922 in Memel
Suppossedly wounded on March 17, 1945 in the area of Veszprem, Hungary
Died around March 20, 1945 in the field hospital in Laz. Götzendorf
Grave:
Community Cemetery Götzendorf/ Bez.Bruck a.d.L./Upper Austria
Row 4, Grave 245

Berg, Hans Obersturmführer
Born: September 29, 1921 in Fischel, Krefeld
Killed on January 2, 1945 near Noville
Grave:
Soldier's Cemetery Recogne-Bastogne, Belgium
Block 1, Row 6, Grave 112

Hellwig, August Oberscharführer
Born February 10, 1921 in Michelbude, East Prussia
Died on April 6, 1945 in the field hospital in Horn, Upper Austria
Grave:
War Graves in Horn, Upper Austria
Block 3, Row 2, Grave 16

Stumber, Günter Oberscharführer
Born April 14, 1918 in Kohlischken, East Prussia
Killed on June 9, 1944 in St. Martin near Caen
Grave:
Soldier's Cemetery in La Cambe, Block 24, Row 5, Grave 165

Schöller, Siegfried Untersturmführer
Born January 6, 1922 in Bollingen, Kreis Ulm
Killed on August 9, 1944 between Laval and le Mans, France
Grave:
Soldier's Cemetery Mont-de-Huisnes, Manche
Tomb 30, Chamber 158

Eismann, Friedrich Unterscharführer
Born on November 4, 1921 in Neukirchen, Chemnitz
Killed on June 9, 1944 near Norrey, west of Caen
Grave:
La Cambe "among the unknown"

Inmann, Ernst Untersturmführer
Born May 22, 1917 in Linz
Died on April 19, 1945 in the field hospital in Schierke, Harz
Grave:
Schierke, Harz, Grave No. 34, Kreis Werningerode

Abel, Werner Untersturmführer
Born on August 15, 1923 in Kranzin, Kreis Arnswalde
Killed in the middle of February in the area of Hornbach, Zweibrücken
Grave:
General Cemetery Nornbach, Row 1, Grave 7

Nerlich, Rudolf Untersturmführer
Born January 13, 1920
Killed in Action on Septermber 6, 1944
Grave:
Soldier's Cemetery in La Cambe, Block 30, Row 4, Grave 160

Egger, Hans Oberscharführer
Born November 24, 1919
Killed in Action on August 7, 1944
Grave:
Soldier's Cemetery La Cambe, Block 19, Row 1, Grave 34

Blank, Walter Untersturmführer
Born on September 14, 1919 in Friedland
Killed in Action on April 23, 1945 in Türnitz
Grave:
Heroe's Cemetery in Türnitz

Szeimies, Willi Oberscharführer
Born on March 3, 1922 in Memel
Found dead on March 11, 1945 on the beach in the Dievenov Forest
Grave:
not determined

Isenberg, Heinrich Untersturmführer
Born Septermber 21, 1923 in Meineringhausen, Kreis Waldeck
Died on July 7, 1946 in the hospital in Garmisch Partenkirchen
Grave:
Community Graveyard in Maineringhausen, private grave

Their Honor Was Loyalty!

Died since the end of the war:

Bendfeldt, Richard
Astegher, Hans
Dr. Clotten, Roman
Hoffmann, Kurt
Klingelhöfer, Oskar
Reisner, Franz
Richter, Willy
Suttner, Karl
Stein, Harald
Stotz, Walter
Westphal, Helmut
Jäger, Anton
Briesemeister, Kurt
Stein, Karl
Mai, Kurt
Kern, Helmut
Giggenbach, Sepp
Schäfgen, August
Schwarz, Wilhelm
Bührer, E. August
Krisch, Karl
Hohmann, Eduard
Reider, Max
Braun, Albert
Döring, Joachim
Römpp, Karl
Wölfel, Heinz
Hermani, Josef
Bergmann, Ludwing
Heuer, Heinz
Deeg, Arthur
Stamer, Karl-Heinz
Krüger, Friedrich
Klein, Kurt
Sternebeck, Werner
Fröhlich, Kurt
Vogg, Georg
Kostal, Johannes
Busch, Leo

PART III
MAPS

LIST OF MAPS

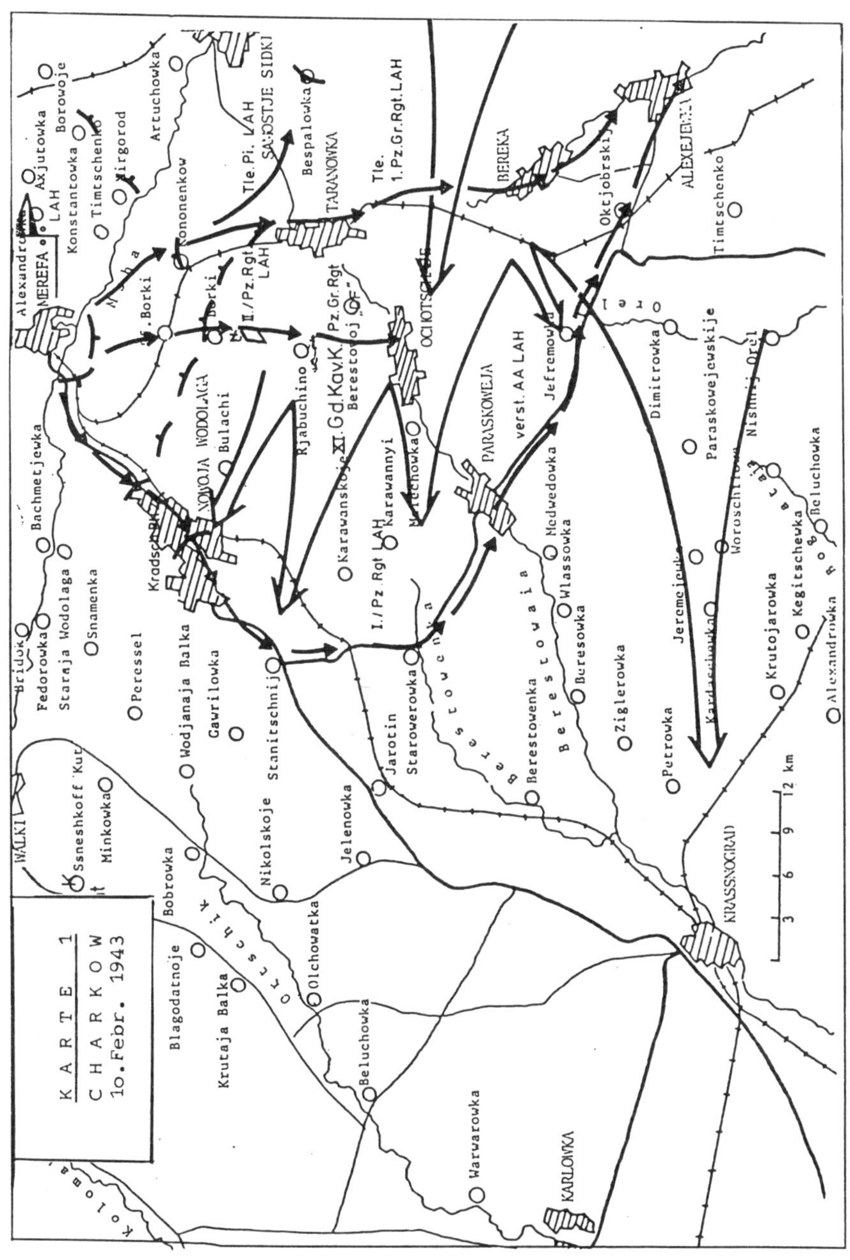
KARTE 1
CHARKOW
1o.Febr. 1943
MEREFA
NOWOJA WODOLAGA
Kradschützen
TARANOWKA
OCHOTSCHAJE
PARASKOWEJA
BEREKA
ALEXEJEWKA
KRASSNOGRAD
KARLOWKA
WALKI
I./Pz.Rgt LAH
II./Pz.Rgt LAH
Tle.Pi. LAH
Tle. 1.Pz.Gr.Rgt.LAH
verst. AA LAH
XI. Gd.Kav.K.
3 6 9 12 km

MAP 1

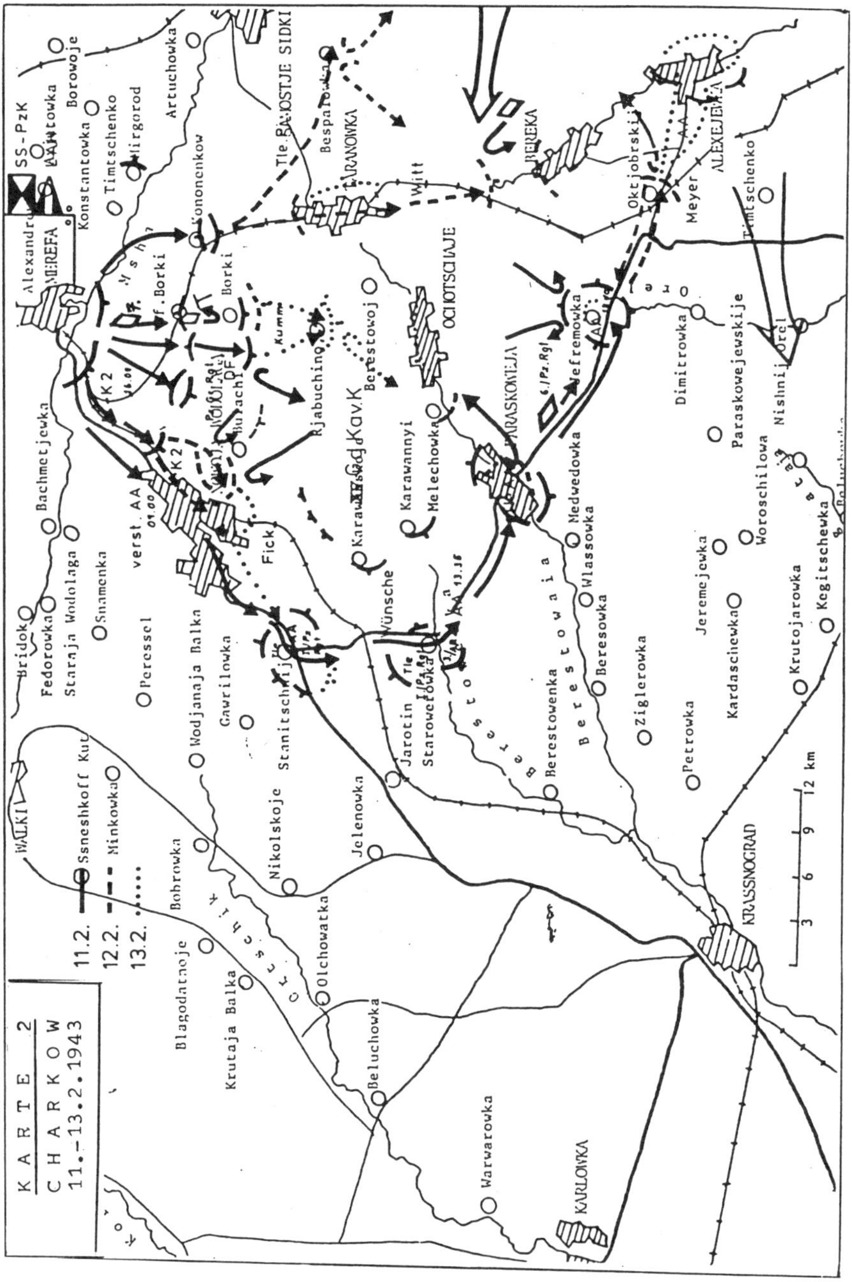

MAP 2

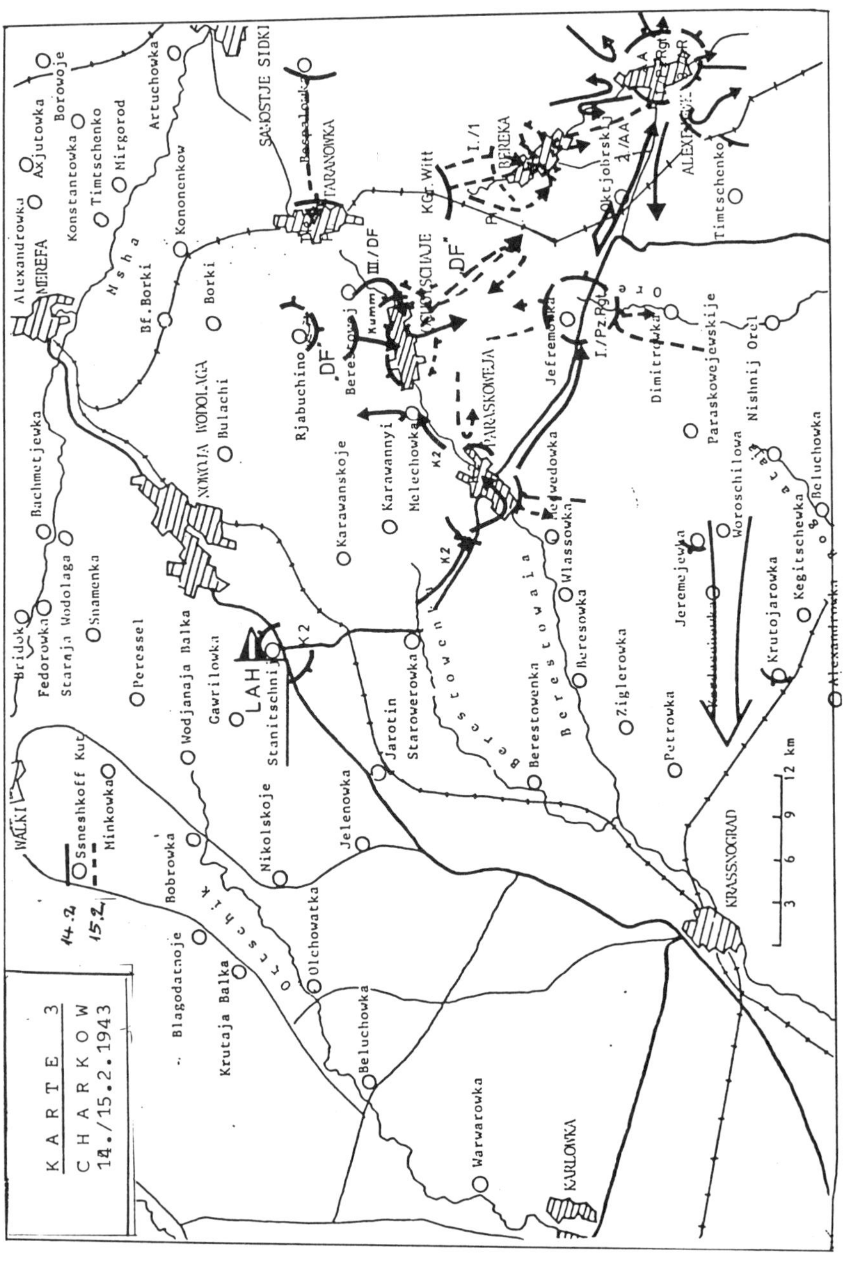
KARTE 3
CHARKOW
14./15.2.1943
Walki
Ssneshkoff Kut
Minkowka
14.2
15.2
Bobrowka
Blagodatnoje
Krutaja Balka
Olchowatka
Nikolskoje
Jelenowka
Beluchowka
Warwarowka
Karlowka
Bridok
Fedorowka
Staraja Wodolaga
Snamenka
Peressel
Wodjanaja Balka
Gawrilowka
LAH
Stanitschnij
K2
Jarotin
Starowerowka
Bachmetjewka
Nowoja Wodolaga
Bulachi
Karawanskoje
Karawannyi
Melechowka
Merefa
Alexandrowka
Konstantowka
Axjutowka
Timtschenko
Borowoje
Mirgorod
Artuchowka
Kononenkow
Bf. Borki
Borki
Msha
Rjabuchino
Berestowoj
DF
III./DF
Taranowka
Sawostje Sidki
Bereka
Parasskoweja
Jefremowka
I./Pz.Rgt.
Medwedowka
Wlassowka
Beresowka
Berestowenka
Ziglerowka
Petrowka
Jeremejewka
Dimitrowka
Paraskowejewskije
Nishnij Orel
Woroschilowa
Beluchowka
Kegitschewka
Krutojarowka
Krassnograd
Oktjobrskij
Timtschenko
3 6 9 12 km

MAP 3

MAP 4

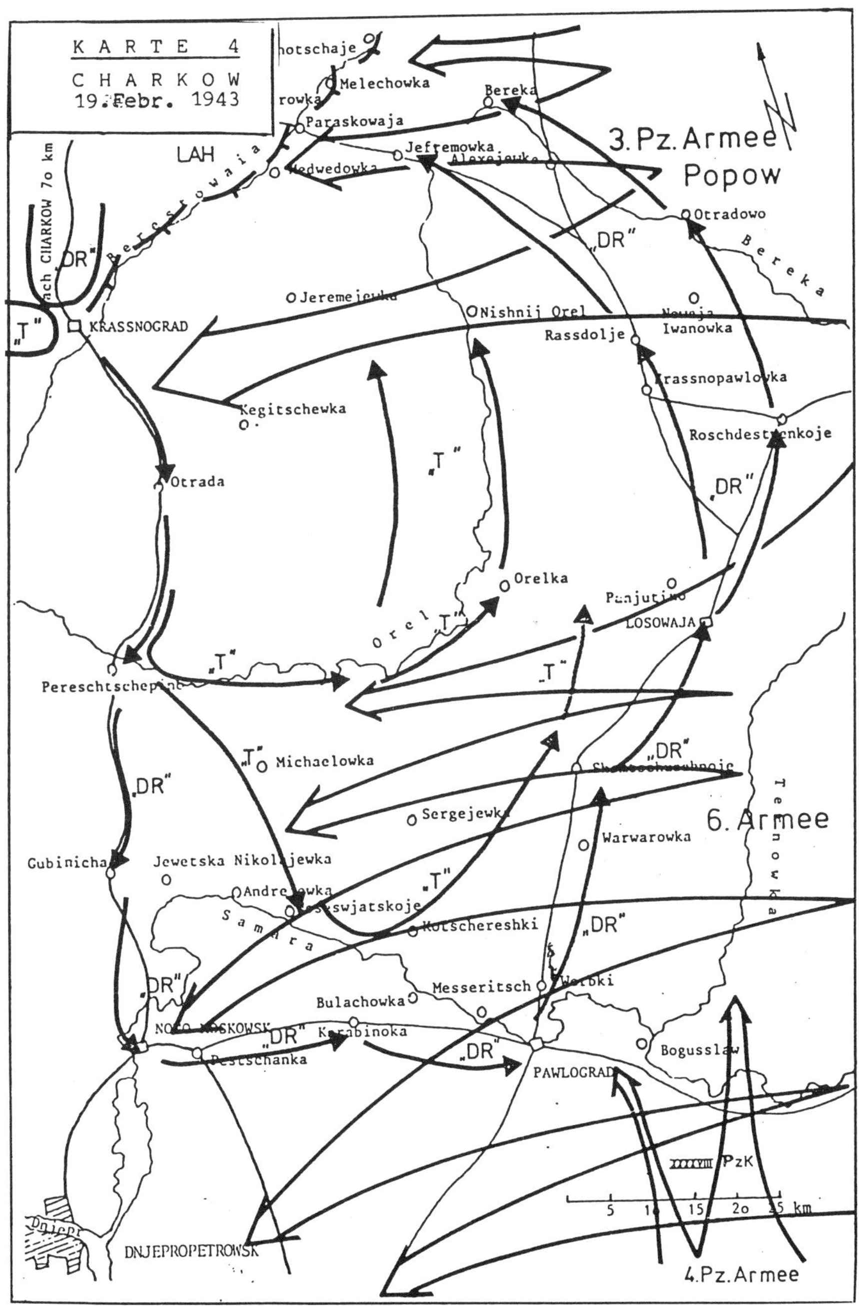
KARTE 4
CHARKOW
19. Febr. 1943
Melechowka
Bereka
Paraskowaja
Jefremowka
LAH
3. Pz. Armee
Popow
Otradowo
Bereka
"DR"
Jeremejewka
Nishnij Orel
Rassdolje
Iwanowka
KRASSNOGRAD
"T"
Kegitschewka
Krassnopawlowka
Roschdestwenkoje
"T"
Otrada
"DR"
Orelka
LOSOWAJA
Orel
Pereschtschepino
Michaelowka
"DR"
Sergejewka
6. Armee
Warwarowka
Gubinicha
Jewetska Nikolajewka
Kotschereshki
Samara
Messeritsch
Bulachowka
Werbki
Karabinoka
Bogusslaw
PAWLOGRAD
PzK
5 10 15 2o 25 km
DNJEPROPETROWSK
Dnjepr
4. Pz. Armee

MAP 5

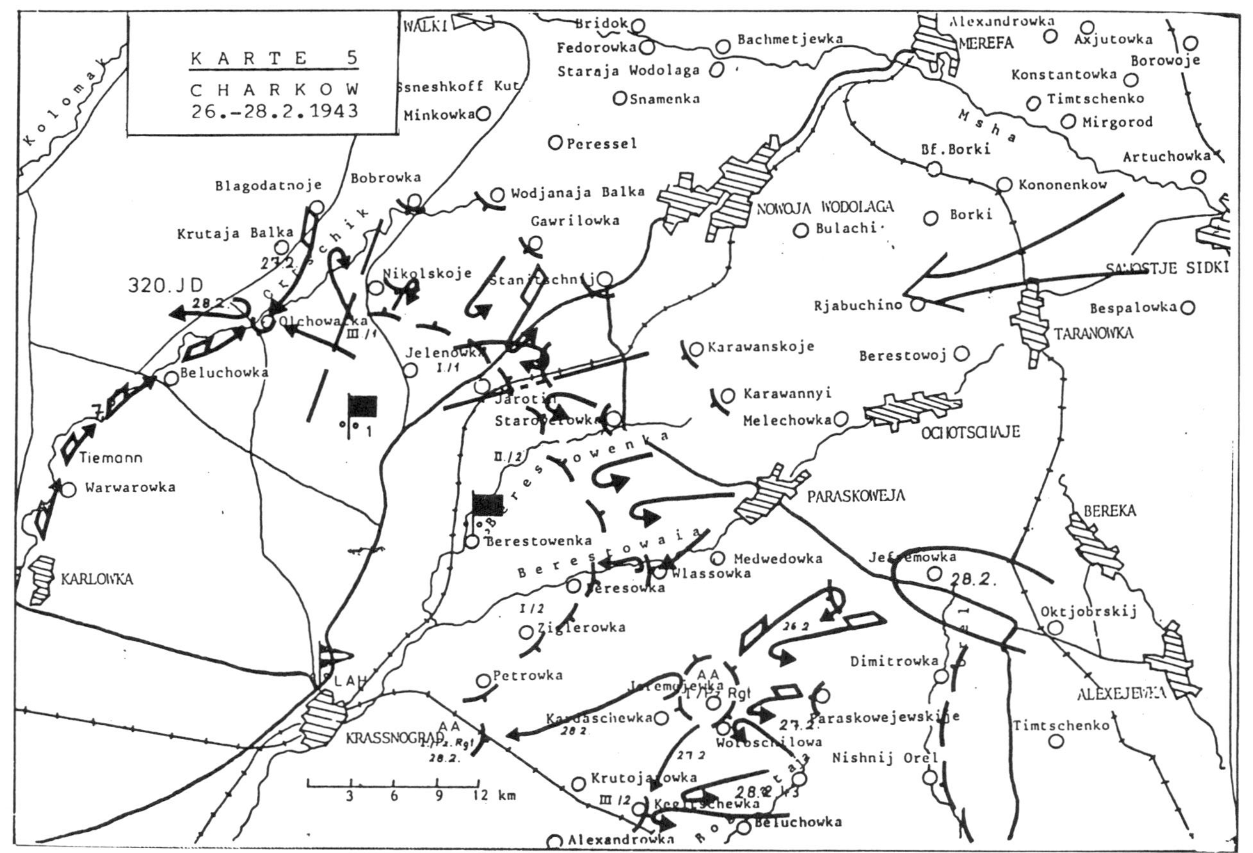
KARTE 5
CHARKOW
26.-28.2.1943
Kolomak
WALKI
Ssneshkoff Kut
Minkowka
Bridok
Fedorowka
Staraja Wodolaga
Snamenka
Bachmetjewka
Peressel
Alexandrowka
MEREFA
Axjutowka
Borowoje
Konstantowka
Timtschenko
Mirgorod
Msha
Bf. Borki
Artuchowka
Kononenkow
Borki
NOWOJA WODOLAGA
Bulachi
Blagodatnoje
Bobrowka
Wodjanaja Balka
Gawrilowka
Krutaja Balka
320. J D
Nikolskoje
Rjabuchino
Bespalowka
TARANOWKA
Olchowatka
Jelenowka
Beluchowka
Karawanskoje
Berestowoj
Karawannyi
Melechowka
OCHOTSCHAJE
Tiemann
Warwarowka
PARASKOWEJA
BEREKA
Berestowenka
Medwedowka
Wlassowka
Jefremowka
28.2.
KARLOWKA
Ziglerowka
Oktjobrskij
Dimitrowka
Petrowka
LAH
KRASSNOGRAD
Kardaschewka
Paraskowejewskije
Woroschilowa
Nishnij Orel
ALEXEJEWKA
Timtschenko
Krutojarowka
Beluchowka
Alexandrowka
3 6 9 12 km

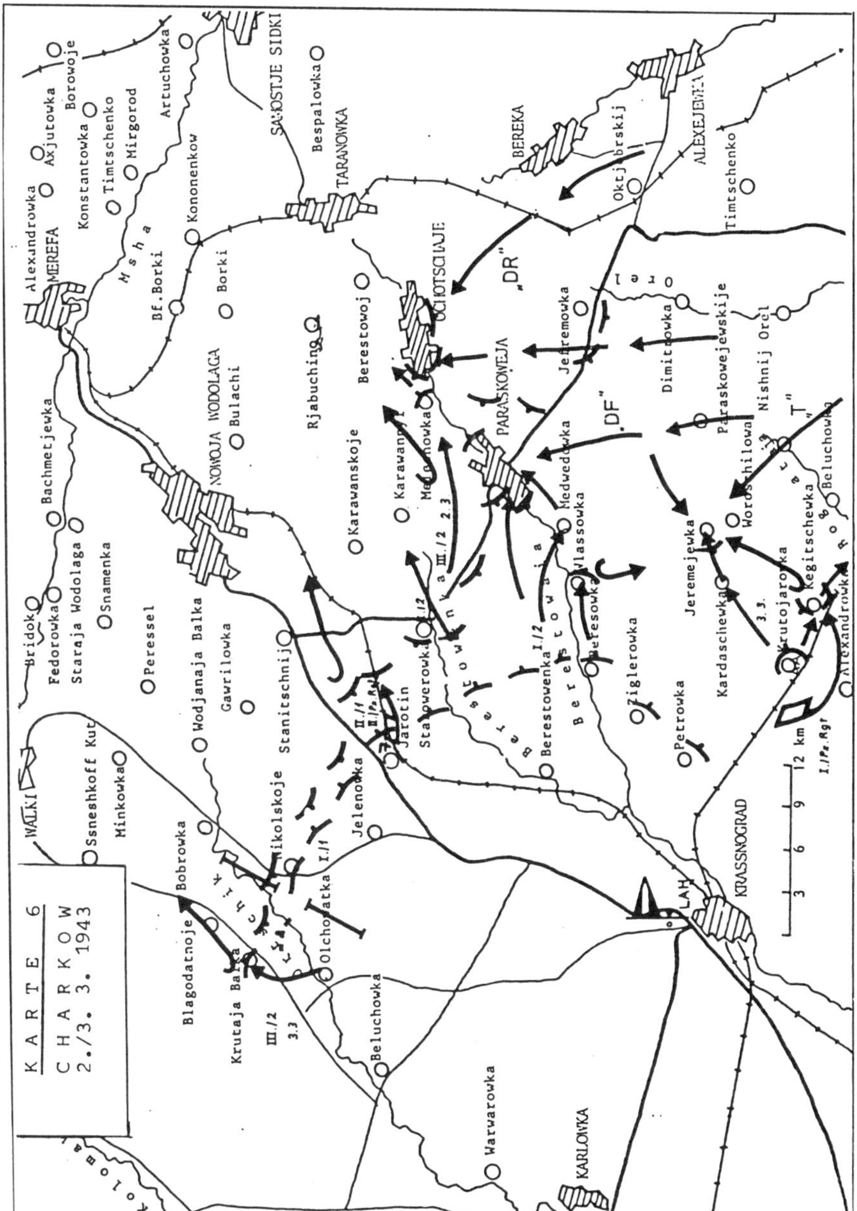
KARTE 6
CHARKOW
2./3. 3. 1943
MEREFA
NOWOJA WODOLAGA
OCHOTSCHAJE
PARASKOWEJA
TARANOWKA
BEREKA
ALEXEJEWKA
KRASSNOGRAD
KARLOWKA
WALKI
"DR"
"DF"
"T"
Alexandrowka
Konstantowka
Timtschenko
Mirgorod
Axjutowka
Borowoje
Artuchowka
Kononenkow
Bespalowka
Bf. Borki
Borki
Bulachi
Rjabuching
Berestowoj
Jefremowka
Dimitrowka
Paraskowejewskije
Nishnij Orel
Oktjabrskij
Bachmetjewka
Staraja Wodolaga
Fedorowka
Bridok
Snamenka
Peressel
Wodjanaja Balka
Gawrilowka
Stanitschnij
Karawanskoje
Medwedowka
Wlassowka
Ziglerowka
Petrowka
Berestowenka
Jeremejewka
Kardaschewka
Krutojarowka
Kegitschewka
Beluchowka
Ssneshkoff Kut
Minkowka
Nikolskoje
Jelenowka
Jarotin
Bobrowka
Blagodatnoje
Krutaja Balka
Olchowatka
Warwarowka
Berestowaja
Orel
Msha
3 6 9 12 km

MAP 6

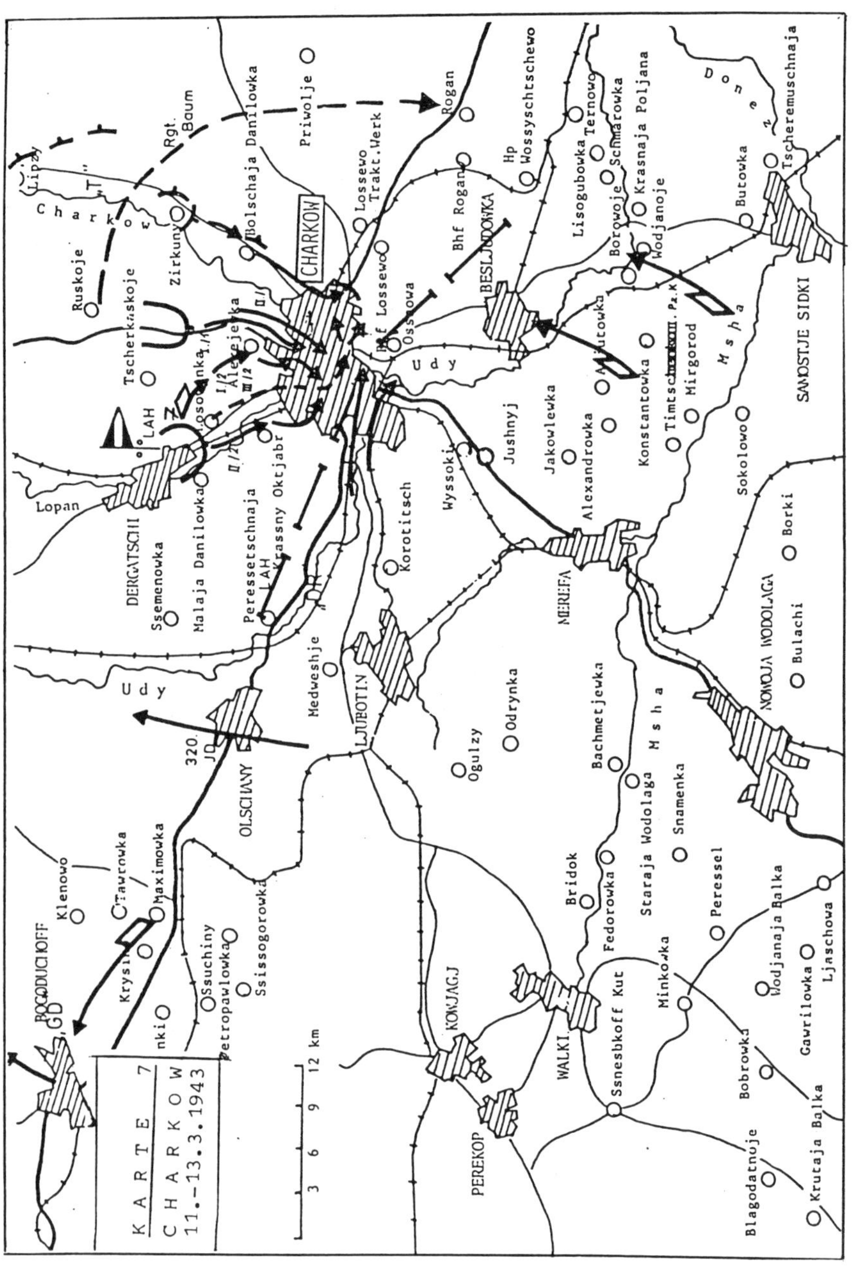
KARTE 7
CHARKOW
11.-13.3.1943
3 6 9 12 km
CHARKOW
Rogan
Priwolje
Bolschaja Danilowka
Rgt. Baum
Lipzy
Ruskoje
Zirkuny
Tscherkasskoje
LAH
Lopan
DERGATSCHI
Ssemenowka
Malaja Danilowka
Peressetschnaja
Krassny Oktjabr
Udy
320. JD
OLSCHANY
LJUBOTIN
Medweshje
Korotitsch
Wyssoki
Jushnyj
Jakowlewka
Alexandrowka
Konstantowka
MEREFA
Bhf Rogan
BESLJUDOWKA
Lisogubowka
Ternowo
Borowoje
Schmarowka
Krasnaja Poljana
Wodjanoje
Butowka
Tscheremuschnaja
Donez
SAMOSTJE SIDKI
Mirgorod
Sokolowo
Borki
NOWOJA WODOLAGA
Bulachi
Bachmetjewka
Staraja Wodolaga
Snamenka
Odrynka
Ogulzy
Bridok
Fedorowka
Peressel
Minkowka
Ssnesbkoff Kut
WALKI
KOWJAGI
PEREKOP
Bobrowka
Gawrilowka
Ljaschowa
Wodjanaja Balka
Krutaja Balka
Blagodatnoje
Klenowo
Tawrowka
Maximowka
Ssuchiny
Petropawlowka
Ssissogorowka
BOGODUCHOFF
GD

MAP 7

MAP 8

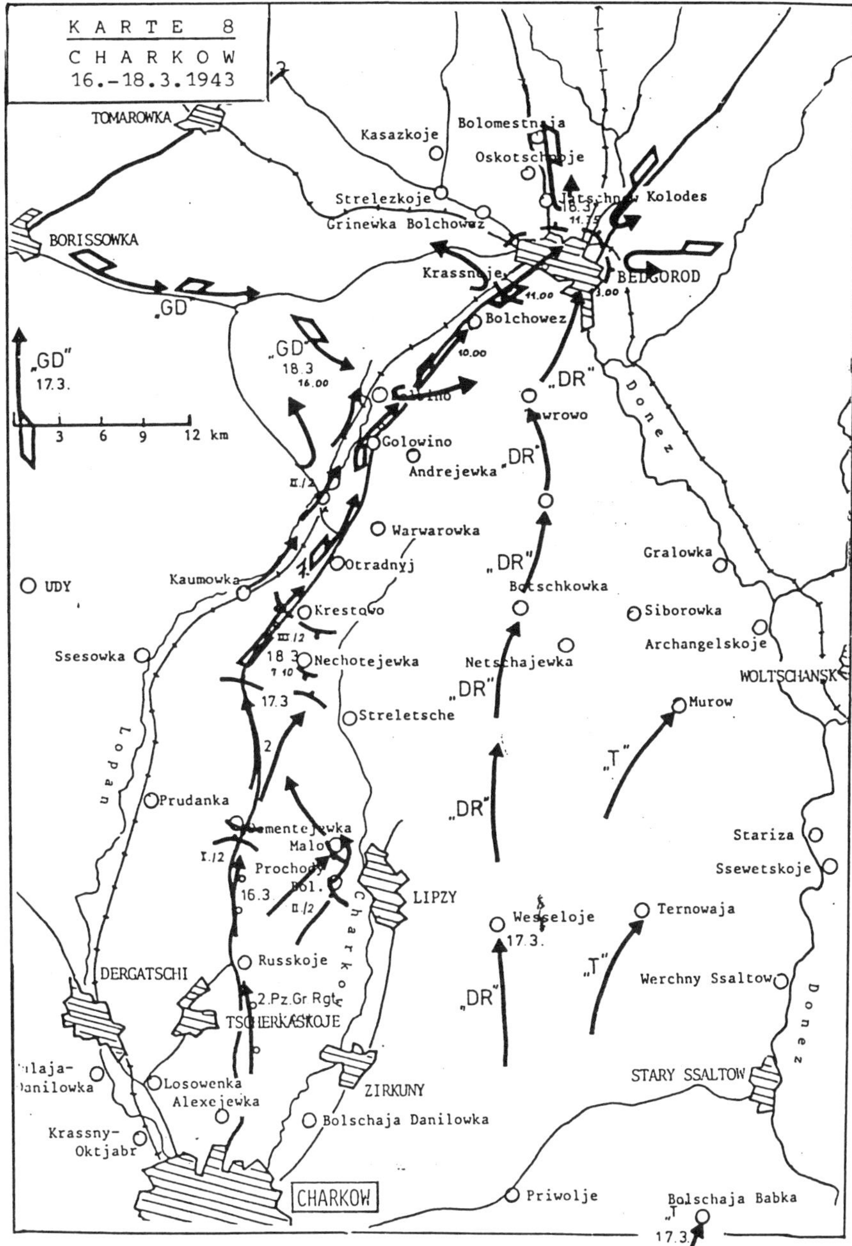
KARTE 8
CHARKOW
16.-18.3.1943
TOMAROWKA
BORISSOWKA
Kasazkoje
Bolomestnaja
Oskotschnoje
Strelezkoje
Grinewka Bolchowez
Kolodes
Krassnoje
BELGOROD
Bolchowez
„GD"
„GD" 17.3.
„GD" 18.3
3 6 9 12 km
Golowino
Andrejewka
„DR"
Warwarowka
Otradnyj
Gralowka
UDY
Kaumowka
Botschkowka
Krestowo
Siborowka
Ssesowka
Nechotejewka
Netschajewka
Archangelskoje
WOLTSCHANSK
Murow
Streletsche
„T"
Lopan
Prudanka
Dementejewka
Malo
Prochody
Bol.
16.3
LIPZY
Charkow
Stariza
Ssewetskoje
Wesseloje
17.3.
Ternowaja
Russkoje
DERGATSCHI
2.Pz.Gr.Rgt.
TSCHERKASKOJE
Werchny Ssaltow
Donez
Losowenka
Alexejewka
ZIRKUNY
STARY SSALTOW
Krassny-Oktjabr
Bolschaja Danilowka
CHARKOW
Priwolje
Bolschaja Babka
17.3.

MAP 9

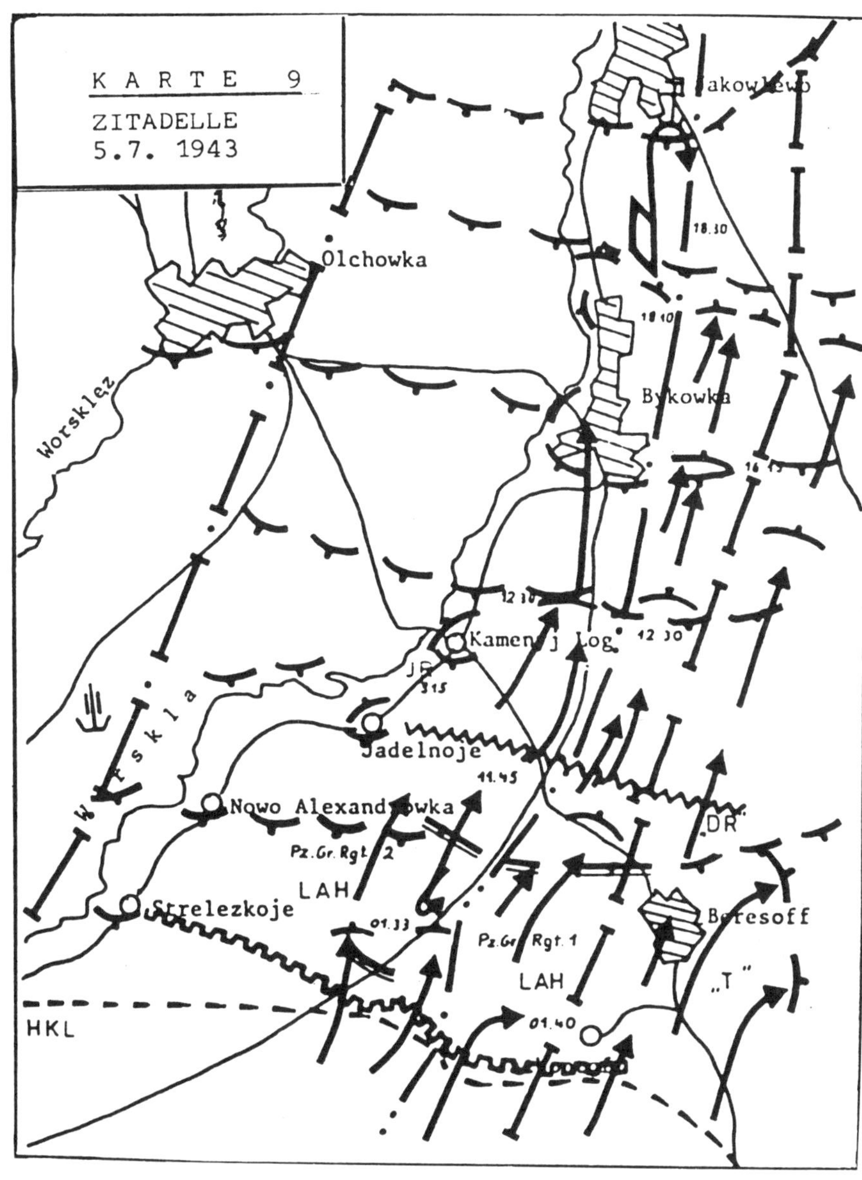
KARTE 9
ZITADELLE
5.7. 1943
Olchowka
Worsklez
Kamenyj Log
12.30
11.45
Pz.Gr.Rgt. 2
LAH
01.33
Pz.Gr. Rgt. 1
LAH
01.40
DR
"T"
HKL
18.30

MAP 10

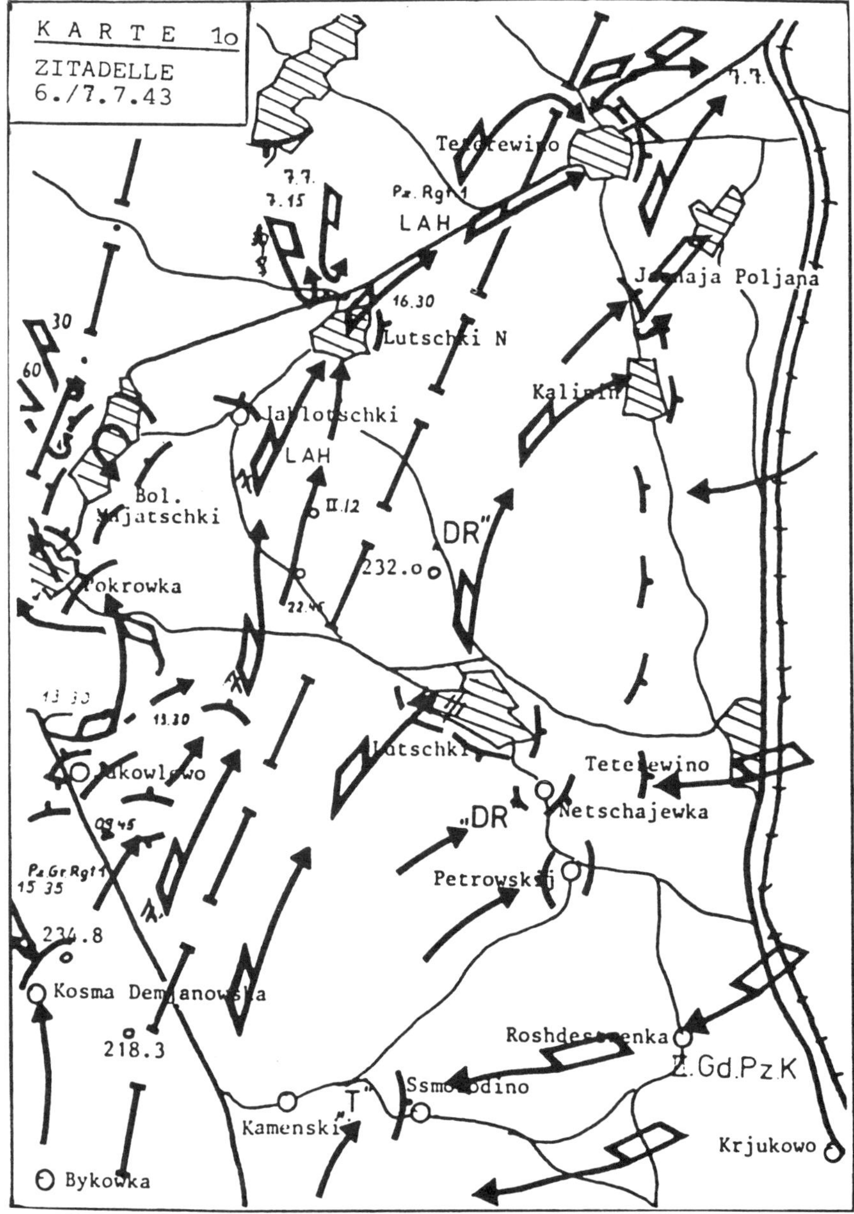
KARTE 1o
ZITADELLE
6./7.7.43
7.7.
7.15
LAH
16.30
LAH
II.12
232.o
Pokrowka
13.30
Netschajewka
"DR"
Petrowskij
Pz.Gr.Rgt1
15 35
Kamenski
"T"
2.Gd.Pz.K
Krjukowo
218.3

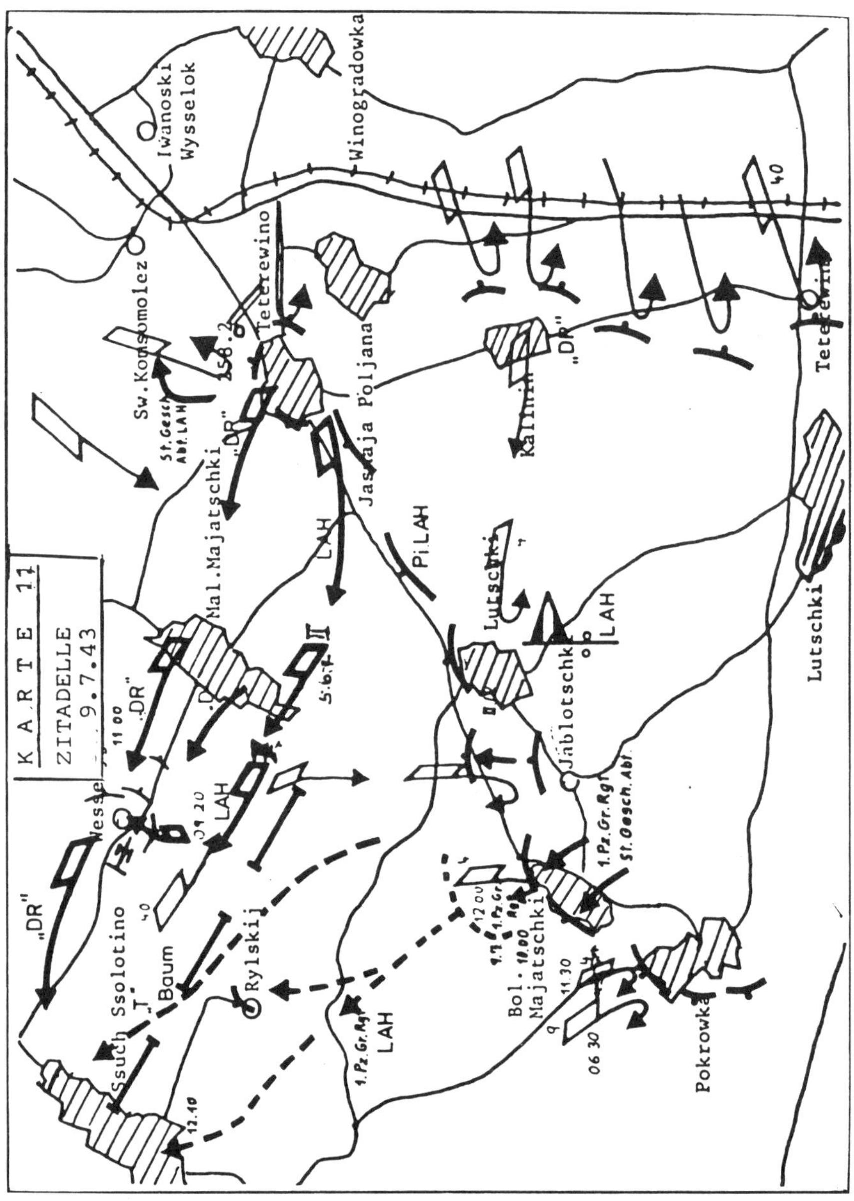
KARTE 11
ZITADELLE
9.7.43
Iwanoski
Wysselok
Winogradowka
Teterewino
Sw. Komsomolez
158.2
St.Gesch.Abt.LAH
„DR"
Jasnaja Poljana
Mal. Majatschki
LAH
Pi.LAH
Kalinin
Lutschki
Jablotschki
1.Pz.Gr.Rgt
St.Gesch.Abt.
Bol. Majatschki
Pokrowka
Rylskij
Ssuch Ssolotino
Baum
11.00
09.20
12.00
10.00
11.30
06.30
12.10

MAP 11

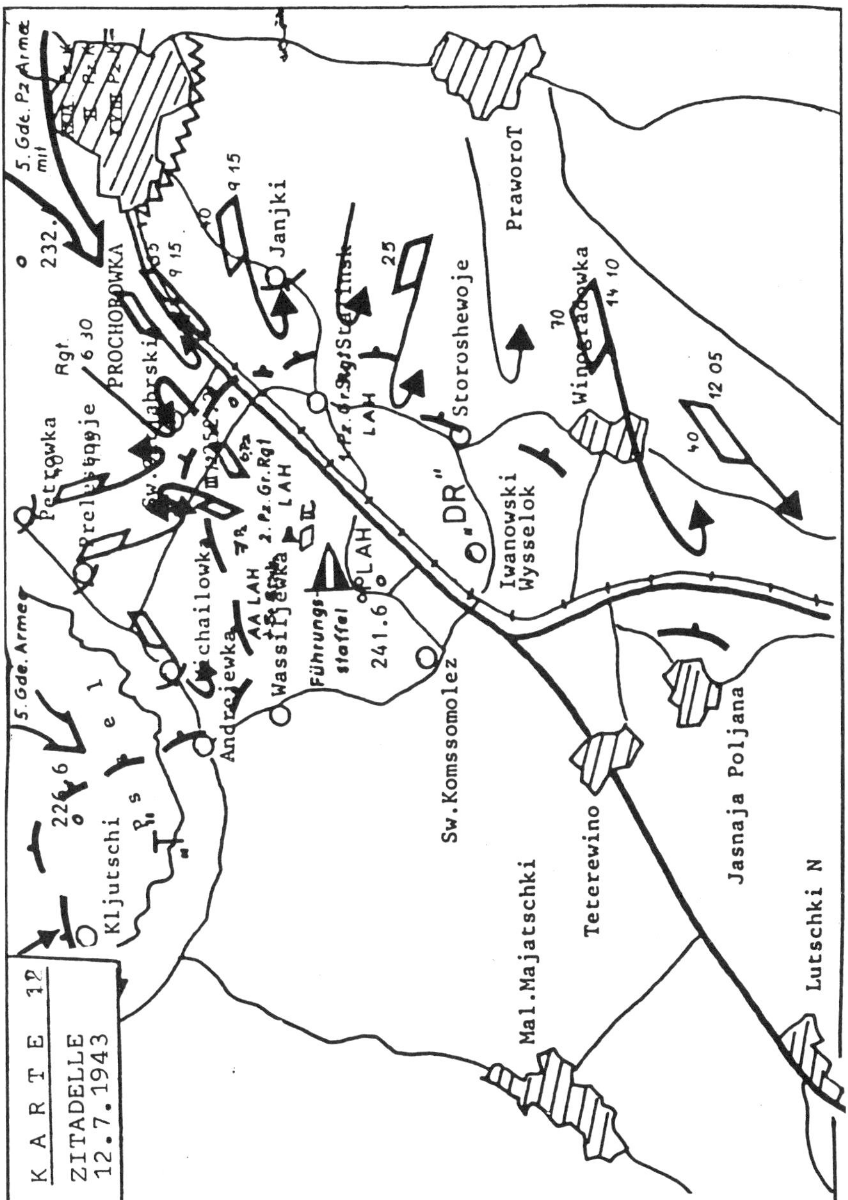
KARTE 12
ZITADELLE
12.7.1943
PROCHOROWKA
Janjki
PraworoT
Storoshewoje
Iwanowski Wysselok
Sw.Komssomolez
Teterewino
Mal.Majatschki
Jasnaja Poljana
Lutschki N
Kljutschi
Andrejewka
Petrowka
Führungs-staffel
241.6
232.
LAH
"DR"
5.Gde.Armee

MAP 12

MAP 13

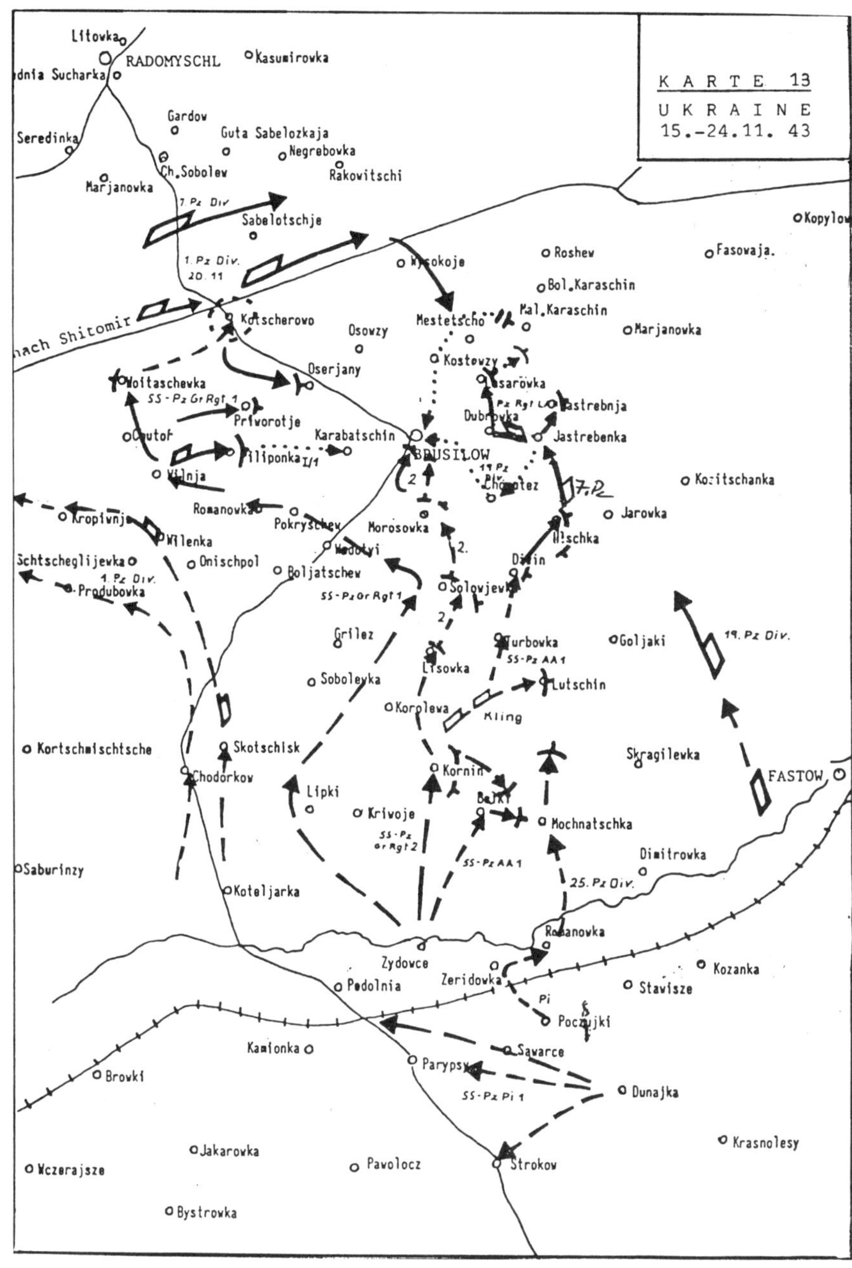
KARTE 13
UKRAINE
15.-24.11. 43
Litowka
RADOMYSCHL
Kasumirowka
Sucharka
Seredinka
Gardow
Guta Sabelozkaja
Negrebowka
Ch. Sobolew
Marjanowka
Rakowitschi
7. Pz. Div.
Sabelotschje
Kopylow
1. Pz. Div.
20. 11
Wysokoje
Roshew
Fasowaja.
Bol. Karaschin
Mal. Karaschin
Marjanowka
nach Shitomir
Kotscherowo
Osowzy
Mestetscho
Kostowzy
Oserjany
Woitaschewka
SS-Pz Gr Rgt 1
Priworotje
Jastrebnja
Dubrowka
Jastrebenka
Chutor
Karabatschin
Filiponka
BRUSILOW
Wilnja
Chomutez
Kozitschanka
Romanowka
Jarowka
Kropiwnja
Pokryschew
Morosowka
Wilenka
Schtscheglijewka
Onischpol
Boljatschew
Solowjewka
1. Pz. Div.
Produbowka
SS-Pz Gr Rgt 1
Grilez
Turbowka
SS-Pz AA 1
Goljaki
19. Pz Div.
Lisowka
Sobolewka
Lutschin
Korolewa
Kling
Kortschmischtsche
Skotschisk
Skragilewka
Chodorkow
Kornin
FASTOW
Lipki
Krivoje
SS-Pz Gr Rgt 2
Mochnatschka
SS-Pz AA 1
Dimitrowka
Saburinzy
25. Pz Div.
Koteljarka
Romanowka
Zydowce
Zeridowka
Kozanka
Pedolnia
Stawisze
Pi
Poczujki
Kamionka
Savarce
Parypsy
Browki
Dunajka
SS-Pz Pi 1
Krasnolesy
Jakarowka
Wczerajsze
Pawolocz
Strokow
Bystrowka

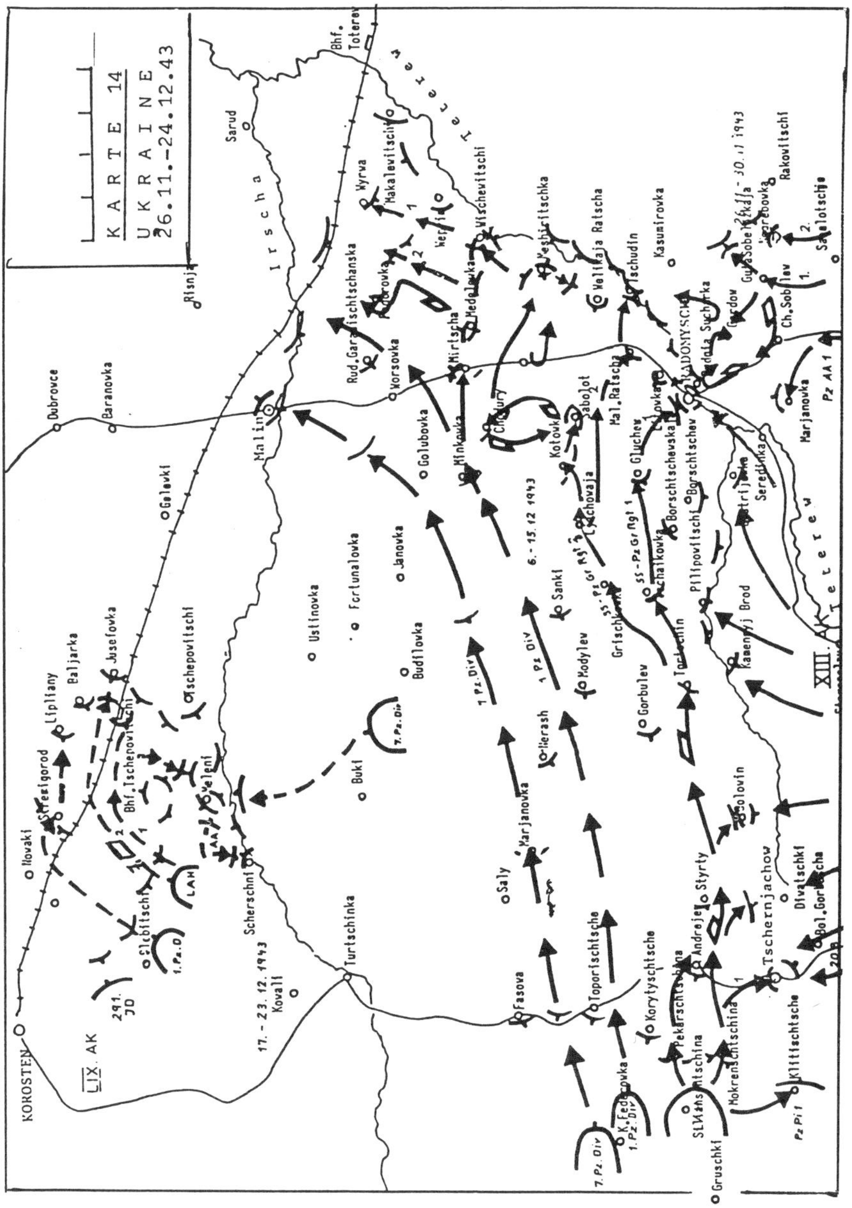
KARTE 14
UKRAINE
26.11.-24.12.43
Malin
Korosten
Turtschinka
Scherschni
Koval!
17.-23.12.1943
6.-15.12.1943
LIX. AK
XIII. AK
Teterew
Irscha
Radomyschl
Sarud
Dubrovce
Baranovka
Golovki
Ustinovka
Fortunalovka
Janovka
Budilovka
Buki
Saly
Marjanovka
Fasova
Toporischtsche
Korytyschtsche
Styrty
Tschernjachow
Gorbulev
Modylev
Sankt
Golubovka
Minkovka
Korsovka
Mirtscha
Kotovka
Gluchov
Grischin
Borschtschev
Pilipovitschi
Kamennyj Brod
Seredinka
Marjanovka
Pz AA 1
Pz Pi 1
291. ID
LAH
1. Pz. Div
7. Pz. Div

MAP 14

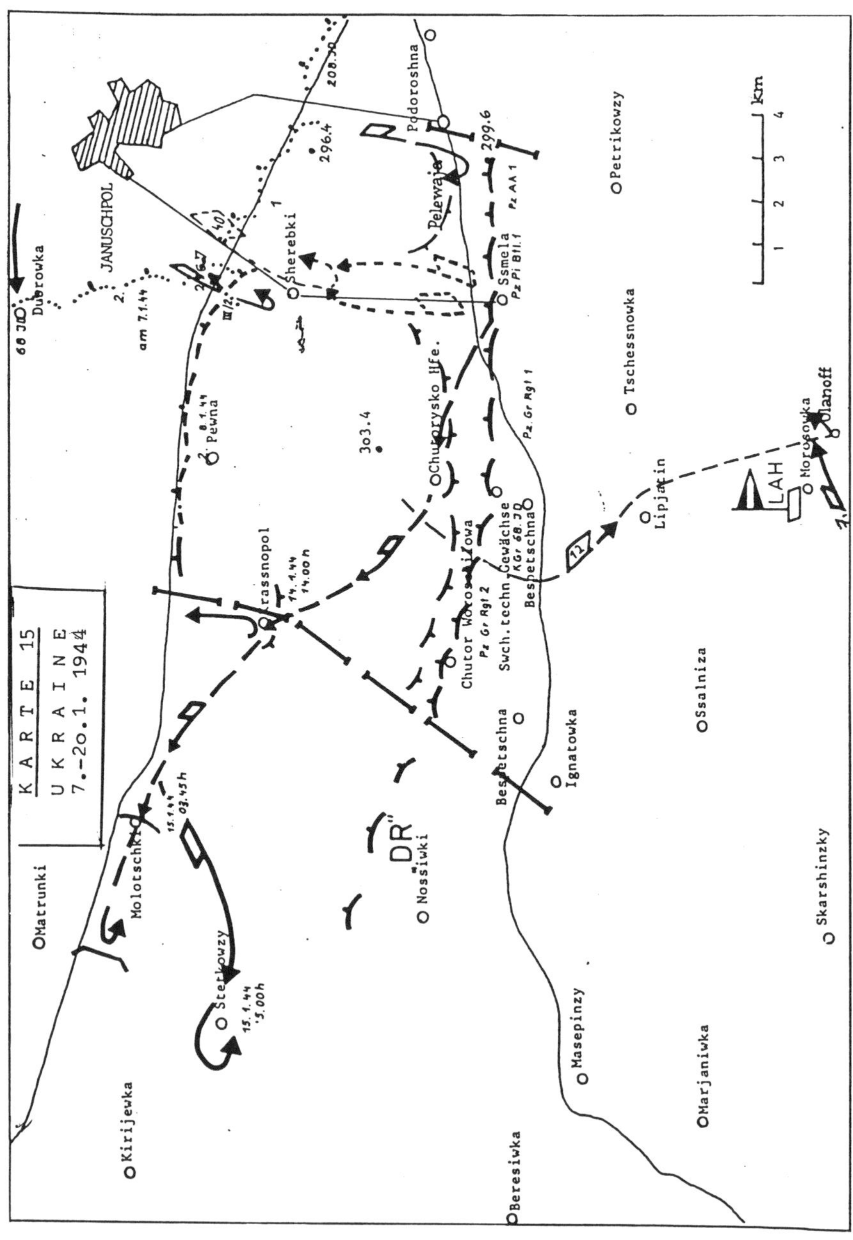

KARTE 15
UKRAINE
7.-20.1.1944
JANUSCHPOL
Dubrowka
Podoroshna
Petrikowzy
Sherebki
Pelewaja
Ssmela
Tschessnowka
Pewna
303.4
296.4
299.6
Chutor Woroschilowa
Swch.techn.Gewächse
Bespetschna
Krassnopol
Lipjatin
Morosowka
Olanoff
LAH
Ssalniza
Ignatowka
Molotschki
Matrunki
Nossiwki
"DR"
Sterkowzy
Kirijewka
Beresiwka
Masepinzy
Marjaniwka
Skarshinzky
km
1 2 3 4

MAP 15

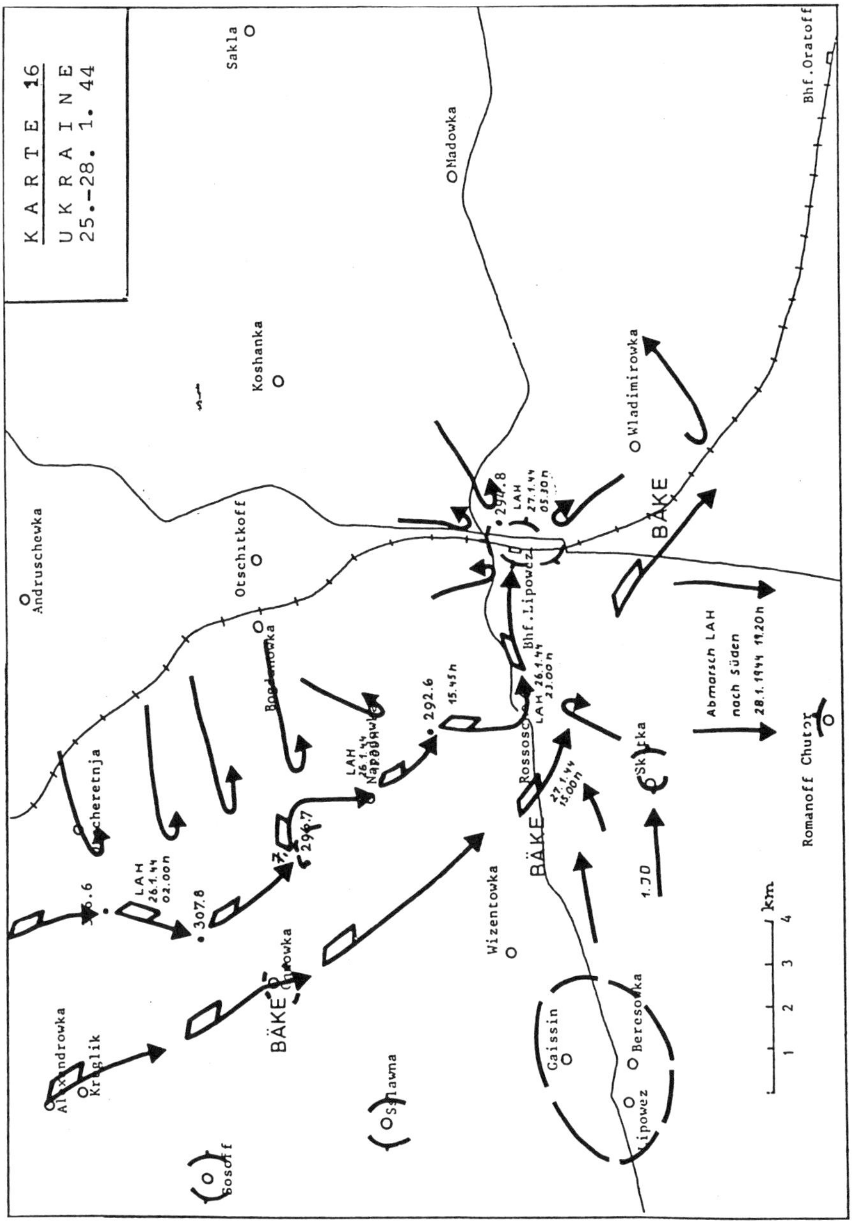

KARTE 16
UKRAINE
25.-28. 1. 44
Sakla
Madowka
Bhf. Oratoff
Koshanka
Wladimirowka
Andruschewka
Otschitkoff
BÄKE
297.8
LAH
27.1.44
05.30h
Bhf. Lipowez
LAH 26.1.44
23.00h
Abmarsch LAH
nach Süden
28.1.1944 19.20h
Romanoff Chutor
Bogdanowka
292.6
15.45h
LAH
26.1.44
Napadowka
Tscheretnja
296.7
Rossosch
27.1.44
15.00h
Skitka
BÄKE
1.JD
LAH
26.1.44
02.00h
307.8
Wizentowka
Beresowka
Gaissin
Lipowez
km
1 2 3 4
Ostrowka
BÄKE
Alexandrowka
Kruglik
Ssolawna
Sosoff

MAP 16

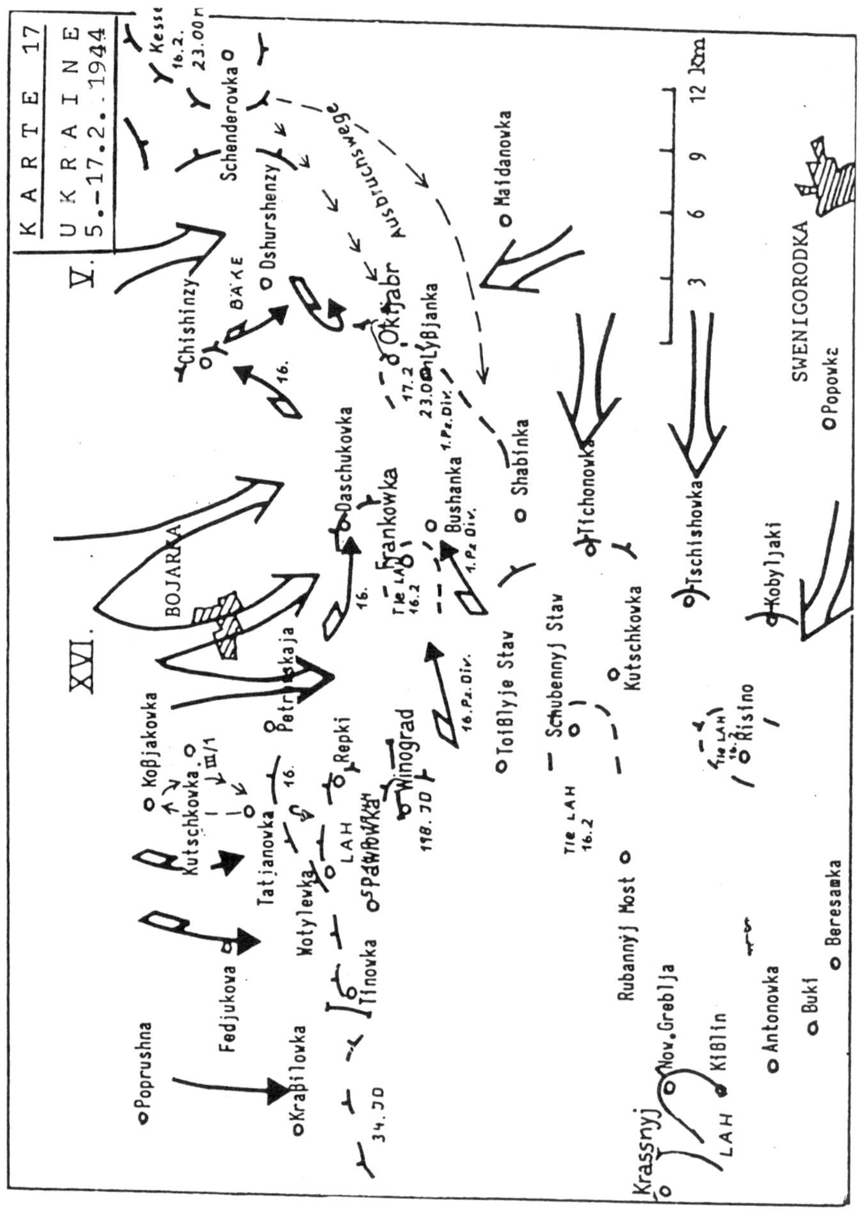
KARTE 17
UKRAINE
5.-17.2.1944
V.
XVI.
BOJARKA
SWENIGORODKA
Ausbruchswege
Schenderowka
Oshurshenzy
Chishinzy
Okijabr
Lyßjanka
Daschukowka
Frankowka
Bushanka
Shabinka
Maidanowka
Tichonowka
Tschishowka
Kobyljaki
Popowka
Petrowskaja
Repki
Winograd
Kutschkowka
Tatjanowka
Kobjakowka
Wotylewka
Tinovka
Fedjukowa
Poprushna
Krabilowka
Rubannyj Most
Beresanka
Antonowka
Buki
Nov. Greblja
Kiblin
Krassnyj
Schubennyj Stav
Tolblyje Stav
Risino
LAH
16. Pz. Div.
1. Pz. Div.
198. JD
34. JD
3 6 9 12 km

MAP 17

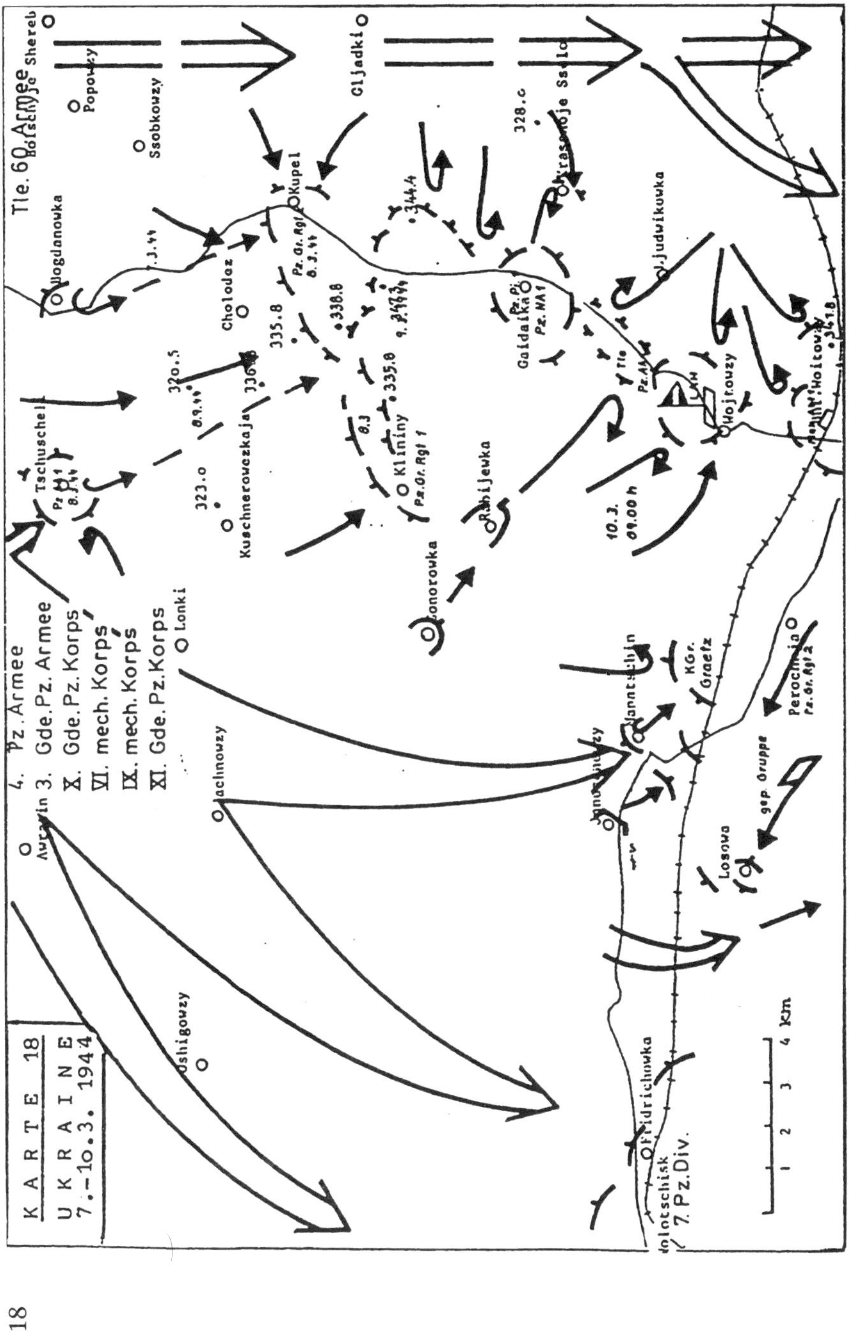

MAP 18

KARTE 18
UKRAINE
7.-1o.3. 1944

4. Pz.Armee
3. Gde.Pz.Armee
X. Gde.Pz.Korps
VI. mech.Korps
IX. mech.Korps
XI. Gde.Pz.Korps

Tle. 60 Armee

Bolschyje Shereb
Popowzy
Ssobkowzy
Bogdanowka
Tschuschel
Cholodez
Kupel
Gljadki
Lonki
Oshigowzy
Kuschnerowczkaja
Klininy
Pz.Gr.Rgt 1
Rabijewka
Gaidaika
Pz.NA1
Krasnoje Sselo
Judwikowka
Wojtowzy
Hoitowzy
Hanntschin
KGr. Graetz
Losowa
gep. Gruppe
Pz.Gr.Rgt 2
Fridrichowka
Wolotschisk
7. Pz.Div.
10.3. 09.00 h
LAH
323.o
320.5
335.8
338.8
344.4
328.c
341.8
1 2 3 4 Km

MAP 19

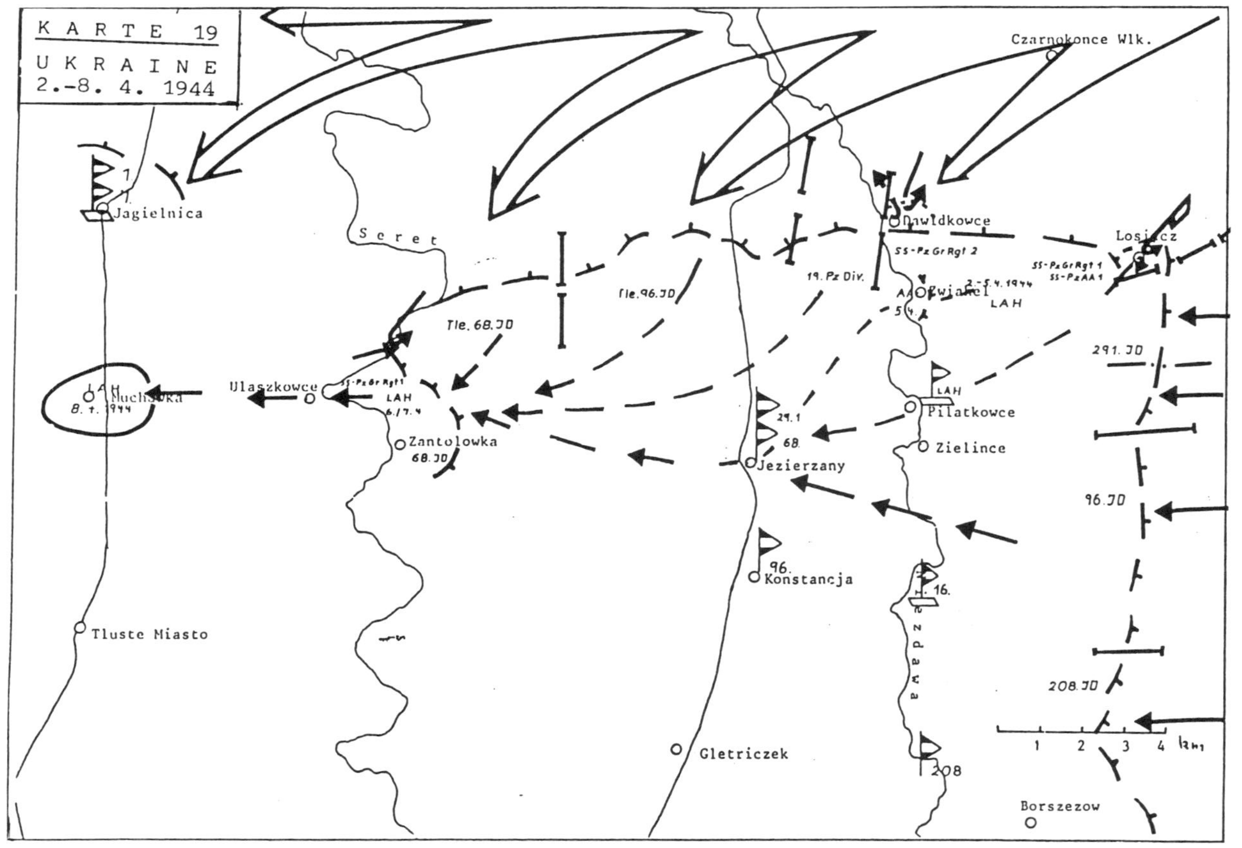
KARTE 19
UKRAINE
2.-8. 4. 1944
Czarnokonce Wlk.
Losiacz
Dawidkowce
Pilatkowce
Zielince
Jezierzany
Konstancja
Gletriczek
Borszczow
Zantolowka
Ulaszkowce
Jagielnicia
Tluste Miasto
Seret
291. JD
96. JD
208. JD
19. Pz Div.
Tle. 96. JD
Tle. 68. JD
68. JD
LAH
SS-PzGrRgt 1
SS-PzGrRgt 2
SS-PzAA 1

MAP 20

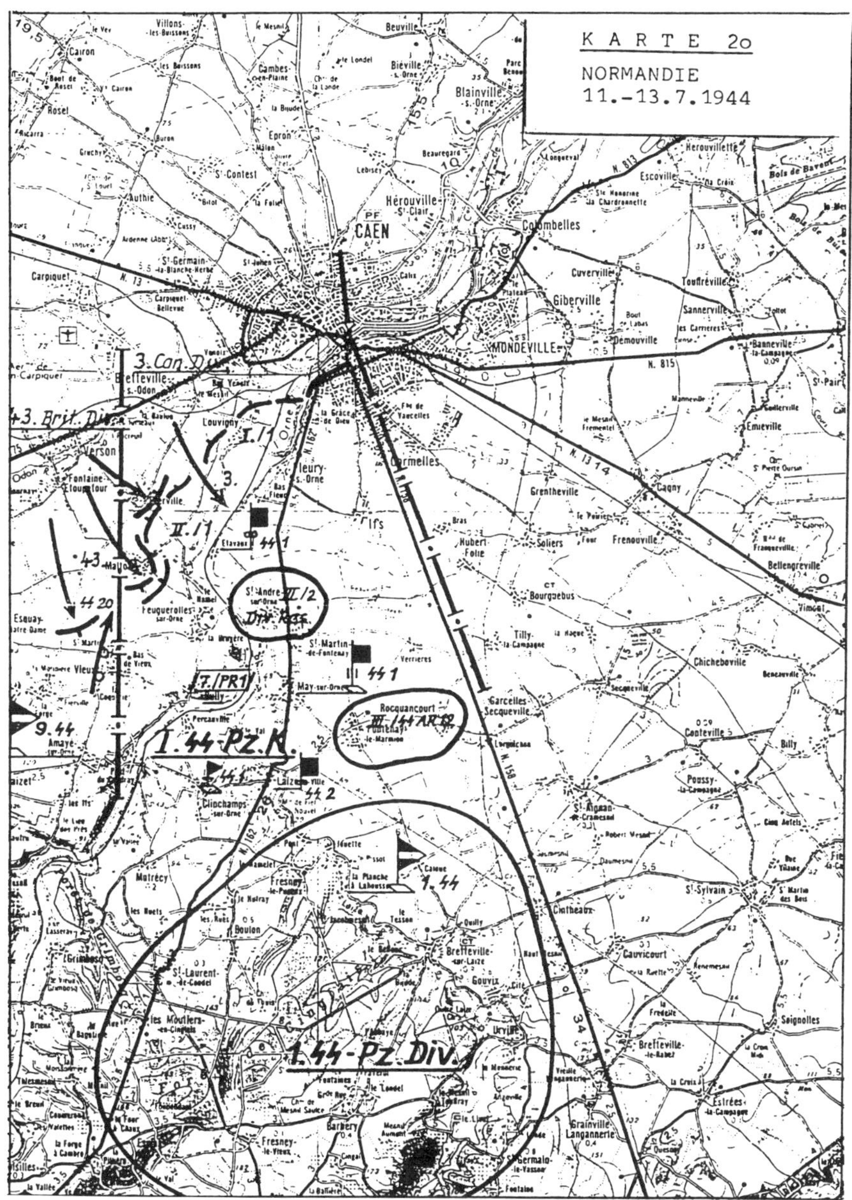
KARTE 20
NORMANDIE
11.-13.7.1944
CAEN
3. Can. Div.
43. Brit. Div.
I. 44-Pz. K.
1. 44-Pz. Div.

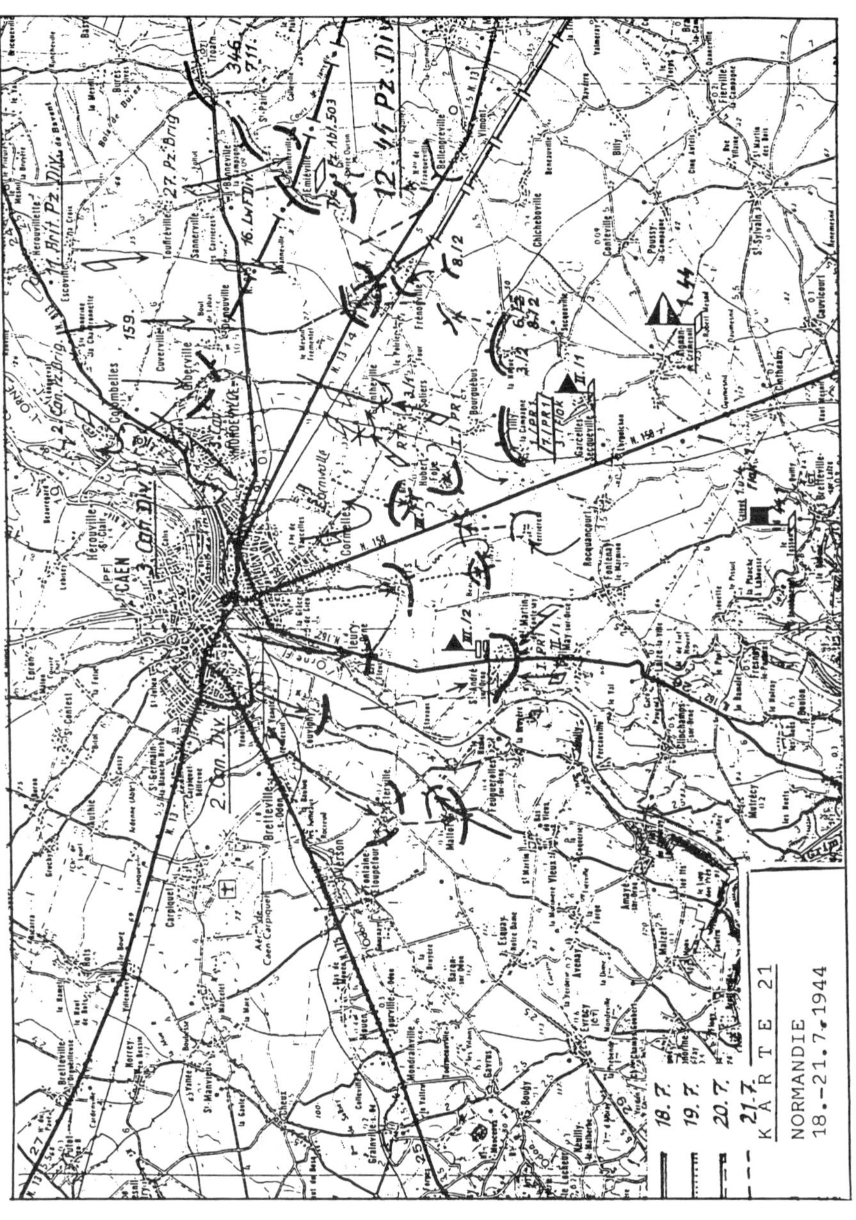

MAP 21

MAP 22

KARTE 22
NORMANDIE
6.-11.8. 1944
7.8.
8.8.
9.8.
10.8.
11.8.
3. Brit. I.D.
11. Brit. A.D.
2. US Div.
29. US Div.
28. US Div.
K. Gr. SCHILLER
4. US Div.
116. PD
84. I.D.
2. PD
9. US Div.
30. US Div.
1. US Div.
80. US Div.
90. US Div.
79. US Div.
St-Germain-de-Tallevende-la-Lande-Vaumont
St-Sever-Calvados
Vire
Mortain
Mesnil-Clinchamps

MAP 23

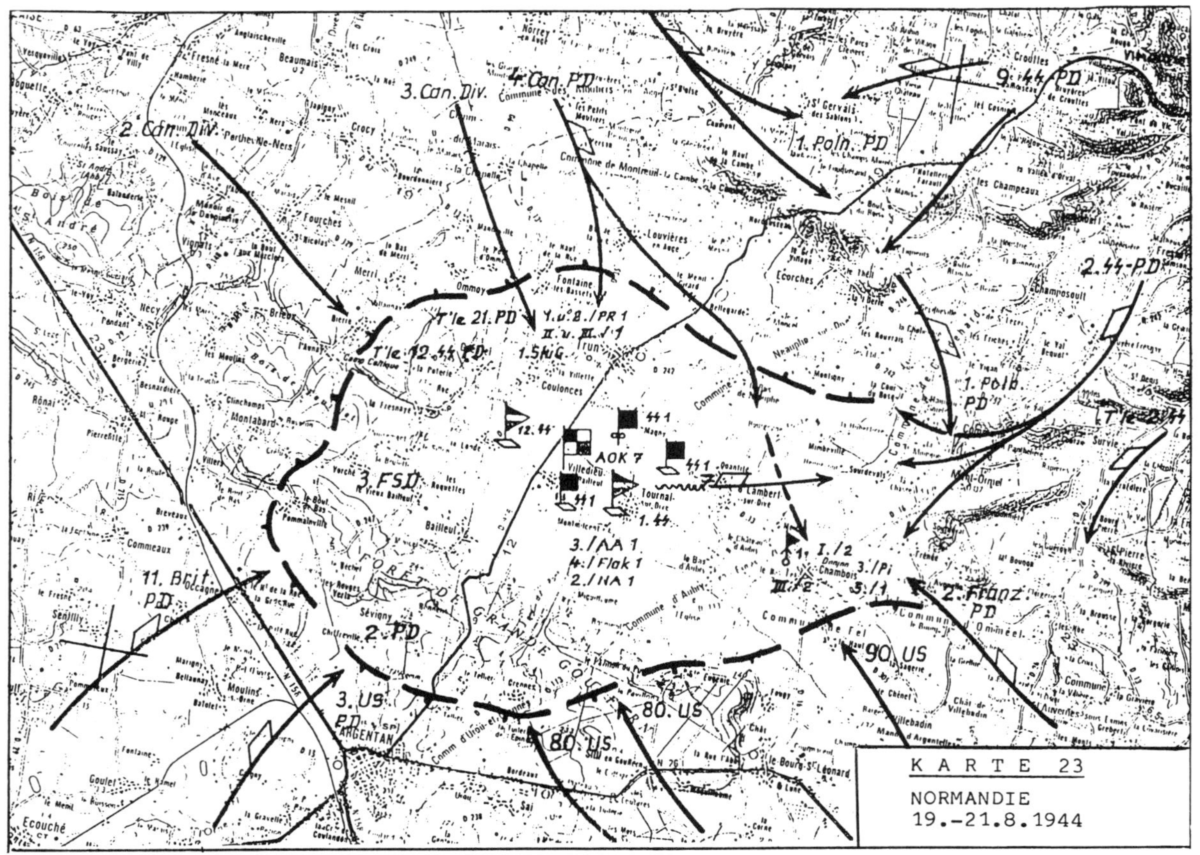
K A R T E 23
NORMANDIE
19.-21.8.1944
3.Can.Div.
4.Can.PD
2.Can.Div.
9.44.PD
1.Poln.PD
2.44-PD
1.Poln.PD
T'le 21.PD
T'le 12.44.PD
1.5.W.G.
AOK 7
3 FSD
3./AA 1
4./Flak 1
2./NA 1
3./Pi
2.Franz.PD
90.US
80.US
80.US
3.US PD
2.PD
11. Brit. PD

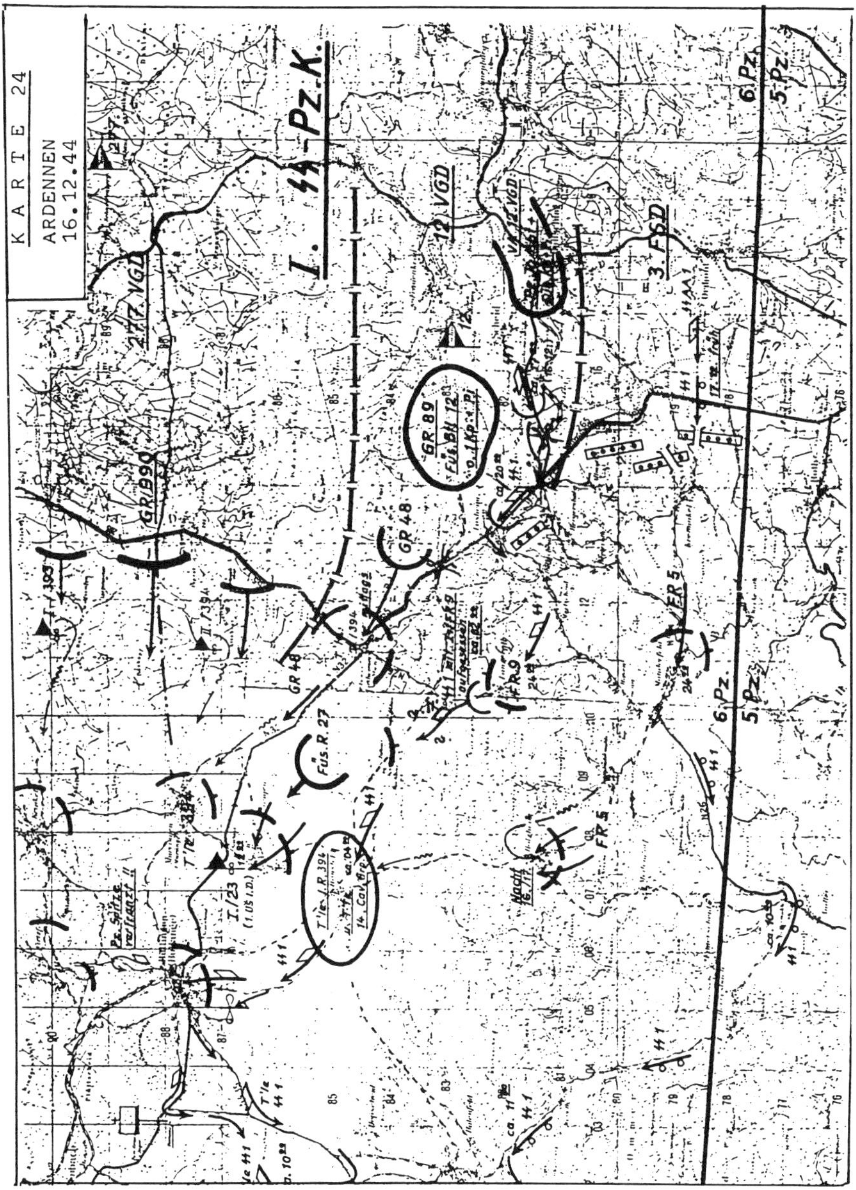
KARTE 24
ARDENNEN
16.12.44
277. VGD
12. VGD
3. FSD
GR 990
GR 48
GR 89
Füs. R. 27
6. Pz.
5. Pz.

MAP 24

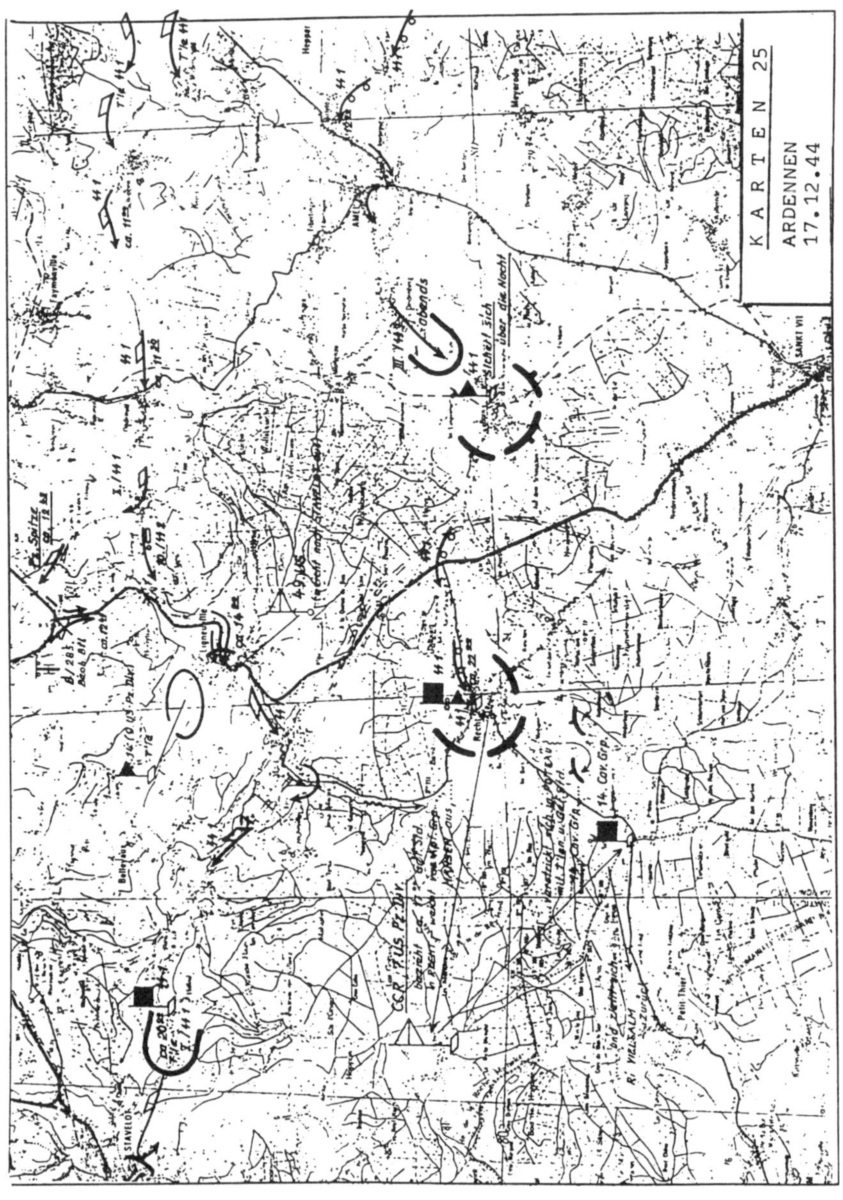

MAP 25

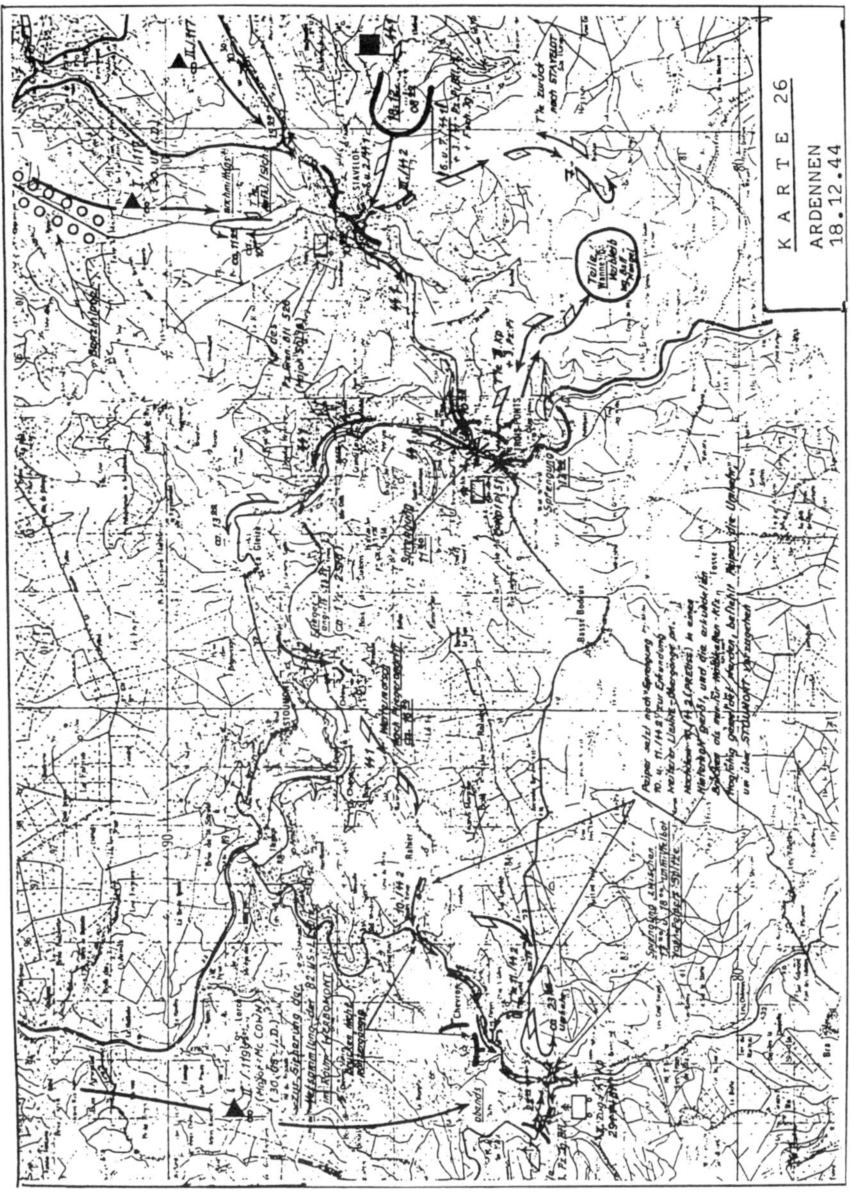

MAP 26

MAP 27

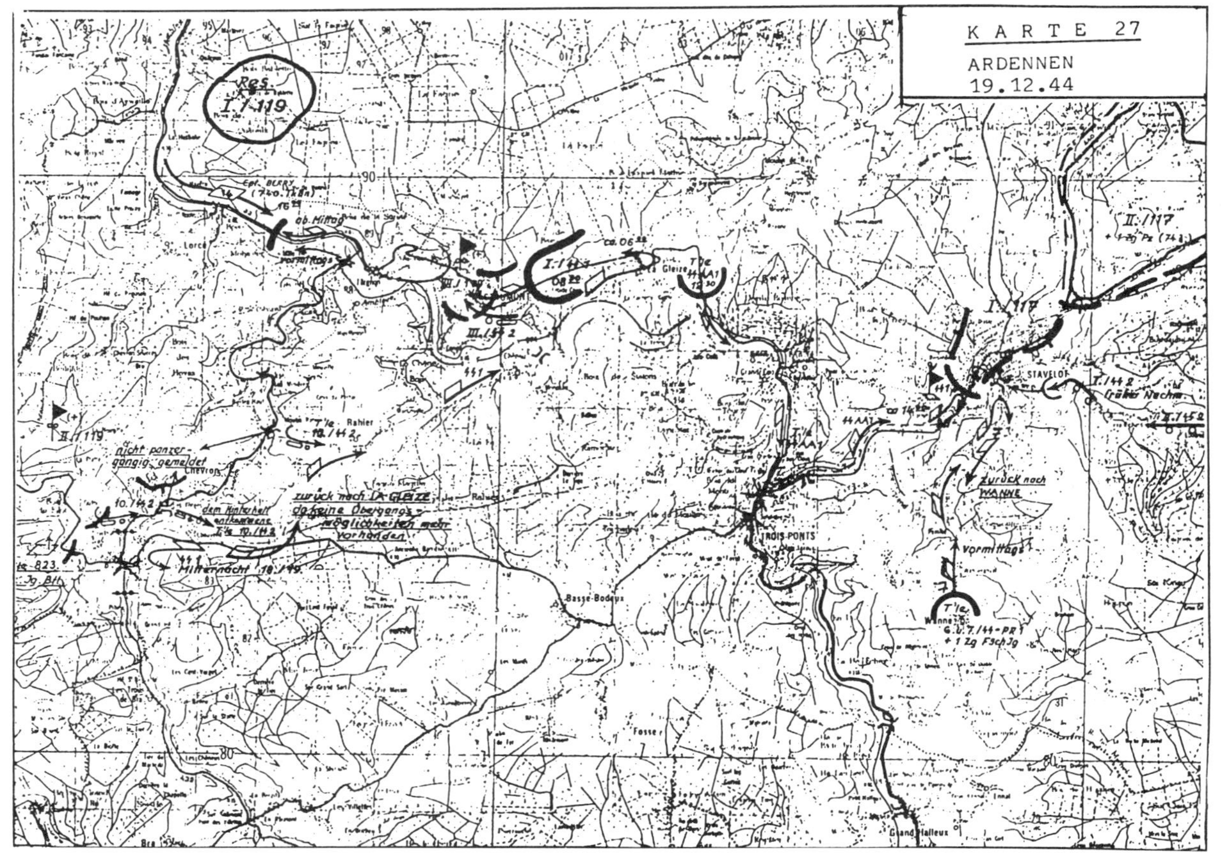
KARTE 27
ARDENNEN
19.12.44
Res.
I./119
STAVELOT
TROIS-PONTS
Basse-Bodeux
zurück nach LA GLEIZE
da keine Übergangs-
möglichkeiten mehr
vorhanden
zurück nach
WANNE
vormittags
nicht panzer-
gängig gemeldet
Mitternacht 18./19.

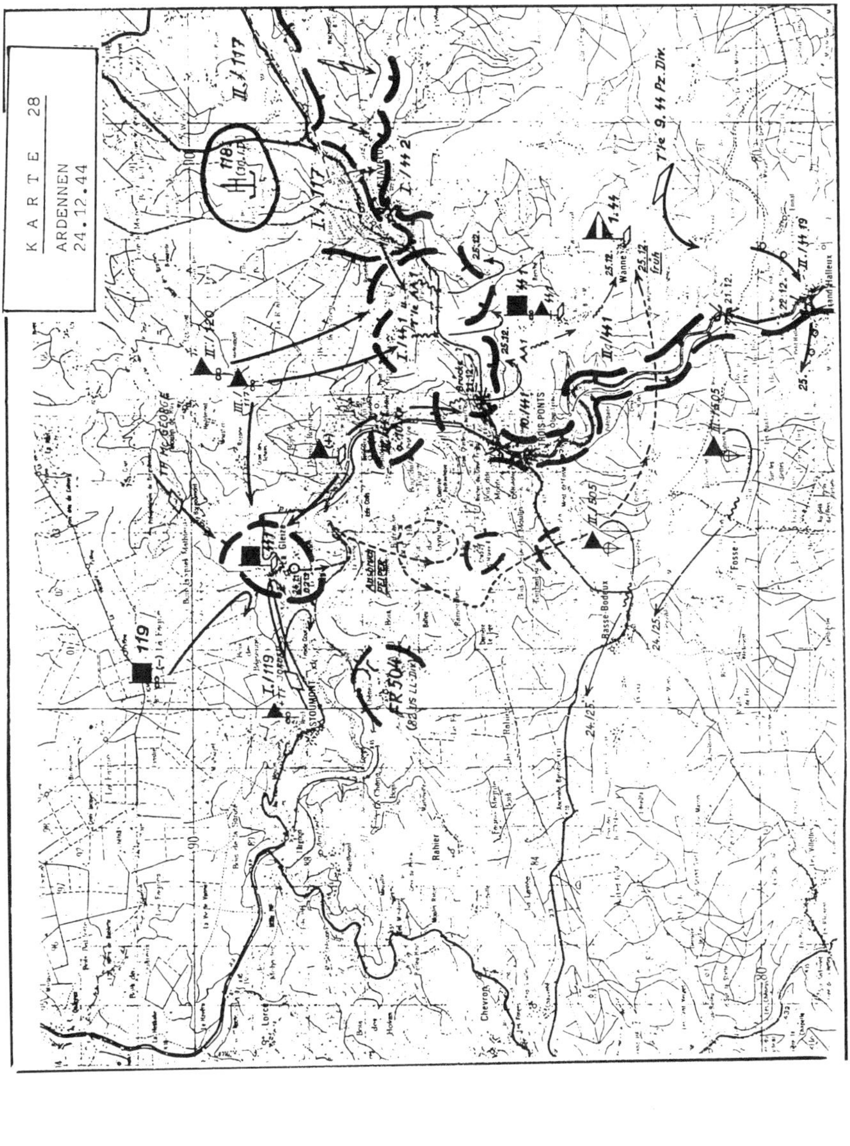

KARTE 28
ARDENNEN
24.12.44

MAP 28

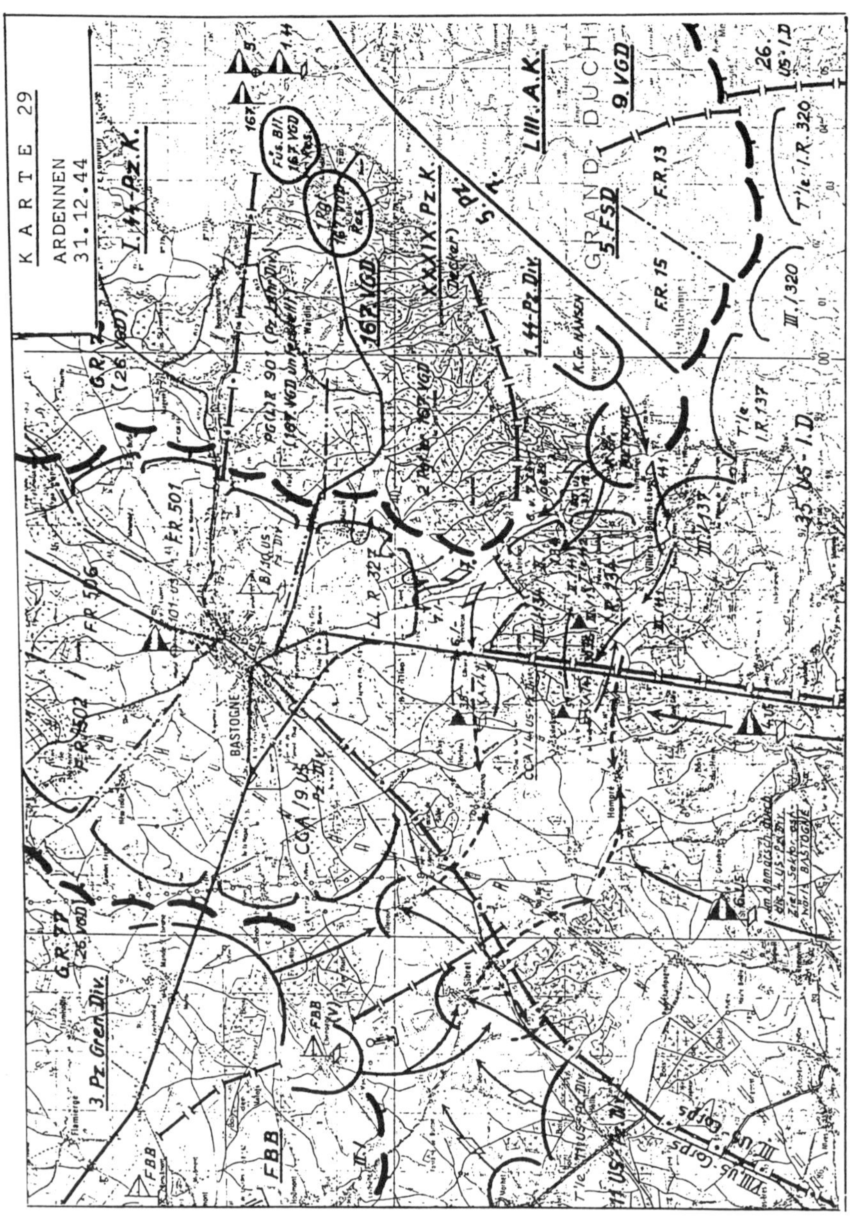

MAP 29

MAP 30

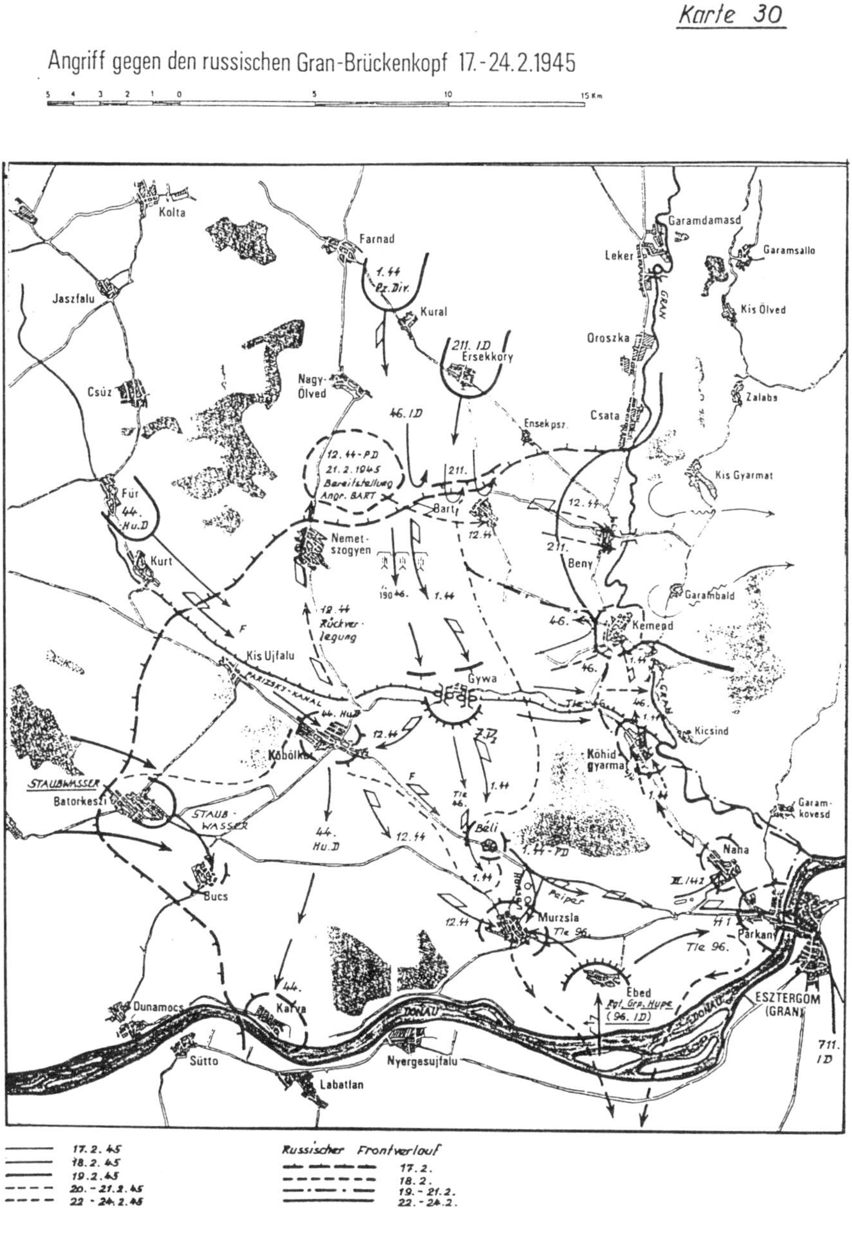

Karte 30

Angriff gegen den russischen Gran-Brückenkopf 17.-24.2.1945

Kolta
Farnad
Garamdamasd
Leker
Garamsallo
Jaszfalu
Kural
Kis Ölved
Oroszka
Ersekkory
Nagy-Ölved
Csúz
Zalaba
Csata
Ensekpsz.
Kis Gyarmat
Für
Bart
Nemet-szogyen
Beny
Kurt
Garambald
Kemend
Kis Ujfalu
Gywa
Kicsind
Köbölkut
Köhid gyarma
Batorkeszi
Garam-kovesd
Béli
Nana
Bucs
Murzsla
Parkany
Ebed
Dunamocs
Karva
ESZTERGOM (GRAN)
Sütto
Nyergesujfalu
Labatlan
DONAU

17.2.45	Russischer Frontverlauf
18.2.45	17.2.
19.2.45	18.2.
20.-21.2.45	19.-21.2.
22-24.2.45	22.-24.2.

MAP 31

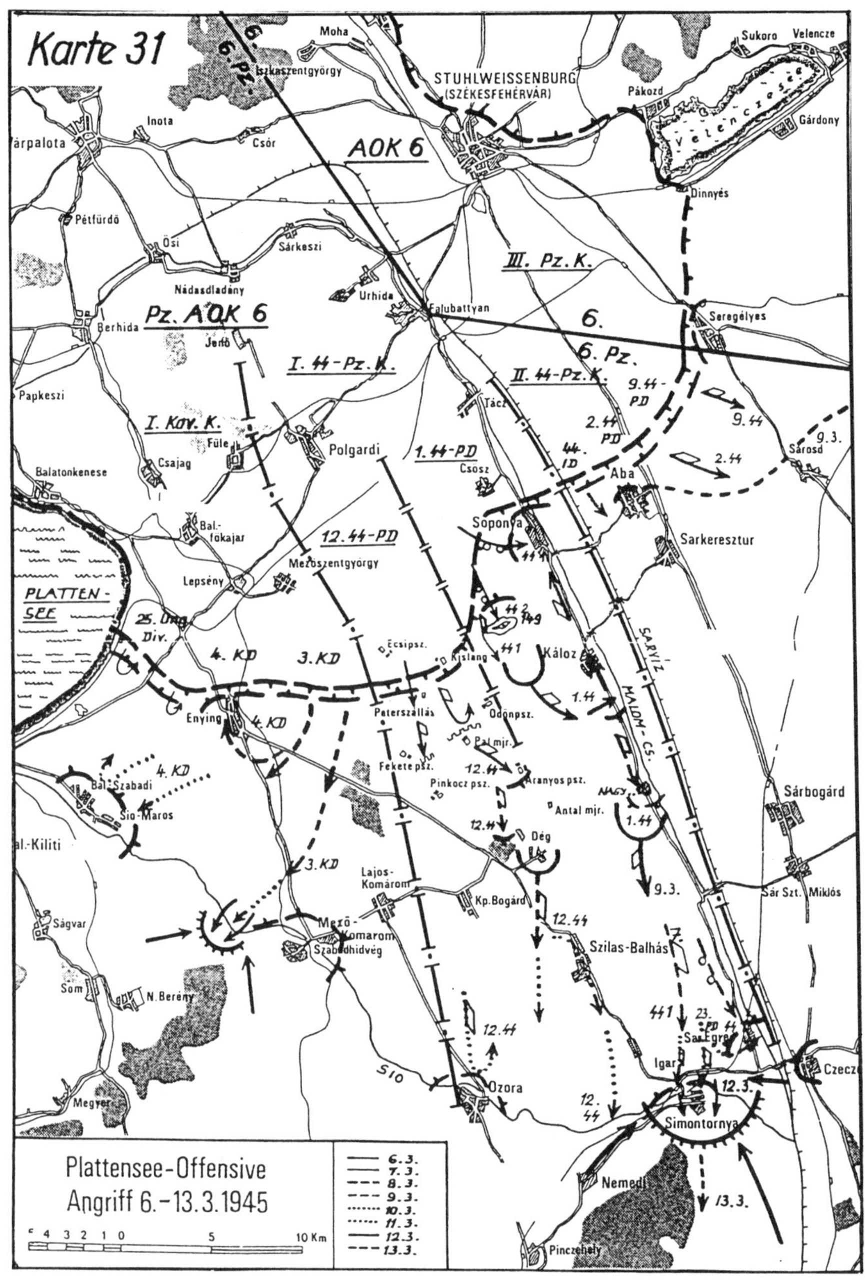
Karte 31
Moha
STUHLWEISSENBURG
(SZÉKESFEHÉRVÁR)
Sukoro
Velencze
Pákozd
Gárdony
Velenczesee
Inota
Csór
AOK 6
Dinnyés
Pétfürdö
Ösi
Sárkeszi
III. Pz. K.
Nádasdladány
Urhida
Falubattyan
Seregélyes
Pz. AOK 6
Berhida
Jenö
I. SS-Pz. K.
6.
6. Pz.
II. SS-Pz. K.
Papkeszi
Tácz
I. Kav. K.
Füle
Polgardi
1. SS-PD
Csosz
Aba
Csajag
Balatonkenese
Sopony
Bal.-fökajar
12. SS-PD
Sarkeresztur
Mezöszentgyörgy
Lepsény
PLATTEN-SEE
25. Ung. Div.
4. KD
3. KD
Ecsipsz.
Kislang
Káloz
SARVIZ
MALOM-CS.
Enying
4. KD
Peterszallás
Odönpsz.
Pal mjr.
Feketepsz.
Pinkocz psz.
Aranyos psz.
Antal mjr.
Bal. Szabadi
Sio-Maros
Dég
Sárbogárd
al.-Kiliti
3. KD
Lajos-Komárom
Kp. Bogárd
9.3.
Sár Szt. Miklós
12. SS
Ságvar
Mezö-Komarom
Szabadhidvég
Szilas-Balhás
Som
N. Berény
Sar Egres
Igar
SIO
Ozora
Czecz
Simontornya
Megyer
Nemedi
13.3.
Pinczehely
Plattensee-Offensive
Angriff 6.-13.3.1945
4 3 2 1 0 5 10 Km
6.3.
7.3.
8.3.
9.3.
10.3.
11.3.
12.3.
13.3.

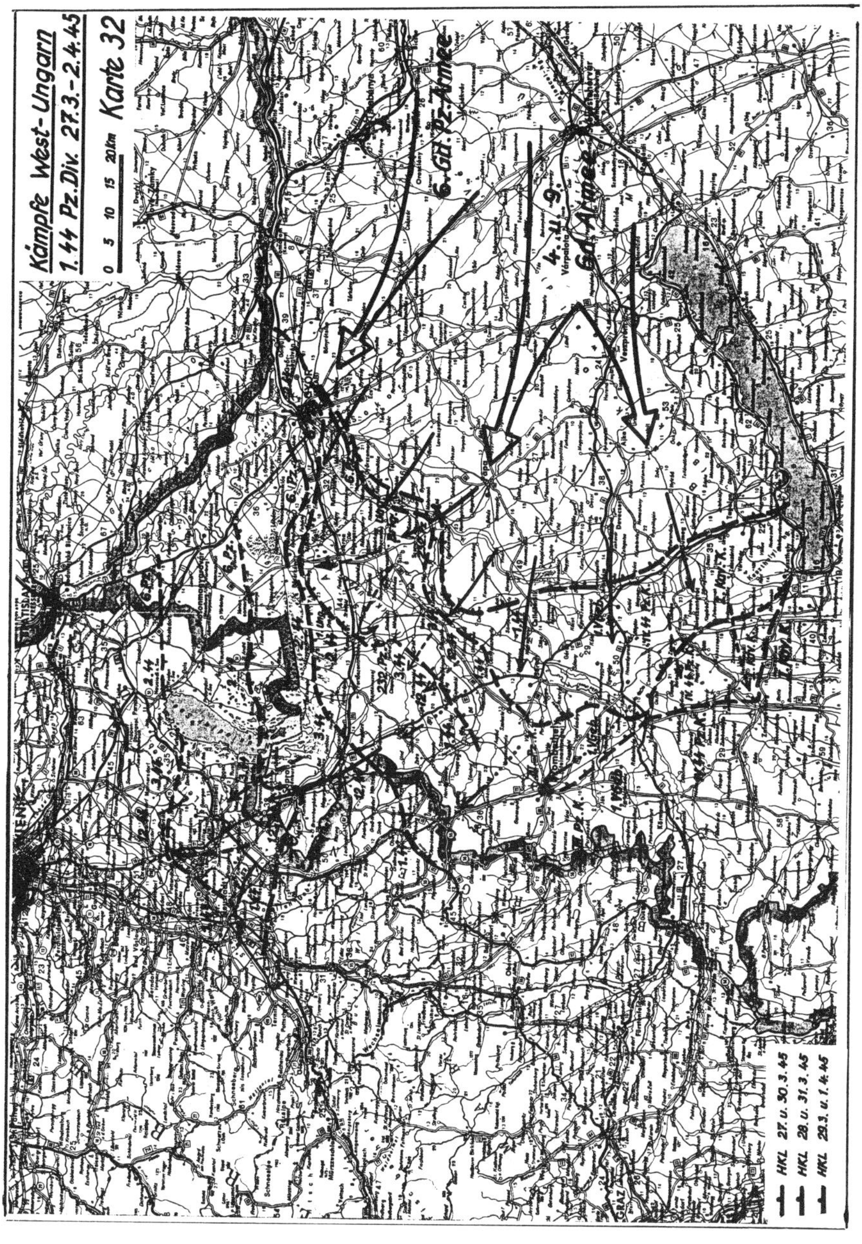

MAP 32

MAP 33

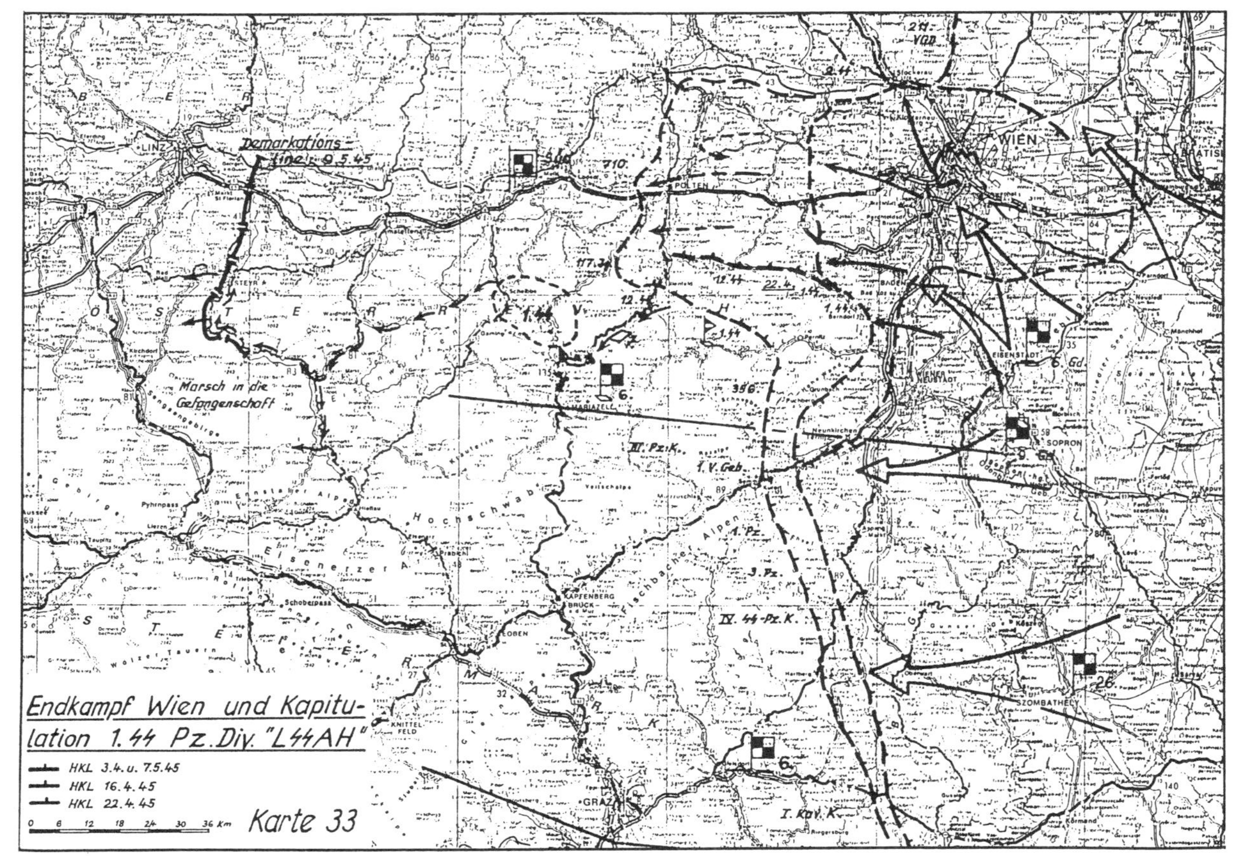
Endkampf Wien und Kapitulation 1. 44 Pz. Div. "L44AH"
HKL 3.4. u. 7.5.45
HKL 16.4.45
HKL 22.4.45
0 6 12 18 24 30 36 Km
Karte 33
WIEN
SOPRON
GRAZ
LINZ
Demarkationslinie 9.5.45
Marsch in die Gefangenschaft

PART IV

ORIGINALS AND DOCUMENTS

BEER NEWSPAPERS

From the time of the formation of the company in Wildflecken and Haustenbeck, from the time in France in the Summer of 1942 and from Kharkov in Spring 1943 some BEER NEWSPAPERS could be "saved."

They are the

BEER NEWSPAPER of the 3. Panzerkompanie from Wildflecken in February 1942

3. Panzerkompanie, Light Platoon, Haustenbeck May, 1942

3. Panzerkompanie, NCO Class, Haustenbeck V/42

BEER NEWSPAPER 7. Panzerkompanie LAH, Evreux, August, 1942

Beer Newspaper 7./SS-Panzer Regiment 1, Kharkov, April, 1943

10 Commandments
for the conducting of war by the German soldier

1. The German Soldier is to fight like a knight for the victory of his people. Atrocities and useless destruction make him unworthy.
2. The fighter must be uniformed or must be seen with easily recognizable special clothing or distinctive markings. Fighting in civilian clothes without such distinguishing clothing is forbidden.
3. No opponent who surrenders is to be killed, not even partisans or spies. They will receive their just punishment through a court of law.
4. Prisoners of war are not to be mistreated or insulted. Weapons, plans and records are to be removed from their person. Other than that, none of their possessions are to be taken away.
5. Dum-Dum bullets are forbidden, bullets are not to be re-made in this manner either.
6. The Red Cross is not to be forgotten. Wounded opponents are to be handled humanely. Medics and field help are not to be prevented from conducting their medical activities or caring for the wounded.
7. The civilian population is not to be forgotten. The soldier may not plunder or destroy mischievously. Historical statues and buildings which serve religion, art, science or charity are to be especially respected. Payment for help or service from the population can only be claimed for reimbursement upon order of superiors.
8. Neutral land may not be entered or flown over, and further, it can not become a part of the field of battle.
9. If a German soldier falls into captivity, then he is required to give his name and rank upon questioning. Under no conditions is he to give any information about which unit he belongs to, or about military, political and economic conditions on the German side. He is not to be persuaded otherwise by promises or threats.
10. Violations of the above orders in these matters are punishable. Enemy violations of the rules 1-8 are to be reported. Retaliatory measures are only to be allowed upon order of higher troop leaders.

Führerbefehl vom 9. Juli 1942 betr. Verlegung von Waffen-SS-Verbänden in den Bereich des OB West

Fernschreiben

9. 7. 15.00 Uhr

An
Gen.St.d.H./Op.Abt.
Chef H.Rüst. u. B.d.E.
Ob.d.M./1. Skl.

Gleichlautend:
OB West
Ob.d.L./Lw.Fü.St.

1. Die schnellen und großen Erfolge im Osten können England vor die Alternative stellen, entweder sofort eine Großlandung zur Bildung einer zweiten Front zu unternehmen oder Sowjet-Rußland als politischen und militärischen Faktor zu verlieren. Es ist daher mit hoher Wahrscheinlichkeit damit zu rechnen, daß feindl. Landungen im Bereich des OB West in Kürze stattfinden.
   Anzeichen sind im besonderen
   a) zunehmende Aussagen von Agenten und sonstige Ergebnisse des Nachrichtendienstes,
   b) starke Ansammlung von Übersetzmitteln in Südengland,
   c) Zurückhaltung der engl. Luftwaffe in den letzten Tagen.
2. Als *besonders gefährdet* sind anzusehen:
   a) In erster Linie die Kanalküste, der Bereich Dieppe—Le Havre und die Normandie, da diese Abschnitte von der feindl. Luftwaffe mit Jagdschutz erreicht werden können und innerhalb der Reichweiten eines großen Teiles der Übersetzmittel liegen,
   b) demnächst der südliche Teil der niederländ. Küste und die Bretagne,
   c) ferner sind durch *Fallschirm- und Luftlandeverbände* sowie durch Sabotage besonders die Hauptverkehrswege, Flugplätze und Hauptquartiere der Stäbe gefährdet.

3. Ich befehle hiernach die sofortige Durchführung folgender Maßnahmen:
   a) *Gen.St.d.H.:*
      1. SS-Reich ist mit den fertiggewordenen Teilen, ohne jeweils die Beendigung der Aufstellung verstärkter Regimenter und die Erreichung voller Beweglichkeit abzuwarten, dem OB West zuzuführen.
         (Vergl. OKW/WFSt/Op. (H) Nr. 002199/42 g.K. vom 1. 7.)
         Die SS-Leibstandarte „Adolf Hitler" ist sofort nach dem Westen abzutransportieren.
         SS-Gen.Kdo. (mot.) ist nach beschleunigtem Abschluß der Aufstellung dem OB West zuzuführen. Zusammenfassen aller im Westen befindlichen SS-Verbände, möglichst auch der Brigade „Göring", unter diesem Gen.-Kdo. ist vorzusehen.
      4. Die befohlene Verlegung eines Regiments der 25. I.D. nach Dänemark wird zunächst zurückgestellt.
   b) *Chef H.Rüst. u. B.d.E.:*
      1. 3 Walküre-II-Verbände sind sofort aufzustellen und nach kurzem Zusammentreten der Truppenteile auf den vorgesehenen Übungsplätzen des Heimatkriegsgebietes beschleunigt dem OB West zuzuführen. Abtransport der ersten Teile der Divisionen von den Truppenübungsplätzen zwischen 18. und 20. 7. 42. Der Einsatz dieser Verbände ist nach Abschluß der Versammlung mit Schwerpunkt im südwestl. Teil der Niederlande und hinter dem belg. Küstenabschnitt vorzusehen.
      2. Die für die personelle und materielle Auffrischung vorgesehenen Transporte sind beschleunigt nach dem Westen zuzuführen.
   c) *OB West* weist Mil.Bef. Frankreich und Mil.Bef. Belgien—Nordfrankreich an, daß wenigstens je eine Haupteisenbahnstrecke und eine Hauptdurchgangsstraße nach den gem. Ziffer 2. a) und b) besonders gefährdeten Abschnitten schwerpunktmäßig so zu sichern ist, daß Zerstörungen und Sabotageakte unterbunden werden können.

In der Nähe von wichtigen Bahnhöfen und besonders gefährdeten Anlagen dieser Verkehrswege sind aus den in der Nähe ansässigen Einwohnern Geiseln zu bestimmen, denen öffentlich anzukündigen ist, daß sie mit ihrem Leben für die Sicherheit der betreffenden Anlagen haften, sobald diese unter der Mitwirkung oder Duldung franz. Einwohner oder Eisenbahnbeamter zerstört werden. Alle holländ., belg. und franz. Gemeinden sind unter Androhung schwerster Repressalien verpflichtet, jede unbekannte Person, die in der Gemeinde auftritt, sofort festzunehmen und der nächsten militärischen Dienststelle zu melden.

Die Zahl der Geiseln ist so festzusetzen, daß der Zweck erreicht wird. In der Nähe besonders wichtiger und gefährdeter Objekte sind Personal und Material zur schnellen Wiederherstellung bereitzustellen.

Führer Order of July 9, 1942
Subject: Transfer of the Waffen-SS Units to the area of the Supreme Commander West

Telegram
To: July 9, 1942, 1500 hours
General Staff of the Army/Operations Department CC: Supreme Commander West
Supreme Commander of the Luftwaffe/ Luftwaffe Leadership Staff

1. The quick and great successes in the east have given England the alternative to either immediately execute a large landing to build a second front or to lose Soviet Russia as a political and military factor. It is therefore calculated upon with all probability that enemy landings in the area of the Supreme Commander West will shortly take place.

Indications are especially:
a) increasing statements from agents and other results of the intelligence service
b) large gatherings of crossing materials in southern England
c) reduced activity of the English Air Force during the last few days.

2. It appears as if the following is especially endangered
a) in the first line the canal coast, the area between Dieppe and La Harre and the Normandy, since theses sections can be reached by the enemy air force with fighter protection and since the majority of crossing supplies lay in this portion of the British Reich.
b) next, the southern portion of the Dutch coast and the Bretagne.
c) further, the main network of roads and railroads, airports and the headquarters of the staff are endangered by para and glider troops, as well as by sabotage.

3.) I therefore order the execution of the following measures:
a.) General Staff of the Army:
1. SS-Reich is to be transferred to the Supreme Commander West with the completed portions of the division, without waiting for the completion of the formation of the strengthened regiments and the conclusion of the measures taken to reach full mobility.
(compare OKW/WFSt/Op.(H) No. 002199/42 g.K. from July 1)
The SS-Leibstandarte "Adolf Hitler" is to be immediately transferred off to the west. SS-General-Kommando (mot.) is to be transferred to the Supreme Commander West after the accelerated conclusion of the formation movements. It is foreseen that other SS units, possibly also the Göring Brigade, will be included within this "General Commando."
4. The ordered transfer of a Regiment of the 23. Infanterie Division to Denmark will be postponed next.

b.) Commander of Army Equipment and Supplies
1. Three Walküre II units are to be immediately formed and to be transferred quickly to the Supreme Commander west after the collecting of the troops at the foreseen troop training grounds. The departure of the first portions of the Division from the training grounds are to take place between July 17 and 20, 1942. The actions of these units is foreseen to take place after the conclusion of the collecting operations with the focal point in the southwestern portion of the Netherlands and behind the Belgian coastal section.
2. The materials and replacements in personnel foreseen for the transport are to be quickly transferred to the west.

c.) The Supreme Commander West instructs the military commander of France and Belgium/ Northern France, that at the very least each should secure a main railway and main road against acts of destruction and sabotage. This should occur according to subparagraph a) and b), especially in the critically endangered sections within the focal point.

In the vicinity of the important train stations and the especially endangered equipment of these transportation networks, hostages are to be taken and the residents are to be publicly informed that they will be liable/held responsible for the destruction with their lives if others cooperate with the French residents or railway officials in destroying anything. It is the duty of all Dutch, Belgian and French communities to take any unknown persons immediately into custody and to take them to the next military station under the threat of severe repercussions.

The number of hostages is to be high enough that its purpose will be reached. In the vicinity of especially important and endangered objects, personnel and material should be on hand to insure their continuous operation in the case of their destruction.

4. *Luftwaffe* zieht im Einvernehmen mit OB West alle für den Einsatz verfügbaren Teile der 7. Fl.Div. und der Brig. „Göring" in ihren Versammlungsräumen zu sofort einsatzfähigen Verbänden zusammen und verlegt entsprechend dem Vorschlag des Ob.d.L. zwei Kampfgruppen aus der Ob.d.L.-Reserve im Osten nach Frankreich.
5. Gen.St.d.H., Ob.d.L., OB West und Chef H.Rüst. u. B.d.E. melden mir über OKW/WFSt täglich 08.00 Uhr über Stand der Durchführung der Maßnahmen zu Ziffer 3 und 4 mit Abschlußstand des Vortages 19.00 Uhr.
6. Ich werde mich im Falle einer feindl. Landung selbst nach dem Westen begeben und von dort aus die Führung wahrnehmen.

Im Entwurf gez. Adolf Hitler
OKW/WFSt Nr. 551 213/42 g.Kdos. Chefs.

[folgt Verteiler]

4. The Luftwaffe, in agreement with the Supreme Commander West, is to immediately transfer all units available for action from the 7. FLAK Division and the "Göring" Brigade into their collecting areas and is to transfer two battle groups to France from the East in accordance with the recommendation of the Supreme Commander of the Luftwaffe.
5. The General Staff of the Army, Supreme Commander of the Luftwaffe, Supreme Commander West and the Commander of Equipment and Supplies are to report their progress with respect to subparagraph 3 and 4 with the figures from the previous day reported at 1900 hours daily at 0800 hours to me through the Supreme Command of the Wehrmacht/Staff of the Army Leadership.
6. In the case of tan enemy landing I will personally depart to the west to take over the leadership.

In planning – signed Adolf Hitler
OKW/WFSt N. 551 213/42 g.Kdos. Chefs.

Operationsbefehl Nr. 2 vom 28. Dezember 1942 betr. weitere Kampfführung auf dem Südflügel der Ostfront

Fernspruch! H.Qu., den 28. Dez. 1942
Geheime Kommandosache
Chefsache!
Nur durch Offizier!

An
Heeresgruppe Don

Operationsbefehl Nr. 2

Mein Bestreben bleibt nach wie vor, die 6. Armee in ihrer Festung zu erhalten und die Voraussetzung für ihre Befreiung zu schaffen.

Trotzdem muß vermieden werden, daß durch Zurückgehen verbündeter Truppen oder durch Eindrücken schwacher eigener Teile oder durch örtlich gebildete starke Feindüberlegenheit neue Kessel entstehen.

Außerdem soll durch bewegliche Kampfführung dem Russen an einzelnen Stellen die Initiative entrissen werden und die Überlegenheit der deutschen Führung wieder zur Geltung kommen. Ich befehle deshalb:

1. *Die Heeresgruppe A* wird unter Beibehalt und besonderer Verstärkung ihrer Küsten- und Gebirgsfront schrittweise Zug um Zug in mehreren Abschnitten in eine verkürzte Stellung Mostowoje (Mostowskoje)—Armawir—ostw. Salsk zurückgenommen. Erster Abschnitt ist die Solka-Kuma-Stellung. Beim Zurücknehmen sind die beweglichen Kräfte (13. und 3. Pz.Div.) auf den Nordflügel zu verschieben, um Umfassungen zuvorzukommen und unsererseits den Feind beweglich anzupacken.
2. *Die Heeresgruppe Don* hat nach wie vor die Pflicht, alles zu tun, um die Voraussetzungen für die Befreiung der 6. Armee zu erhalten. Sie darf deshalb ihre Verbände nur dann nach Westen zurücknehmen, wenn es unbedingt notwendig ist und auch dann nur im ständigen Kampf, um dem Feind möglichst große Verluste beizubringen und um Raum und Zeit für den Aufmarsch der anrollenden Verstärkungen zu erhalten bzw. zu schaffen.

   Die Kräfte südl. des Don sind unter dieser Voraussetzung zunächst nicht über die allgemeine Linie Höhengelände 60 km nordostw. Salsk—Brückenkopf Zymljanskaja, sodann im Zusammenhang mit den Bewegungen der Heeresgruppe A nicht über die Linie Salsk—Konstantinowskaja zurückzunehmen. Letztere ist zu halten. Die Kräfte nördlich des Don sind unter denselben Voraussetzungen nicht über die Linie Brückenkopf Zymljanskaja—Morozowski, sodann nicht über die Linie Konstantinowskaja—Donez zurückzunehmen. Letztere ist zu halten.
3. Bei den *Rückzugsbewegungen*, insbesondere denen der Heeresgruppe A, kommt es darauf an,
   a) die innere Haltung der Truppe und ihr Überlegenheitsgefühl über den Russen mit allen Mitteln, insbesondere durch Offensivstöße größeren und kleineren Ausmaßes, zu erhalten,
   b) dem Feind durch bewegliche Kampfführung, Verminungen, durch pak-beherrschte Minengassen, Zeitzünderminen, Hinterhalte usw. den größtmöglichen Schaden zuzufügen,
   c) sämtliche Waffen, Gerät, Material und Vorräte rechtzeitig zu bergen bzw. mitzuführen,
   d) sämtliche Verwundeten rechtzeitig abzutransportieren,
   e) sämtliche Bahnstrecken gründlich zu zerstören und das auf ihnen noch befindliche Breitspurmaterial zu vernichten,
   f) die in den geräumten Gebieten vorhandenen Unterkunftsmöglichkeiten für den Gegner im weitesten Umfange unbenutzbar zu machen, insbesondere die Heizmöglichkeiten zu zerstören,

Operational Order No. 2 of December 28, 1942
Subject: the conducting of further battles on the Southern wing of the eastern front.

Headquarters, December 28, 1942
Telegraph!
Secret Command Document
Commanders only!
Only for Officers

To:
Army Group "Don"

Operational Order No. 2

My intents remain as before, to keep the 6th Army in its fort and to achieve the necessary requirements to free it.

Despite this the formation of new pockets must be avoided which would be the result of retreating troops or the foreseen collapse of our troops by local strongpoints of enemy superiority.

Besides, the Russians should be deprived of their initiative by conducting a mobile battle leadership in certain local points. This will once again confirm the superiority of German leadership. Therefore I order:

1 Army Group A be taken back to a shorter line running from Mostovoje (Mosotvshkofe) to Armavir to the east of Salk – move for move – and be held by strengthening the sections of the coastal and mountain front. The first section is the Sulka-Kuma Position. During the pull back the mobile forces (13. and 3. Panzer Divisions) are to be shoved to the northern flank, to prevent encirclement and to seize the enemy on the move.

2. The Army Group "Don" continues to have the duty to maintain / to achieve all requirements for the freeing of the 6th Army. Therefore the Army group will only be allowed to pull back its units to the west if it is absolutely necessary, and then only in constant battle, in order to inflict as many casualties as possible on the enemy and to maintain and acquire land and time for the transportation of supplies and replacements.

The forces south of the Don are not to be pulled back over the general line 60 km north east of the Salsk Bridgehead Zumljanskaja, so it can then pull back over the line Salsk-Konstantinovskaja in conjunction with the movements of Army Group A. The last mentioned is to be held. The forces north of the Don are not to be taken back over the line between the bridgehead in Zymljanskaja and Morozovski and not over the line between Konstantinovskaja and the Donez under the same requirements. The latter mentioned is to be held.

3. During the retreat movements, especially during those of Army Group A, success depends on:
- a.) the inner posture of the troops and their feeling of superiority over the Russians with all means, especially through large and small scale offensive thrusts.
- b.) to inflict the most possible damage on the enemy through mobile battle leadership, mining and through mined alleys ruled by anti-tank guns, time capsule mines, obstacles, etc.
- c.) the protection and maintaining possession of all weapons, equipment, material and supplies. In a timely fashion.
- d.) by transporting off all wounded in a timely fashion.
- e.) by destroying all train tracks and by destroying all building materials.
- f.) by making all shelter possibilities available in the evacuated areas unusable, especially by destroying all possibilities for heating.

g) in das neue Gebiet schon jetzt vorausschauend Bevorratung zu schaffen, insbesondere Lebensmittel aus den fruchtbaren Ebenen.

4. Um die *Einheitlichkeit der Bewegungen* der Heeresgruppe A und Don, insbesondere der Panzerkorps auf dem Nordflügel der Heeresgruppe A und der 16. I.D. (mot.), sicherzustellen, wird die Heeresgruppe A der Heeresgruppe Don unterstellt. Der Oberbefehlshaber der Gruppe Don meldet, zu welchem Zeitpunkt er den Befehl übernehmen kann. Heeresgruppe Don führt von diesem Zeitpunkt ab die Bezeichnung Heeresgruppe Süd.

   Über spätere Auflösung des Oberkommandos der Heeresgruppe A ergeht zeitgerecht Befehl.

5. Die für die *Schließung der Front zwischen Heeresgruppe Don und Heeresgruppe B* gegebenen Befehle behalten weiter Gültigkeit. Vor allem kommt es darauf an, daß die Heeresgruppe B unverzüglich ihre Kräfte an den Kalitwa-Abschnitt heranschiebt und die gesicherte Verbindung zur Armeegruppe Hollidt hergestellt wird. Die Heeresgruppe B ist für diese Verbindung verantwortlich.

6. Als Rückhalt-Stellung für die Heeresgruppe A bleibt es bei der mit OKH/Op.-Abt. Nr. 421034/42 geh. Kdos. Chefs. vom 27. 12. 42, Ziff. II, Abs. 1 d) festgelegten. Ihr Ausbau ist zu beschleunigen.

   Ebenso ist für die Heeresgruppe Don ein großer Brückenkopf Rostow etwa in Linie SSW. Semibalka—Tschjornij—Sal-Mündung festzulegen und mit dem Ausbau zu beginnen.

7. Heeresgruppe A und Don melden
   a) baldmöglichst ihre Absicht im großen,
   b) täglich ihre Absichten.

gez. Adolf Hitler
OKH/Gen.St.d.H./Op.Abt.
Nr. 421042/42 geh.Kdos. Chefs. v. 28. 12. 42

[folgt Verteiler]

36.

Ergänzung zum Operationsbefehl Nr 2 vom 31 Dezember 1942

Geheime Kommandosache
Chefsache!
Nur durch Offizier!
An Heeresgruppe Don
Abgang 31. 12. 42
Aufgenommen 1. 1. 43 — 04.10 Uhr

I. Ergänzung zum Operationsbefehl Nr. 2:

1. Um die Befreiung der 6. Armee durchführen zu können, wird eine starke Kräftegruppe von Panzerverbänden bis Mitte Februar im Gebiet südostwärts Charkow versammelt werden.

   Hierzu werden im größtmöglichen Tempo antransportiert aus dem Westen: SS-Adolf Hitler, SS-Reich, SS-T, von Heeresgruppe Mitte Div. „Großdeutschland". Außerdem werden bis zum gleichen Zeitpunkt 3 weitere Inf.Div.en aus dem Westen in Gegend südl. Kiew versammelt, um von hier im Anschluß an die mot.Gruppe mit der Bahn vorgezogen zu werden.

2. Ist beabsichtigt, ab Mitte Februar je nach Wetterlage mit der Panzergruppe und weiteren aus der Heeresgruppe A und Don zu gewinnenden schnellen Verbänden, voraussichtlich nördl. des Don in Richtung Stalingrad, zur Befreiung der 6. Armee anzutreten.

3. Heeresgruppe Don und B haben die bestmöglichen Voraussetzungen für den Aufmarsch und den Ansatz der mot.Gruppe zu erhalten bzw. zu schaffen. Hierzu gilt nach wie vor Op.-Befehl Nr. 2.

OKH/Gen.St.d.H./Op.Abt. (I S/B) Nr. 421052/42
g.Kdos. 31. 12. 42

[folgt Verteiler]

g.) by acquiring prospective provisions and supplies in the new areas, especially food stuffs from the fruit bearing areas.

4. In order to secure the *unity of movements* of Army Group A and Don, especially of the Panzerkorps on the northern flank of Army Group a and the 16. (mot.) Infanterie Division, Army Group A will be subordinated to Army Group Don. The Supreme Commander of the Group Don is to report at which point in time it will be able to take command. Army Group Don is from this point in time to be called Army Group South.

The order to later dissolve the Supreme Command of Army Group A will be issued at the appropriate time.

5. The given orders for the closing of the Front between Army Group Don and Army Group B are once again valid. Above all it depends on whether Army Group B can shove its forces to the Kalitva Section without delay and established contact with Army Group Hollidt. Army Group B is responsible for establishing this contact.

6. The Supreme Command of the Army is to determine the point at which Army Group A is to halt their retreat. (Op.Abt.Nr. 421034/42 Secret Commander from Dec. 27, 1942 Subsection II, Paragraph D). This build up is to take place at an accelerated pace.

At the same time the Army Group Don is to form a large Bridgehead in Rostov at about the line south-southwest of Semibalka-Tshjornij – mouth of the Sal river and to begin with its construction.

7. Army Groups A and Don are to report
   a) their intentions asap
   b) their intentions on a daily basis.

Signed Adolf Hitler
OKH/Gen.St.d.H./Op.Abt.
Secret Command No. ..... Dec. 28 1942.

Supplement to the Operational Order

Secret Command Document
Command Document!
Only for Officers!
To Army Group Don
Submitted December 31, 1942
Received January 1, 1943 at 0410 hours

I. Supplement to operational order no. 2

1. In order to execute the freeing of the 6th Army, a strong group of Panzer troop forces must be collected in the area southeast of Kharkov until the middle of February.

For this the following units will be transported from the West at the quickest pace:

SS-Adolf Hitler, SS-Reich, SS-T, From Army Group "Mentor" the Division "Großdeutschland." Besides that at the same time three further infantry divisions will be collected from the west into the area south of Kiev, and hook up with the motorized groups and transferred by train.

2. It is intended that the fast units will advance to the north of the Don in the direction of Stalingrad and depending on the weather with the Panzer Group and further the units of Army Group A and Don to free the 6th Army.

3. Army Group Don and B must prepare the best possible situation for the departure and the start of the motorized group. For this, as before, the operational order No. 2 is valid

Bundesrepublik Deutschland
Der Bundeskanzler

Bonn, den 17. 12. 1952

Herrn
Generaloberst a.D. H a u s e r
Ludwigsburg / Wttbg.
Asperger Str. 48

Sehr geehrter Herr Generaloberst!

Einer Anregung nachkommend teile ich mit, daß die von mir in meiner Rede vom 3. Dezember 1952 vor dem Deutschen Bundestag abgegebene Ehrenerklärung für die Soldaten der früheren deutschen Wehrmacht auch die Angehörigen der Waffen-SS umfaßt, soweit sie ausschließlich als Soldaten ehrenvoll für Deutschland gekämpft haben.

Mit dem Ausdruck vorzüglicher Hochachtung
bin ich Ihr

Adenauer
(Adenauer)

OKH/Gen.St.d.H./Op.Abt. (I S/B) Nr. 421052/42
g.Kdos. 31.12.42

Bundesrepublik Deutschland
Der Bundeskanzler

Bonn, December 17, 1952

Herrn
Generaloberst a.D. Hausser
Ludwigsburg, Württemberg
Asperger Str. 48

Very Honored Herr Generaloberst

Upon suggestion I am writing you to inform you that the speech I gave on December 3, 1952 in front of the German Congress which included an apology to the soldiers of the German Wehrmacht also includes the members of the Waffen-SS as far as they exclusively fought as honorable soldiers for Germany.

With an expression of the highest respect

yours truly,

(signed) Adenauer

Der Bundesminister der Justiz

- 925o/1 II - 25 244/6o -

Bonn, den 2. Januar 1961
Postfach
Tel. 20171
Hausruf 223

Betr.: Rechtswirkung des Urteils im Nürnberger Kriegsverbrecherprozeß gegen die Waffen-SS

Bezug: a) Ihre Schreiben vom 14. Juni und 3o.September 196o
b) mein Schreiben vom 19. November 196o

Das Urteil des Internationalen Militärgerichtshofs in Nürnberg vom 1. Oktober 1946, durch das die SS einschließlich der Waffen-SS zu einer verbrecherischen Organisation erklärt worden ist, hat nach dem Recht der Bundesrepublik k e i n e Rechtswirkungen für die ehemaligen Angehörigen der SS und der Waffen-SS. Das Urteil hat nur deklaratorische Bedeutung. Niemand kann auf Grund dieses Urteils wegen seiner bloßen Mitgliedschaft in der SS strafrechtlich verfolgt werden. Eine Strafverfolgung ist nach den in der Bundesrepublik geltenden Gesetzen nur möglich, wenn sich ein Mitglied der SS persönlich einer Straftat schuldig gemacht hat.

Ich darf Sie weiter darauf hinweisen, daß die Bundesrepublik - aus hier nicht näher zu erörternden Erwägungen - eine ausdrückliche, vertragliche Anerkennung der von alliierten Militärgerichten in Deutschland gefällten "Kriegsverbrecherurteile" - dazu gehört auch das Urteil des IMT vom 1. Oktober 1946 - vermieden hat. Dies ergibt sich aus §§ 6 und 7 des Überleitungsvertrages in der Fassung der Bekanntmachung vom 3o. März 1955 (Bundesgesetzbl. II, S. 4o5).

Nach internationalem Recht, d.h. nach Völkerrecht, ist die Rechtslage nicht anders. Wie die Frage nach dem Recht der sowjetisch besetzten Zone zu beurteilen ist, kann ich Ihnen nicht sagen. Mir ist jedoch nicht bekannt geworden, daß in der sowjetisch besetzten Zone jemand allein deshalb Verfolgungen oder Nachteilen ausgesetzt ist, weil der Internationale Militärgerichtshof in Nürnberg die SS als verbrecherische Organisation erklärt hat.

Mit vorzüglicher Hochachtung
Im Auftrag
Schätzler

Beglaubigt
[signature]
Regierungsangestellte

Der Bundesminister for Justice Bonn, the 2nd of January, 1961
P.O. Box
– 9250/1 II – 25 244/60 - Tel. 20171
Ext. 223

Subject: Validity of the judgment against the Waffen-SS during the Nürnberg War Criminal Trials.

Reference: a) your letter of June 14 and September 30, 1960
b) my letter of November 19, 1960

The judgment of the international Military Court in Nürnberg on October 1, 1946, by which the SS, including the Waffen-SS, was judged a criminal organization has, according to the rights of the Bundesrepublik, no validity for the former members of the Waffen-SS. The judgment has only declaratory meaning. No one can be prosecuted as a criminal for just his membership in the SS as a result of this judgment. According to the laws enforced by the Bundesrepublik a criminal prosecution can only be possible when a member of the SS personally committed a crime.

May I also point out to you that the Bundesrepublik – which doesn't want to discuss the details thereof in this letter – denied the expressly stipulated case of the "War criminal judgments," the judgment of the International Military Tribunal of Oct. 1, 1946 is also is included here. This is the result of §§ 6 and 7 of the transitional agreement in the wording of the proclamation of March 30, 1955 Bundeslaw Order II, Page 405.

According to international rights, that means that according to the rights of the people, this legal status is no different. As to the question of the Soviet occupied zone, I can't say. I don't know if someone can be prosecuted in the Soviet occupied zones because of the International Militate Tribunal in Nürnberg declared the SS as a criminal organization.

With highest respect

(signed) Schätzler

Leibstandarte SS Adolf Hitler
SS-Panzer-Regiment 1 — Rgt.Gef.Std., den 1.3.1943

Gefechtsbericht

Für den Einsatz der Kampfgruppe 7. Pz.Kp., Kampfstaffel Panz.Rgt. am 27. u. 28.2.1943 auf Olchowatka

Am 27.2.1943, 8,00 Uhr wurden auf Anruf des Ia sämtliche in der Werkstatt befindlichen Pz.Kpfw. der 7. Kp. zusammen mit dem le. Zug des Rgt.Stabes unter Führung des Rgt.-Adjutanten zu einer Kampfgruppe zusammengestellt, mit dem Auftrag, eine russische Kräftegruppe, bestehend aus Panzern, Pz.Jäg. und Inf., die beim linken Nachbarn des 1. Pz.Gr.Rgt. der 320. I.D. auf Olchowatka durchgebrochen war und in Richtung auf die Versorgungsstraße der Div. Krassnograd - Poltawa vorging, aufzuhalten.

09,00 Uhr trat die Kampfgruppe mit le. Zug als Spitze in Richtung Karlowka an. Von den Pz.Kpfw. der 7. Kp. konnten vorerst nur 2 antreten, wovon einer auf halber Strecke durch Bremsschaden ausfiel. Somit bestand die Kampfgruppe aus 3 Pz.Kpfw. III und 1 Pz.Kpfw. IV (4 Pz.Kpfw. II). Le. Zug zog bis Nordrand Popowka vor und sicherte in Richtung Warwarowka. Nachdem Rest Kampfgruppe aufgeschlossen war, klärte le. Zug weiter auf bis Nordrand Warwarowka. Warwarowka wurde ebenfalls feindfrei gemeldet. Nordrand Warwarowka wurde in Richtung Wessnjanoje gesichert. Kampfgruppe schloß auf. Von Wessnjanoje trat Kampfgruppe um 11,00 Uhr auf Beluchowka an. Bei Annäherung an den Ort wurde die Spitze der Kampfgruppe mit starkem Pak- und Pz.K.-Feuer empfangen. Die beiden Pz.Kpfw. III des le. Zuges wurden abgeschossen. Die Besatzung Oscha. Scharna bootete nach Volltreffer aus. Oscha. Scharna gefallen. Pz. Uscha.Witt nach 4 Pak-Treffern brennend,konnte sich Richtung Wessnjanoje zurückziehen und dort gelöscht werden. Uscha. Witt und Funker leicht verwundet. Nunmehr bestand die Kampfgruppe noch aus 1 Pz.Kpfw. III und 1 Pz.Kpfw. IV (4 Pz.Kpfw. ~~II~~). Kampfgruppe zog sich auf Nordrand Wessnjanoje zurück, sicherte Richtung Beluchowka und setzte Aufklärung nach Südosten und Südwestrand Beluchowka an.

12,00 Uhr traf Ustuf. Stollmayer mit einem Pz.Kpfw. IV ein. Ein Spähtrupp des Ersatzes des 1. Gr.Rgt. in Stärke 1/11 erreichte die Kampfgruppe und wurde eingegliedert. In der Zeit von 16,00 Uhr - 22,00 Uhr trafen unter Führung von Ustuf. Sternebeck weitere 4 Pz.Kpfw. IV und 2 Pz.Kpfw. III ein. Hstuf. Schürer vom 1. Rgt. meldete sich mit 60 Mann Ersatz für das 1. Rgt. und unterstellte sich.

Sehr vorteilhaft wirkte sich aus, daß von der Nachr.Abt. der Div. sofort Fernsprech bis zum Gef.Std. gelegt wurde (Oscha. Wonnenberg).

Auf Befehl der Div. Ia (fernmündlich) sperrte die Kampfgruppe die Straßen nach Beluchowka von Südosten und Südwesten. Laufende Aufklärung (Inf.-Spähtrupps) meldete am 28.2.1943, 4,00 Uhr, daß sich feindl. Panzer aus Beluchowka in Richtung Olchowatka lösen.

- 2 -

Leibstandarte SS Adolf Hitler
SS-Panzer Regiment 1 Regimental Command Post, the 1st of March, 1943

Action Report

For the attack Olchovatka by the Battle Group 7. Panzer Kompanie, Battle Squadron Panzer Regiment
on the 27th and 28th of February, 1943

On February 27, 1943 at 0800 hours the Ia called and ordered that a battlegroup was to be formed from all of the Pz.Kpfw. of the 7. Kp. that were in the work shop together with the light platoon of the regimental staff. The battle group was to be led by the regimental adjutant and had the task of holding up a Russian battle group consisting of tanks, anti-tank guns and infantry. This Russian battle group had broken through the left neighbor of the 1. Pz.Gr.Rgt. of the 320. Infanterie Division and then into Olchovatka. It then started in the direction of the division's supply road between Krassnograd and Poltava.

At 0900 hours the Kampfgruppe together with the light platoon in the lead departed in the direction of Karlovka. At first only two Panzer Kampfwagen of the 7. Kompanie could depart, and shortly thereafter one of them fell out due to brake damage after traveling half way. Due to that the Kampfgruppe consisted of three Panzer Kampfwagen III and one Panzer Kampfwagen IV (4 Panzer Kampfwagen II). The light platoon advanced until reaching the northern edge of Popovka and secured the direction to Varvarovka. After the rest of the Kampfgruppe caught up, the light platoon reconnoitered the northern edge of Varvarovka. Vavarovka was reported to be free of the enemy. The northern edge of Vavarovka was then secured in the direction of Vessnjanoje. All elements of the Kampfgruppe were present. The Kampfgruppe departed from Vessnjanoje at 1100 hours and advanced towards Beluchovka. Upon approaching the village, the lead unit of the Kampfgruppe received strong anti-tank and tank fire. Both of the Panzer Kampfwagen IIIs of the light platoon were knocked out. The crew of Oberscharführer Scharna's Panzer disembarked after a direct hit. Oberscharführer Scharna was killed. The Panzer of Unterscharführer Witt started to burn after four hits from anti-tank guns but was still able to pull back in the direction of Vessnjanoje where the fire was put out. Unterscharführer Witt was lightly wounded. At this point the Kampfgruppe consisted still of 1 Panzer Kampfwagen III and 1 Panzer Kampfwagen IV (4 Panzer Kampfwagen II). The Kampfgruppe pulled back to the northern edge of Vessnjanoje, secured in the direction of Beluchovka and conducted reconnaissance to the southeast and southwest edge of Beluchovka.

At 1200 hours Untersturmführer Stollmayer arrived with a Panzer Kampfwagen IV. A patrol troop consisting of replacements from the 1. Grenadier Regiment with a strength of one officer and eleven NCOs and men reached the Kampfgruppe and was absorbed by it. Between 1600 and 2200 hours a further four Panzer Kampfwagen IV and two Panzer Kampfwagen III arrived under the leadership of Untersturmführer Sternebeck. Hauptsturmführer Schürer from the 1. Regiment reported with sixty replacements for the 1. Regiment and subordinated himself and his men to them.

It proved to be very advantageous that communications were established between the signals battalion and the Division (thanks to Oberscharführer Wonnenberg).

Upon the order of the Divisional Ia (by wire) the Kampfgruppe blocked the road to Beluchovka from the southeast and the southwest. Continuos reconnaissance (infantry patrol troops) determined that enemy tanks were retreating from Beluchovka in the direction of Olchovatka on February 28, 1943 at 0400 hours.

- 2 -

04,45 Uhr trat Kampfgruppe zum Angriff an. Zug Janke mit Feuer auf Südwestrand frontal bindend. Zug Stollmayer entlang der Straße Swch Chalturino – Beluchowka, mit Inf. auf Südostrand Beluchowka. Ort war zum großen Teil feindfrei. Feindl. Inf., die sich versteckt hielt, wurde niedergemacht. Kampfgruppe stieß zum Nordostrand durch, Inf. aufgesessen. Zug Stollmayer übernahm Sicherung am Nordostausgang. Zug Janke wurde 06,30 Uhr angesetzt zur Aufklärung in Richtung Olchowatka und zur Verbindungsaufnahme mit Stu.Gesch.Battr. Wiesemann in Krassnosnamenka. Am Südrand Olchowatka bekam Aufklärung starkes Pak- und Kw.K.-Feuer. Ein Pz.Kpfw. IV wurde abgeschossen und brannte aus. Richt- und Ladeschütze gefallen, übrige Besatzung bootete mit starken Verbrennungen aus. Zug Stollmayer eröffnete auf erkannte Mündungsfeuer sofort das Feuer und vernichtete dabei einen feindl. Panzer und eine feindl. Pak. Unter gegenseitiger Feuerunterstützung zog Rest Zug Janke zurück, vernichtete dabei eine feindl. Pak. Pz.Kpfw. Janke erhielt 4 Pak-Treffer und fiel aus. Zug Stollmayer nahm nach Rückkunft Janke aus Feuerstellung am Ortsrand Feuer auf erkannte Ziele am Westrand Olchowatka auf und vernichtete eine weitere feindl. Pak. Feindl. Kw.K.- und Pak-Feuer und vereinzeltes Inf.-Feuer Auf Stellung Nordrand Beluchowka hatte weiter keine Wirkung (1 leicht Verwundeter).

12,00 Uhr wurde durch fernmündliche Verbindungaufnahme Kampfgruppe durch Staf. Witt in die Lage eingewiesen. Str. Olchowatka war in eigener Hand. Stu.Gesch.Battr. Wiesemann war in Südwestteil Now. Olchowatka eingedrungen. 5. Pz.Kp. sollte von Osten herangezogen werden und mit Btl. Frey nach vorangegangener Artl.-Unterstützung Now. Olchowatka angreifen. Kampfgruppe erhielt Befehl, bei Anlaufen des Angriffs Westrand Olchowatka mit Feuer zu belegen und im Ver-~~laufe des Angriffs aus Beluchowka auf Olchowatka ebenfalls anzutreten.~~ Nach Abflauen des Artl.-Feuers auf Olchowatka sah Kampfgruppe um 14,00 Uhr eigene Inf. und Sturmgeschütze in den Südrand Olchowatka eindringen. Kampfgruppe eröffnete mit Zug Janke Feuer auf Westrand und setzte Zug Stollmayer rechts umfassend auf Südwestrand an. 14,30 Uhr war zu erkennen, wie russ. Panzer und Inf. in Stärke von 2 Kpn. aus Olchowatka über den Sumpf nach Nagornaja zu entkommen versuchten. Die 2 erkannten Panzer blieben im Sumpf stecken und wurden abgeschossen. Die am Hang fliehende russ. Inf. wurde von Zug Janke und le. Zug unter Feuer genommen und zum großen Teil vernichtet. Zug Stollmayer und Halbzug Sternebeck griffen unter Führung des Rgt.-Adjutanten verfolgend am Westrand Olchowatka entlang auf Nagornaja an, bis Vorwärtsbewegung durch Sumpf unmöglich gemacht wurde. Aus Stellungen am Sumpfrand wurden die letzten in Nagornaja verschwindenden feindl. Infanteristen unter Feuer genommen und Häuser teilweise in Brand geschossen. Stärke der entkommenen feindl. Inf. 80 – 100 Mann.

Bei Erreichen des Sumpfrandes stieß Zug Stollmayer an der Nordost-Ecke des Dorfes auf eigene Panzer, die Olchowatka von Nordosten her durchstoßen hatten (5.Pz.Kpf).

Kampfgruppe brach Angriff ab und führte 7. Kp. befehlsgemäß der II. Abt. wieder zu. Inf. (Ersatz) wurde auf Befehl Staf. Witt durch Hstuf. Schürer dem 1. Rgt. nach Jegorjewka zugeführt. Le. Zug Rgt. rückte 19,00 Uhr aus Beluchowka über Popowka in die Unterkunft zurück.

SS-Obersturmführer und
Rgt.-Adjutant
[signature]

At 0445 hours the battle group departed for the attack. Platoon Janke fired forward on the southwestern edge. Platoon Stollmayer fired along the roach from Swch Chalturino to Beluchovka and infantry attacked the southeastern edge of Beluchovka. The village was for the most part free of the enemy. Enemy infantrymen, which remained hidden, were knocked out. The Kampfgruppe broke through to the northern edge of the village with the Panzers mounted without infantry. Platoon Stollmayer overtook the security on the northeastern exit of the village. Platoon Janke set out on a reconnaissance mission in the direction of Olchovatka and also to try and take up contact with the Sturmgeschütz Battery Wiesemann in Krassnosnoamenka. On the southern edge of Olchovatka the reconnaissance party received strong anti-tank and tank fire. A Panzer Kampfwagen IV was knocked out and burned. The no. 1 gunner and the loader were killed, the rest of the crew disembarked and had suffered bad wounds. Platoon Stollmayer opened his hatch and immediately noticed muzzle fire and was then able to knock out an armored car and an enemy anti-tank gun. Under the protection of fire support the rest of the Platoon Janke pulled back during which they annihilated an enemy anti-tank gun. Panzer Kampfwagen Janke received four ant-tank gun hits and was knocked out. Platoon Stollmayer took firing position on the edge of the village after Janke arrived back and aimed his fire on recognized targets on the western edge of Olchovatka and annihilated a further enemy anti-tank gun. Fire from enemy armored cars and anti-tank guns, as well as infantry fire on the position in Buluchovka had no further effect (1 lightly wounded soldier).

At 1200 hours, after establishing wire contact the Kampfgruppe (Standartenführer Willt) was informed of the situation. Star. Olchovatka was in our hands. Sturmgeschütz Battery Wiesemann had penetrated the southwestern part of Nov. Olchovatka. The 5. Panzerkompanie was to be pulled up from the east and attack Nov. Olchovatka with Battalion Frey after artillery preparation and with their continued support. The Kampfgruppe received the order to lay the western edge of Olchovatka with fire and during the course of the attack to advance from Beluchovka to Olchovatka. After the conclusion of the artillery preparation on Olchovatka the Kampfgruppe saw its own infantry and Sturmgeschütze penetrate the southern edge of Olchovatka at 1400 hours. The Kampfgruppe opened fire on the western edge with Platoon Janke and sent platoon Stollmayer to come around from the right towards the southwestern edge. At 1430 hours it was recognized that Russian tanks and infantry in the strength of two companies were trying to escape from Olchovatka through the swamp to Nagornaja. The two tanks that were discovered got stuck in the swamp and were knocked out. The fleeing Russian infantry was taken under fire and was for the most part annihilated. Platoon and Half-Platoon Sternebeck pursued the attack on the western edge of Olchovatka to Nagornaja under the leadership of the Regimental Adjutant. The attack continued until forward movement was made impossible by the swamp. The fragments of enemy infantry forces fleeing from the edge of the swamp and disappearing in Nagornaja were taken under fire and the houses were partly set on fire by our guns. The strength of the surviving enemy infantry was some eighty to one hundred men.

Upon reaching the edge of the swamp platoon Stollmayer pushed on to the northeast corner of the village and happened upon some of our Panzers that had broken through Olchovatka from the northeast (5. Panzerkompanie).

The Kampfgruppe broke off the attack and brought back the 7. Panzerkompanie according to an order issued by the IInd Battalion. The (replacement) infantry was taken back to Jegorjevka upon the orders of Standartenführer Witt (received through Hauptsturmführer Schürer of the 1. Regiment). The Regiment's Light Platoon went back to its camp from Beluchovka through Popovka at 1900 hours.

(signed)
SS-Obersturmführer and
Rgt. Adjutant

7./SS-Panzer Regiment 1 "LSSAH" O.U., den 6.6.44

Bericht ueber die Abgaengigkeit
des SS-Schtz. Anton W o l f r a m

Wolfram wurde bei den Kaempfen in Balkowzi Krs. Tarnopol in der Nacht v. 5./6.3.44 zuletzt gesehen. Nachdem sich die Kp. am anderen Morgen wieder gesammelt hatte fehlte er. Da auch die Eltern seit Februar ohne jede Nachricht von ihm sind, ist anzunehmen, dass W. gefallen oder verwundet in Gefangenschaft geraten ist.

SS-Obersturmfuehrer
und Kompaniefuehrer

7./SS-Panzer Regiment 1 "LSSAH" Village Quarters, June 6, 1944

Report about the disappearance of
the SS-Schütze Anton Wolfram

Wolfram was last seen during the night of March 5/6, 1944 during the battles in Balkovzi in the area of Tarnopol. After the company collected the next morning, he was missing. Since the parents have not heard from him since February, it is to be assumed that W. was killed or wounded and fell into captivity.

(signed)
SS-Obersturmführer
and Company Commander

7./SS-Panzer Regiment 1 "LSSAH" O.U., den 6.6.44

FPN 31 820

Volksdeutscher

Vermissten - Meldung

1.) W o l f r a m , Anton SS-Schuetze

2.) geb. 3.3.1924 in Johannisfeld

3.) Besondere koerperl.Merkmale : k e i n e

4.) Erkennungsmarkenbeschriftung: 5./SS-Pz.Gren.A.u.E.Btl.12 28639

5.) Ers.Tr.Teil und dessen Anschrift: SS-Pz.A.u.E.Rgt.Riga-Strand

6.) Anschrift der naechsten Angehoerigen:

Hans W o l f r a m (Vater)
Johannisfeld Nr.142
Kreis Prinz Eugen /Rumaenien

7.) Vermisst seit 6.3.44 in Balkowzi Krs.Tarnopol

8.) Mutmassliches Schicksal und Anhaltspunkte:

Wolfram wurde bei den naechtlichen Kaempfen in Balkowzi zuletzt gesehen. Nachdem sich die Kp. ... abgesetzt und ... gesammelt hatte, fehlte er. Es ist anzunehmen, dass W. entweder gefallen oder in Gefangenschaft geraten ist.

9.) Angabe ueber Sicherstellung und Verbleib der Eigensachen:

W. trug seine eigenen Sachen saemtlich bei sich. bei der Kp. liegt nichts vor.

10.) Bisher zur Nachforschung getroffene Massnahmen:

Nachfragen bei Kameraden.

11.) Meldung ueber unerlaubte Entfernung wurde nicht erstattet.

12.) Angehoerige benachrichtigt am 6.6.44 durch Ostuf.Sternebeck

SS-Obersturmfuehrer
und Kompaniefuehrer

7./SS-Panzer Regiment 1 "LSSAH" Village Quarters, 6/6/44
FPN 31820
Ethnic German

MIA Report

1.) Wolfram, Anton SS-Schütze
2.) Born March 3, 1924, in Johannisfeld
3.) Special physical characteristics: none
4.) Dog Tag number: 5./SS-Pz.Gren. A. u. E. Btl. 12 28639
5.) Replacement unit and its address: SS-Pz. A. u. E. Rgt. Riga-Strand
6.) Family Address:

Hans Wolfram
Johannisfeld Nr. 142
Kreis Prinz Eugen / Rumania

7.) Missing since March 6, 1944, in Balkovzi in the district of Tarnopol
8.) Fate of the MIA: Wolfram was last seen during the battles in Balkovzi. It is assumed that he was either killed or was taken prisoner.
9.) Information concerning his possessions: Wolfram carried his belongs. Nothing was left behind with the company.
10.) Current attempts to find out information about the MIA: Inquiries with comrades.
11.) Reports of AWOL were not made.
12.) Family members were informed on June 6, 1944, by Obersturmführer Sternebeck.

(Signed)
SS-Obersturmführer
and Company Commander

NOTICE.

1. IT IS VORBIDDEN:
   a. For Internees to turn off lights in the cells or unscrew the light bulbs.
   b. Excessive conversation, singing, whistling, or any other loud noises.

2. Windows in the cells will be opened during the night from the time the lights are turned off (By the Guards) until daylight.

3. Violations of above rules will be punished.

JOHN T. EVANS
Prison Commander.

1. Es ist verboten:
   a. Für die Internierten Lichter in den Zellen auszudrehen oder die Birnen loszuschrauben.
   b. Übertrieben laute Unterhaltung, Singen, Pfeifen oder irgend welche andere laute Geräusche.

2. Die Fenster in den Zellen sind während der Nacht, vom Zeitpunkt des Abdrehens des Lichtes (Durch die Wachen) bis zum Einbruch des Tageslichts zu öffnen.

3. Übertretungen der obigen Vorschriften werden bestraft.

MALNUTRITION CARD
10 Nov. 1945

The holder of this card
Wölfel Heinz D-3137
will receive THREE meals per day

By order

Camp physician

15 NOV 1945

GEFANGENEN-AUSWEIS
Stets bei sich tragen

Name Wolfel, Heinz

Nr. 2058OE042 Baracke Cellenbn

Zimmer

Schwäbisch-Hall-

NOTICE

1. IT IS FORBIDDEN:
a. For Internees to turn off lights in the cells or unscrew the light bulbs.
b. Excessive conversation, singing, whistling, or any other loud noises.
2. Windows in the cells will be opened during the night from the time the lights are tuned off (By the guards) until daylight.
3. Violations of the above rules will be punished.

John T. Frans
Prison Commander.

Malnutrition Card
Nov. 10, 1945

The holder of this card Name: Wolfel, Heinz
Wolfel, Heinz D-3137
will receive THREE meals per day Nr. 20580E042 Barracks: Cellenbu

By order Room: ________________

Camp physician

15 Nov 1945

Schwäbisch Hall

Bekanntmachung.

1. **Es ist verboten:**

   a. Lichter in den Zellen auszudrehen oder die Birnen loszuschrauben.
   b. Übertrieben laute Unterhaltung, Singen, Pfeifen, oder irgend welche andere laute Geräusche.

2. Die Fenster sind während der Nacht, vom Zeitpunkt des Lichtausdrehens (durch die Wachen) bis zum Einbruch des Tageslichts zu öffnen.

3. Die Gefangenen einer Zelle dürfen nicht mit denen einer anderen Zelle in Verbindung treten. Jeder, der versucht, solche Verbindung auf irgend eine Art aufzunehmen, wird der härtesten Bestrafung unterworfen sein.

4. Die Gefangenen dürfen keinesfalls mit deutschem Personal innerhalb oder ausserhalb dieses Gefängnisses in Verbindung treten. Alle Gesuche und Wünsche dürfen nur an amerikanische Wachen gegeben werden.

5. Übertretungen der obigen Vorschriften werden bestraft.

---

1. Sie werden mit Wasser und Brot bestraft, weil viele von Ihnen ihre Namen, Einheit und andere Daten auf ihre Essgeschirre geschrieben haben. Dies ist strengstens verboten. Diejenigen, deren Name auf solchen Essgeschirren zu lesen ist, werden, sobald sie entlarvt sind, weiterhin bestraft werden.
   Sie sind keine Kriegsgefangenen und weitere Verletzungen der Bestimmungen dieses Gefängnisses werden sehr schwer bestraft werden.

   Jeder weitere Versuch, auf irgend eine erdenkliche Art mit Personen, ausserhalb ihrer Zellen und die kein ermächtigtes amerikanisches Personal sind, in Verbindung zu treten, wird den Schuldigen der schwerst-möglichen Bestrafung zuführen.

Announcement

1. IT IS FORBIDDEN:
   a. For Internees to turn off lights in the cells or unscrew the light bulbs.
   b. Excessive conversation, singing, whistling, or any other loud noises.

2. Windows in the cells will be opened during the night from the time the lights are tuned off (by the guards) until daylight.

3. Violations of the above rules will be punished.

4. The prisoners are in no case allowed to come into contact with German personnel in or outside of the prison. All attempts or wishes are only to be submitted to an American guard.

5. Excessive violations of the above rules will be punished.

---

1. You will be punished with bread and water because many of you have engraved your name, unit and other dates on your utensils. This is extremely forbidden. Those of you whose names are readable on such utensils will be further punished after you have been de-loused. You are not a prisoner of war and further ??????? will be punished in the worst way.

2. Further attempts to come into communication with persons which are not American personnel outside of the cells will lead to the most stringent punishment possible.

Release No. 5557

RELEASE FROM CIVILIAN INTERNMENT CAMP NO. DACHAU

ENTLASSUNGSSCHEIN FÜR ZIVILPERSONEN AUS DEM INTERNIERUNGSLAGER NR. DACHAU

* Discharged ader provisions ltr. HQ USFET AG file 383.7 GHL AGO subj: "Arrest and Detention" dtd. 9.10.46 TWX HQ TUSA, ref. No. F-271 dtd. 11.1.47 and VO CG USFET.

HEADQUATERS FIRST MILITARY DISTRICT

Third US Army
Dritte Amerikanische Armee

This is to certify that
Hiermit wird bestätigt, daß WOELFEL, Heinz (name and address) (Name und Adresse)

Nuernberg, Zwickauerstr.7

whose signature appears below and who has been interned at Civilian Internment Camp as indicated above for t following reasons:

die/der Unterzeichnete, die/der aus folgenden Gründen im Internierungslager für Zivilpersonen, wie oben angeführ interniert war:

WAR CRIMES SUSPECT*

has been released, ~~provisionally released, paroled~~ (Strike out words not applying) from internment ~~upon order of the du~~ ~~Military Government Review Board for~~ *CLEARED BY WAR CRIMES

ist auf Grund ~~einer Entscheidung des kürzlich eingesetzten Prüfungsausschusses für~~

von der Internierung entlassen, ~~vorläufig entlassen, ehrenwörtlich entlassen~~ worden. (Nicht zutreffendes durchstreiche

The bearer will not be rearrested for any of the reasons stated in the first paragraph of this letter, except by expr order of the Director of Military Government for Bavaria

Der Inhaber dieses Entlassungsscheines darf nicht wieder verhaftet werden aus einem in Paragraph 1 dieses Briefes an führten Grund, außer auf Grund eines ausdrücklichen Befehles des Direktors der Militärregierung für Bayern

If provisionally released or paroled: Under terms of the provisional release or parole bearer will (State provisions).

Bei nur vorläufiger oder ehrenwörtlicher Entlassung: Unter den Bedingungen der vorläufigen oder ehrenwörtlichen E lassung hat Entlassene/r: (Angabe der Bedingungen.)

None

Bearer will upon his arrival home report to the Landrat of the Kreis nearest to his place of abode and to the near Military Government Office and register his name, date of registery and the Military Government Review Board wh has ordered his release.

Der Inhaber dieses Entlassungsscheines hat sich bei seiner Ankunft in seinem Wohnort sofort beim Landrat des sein Wohnort nächsten Kreises zu melden (XXXX) und zu registrieren, unter Angabe des Prüfungsa schusses, der seine Entlassung veranlaßt hat.

EXHIBIT "A" (Continued)

Bearer has been instructed that his continued freedom is dependent upon his conduct and compliance with the laws and regulations of Allied Military Government.

Der Inhaber dieses Entlassungsscheines ist darüber aufgeklärt worden, daß seine Freiheit von seinem jeweiligen Verhalten sowie seiner Einfügung in die Gesetze und Verordnungen der Alliierten Militärregierung abhängig ist.

Bearer will retain this release as evidence of the validity of his release, and in the event of his arrest in the future this release will be attached to the original of the arrest report.

Der Inhaber dieses Entlassungsscheines hat diesen als Beweis seiner rechtmäßigen Entlassung selbst aufzubewahren. Im Falle einer zukünftigen Inhaftierung muß dieses Schriftstück dem Originalverhaftungsbericht angeheftet werden.

For the Commanding Officer:
Für den Kommandanten:

Interne's signature — Unterschrift des Internierten

Name (signed) (Unterschrift)

Date

Right Thumb

Name RAY L. INZER
(Printed or typed)
(Druckbuchstaben oder Maschinenschrift)

LT. COL. INF.
COMPOUND EXECUTIVE OFFICER

Unit

Name

This is a valuable paper and internee should keep it on his person always. If lost application for duplicate should at once be made to ~~Director Military Government for~~ ... ~~Military Government Review~~

Dies ist ein wertvolles Papier, welches Sie immer bei sich führen sollten. Wenn Sie dieses verlieren, ist sofort ein Antrag für ein Duplikat an den ~~Director Military Government~~ ... ~~Überprüfungsausschuß~~ für ... zu stellen.

HEADQUARTERS WAR CRIMES ENCLOSURE
CI SCREENING STAFF CIE DACHAU APO 407 US ARMY

Arbeitsamt Nürnberg
29. 4. 47.

Lebensmittelkarten ... 28.4. bis 4.5.47
... 29. April 1947

Die Lebensmittel... versorgung aufgenommen ... 5. 5. 47
... den 9. 5. 47

Nürnberg, den 29. 4. 47
Der Stadtrat zu Nürnberg
I.A.

Release No.,2946

RELEASE FROM CIVILIAN INTERNMENT CAMP NO. DACHAU

ENTLASSUNGSSCHEIN FÜR ZIVILPERSONEN AUS DEM INTERNIERUNGSLAGER NR. DACHAU

* Discharged under provisions ltr. HQ USFET AG file 383.7 GBL-AGO, subj. "Arrest a nd Detention" dtd. 9.10.46, TWX HQ TUSA, ref. No. F-271,dtd. 11.1.47

HEADQUARTERS FIRST MILITARY DISTRICT
Third US Army
Dritte Amerikanische Armee

This is to certify that M U E L L E R , Wolfgang Dieter
Hiermit wird bestätigt, daß (name and address)
(Name und Adresse)

E S S E N - Stadtwald , Sundernholz 53

whose signature appears below, and who has been interned at Civilian Internment Camp as indicated above for the following reasons:

die/der Unterzeichnete, die/der aus folgenden Gründen im Internierungslager für Zivilpersonen, wie oben angeführt, ~~interniert war~~ ~~War Crimes Suspect~~

has been released, ~~provisionally released, paroled~~. (Strike out words not applying) from internment ~~upon order of the duly appointed Military Government Review Board for~~ * Cleared by War Crimes

ist ~~auf Grund einer Entscheidung des kürzlich eingesetzten Prüfungsausschusses für~~

von der Internierung entlassen, vorläufig entlassen, ehrenwörtlich entlassen worden. (Nicht zutreffendes durchstreichen.)

The bearer will not be rearrested for any of the reasons stated in the first paragraph of this letter, except by express order of the Director of Military Government for Bavaria.

Der Inhaber dieses Entlassungsscheines darf nicht wieder verhaftet werden aus einem in Paragraph 1 dieses Briefes angeführten Grund, außer auf Grund eines ausdrücklichen Befehles des Direktors der Militärregierung für

If provisionally released or paroled: Under terms of the provisional release or parole bearer will (State provisions).

Bei nur vorläufiger oder ehrenwörtlicher Entlassung: Unter den Bedingungen der vorläufigen oder ehrenwörtlichen Entlassung hat Entlassene/r: (Angabe der Bedingungen.)

None

Bearer will upon his arrival home report to the Landrat of the Kreis nearest to his place of abode and to the nearest Military Government Office and register his name, date of registery and the Military Government Review Board which has ordered his release.

Der Inhaber dieses Entlassungsscheines hat sich bei seiner Ankunft in seinem Wohnort sofort beim Landrat des seinem Wohnort nächsten Kreises zu melden (xxxxxxxxxxxxxxxxxx) und zu registrieren, unter Angabe des Prüfungsausschusses, der seine Entlassung veranlaßt hat.

CONTROL FORM D. 2
Kontrollblatt D. 2.
344934

ALL ENTRIES WILL BE MADE IN BLOCK LATIN CAPITALS AND WILL BE MADE IN INK OR TYPESCRIPT. 6

CERTIFICATE OF DISCHARGE
Entlassungsschein

CERTIFICAT DE CONGE LIBENABLE

I

PERSONAL PARTICULARS
Personalbeschreibung

Dieses Blatt muß in folgender Weise ausgefüllt werden:
1. In lateinischer Druckschrift und in großer Buchstaben.
2. Mit Tinte oder mit Schreibmaschine

SURNAME OF HOLDER / Familienname des Inhabers / SURNOM DU PORTEUR: MÜLLER
CHRISTIAN NAMES / Vorname des Inhabers / PRENOMS: WOLFGANG
CIVIL OCCUPATION / Beruf oder Beschäftigung / EMPLOI CIVIL: PUPIL
HOME ADDRESS / Heimatanschrift / RESIDENCE: Straße ... Ort DACHAU ... Kreis ... Regierungsbezirk / Land / MUENCHEN/BAYERN

DATE OF BIRTH / Geburtsdatum (DAY / MONTH / YEAR / DATE DE NAISSANCE (Tag / Monat / Jahr): 24.10.1924
PLACE OF BIRTH / Geburtsort / LIEU DE NAISSANCE: ESSEN/RUHR
FAMILY STATUS / Familienstand / ETAT DE FAMILLE: SINGLE Ledig / MARRIED Verheiratet / WIDOW(ER) Verwitwet / DIVORCED Geschieden — SINGLE
NUMBER OF CHILDREN WHO ARE MINORS / Zahl der minderjährigen Kinder / NOMBRE D'ENFANTS MINEURS: NONE

I HEREBY CERTIFY THAT TO THE BEST OF MY KNOWLEDGE AND BELIEF THE PARTICULARS GIVEN ABOVE ARE TRUE.

Ich erkläre hiermit, nach bestem Wissen und Gewissen, daß die obigen Angaben wahr sind.

I ALSO CERTIFY THAT I HAVE READ AND UNDERSTOOD THE "INSTRUCTIONS TO PERSONNEL ON DISCHARGE" (CONTROL FORM D. 1)

Ich bestätige außerdem, daß ich die „Anweisung für Soldaten und Angehörige Militär - ähnlicher Organisationen" usw. (Kontrollblat D. 1) gelesen und verstanden habe

SIGNATURE OF HOLDER / Unterschrift des Inhabers: WOLFGANG MÜLLER

II

MEDICAL CERTIFICATE
Ärztlicher Befund

DISTINGUISHING MARKS / Besondere Kennzeichen: SCARS ON THE FOREHEAD, ON BOTH SIDES OF THE SHOULDE

DISABILITY, WITH DESCRIPTION / Dienstunfähigkeit, mit Beschreibung: SHOT THROUGH THE LUNG, PLEXUS LAESION, LEFT ARM ACTION IMPEDED.

MEDICAL CATEGORY / Tauglichkeitsgrad

I CERTIFY THAT TO THE BEST OF MY KNOWLEDGE AND BELIEF THE ABOVE PARTICULARS RELATING TO THE HOLDER ARE TRUE AND THAT HE IS NOT VERMINOUS OR SUFFERING FORM ANY INFECTIOUS OR CONTAGIOUS DISEASE.

Ich erkläre hiermit, nach bestem Wissen und Gewissen, daß die obigen Angaben wahr sind, daß der Inhaber ungezieferfrei ist und daß er keinerlei ansteckende oder übertragbare Krankheit hat.

SIGNATURE OF MEDICAL OFFICER / Unterschrift des Sanitätsoffiziers

NAME AND RANK OF MEDICAL OFFICER IN BLOCK LATIN CAPITALS / Zuname / Vorname / Dienstgrad des Sanitätsoffiziers (In lateinischer Druckschrift und in großen Buchstaben): JOHN E MILLER CAPT MC

† DELETE THAT WHICH IS INAPPLICABLE
Nichtzutreffendes durchstreichen

III

PARTICULARS OF DISCHARGE
Entlassungsvermerk

DETAILS DE CONGE DEFINITIF

THE PERSON TO WHOM THE ABOVE PARTICULARS REFER / Die Person, auf die sich obige Angaben beziehen / WAS DISCHARGED ON (Date) / wurde am (Datum der Entlassung) / LA PERSONNE A QUI LES DETAILS S'APPLIQUENT A ETE CONGEDIEE LE ... FROM THE* / vom/von der* / DE* WAFFEN-SS entlassen

RIGHT THUMBPRINT
Abdruck des rechten Daumen
EMPREINTE DU POUCE DROIT

CERTIFIE PAR / CERTIFIED BY / Beglaubigt durch

SCEAU OFFICIEL / OFFICIAL EMBOSSED SEAL / Amtlicher Einprägestempel

NAME, RANK AND APPOINTMENT OF ALLIED DISCHARGING OFFICER IN BLOCK CAPITALS / NOM, RANG ET EMPLOM (EN LETTRES MAJUSCULES DE L'OFFICIER ALLIE CONGEDIANT: DONALD C MILLER MAJ F A — HQ 774th TANK BN

* INSERT "ARMY," "NAVY", "AIR FORCE," "VOLKSSTURM," OR PARAMILITARY ORGANIZATION, e.g., "R. A. D.", "N. S. F. K.", ETC.

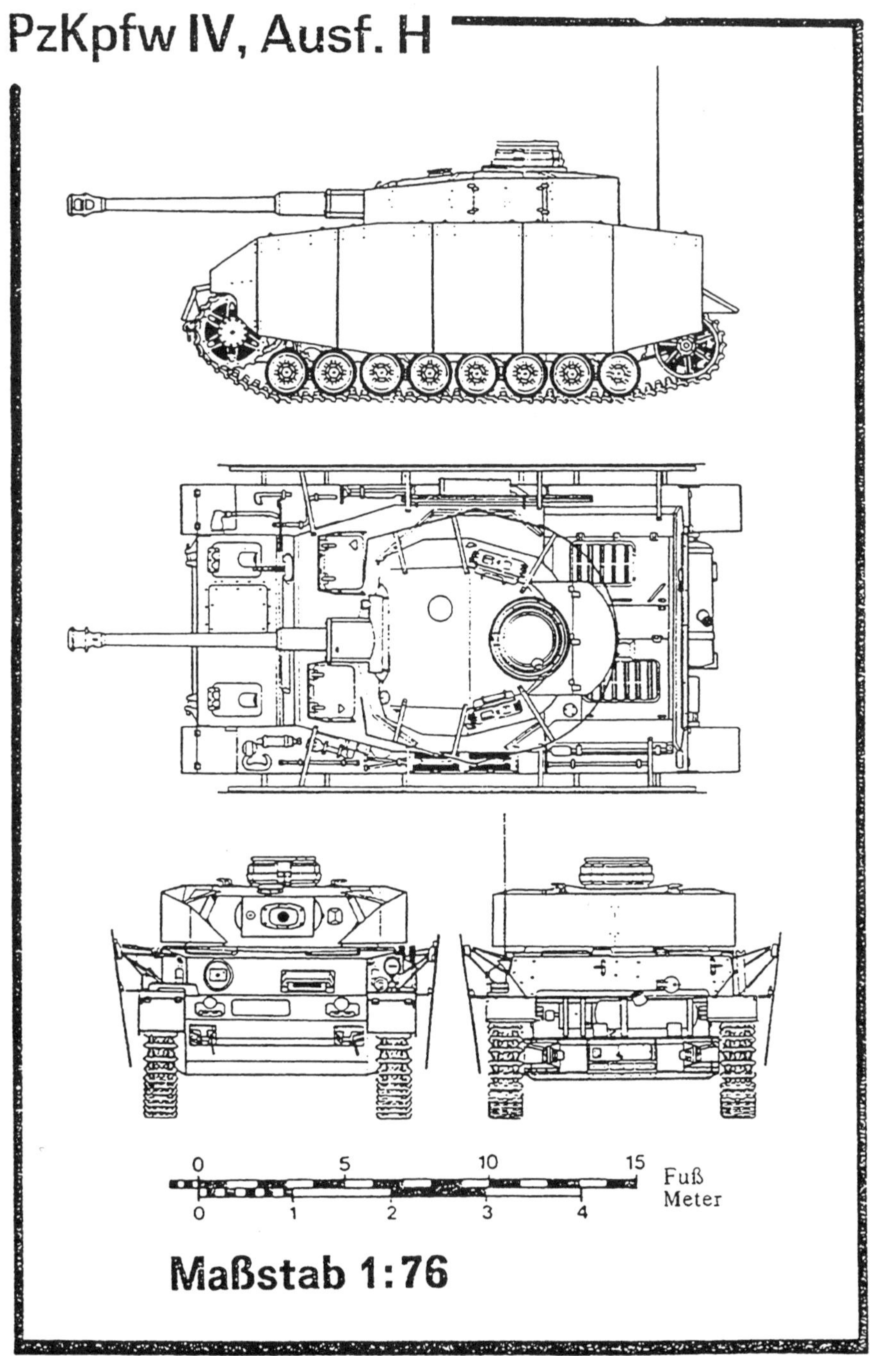
PzKpfw IV, Ausf. H
0
5
10
15
Fuß
Meter
0
1
2
3
4
Maßstab 1:76

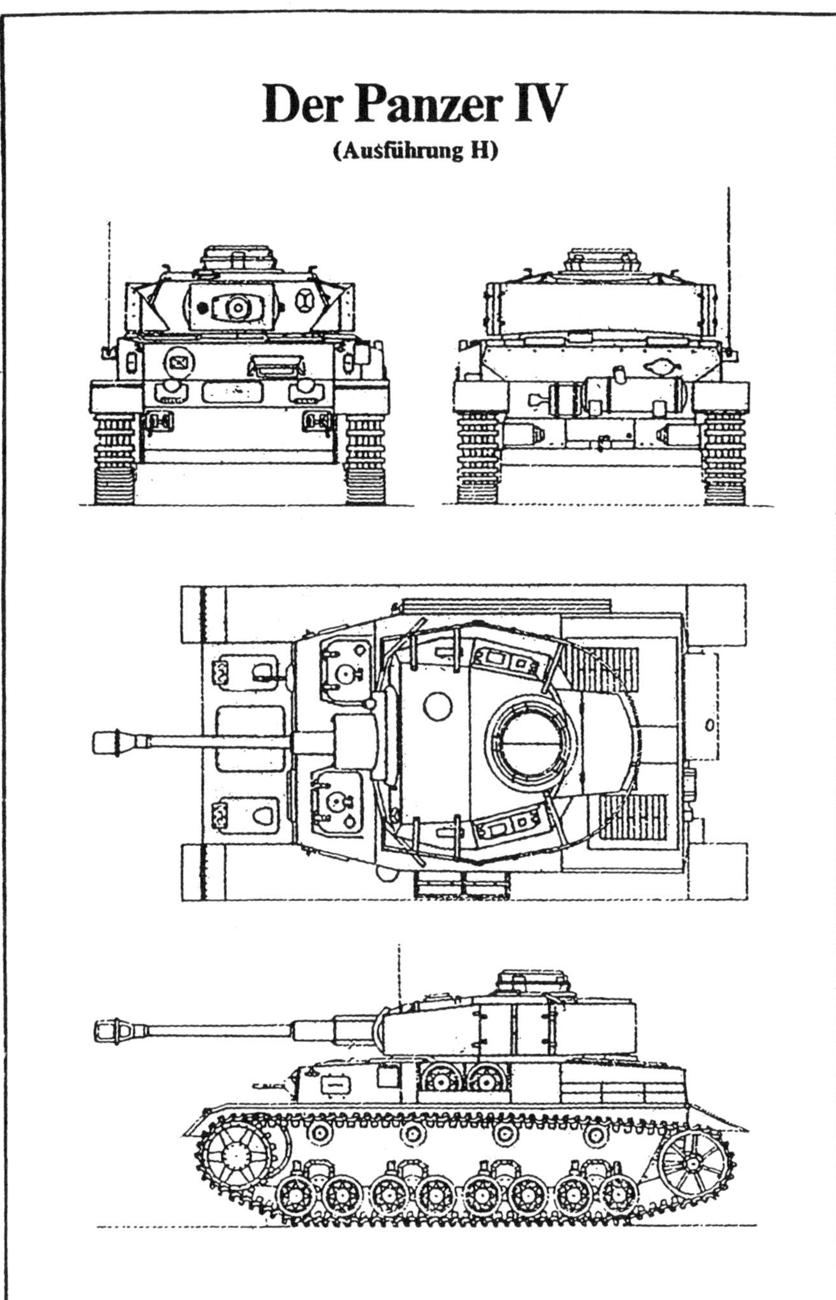
Der Panzer IV
(Ausführung H)

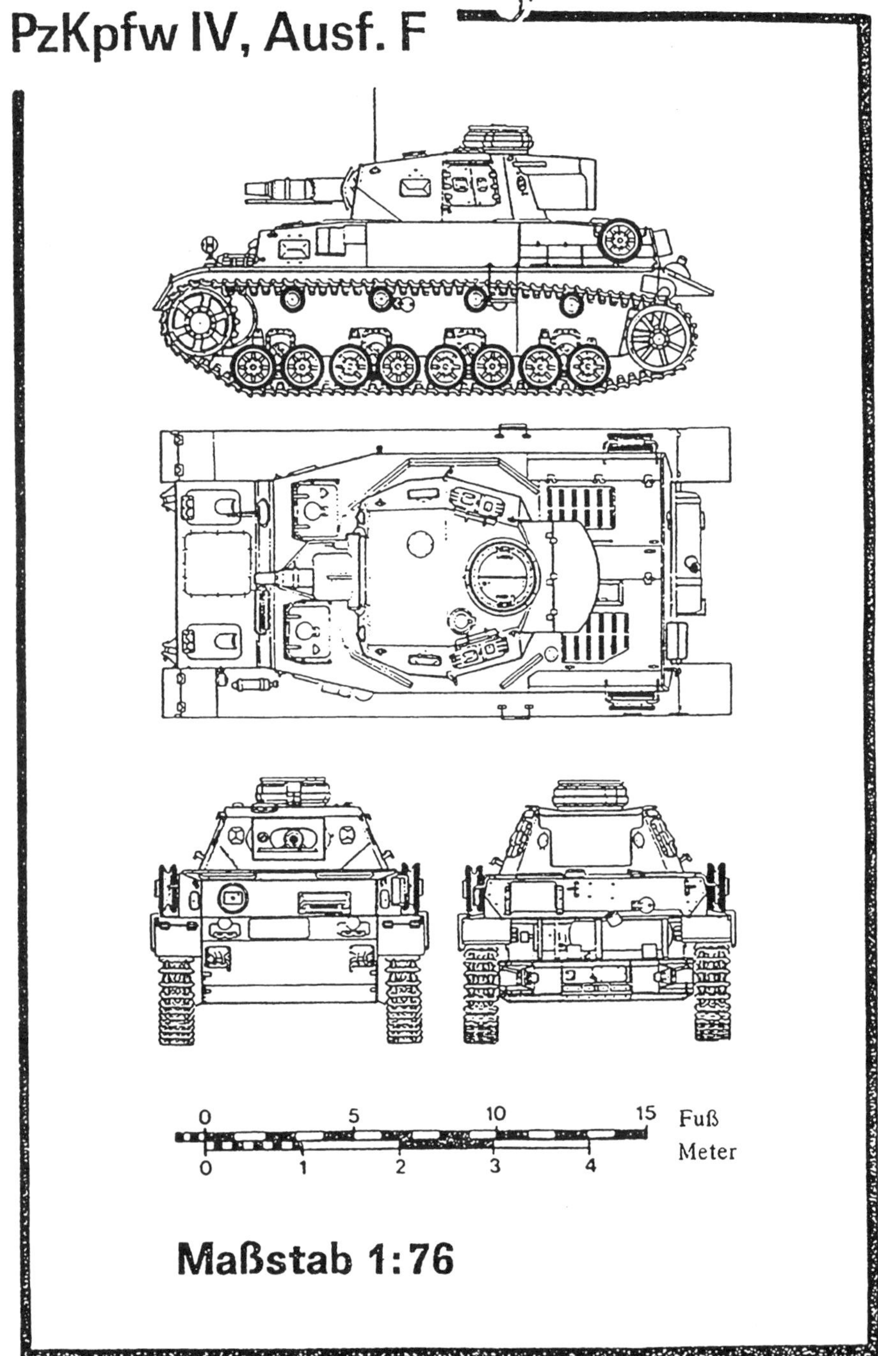
PzKpfw IV, Ausf. F
0
5
10
15
Fuß
Meter
0
1
2
3
4
Maßstab 1:76

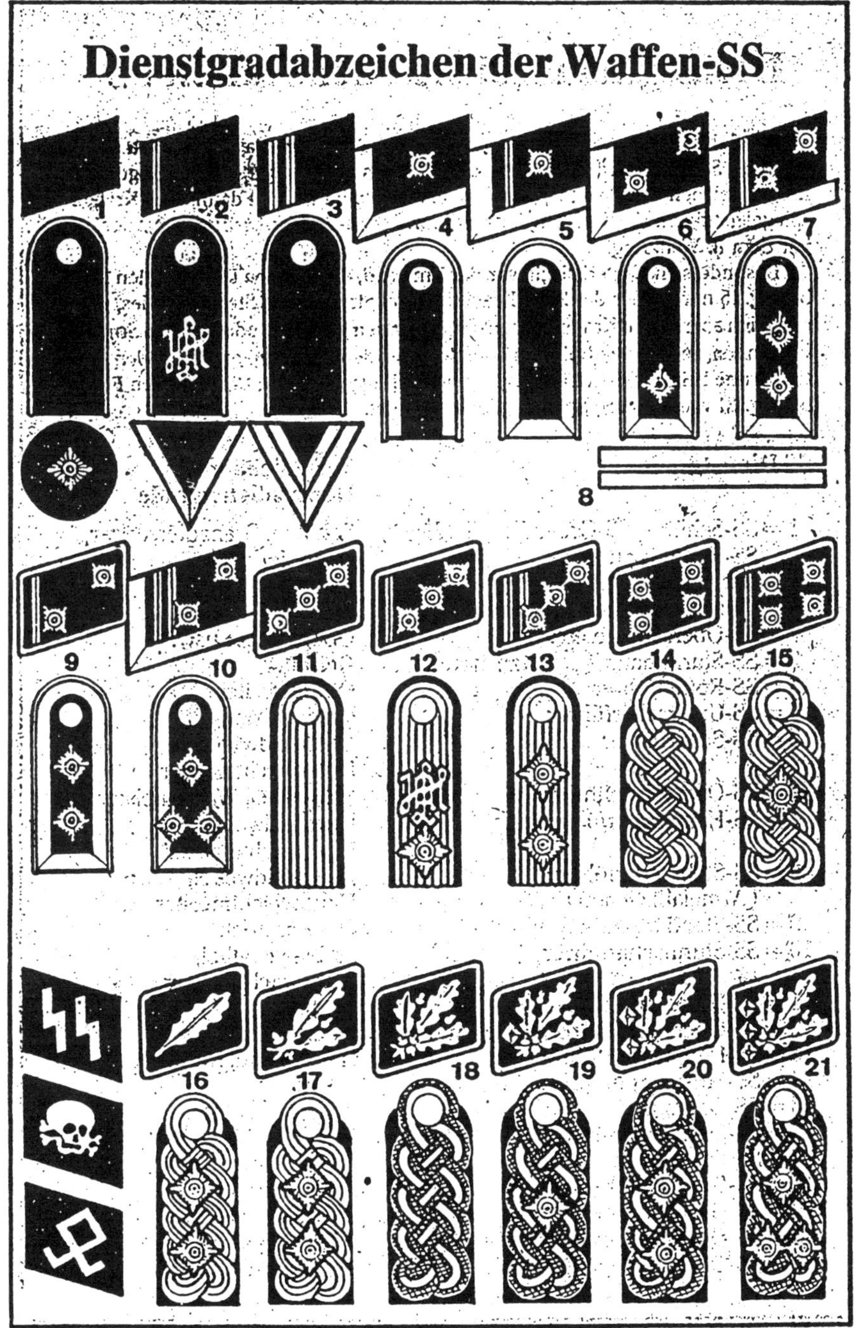
Dienstgradabzeichen der Waffen-SS
1
2
3
4
5
6
7
8
9
10
11
12
13
14
15
16
17
18
19
20
21

INDEX

Also from the Publisher

RIDING EAST
The SS Cavalry Brigade in Poland and Russia 1939-1942
MARK C. YERGER

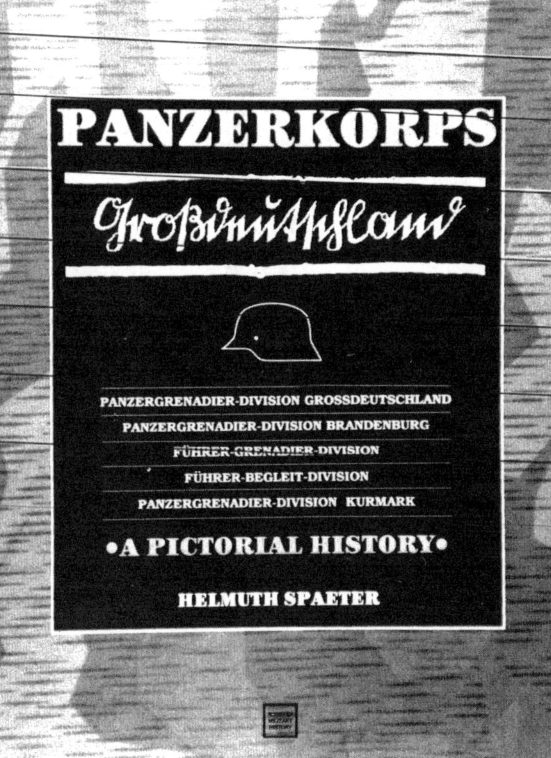
PANZERKORPS
Großdeutschland
PANZERGRENADIER-DIVISION GROSSDEUTSCHLAND
PANZERGRENADIER-DIVISION BRANDENBURG
FÜHRER-GRENADIER-DIVISION
FÜHRER-BEGLEIT-DIVISION
PANZERGRENADIER-DIVISION KURMARK
•A PICTORIAL HISTORY•
HELMUTH SPAETER